AF771312

CORPORATE GOVERNANCE AND CULTURE IN FINANCIAL INSTITUTIONS

ELGAR FINANCIAL LAW AND PRACTICE

Series Editor: Jeffrey Golden KC (Hon), *Arbitrator and Mediator, 3 Hare Court; Founder and Chair Emeritus of the P.R.I.M.E. Finance Foundation*

The Elgar Financial Law and Practice series is a library of works by leading practitioners and scholars covering discrete areas of law in the field of banking and finance. Titles in the series are both analytical and descriptive in approach, highlighting and unpicking the legal issues that are most critical and relevant to practice. Designed to be detailed, focused reference works, the books in this series offer an authoritative statement on the law and practice in key topics within the field, from Financial Collateral to Private Equity, from Secured Transactions to Financial Crime, and from Financial Derivatives and Hedge Funds to Bank Resolution and Bank Capital.

For a full list of Edward Elgar published titles, including the titles in this series, visit our website at www.e-elgar.com.

CORPORATE GOVERNANCE AND CULTURE IN FINANCIAL INSTITUTIONS

Edited by

ANDREAS KOKKINIS
Associate Professor, University of Birmingham, UK

ANAT KELLER
Reader in Law, King's College London, UK

ELGAR FINANCIAL LAW AND PRACTICE

Edward Elgar PUBLISHING

Cheltenham, UK • Northampton, MA, USA

© The Editors and Contributors Severally 2025

All rights reserved. No part of this publication may be reproduced, stored in a retrieval system or transmitted in any form or by any means, electronic, mechanical or photocopying, recording, or otherwise without the prior permission of the publisher.

Published by

Edward Elgar Publishing Limited
The Lypiatts
15 Lansdown Road
Cheltenham
Glos GL50 2JA
UK

Edward Elgar Publishing, Inc.
William Pratt House
9 Dewey Court
Northampton
Massachusetts 01060
USA

Authorised representative in the EU for GPSR queries only: Easy Access System Europe – Mustamäe tee 50, 10621 Tallinn, Estonia, gpsr.requests@easproject.com

A catalogue record for this book is available from the British Library

Library of Congress Control Number: 2025940941

This book is available electronically in the **Elgar**online
Law subject collection
https://doi.org/10.4337/9781035317905

MIX
Paper | Supporting responsible forestry
FSC® C013604

ISBN 978 1 0353 1789 9 (cased)
ISBN 978 1 0353 1790 5 (eBook)
ISBN 978 1 0353 7151 8 (ePub)

Printed and bound by CPI Group (UK) Ltd, Croydon, CR0 4YY

CONTENTS

EXTENDED CONTENTS

LIST OF CONTRIBUTORS

Fliss Berridge began as a professional musician (trombone, in case you were wondering). After several years of orchestral music, she wanted a job where she wouldn't have to worry about money. So Fliss went to law school in the evenings and re-trained to become a lawyer. Qualifying in corporate and commercial, Fliss worked in private practice at City firms, and moved in-house in 2013 to work for the UK's central not-for-profit payment systems. She then became Head of Legal, Regulatory and Corporate Governance for the UK's online and mobile payment scheme, Faster Payments, and mobile service, Paym. Following the Faster Payments' team award for innovation and competition, Fliss co-founded payments fintech Ordo. Ordo helps consumers and businesses manage their finances better and improve their financial wellbeing, and provides competition to the dominant banks and card schemes. Exploiting open banking technology, Ordo is bringing instant, low-cost, secure account-to-account payments and data access to businesses and consumers.

Alan Brener is Associate Professor at University College London's Laws Faculty and Deputy Director of the Faculty's Centre for Ethics and Law. He is a qualified Chartered Accountant and a Fellow of the Chartered Banker Institute. Prior to starting his PhD Alan worked for Santander UK and was responsible, at different times, for the compliance and retail legal departments and regulatory policy. He also worked at other banks before this and as a senior prudential and conduct of business regulator for the insurance and collective investments sectors, having previously worked on aspects of public policy at the Department of Trade and Industry.

Sarah Cichon completed the German First State Examination at Humboldt-Universität zu Berlin, a French maîtrise en droit in European Law at Université Paris Panthéon-Assas (Paris 2) and an LLM in international financial law at King's College London, where she also worked as a research assistant for Dr Anat Keller. She is currently a PhD candidate in EU financial law at Humboldt-Universität zu Berlin and works as a research assistant in the financial services regulatory practice of a US law firm in Berlin, Germany.

Blanaid Clarke is the McCann FitzGerald Chair in Corporate Law, Trinity College Dublin. She is also Deputy Chairman of the Irish Banking Culture Board, the Irish representative on the OECD's Corporate Governance Committee, a member of ESMA's Shareholder Transactions Working Group and a Vice President of the Academic Board of the European Banking Institute. Previously, she was a member of the Irish Central Bank Commission, the IMF's Safeguards Assessments – 2022 External Expert Panel, ESMA's Securities Markets Stakeholder Group and the European Commission's Informal Expert Group on Company Law and Reflection Group on the Future of EU Company Law.

Jo Goddard is Co-founder of ESG Experts Ltd. She has been a sustainability professional for 17 years and works with businesses to implement sustainability strategy and catalyse climate action. Her clients have included large global organisations such as Allianz and Sabre Technologies, as well as smaller fast-growth businesses such as Moonpig and Matter Real Estate LLP. Her background is within financial services leading sustainability functions at Aviva, Old Mutual and Barclays. She has an MSc in Environmental Assessment and Management. She is a Council member for Heart of the City, a judge for the Royal Academy of Engineering Innovation, a Non-Executive Director for Petrolube and a trustee for Street Trees for Living.

Eleanore Hickman is Senior Lecturer in corporate law and governance at the University of Bristol, a co-director of the University of Bristol Centre for Private and Commercial Law and a member of the UK Young Academy. Having returned to academia from legal practice, Eleanore completed her doctoral studies at University College London, going on to carry out post-doctoral research at the University of Cambridge. Eleanore's research spans issues relating to corporate governance, financial regulation and the digital transformation. Her monograph *Diversity, Merit and Power in the C-suite* was published with Hart in 2023. She has also published a variety of chapters and articles in leading academic outlets.

Kosmas Kaprinis is Regulatory Advisor for Binance and an Adjunct Professor of Fintech at IE University (Madrid). In the past, he held assignments at HSBC, the European Central Bank, the World Bank and legal private practice, as well as teaching and research appointments at Harvard, Oxford and Frankfurt Universities. An economist and lawyer by training, Kosmas completed a Masters and doctorate in law and finance at Oxford University and a Masters in public policy at Harvard University.

Anat Keller is Reader (Associate Professor) in Financial Law. She joined the Dickson Poon School of Law in April 2016 and has previously taught at UCL (2007-2016). Dr Keller holds a PhD from the Centre for Commercial Law Studies at Queen Mary University of London, an LLM from the London School of Economics and first-class degrees in Management and Law (magna cum laude). Dr Keller is a qualified solicitor of England and Wales. Her influential monograph *Legal Foundations of Macroprudential Policy: An Interdisciplinary Approach* was published in 2020 (Cambridge: Intersentia). Dr Keller is also Global Associate Professor of Law at the University of Notre Dame and a Fellow of the Higher Education Academy.

Isabel Kelly, ESG Experts Ltd co-founder, is Non-Executive Director and ESG Committee Chair at TPXimpact, an AIM-listed BCorp delivering digital transformation. She is Board Advisor to the Social Impact Committee at SME insurance company Simply Business, also a BCorp. She is an impact careers advisor for MBA students at the Said Business School, Oxford University, and in 2015 founded Profit with Purpose, a social impact consultancy. She is a Trustee at Big Give, the UK's largest match funding charity. From 2002 to 2014 she was International Director of the Salesforce Foundation, and before that she worked for 11 years at Amnesty International on the East Asia desk. Her first job was at Oxfam.

Andreas Kokkinis joined Birmingham Law School as Associate Professor in 2020, having previously worked at the University of Warwick, UCL and the University of Kent. He holds a PhD from UCL (2014), an LLM from LSE (2009) and an LLB from the National University of Athens (2008). Dr Kokkinis has published widely in the areas of corporate governance and financial regulation, and engages regularly with policy makers and the media. His work has been published in journals such as the *Journal of Corporate Law Studies*, *Journal of Financial Regulation*, *Singapore Journal of Legal Studies*, *Indiana Journal of Global Legal Studies* and *Journal of Banking Regulation*. Dr Kokkinis has presented his research in several countries, including the US, Colombia, Singapore, Malaysia, Norway, Germany, France, Italy, Spain, Poland and Latvia.

Longjie Lu is Lecturer in Banking, Corporate and Financial Law, School of Law, University of Edinburgh and writes on both financial regulation and corporate governance. She recently published the book *Market or State: The Regulation and Practice of Bankers' Remuneration in the UK and China* (CUP 2022). Prior to Edinburgh, Longjie taught law at the Dickson Poon School of Law, King's College London, and completed her PhD in law at the University of Leeds.

Peter McCormack is Trustee of the Chartered Banker Institute and started his banking career in 1981. In the early part he worked in branch banking, serving customers, for three different banks in three different countries. For the past 25 years he has mainly worked in regulatory roles with the Financial Services Authority, the Guernsey Financial Services Commission, the Prudential Regulation Authority, the Financial Conduct Authority and most recently the Financial Reporting Council. In addition to legal education, he completed a PhD in Management at King's College, London and is a Fellow of the Chartered Banker Institute, the Chartered Governance Institute and the Institute of Directors.

Babajide Oniwinde obtained a Doctorate in Business Administration (DBA) from the Faculty of Business and Law at Anglia Ruskin University, where his thesis focused on the interplay between Regulatory Compliance and Senior Management Individual Accountability in Financial Services. He has held the position of Compliance Officer and MLRO with regulated firms in London since 2017 and prior to that worked for regulators in the UK and overseas. He holds an LLB, LLM and MBA and is a Qualified Solicitor (non-practising) admitted in England and Wales. In addition, he has held Associateship of the Chartered Institute of Securities and Investment.

Michael Schillig is Professor of Law at King's College London, Dickson Poon School of Law. Professor Schillig has published broadly in the areas of transnational, European and comparative private and commercial law with particular emphasis on contract, company and corporate insolvency law. Michael joined King's in 2007, following three years as the DAAD Lecturer in Law at the University of Sheffield. Michael read law at the University of Erlangen-Nuremberg and obtained his LLM from King's College London and his PhD from Humboldt University Berlin. He has been a Visiting Scholar at the University of California, Berkeley, and at the University of California, Los Angeles.

FOREWORD: THE ROLE OF CORPORATE CULTURE IN THE FINANCIAL SECTOR

For any experienced business leader, it is self-evident that corporate culture matters. Beliefs and assumptions shared across the organisation are crucial drivers of success. However, what is less self-evident is why such a critical success factor should have been neglected by governance thinkers and regulators until relatively recently. Such an omission is particularly hard to fathom in the context of the financial sector. Financial institutions must sustain high levels of confidence and trust. This is likely to be elusive if key players within the organisation are seen as conducting themselves in a toxic or disreputable manner, or are failing to meet the behavioural expectations of wider society.

Financial institutions have not always been so oblivious to matters of culture. Historically, great store was placed on the recruitment of individuals demonstrating 'character' and 'integrity'. However, as the sector became more sophisticated and incentive structures changed, the emphasis placed on such 'soft' qualities diminished relative to technical prowess in areas like financial engineering, trading, deal-making and risk management.

However, the technical complexity of finance – which is only likely to increase – does not obviate the need to operate within a strong ethical culture. Without such a framework, financial organisations are acutely vulnerable to scandal, mishap or reputational implosion. The tone must be set from the top. If those in leadership positions do not set the right example, then it is likely that poor attitudes will pervade the entire organisation. And if inappropriate attitudes are endemic across the sector as a whole, then culture can easily become a significant source of systemic financial risk.

Shaping a positive corporate culture is not necessarily easy. It requires time, effort and expertise from board members, senior managers and external regulators. However, this is not a challenge that can be ignored or downplayed. Boards and regulators increasingly acknowledge that oversight of organisational culture is a key part of their remit, not just something that exists and cannot be altered. The Institute of Directors recently published its first Code of Conduct for Directors, which seeks to articulate how directors can nurture a positive corporate culture.

As this fascinating new book demonstrates, corporate culture is rapidly gaining a central place in the pantheon of corporate governance. I have no doubt that it will continue to be an important frontier of research for governance scholars and practitioners alike for some time to come.

Dr. Roger Barker
Director of Policy and Corporate Governance
Institute of Directors

TABLE OF CASES

EUROPEAN UNION

IRELAND

UNITED KINGDOM

TABLE OF LEGISLATION

EUROPEAN UNION

Regulations

Directives

INTERNATIONAL

Ireland

Statutes

Statutory Instruments

United Kingdom

Statutes

Statutory Instruments

Assimilated Law (formerly Retained EU Law)

United States

INTRODUCTION TO CORPORATE GOVERNANCE AND CULTURE IN FINANCIAL INSTITUTIONS

Andreas Kokkinis and Anat Keller

Not so long ago, organisational culture and corporate governance were not seen as integral to regulatory perimeter and focus. Culture was viewed as a business matter rather than a regulatory concern and soft law was the only source of guidance for corporate governance across all sectors. As the global financial crisis of 2007–9 exposed the unstable foundations of laissez-faire financialised capitalism, evident in instances of scandalising misconduct or risk-taking by the likes of Fred Goodwin and Richard Severin Fuld Jr, public discourse shifted from a market-oriented to a public good-oriented view of culture and governance in financial firms. Post-crisis executive remuneration, risk management and the function of boards have attracted the attention of regulators. However, the most fundamental shift in regulatory thinking is arguably the inclusion of purposeful culture as a key regulatory objective. While it has by now become an axiom that culture falls within the regulatory perimeter, the remaining challenge is the way to conceptualise, observe and assess culture and the types of rules that are more likely to be effective in instigating cultural change (e.g., prescriptive rules vs principles). **I.1**

This book takes the reader through the manifestations of organisational culture in finance through its interplay with corporate governance and various regulatory regimes and policy debates. These investigations will hopefully contribute to the public debates that seek to concretise purposeful culture by giving it a tangible meaning and making it a workable locus for regulatory action. To do so, this book brings together experts from a range of financial services professions and academia to shed light on crucial aspects of culture in finance. The idea of the book came about as a continuation and expansion of a British Academy/Leverhulme-funded research project on 'Operationalising Purposeful Culture in Financial Firms to Deliver Better Outcomes for Consumers: An Empirical Analysis' (SG2122\210367, July 2022–December 2024). The editors, Dr Anat Keller and Dr Andreas Kokkinis, are deeply grateful to the 12 contributing authors for their hard work and frank reflection of their professional and/or **I.2** research expertise. Following this introduction, the book is divided into 12 main chapters that reflect the various aspects of culture in finance. In the following paragraphs, we provide a brief overview of each chapter.

I.3 *Cichon, Keller and Kokkinis* critically examine the legal and regulatory frameworks shaping governance and culture in financial institutions. As governance and culture influence decision-making, organisational resilience and outcomes for consumers and markets, deficiencies in these areas expose firms to reputational, operational and financial risks, including threats to liquidity and solvency. As a result, governance and culture have become key focus areas for both global and national regulators. The authors detail the legal and regulatory frameworks related to governance and culture, providing an overview of the foundations and recent developments of governance requirements applicable to financial institutions, the Senior Managers and Certification Regime (SMCR), executive remuneration rules, the Consumer Duty and diversity and inclusion and related developments. The authors identify enforcement as a persistent weakness and highlight inconsistencies in rule design such as the removal of the bonus cap without strengthening other remuneration regulations such as malus, clawback and deferral mechanisms. Furthermore, the incremental layering of policies with mixed objectives – financial stability, consumer protection and social justice – risks creating ambiguity and inefficiency. The authors advocate for a more holistic, coherent regulatory framework to reduce compliance costs and better achieve policy goals.

I.4 *Brener* examines how boards and regulators can assess and influence organisational culture using quantitative and qualitative approaches. He highlights that poor cultural practices undermine compliance and threaten a firm's survival. Large complex organisations often face challenges from multiple subcultures operating in silos, complicating efforts to build cohesive, purpose-driven cultures. *Brener* argues that both boards and regulators must proactively assess and measure these cultures to identify and address unacceptable practices. He suggests several practical measures for board members, including recruiting and onboarding individuals who align with desired cultural values, setting targets consistent with a positive culture and promoting stakeholders who exemplify these values. Obstacles to personal accountability, such as the 'three lines of defence' model and reliance on non-disclosure agreements, should be removed to foster transparency and trust. Encouraging employees to raise concerns without fear of retaliation is crucial for two-way communication and building trust. Additionally, continual training for all stakeholders, including senior executives and board members, may promote a deeper understanding of the cultural impact of decisions and behaviour. Brener concludes that regulatory focus on culture remains limited and must be significantly enhanced and that boards must recognise that culture is not secondary to compliance but integral to organisational success.

Hickman addresses gender diversity in the UK financial services sector and its interaction with corporate culture, stressing the need to address systemic issues beyond board representation. While progress has been made, including increased representation of women in boardrooms and management, disparities persist. Women are disproportionately represented in non-executive roles with limited decision-making power and are overrepresented in supporting functions. Moreover, the gender pay gap in financial services remains nearly double that of other industries. Hickman explores the historical perception of finance as male-dominated and highlights that cultural challenges such as sexual harassment and differential treatment are particularly pronounced in financial services. In the author's view, embedding core values such as respect, fairness, and integrity, along with infrastructures that encourage speaking up, are essential for fostering diversity and inclusivity within the sector. In Hickman's view, regulatory initiatives focused on processes and data may detract from meaningful cultural change. Instead, initiatives aimed at strengthening cultural infrastructure and fostering inclusivity are advocated as more effective solutions. In this sense Hickman emphasises the need to challenge societal narratives that perpetuate finance as a masculine domain, promoting the perception of financial services as open to all. **I.5**

Lu examines the evolving role of executive remuneration in financial firms, focusing on its use as a tool for influencing behaviour and cultural norms to achieve economic and societal goals through regulatory intervention. According to Lu, while traditionally aimed at maximising shareholder value, executive remuneration is now transitioning into a quasi-regulatory tool mechanism for aligning executives' interests with broader objectives such as financial stability and environmental, social and governance (ESG) goals. These reforms embed societal goals into performance targets, aligning them with executives' personal interests. However, Lu cautions that increased effort and uncertainty associated with these goals may lead executives to adopt alternative strategies that undermine the intended regulatory objectives. This reflects a fundamental conflict between the self-interest of executives and the regulatory push for responsibility. The author argues that driving cultural change through ESG metrics is particularly challenging due to the lack of standardisation, making alignment with stakeholder interests more difficult and creating opportunities for circumvention. In the author's view executive remuneration alone cannot instigate a cultural shift but can serve as an accelerator when complemented **I.6** by broader efforts. According to Lu, regulators must therefore carefully design reforms to avoid unintended consequences and to ensure alignment between corporate behaviour and regulatory objectives.

I.7 *Clarke* gives an introduction to Ireland's Individual Accountability Framework (IAF) and its role in fostering cultural change in financial institutions. The IAF emerged following the Central Bank of Ireland's review of cultural and behavioural issues in Ireland's main retail banks, prompted by public outrage over the tracker mortgage scandal. Enacted in 2023, the IAF includes Conduct Standards, the Senior Executive Accountability Regime (SEAR), enhancements to the Fitness and Probity Regime and a unified enforcement process. Clarke focuses on SEAR and Conduct Standards, which impose individual accountability on specified persons, requiring them to take 'reasonable steps' to ensure compliance. These measures aim to strengthen governance and align leadership with cultural objectives. Clarke welcomes the IAF, as it strengthens the accountability of senior executives and should encourage good governance and positive culture within firms. Nevertheless, Clarke highlights challenges, including tensions between individual accountability and collective decision-making, and the inclusion of non-executive directors in SEAR. Moreover, firms must allocate resources to prepare responsibility statements, monitor compliance, and adapt employment contracts. She emphasises the importance of clarity in defining responsibilities and enforcement to generate confidence and facilitate consistent and effective implementation. Clarke advocates for an IAF 'sandbox' for collaborative engagement between regulators and firms, enabling clearer expectations and better-informed regulatory practices.

I.8 *McCormack* explores the role of professionalism, corporate governance and purposeful culture in reconnecting the banking sector with its customers. The author highlights the historical importance of vocational education provided by professional banking institutes, which fostered trusted banker–customer relationships and positioned bankers as 'pillars of the community'. However, structural shifts, including profit-maximisation, transactional cultures and cost-reducing technologies, have eroded trust and distanced financial institutions from their customers. Beyond regulatory initiatives such as the FCA's Consumer Duty, McCormack advocates for a renewed focus on collaborative governance and professional training to restore confidence and trust in the sector. The closure of key industry bodies, underscores the need for renewed commitment to professionalism and collaborative governance. McCormack argues that rebuilding trust and fostering long-term customer relationships is in the national interest and requires collaboration among policymakers, regulators, professional institutes, and banks. Moreover, professionalism, supported by ethical and technical training, is critical to achieving a purposeful culture benefiting bankers, customers and society at large.

Kelly and Goddard delve into the evolution of environmental, social and governance (ESG) strategies and their impact on corporate culture in financial services. The authors trace the progression from early voluntary Corporate Social Responsibility (CSR) initiatives through expanded accountability after the 2008 financial crisis to current ESG legislative requirements. The authors identify the emergence of a new culture in the financial services sector, driven by purpose and ESG considerations. Over the past decade, ESG factors have gained recognition as essential considerations for boards, employees, leadership and regulators. These developments have professionalised ESG practices and fostered broader acceptance of non-financial concerns alongside commercial priorities. However, challenges remain in embedding a 'profit with purpose' ethos across the sector. While many firms now accept the legitimacy of ESG concerns, they often balance these against the imperative to remain commercially viable. This tension indicates that significant cultural shifts are still required for ESG principles to be fully integrated into the sector. The authors advocate for a deeper commitment to embedding purpose-driven ESG strategies within corporate culture, emphasising their potential to redefine the values and priorities in financial services. **I.9**

Berridge examines purpose-led companies in financial services through a case study on Ordo, an open banking FinTech. The author locates the UK financial services sector within the broader societal context, exploring wealth disparities and the evolving purpose of financial services. Berridge highlights key innovations in the UK payments sector, including the Faster Payments Scheme and Open Banking. The discussion of Open Banking includes an analysis of its legal and regulatory framework, ultimately building a case for embedding purpose within Open Banking. Berridge introduces Ordo, charting the company's development from its origins to its present operations and future ambitions. Central to this narrative is the role of purpose in shaping Ordo's mission, operations, and customer relationships. By operationalising purpose, Ordo illustrates how a mission-driven approach can enhance financial wellbeing and foster resilience. The author reflects on the broader implications of purpose-driven business models, emphasising the responsibility of the financial services sector. **I.10**

Kaprinis investigates how internal compliance and risk management processes shape organisational culture, highlighting the increasing regulatory focus on risk culture as a critical component of risk management. Kaprinis argues that **I.11** fostering an effective risk culture requires addressing conceptual ambiguities rather than relying on organisational restructuring. Risk culture is inherently multifaceted, encompassing formal procedures and informal practices, with its qualitative nature posing significant challenges for compliance functions. Effective risk culture encourages prudent risk-taking aligned with sustainable growth, rather than over-regulation or excessive caution. He advocates for tailoring risk culture to align with each institution's unique business strategy and operational context. The author offers practical recommendations to enhance compliance culture. These include empowering middle management as role models, fostering informal networks among compliance professionals to share knowledge and best practices and encouraging experimentation in compliance practices to drive adaptability and continuous improvement. The author also points to the strategic role of compliance and risk managers in business decision-making and advocates for the responsible integration of AI to enhance compliance efficiency while addressing associated ethical and regulatory challenges.

I.12 *Oniwinde* looks at how RegTech and AI are transforming anti-money laundering (AML) efforts and shaping internal culture within financial institutions. Advanced technologies, such as artificial intelligence and machine learning, enhance monitoring systems, detect suspicious activities and improve adherence to regulatory requirements. However, Oniwinde stresses that technology must be accompanied by a strong compliance-oriented culture to guarantee AML compliance. Challenges related to culture and compliance include a 'tick-box' mentality, resistance to change, lack of accountability, and prioritisation of revenue over market integrity, hinder effective AML implementation even when sophisticated technologies are in place. Compliance officers report that while technology offers significant advantages, it can also be exploited to bypass controls. Additionally, the rapid pace of technological and market developments often outpaces regulatory frameworks, complicating compliance efforts. Oniwinde argues that achieving long-term compliance and public trust requires more than deterrence-based approaches. Financial institutions must allocate sufficient resources to compliance functions, integrate technological solutions and instil a culture of accountability across all organisational levels to effectively fight money laundering and financial crime, rendering this a strategic objective.

I.13 *Schillig* examines the potential of new technologies, particularly natural language processing and machine learning, to measure and influence corporate governance and culture in the financial sector. Schillig notes that the theoretical framework underpinning corporate governance in the financial sector requires significant modifications, as de facto state guarantees shift residual risk from shareholders to taxpayers. Corporate culture thus becomes a critical tool for aligning management incentives with taxpayer interests. Against this backdrop, Schillig explores how AI technologies can enhance corporate governance and culture. The author acknowledges the promise of these tools but cautions against viewing them as a panacea. While AI may be able to measure culture more reliably and influence it through improved decision-making, its deployment introduces governance challenges of its own. Schillig advocates for targeted legal and regulatory frameworks with a focus on algorithm design, robust testing, adequate training and effective supervision. Such tailored regulation could accommodate sector-specific idiosyncrasies while being less intrusive. Despite AI's potential, Schillig emphasises the continued importance of human expertise and accountability at all levels – board, senior management and regulators alike – ensuring robust governance arrangements remain central to fostering effective corporate governance and culture.

In the short final chapter, *Keller and Kokkinis* take us on a journey to the **I.14** future, or at least to one possible future for corporate governance and culture in finance. In looking ahead to the future, our thoughts return to the past, to the fundamental concepts of ethics and expertise as embodied by professionalism.

1

LEGAL AND REGULATORY FRAMEWORK FOR CORPORATE GOVERNANCE AND CULTURE IN FINANCIAL INSTITUTIONS

Sarah Cichon, Anat Keller and Andreas Kokkinis

A. INTRODUCTION

The 2007–9 global financial crisis (GFC) exposed significant weaknesses in the governance and culture of financial institutions.[1] This prompted calls for improvement[2] which have since been met with the response of a wide range of micro- and macroprudential as well as conduct-related reforms. Post-crisis there has been much greater emphasis on macroprudential regulation (regulation that focuses on the stability of the financial system as a whole). At the same time, macroprudential regulation has been strengthened with more demanding capital adequacy rules, a novel set of liquidity rules and, most importantly for our purposes, a raft of rules on executive remuneration, risk management and individual accountability. In parallel, in the past decade there have been significant developments in conduct of business regulation, such as the new FCA Consumer Duty, and expectations around purposeful culture, including diversity and inclusion. **1.1**

Effective governance and healthy culture, however, underpin all aspects of a firm's organisational life, including all financial regulation policies, being prerequisites for, and integral to, achieving the safety and soundness of individual institutions, the stability of the financial system, market integrity and fair treatment of customers. Governance and culture shape an institution's structure, values, norms and behaviours, influencing its decision making and resilience as well as outcomes for consumers and markets.[3] Conversely, deficiencies can lead to reputational and operational risk that can give rise to risks to capital, liquidity and solvency. Culture and governance have therefore gained a prominent position in regulatory policy at global and national levels.[4] In the UK, the Financial Conduct Authority (FCA) has put a special focus on governance **1.2**

---

1 All weblinks were last accessed on 25 November 2024. This chapter examines the regulatory framework for 'financial institutions' regulated by the PRA and FCA. Insofar as specific rules apply to specific types of institutions, this will be indicated.

2 Cf. In the UK: FSA, 'The Turner Review: A Regulatory Response to the Global Banking Crisis' (The Financial Services Authority 2009); PCBS, 'Changing Banking for Good' (2013) HL Paper 27-II, HC 175-II paras 356–365. Jacques de Larosière and others, 'Report by the High-Level Group on Financial Supervision in the EU' (Brussels, 25 February 2009); see also for example the Salz Review, which criticised Barclays' lack of a group-wide culture of shared values: Anthony Salz, 'Salz Review: An Independent Review of Barclays' Business Practices' (April 2013) paras 2.15 et seq.

3 FCA, 'Our approach to supervision' (March 2024) https://www.fca.org.uk/publications/corporate-documents/our-approach-to-supervision>. For further resources related to the FCA's work on governance and culture see FCA, 'Culture and governance' (July 2024) https://www.fca.org.uk/firms/culture-and-governance.

4 Standards and supervisory guidance have been provided at international level by the Basel Committee on Banking Supervision (BCBS), the Financial Stability Board (FSB) and the Group of Thirty (G30).

and healthy purposeful culture as part of its supervisory approach.[5] According to the FCA, the four drivers of culture are purpose, leadership, people and governance,[6] which provide a benchmark for assessing the quality of culture in regulated firms. These drivers are embedded in legal and regulatory frameworks, most notably the Financial Services and Markets Act 2000 (FSMA 2000),[7] as well as further pieces of legislation and regulation including the Prudential Regulation Authority (PRA) Rules[8] and Guidance[9] and the *FCA Handbook*.[10]

1.3 This chapter provides an in-depth analysis of this expanding area that will be of use to both academics and practitioners. The discussion is anchored in both policy and academic debates and seeks to evaluate the effectiveness of the current regime and identify remaining challenges in its design and implementation. The chapter begins with an outline of structural governance requirements (section B), covering both the general corporate governance framework and the special rules that apply to financial institutions. Then, it proceeds to examine particular policy areas that shape governance and culture. Section C discusses the Senior Managers and Certification Regime (SMCR) and its *raison d'etre* of enhancing individual accountability. Section D analyses the complex rules around executive remuneration which intend to reduce excessive risk taking and embed non-financial performance targets in senior managerial practice. Section E discusses the FCA Consumer Duty that was introduced in 2023 as a flagship policy that aims at instigating a shift in culture and behaviours to strengthen consumer protection in the financial services and put customers' needs first. Section F introduces regulatory policies and expectations on diversity and inclusion which, as we shall demonstrate, take an instrumental view of diversity as a means to enhanced compliance with regulatory objectives. Section G concludes.

---

5 FCA, 'Culture and governance' (7 April 2024) https://www.fca.org.uk/firms/culture-and-governance.

6 Ibid.

7 See the most recent amendments by the Financial Services and Markets Act 2023 (FSMA 2023).

8 PRA, *PRA Rulebook* https://www.prarulebook.co.uk/pra-rules. The *PRA Rulebook* contains prudential requirements applicable to all PRA-authorised persons and firms and certain unauthorised persons.

9 PRA, *PRA Guidance* https://www.prarulebook.co.uk/guidance. The PRA provides guidance in the form of Supervisory Statements ('SS') and Statements of Policy ('SoP').

10 FCA, *FCA Handbook* https://www.handbook.fca.org.uk. The *FCA Handbook* containing rules and guidance is applicable to FCA regulated persons and firms. Firms regulated by both the FCA and PRA ('Dual-regulated firms') are subject to both the FCA's and PRA's rules and guidance. See the Financial Services and Markets Act 2000 (PRA-regulated Activities) Order 2013/556 last amended by the Financial Services Act 2021 (Prudential Regulation of Credit Institutions and Investment Firms) (Consequential Amendments and Miscellaneous Provisions) Regulations 2021 (S.I. 2021/1376).

B. STRUCTURAL GOVERNANCE REQUIREMENTS

1. The Conventional UK Corporate Governance Framework

The UK corporate governance framework is anchored in the Corporate Governance Code (Code), issued by the Financial Reporting Council and updated biennially.[11] Although the Code is not legally binding, listed companies must disclose their adherence to its principles, providing explanations for any non-compliance.[12] As such it applies directly to large banks, insurance firms and investment management firms and funds the securities of which are admitted to the official list. Beyond its immediate relevance to listed companies, the Code is influential in shaping standards for large non-listed companies and thus constitutes a formative influence on corporate governance practices for a wide range of financial institutions. **1.4**

The Code aims to promote effective and entrepreneurial corporate boards that promote the long-term sustainable success of the company[13] and culture that emphasises integrity, openness and diversity.[14] In particular, the Code addresses the principal–agent problem, which arises when one party (the principal) appoints another (the agent) to act on their behalf.[15] In a corporate context, shareholders (principals) rely on managers (agents) to manage the company in their best interests.[16] An agency relationship arises from the separation of ownership and control, where share ownership is dispersed, limiting **1.5**

11 FRC, 'UK Corporate Governance Code' https://www.frc.org.uk/library/standards-codes-policy/corporate-governance/uk-corporate-governance-code/. The 2024 Code will apply to financial years beginning on or after 1 January 2025 and is referred to in this section as the '2024 Code'. The 2024 Code is supported by the FRC's Corporate Governance Code Guidance: FRC, 'Corporate Governance Code Guidance' https://www.frc.org.uk/library/standards-codes-policy/corporate-governance/corporate-governance-code-guidance/.

12 Under the UK Listing Rules (LR) UK-incorporated companies must include a corporate governance disclosure in their annual financial report, 6.6.6 LR. Overseas companies with the same listing category are similarly required to disclose this information, 6.6.17 LR. Companies listed under the closed-end investment funds category must also comply with this requirement, 11.4.1 and 11.4.2 LR. Additionally, issuers subject to *FCA Handbook*'s Disclosure Guidance and Transparency Rules sourcebook (DTR) Section 7 are required to make corporate governance disclosures either in their directors' report or in a separate corporate governance statement. Cf. Principle C of the 2024 Code.

13 Principle A of the 2024 Code.

14 Introduction to the 2024 Code.

15 Tackling the agency problem has been central to the corporate governance movement since its inception. See Daniel R Fischel, 'The Corporate Governance Movement' (1982) 35 *Vanderbilt Law Review* 1259.

16 John Black, Nigar Hashimzade and Gareth D Myles, 'Principal and Agent' in *A Dictionary of Economics* (5th edn, Oxford University Press 2017, online edn). See also Sanford J Grossman and Oliver D Hart, 'An Analysis of the Principal-Agent Problem' (1983) 51 Econometrica 7 and Frank H Easterbrook, 'Managers' Discretion and Investors' Welfare: Theories and Evidence' (1984) 9 *Delaware Journal of Corporate Law* 540.

individual shareholders' ability to exert effective control.[17] Divergent interests between managers and shareholders may then result in agency costs, as managers may pursue personal gains over shareholder interests. Shareholders, however, face significant costs in attempting to influence corporate decisions. They must gather information, form coalitions, and engage with the board, whilst confronted with uncertainty as to the outcome and benefits that are shared among all shareholders. This leads to shareholder passivity, known as rational apathy, where board recommendations are typically approved with little resistance.[18] To mitigate this risk, the Code's principles and provisions on board independence and board committees aim to reduce these agency costs.[19] The Code requires at least half the board, excluding the chair, to be independent non-executive directors.[20] The chairman must be distinct from the CEO and have no significant prior relationship with the company.[21] Most UK-listed financial institutions follow these guidelines, maintaining a high proportion of independent directors on their boards.[22] Moreover, as nominations, remuneration, and audit carry notable potential for conflicts between senior management and shareholders, the Code mandates establishing a nominations committee for board appointments;[23] an audit committee to oversee external auditors, financial controls and statements;[24] and a remuneration committee to set remuneration policies and determine compensation.[25] In addition to the Code, UK company law employs various mechanisms to address these costs, including granting shareholders decision-making authority, providing them

17 This phenomenon has been common in the UK since the late 1960s. On an agency relationship in this scenario see Adolf Berle and Gardiner Means, *The Modern Corporation and Private Property* (rev edn, Harcourt, Brace & World, 1967) 108–109.

18 For a modern explanation of the dynamics of shareholder voting and the rational apathy of the shareholders from a US perspective, see Christopher Gulinello, 'The Retail Investor Vote: Mobilizing Rationally Apathetic Shareholders to Preserve or Challenge the Board's Presumption of Authority' (2010) *Utah Law Review* 547, 573–576.

19 Theoretical and empirical research supports the significance of board structure and independence in mitigating agency costs. A review of general economic literature on the functioning of boards of directors can be found in Renee Adams, Benjamin Hermalin and Michael Weisbach, 'The Role of Boards of Directors in Corporate Governance: A Conceptual Framework and Survey' (2010) 48 *Journal of Economic Literature* 58.

20 Provision 11 of the Code. Provision 10 also contains a list of relationships and circumstances which are likely to impair independence. This includes shareholders, employees, business partners, family ties, interlocking directorships, and other associations.

21 Provision 9 of the 2024 Code.

22 The UK has one of the highest proportions of independent directors. With reference to S&P 500 see Spencer Stuart, '2023 Spencer Stuart Board Indexes' https://www.spencerstuart.com/research-and-insight/boards-around-the-world?category=all-board-composition&topic=all-topics.

23 Provision 17 et seq. of the 2024 Code.

24 Provision 24 et seq. of the 2024 Code.

25 Provision 32 et seq. of the 2024 Code.

the power to appoint and remove directors, imposing fiduciary duties on directors and aligning director incentives with shareholder interests.[26]

With regard to culture and diversity and inclusion, the Code requires boards not only to assess and monitor culture but also to report on how effectively the desired culture has been embedded within the company.[27] Moreover, the Code highlights that board appointments and succession plans should promote diversity, inclusion and equal opportunities. The most recent version of the Code, however, removed diversity characteristics pertaining to diversity of gender, social and ethnic backgrounds, cognitive and personal strengths.[28] While the FRC contends that broader interpretations of diversity policies enable flexibility,[29] this approach risks diluting strategies and actions to increase diversity.[30] Emphasising concrete diversity characteristics enhances public accountability and as a consequence increases the incentive to focus on achieving more diversity. For instance, the Davies Review (2011–2015) contributed to doubling female representation on FTSE 350 boards[31] and sustained focus on gender diversity again doubled female representation in the decade following the review.[32] **1.6**

2. Specific Corporate Governance Requirements for Financial Institutions

In the aftermath of the latest global financial crisis, the corporate governance of financial institutions attracted the attention of regulators at the global, regional and national levels. Regulators increased focus on corporate governance[33] in response to concerns about shareholder-centric governance models due to the negative externalities arising from institutions' failures – often leading to government bailouts and undermining financial stability.[34] A key devel- **1.7**

26 Reinier Kraakman et al, *The Anatomy of Corporate Law: A Comparative and Functional Approach* (3rd edn, OUP, 2017) 31 et seq.

27 Provision 2 of the 2024 Code.

28 Principle J of the 2018 Code referred to these characteristics, which were not included in the 2024 Code.

29 Provision 23 and Principle J of the 2024 Code.

30 On diversity and inclusion cf. ibid Section E.

31 Female representation on FTSE 100 boards increased from 12 per cent in 2011 to 25 per cent in 2015, and on FTSE 250 boards from 9 per cent to 22 per cent in the same period. FTSE Women Leaders, '2011–2015 The Davies Review' https://ftsewomenleaders.com/2011-2015-the-davies-review.

32 Female representation on FTSE 350 boards lies at 40.2 per cent. FTSE Women Leaders, 'FTSE Women Leaders Review' (February 2024) 35 https://ftsewomenleaders.com.

33 See responses of the OECD: Grant Kirkpatrick, 'The Corporate Governance Lessons from the Financial Crisis' (2009) *OECD Journal: Financial Market Trends* 61 and the EU: Commission, 'Corporate governance in financial institutions and remuneration policies' COM (2010) 284 final, 2.

34 See e.g. Jaap Winter, 'The Financial Crisis: Does Good Corporate Governance Matter and How to Achieve it?' in Eddy Wymeersch, Klaus Hopt and Guido Ferranini (eds), *Financial Regulation and Supervision: A Post-crisis Analysis* (OUP 2012).

opment was the publication of the Basel Principles for Enhancing Corporate Governance in 2010.[35] These principles emphasise the importance of corporate governance at both the micro-level, for individual institutions, and the macro-level, for the stability of the financial system through appropriate incentives, facilitating regulatory supervision and enhancing market confidence.[36] The Basel Principles stress the need for effective boards, sound risk management, executive remuneration, simplified group structures and transparency, thereby complementing general cross-sectoral governance requirements with rules to ensure effective risk management.[37] These include, for instance, the establishment of a board risk committee and the appointment of a Chief Risk Officer (CRO).[38] The Basel Principles also underline the important role of supervisors in assessing governance structures and the need to possess the power to intervene when necessary.[39]

1.8 In the UK, the Walker Review introduced reforms relating to the governance of financial institutions, which were later adopted by the regulatory frameworks of the PRA and FCA.[40] The Walker Review did not challenge the shareholder-value orientation of financial institutions' governance due to concerns that this would cause uncertainty and raise capital costs driving away investors.[41] The Parliamentary Commission on Banking Standards (PCBS), which was appointed by both Houses of Parliament to consider and report on the professional standards and culture of the UK financial sector, adopted a more critical view.[42] It proposed reviewing directors' duties under the Companies Act 2006 in view of prioritising financial stability over shareholder interests,[43] which was however never implemented. Nevertheless, the Walker

---

35 Working Group on Corporate Governance of the Basel Committee, 'Principles for Enhancing Corporate Governance' (Bank of International Settlements 2010).

36 Ibid 1–2.

37 Ibid 7 et seq.

38 Ibid 17.

39 Ibid 30 et seq.

40 Sir David Walker, 'A Review of Corporate Governance in UK Banks and Other Financial Industry Entities: Final Recommendations' (2009) (Walker Review) para 1.22 https://www.icaew.com/en/library/subject-gateways/corporate-governance/codes-and-reports/walker-report.

41 Sections 168, 171, 172, 304, 305, 314, 561 and 983 of the Companies Act 2006; 'Walker Review', Annex 3, 137.

42 PCBS, 'Changing Banking for Good' (2013) HL Paper 27-II, HC 175-II para 119.

43 Ibid para 708. The PCBS recommended revising the Code to require bank directors to prioritise the institution's safety and soundness and consider duties to customers, taxpayers, and others. It also suggested amending the PRA Principles to ensure banks operate with a focus on stability, interpreting directors' shareholder responsibilities. Additionally, Senior Persons in director roles were to explicitly uphold the firm's safety and soundness. The PCBS recommended amending section 172 of the Companies Act 2006, removing shareholder primacy in banks in favour of prioritising financial stability. On the parallel academic debate see eg Iris H-Y Chiu, 'Comparing Directors' Duties in the Financial Services Sector with

Review led to reforms addressing certain aspects of boards' composition and role[44] and introduced recommendations pertaining to risk governance[45] and remuneration.[46]

Beyond UK-led reforms, a vast part of governance requirements applicable today was introduced under EU law – in particular, the EU Capital Requirements Directive (CRD IV)[47] as well as the Markets in Financial Instruments Directive (MiFID II).[48] While many of these requirements aligned with the recommendations of the Code and regulatory practice, the EU Directives rendered them legally binding. In general, institutions must establish effective governance systems, including robust risk strategies and management systems,[49] and ensure their affairs are organised and controlled responsibly and effectively.[50] Extensive governance requirements apply to CRR firms[51] as well as certain FCA-regulated institutions,[52] in particular significant institutions.[53] CRR and SYSC firms are required to establish robust governance arrangements, including a clear organisational structure with well-defined, transparent, and consistent lines of responsibility.[54] They must implement effective processes to identify, manage, monitor and report risks 1.9

Regulatory Duties under the Senior Persons Regime – Some Critical Observations' (2016) 27 *European Business Law Review* 261; Mads Andenas and Iris H-Y Chiu, *The Foundations and Future of Financial Regulation: Governance for Responsibility* (Routledge 2014) 392; Andreas Kokkinis, *Corporate Law and Financial Instability* (Routledge 2018).

44 Sir David Walker (n 40) chs 2–5.

45 Ibid 6.

46 Ibid 7.

47 Directive 2013/36/EU of the European Parliament and of the Council of 26 June 2013 on access to the activity of credit institutions and the prudential supervision of credit institutions and investment firms, *OJ L* 176, 27.6.2013, p. 1–337.

48 Directive 2014/65/EU of the European Parliament and of the Council of 15 May 2014 on markets in financial instruments and amending Directive 2002/92/EC and Directive 2011/61/EU, *OJ L* 173, 12.6.2014, p. 349–496.

49 *PRA Rulebook*, Fundamental Rule 5.

50 *PRA Rulebook*, Fundamental Rule 6.

51 CRR firms are UK banks, building societies or UK-designated investment firms that were subject to the CRR and authorised within the meaning of section 31(1)(a) of the FSMA 2000. These are credit institutions with the permission under Part 4A of FSMA to carry on the regulated activity of accepting deposits or PRA-designated investment firms with their registered or head offices in the UK. This does not include credit unions or friendly societies, cf. Article 4(2)(A) of the retained EU law version of Regulation (EU) No 575/2013 of the European Parliament and of the Council of 26 June 2013 on prudential requirements for credit institutions and investment firms and amending Regulation (EU) No 648/2012 (UK CRR) brought into UK law through the European Union (Withdrawal) Act 2018.

52 *FCA Handbook*, Senior Management Arrangements, Systems and Controls (SYSC), 1.1A.

53 Significant institutions within the meaning of the UK CRR; Significant SYSC firms are defined in *FCA Handbook*, SYSC, 1.5.2. Specific rules apply to limited scope FCA-regulated institutions, cf. *FCA Handbook*, SYSC, 4.4.

54 *PRA Rulebook*, CRR Firms, General organisational requirements, 2.1; *FCA Handbook*, SYSC, 4.1.1. Cf. Art. 74(1) CRD IV and Art. 16(5) MiFID II.

and internal control mechanisms.[55] These requirements are applied proportionally, taking into account the institution's size, complexity, operations and risk exposure.[56]

1.10 The management body is responsible for defining and overseeing governance arrangements that ensure the firm's effective and prudent management, including the segregation of duties and the prevention of conflicts of interest.[57] Given its critical role, the management body is subject to specific structural governance requirements in light of its essential and sensitive governance and risk management functions. Members of the management body must be of good repute and possess sufficient experience to ensure the firm's sound and prudent management.[58] Moreover, it is prohibited to combine the roles of CEO and board chairman without regulatory approval.[59] Members of the management body may also not hold more directorships than is appropriate considering individual circumstances and the nature, scale and complexity of the institution's activities.[60] In significant institutions,[61] individuals' board appointments are generally limited to one executive, two non-executive or four non-executive roles.[62] Furthermore, significant institutions are required to establish nomination committees composed exclusively of non-executive directors.[63] For institutions without a nomination committee, a diverse set of qualities and expertise must nevertheless be considered when recruiting

55 *PRA Rulebook*, CRR Firms, General organisational requirements, 2.1; *FCA Handbook*, SYSC, 4.1.1. Cf. Art. 74(1) CRD IV and Art. 16(5) MiFID II.

56 *PRA Rulebook*, CRR Firms, General organisational requirements, 2.2; *FCA Handboo*k, SYSC, 4.1.2. Cf. Art. 74(2) CRD IV.

57 *PRA Rulebook*, CRR Firms, General organisational requirements, 5.1; *FCA Handbook*, SYSC, 4.3A.1. Cf. Art. 88(1) CRD IV and Art. 9(3) MiFID II.

58 *PRA Rulebook*, CRR Firms, General organisational requirements, 5.2; *FCA Handbook*, SYSC, 4.2.1 Cf. Art. 91(1)-(2) and (7)-(8) CRD IV and Art. 9(1) and (4) MiFID II. Cf. also Section B.3(a) and (b) in this chapter on fitness and propriety requirements.

59 *PRA Rulebook*, Senior Management Functions, 8.2; FCA Handbook, SYSC, 4.3A.2. Cf. Art. 88(1)(e) CRD IV and Art. 9(1) MiFID II.

60 *PRA Rulebook*, CRR Firms, General organisational requirements, 5.4; FCA Handbook, SYSC, 4.3A.5. Cf. Art. 91(3) CRD IV and Art. 9(1) MiFID II.

61 *FCA Handbook*, SYSC, 1.5. The PRA categorises its supervised firms into four impact levels, determined by their potential influence. PRA, 'The Prudential Regulation Authority's Approach to Banking Supervision' (2023) para 35 https://www.bankofengland.co.uk/-/media/boe/files/prudential-regulation/approach/banking-approach-2023.pdf.

62 *PRA Rulebook*, CRR Firms, General organisational requirements, 5.5; FCA Handbook, SYSC, 4.3A.6. Cf. Art. 91(3) CRD IV and Art. 9(1) MiFID II. Cf. Exceptions in *PRA Rulebook*, CRR Firms, General organisational requirements, 5.6; *FCA Handbook*, SYSC, 4.3A.7. Cf. Art. 91(4) and (5) CRD IV and Art. 9(1) MiFID II.

63 *PRA Rulebook*, CRR Firms, General organisational requirements, 6.1–6.2; *FCA Handbook*, SYSC, 4.3A.8-9. Cf. Art. 88(2) and Art. 91(10) CRD IV and Art. 9(1) MiFID II.

members of the management body, with a policy in place promoting diversity within the management body.[64]

In addition to governance, the management body holds overall responsibility for risk management.[65] It must approve and periodically review strategies and policies for managing, monitoring and mitigating the institution's risks.[66] Risk management functions must operate independently from operational functions and report directly to the board.[67] Significant financial institutions are required to appoint a CRO to lead the risk management function[68] and establish a risk committee, composed of non-executive directors.[69] The risk committee advises the management body on the institution's overall risk appetite and assists in overseeing the implementation of risk strategies.[70] It must also cooperate with the remuneration committee to ensure risk management is integrated into the institution's remuneration policies.[71] **1.11**

C. SENIOR MANAGERS AND CERTIFICATION REGIME (SMCR)

Beyond structural governance requirements, a wide range of financial institutions in the UK are now also governed by the Senior Managers and Certification Regime (SMCR) outlined in the FSMA[72] and PRA and FCA rules and guidance. The SMCR was introduced in 2016 to replace the pre-existing Approved Persons Regime with a view to overcoming the accountability deficit which was evident during the 2007–9 crisis and which results from the collective nature of board responsibility under company law principles. The SMCR is designed to promote a culture of individual responsibility and accountability of managers to drive cultural change and reduce consumer harm thereby also strengthening market integrity and risk management within financial **1.12**

64 *PRA Rulebook*, CRR Firms, General organisational requirements, 6.3; *FCA Handbook*, SYSC, 4.3A.10. Cf. Art. 91(10) CRD and Art. 9(1) MiFID II.

65 *PRA Rulebook*, CRR Firms, Risk Control, 2.7. Cf. Art. 76(2) CRD IV.

66 *PRA Rulebook*, CRR Firms, Risk Control, 2.3; FCA Handbook, SYSC, 4.3A.1A. Cf. Art. 76(1) CRD IV and Art. 9(3) MiFID II. Common platform firms other than credit institutions or AIFM investment firms must have alternative arrangements in place which ensure sound and prudent management of the firm, *FCA Handbook*, SYSC, 4.2.6 FCA. Cf. Art. 9(6) MiFID II.

67 *PRA Rulebook*, CRR Firms, Risk Control, 3.4. Cf. Art. 76(5) CRD IV.

68 *PRA Rulebook*, CRR Firms, Risk Control, 3.5. Cf. Art. 76(5) CRD IV.

69 *PRA Rulebook*, CRR Firms, Risk Control, 3.1(1) Cf. Art. 76(3) CRD IV.

70 *PRA Rulebook*, CRR Firms, Risk Control, 3.1(2) Cf. Art. 76(3) CRD IV.

71 *PRA Rulebook*, CRR Firms, Risk Control, 3.1-3.3. Cf. Art. 76(3)–(4) CRD IV.

72 Financial Services & Markets Act 2000 amended by Part 4 of the 2013 Financial Services Banking Reform Act (hereinafter: the FSBRA 2013). The relevant provisions were brought into force on 7 March 2016 by the FSBRA 2013 (Commencement No. 9) Order 2015 (S.I. 2015/490).

institutions.[73] This section examines: the development of the SMCR (1); its scope and applicable legal framework (2); core elements (3); enforcement (4); and ongoing review (5).

1. Development of the SMCR

1.13 The SMCR was introduced in the aftermath of the GFC, primarily in response to the failings in governance and culture within the financial sector. It follows recommendations stemming from the PCBS report, which identified significant shortcomings in the previously applicable Approved Persons Regime, in particular concerning the accountability of senior managers.[74] The PCBS report advocated for a more rigorous framework focused on accountability and fitness and propriety of senior management as well as enhanced conduct standards.[75] The report also reflected widespread public outrage towards senior bank managers, who were widely seen as responsible for the crisis and the LIBOR scandal[76] but largely avoided regulatory sanctions.[77] Most of the PCBS recommendations were enacted through the Financial Services Banking Reform Act 2013, which replaced the Approved Persons Regime with the SMCR, effective from April 2016.

2. Scope and Applicable Framework

1.14 The SMCR was initially introduced for CRR firms but has since been extended to include insurance firms,[78] benchmark administrators,[79] investment exchanges, credit rating agencies and financial market infrastructures (FMIs).[80] While payment, e-money and crypto firms were not included in the

---

73 FCA, 'Senior Managers and Certification Regime' (19 April 2016) https://www.fca.org.uk/firms/senior-managers-certification-regime. For an extensive analysis of the SMCR and its link to organisational culture see Anat Keller and Andreas Kokkinis, 'The Senior Managers and Certification Regime in Financial Firms: An Organisational Culture Analysis' (2022) 22 *Journal of Corporate Law Studies* 299.

74 PCBS, 'Changing Banking for Good' (2013) HL Paper 27-II, HC 175-II paras 105 et seq.

75 Ibid para 283 et seq.

76 For a detailed analysis, see Patrick McConnell, 'Systemic Operational Risk: the LIBOR Manipulation Scandal' (2013) 8 *Journal of Operational Risk* 59.

77 For a discussion of post-crisis regulatory enforcement cases against bank senior managers, see Andreas Kokkinis, 'The Regulation of Bank Corporate Governance, Executive Remuneration and Senior Managers Accountability' in Andreas Kokkinis and Andrea Miglionico, *Banking Law* (Routledge 2021) 131–134.

78 FCA 'Policy Statement PS18/16: Final guidance: The Duty of Responsibility for insurers and FCA solo-regulated firms' (July 2018) https://www.fca.org.uk/publication/policy/ps18-16.pdf.

79 FCA 'Policy Statement PS20/5: Extending the Senior Managers Regime to benchmark administrators: Final rules' (June 2020), https://www.fca.org.uk/publications/policy-statements/ps20-5-extending-senior-managers-regime-benchmark-administrators-final-rules.

80 The SMCR was extended to FMIs considered systemically important to the UK's economy and financial system. Schedule 10 FSMA 2023 introduces sections 309A to 309Z8, which apply the regime to

most recent extension of the SMCR's scope, the FCA sees value in this and is exploring potential options with HM Treasury for extending the regime to these firms.[81] In line with this, the FCA issued a 'Dear CEO letter' to Payments and E-Money Firms in March 2023, highlighting expectations regarding leadership, oversight and governance.[82] The FCA emphasised that these firms should ensure their directors and those providing payment services are fit and proper and possess appropriate knowledge and experience, mirroring the expectations applied to institutions within the SMCR's scope.[83] However, the absence of explicit regulatory progress suggests that extending the SMCR to these institutions has been paused, pending the outcome of the SMCR review.[84] With regard to financial institutions within the scope of the SMCR, the applicable requirements vary depending on whether an institution is regulated solely by the FCA ('solo-regulated') or by both the FCA and the PRA ('dual-regulated'). The scope of responsibilities for solo-regulated institutions differs across three categories of institutions: enhanced, core and limited scope. Core firms adhere to a standard set of requirements, while limited scope firms face reduced obligations. In contrast, larger and more complex enhanced firms must comply with additional rules.[85] Dual-regulated institutions, such as CRR firms, are subject to specific rules and guidance issued by the PRA which vary based on the institution's classification. The PRA holds primary responsibility for the oversight and approval of most Senior Management Functions (SMFs) in dual-regulated institutions, with FCA consent required.[86] However, for certain SMFs, the FCA alone is responsible for approval.[87]

---

exempt persons in chapter 18 (Central Counterparties, Central Securities Depositories and Recognised Investment Exchanges).

81 FCA, 'FCA Perimeter Report' (5 April 2024) https://www.fca.org.uk/publications/annual-reports/perimeter-report.

82 FCA, 'Dear CEO Letter: FCA priorities for payments firms' (16 March 2023) https://www.fca.org.uk/publication/correspondence/priorities-payments-firms-portfolio-letter-2023.pdf.

83 Ibid, B.

84 See below Section B.5.

85 FCA, 'The Senior Managers and Certification Regime: Guide for FCA solo-regulated irms' (2019) chs 5–7 https://www.fca.org.uk/publication/policy/guide-for-fca-solo-regulated-firms.pdf.

86 Cf. Section 59 of the FSMA as amended by the FSBRA 2013 (c. 33), s. 148(5). Cf. also *FCA Handbook*, Supervision (SUP), 10C.9.

87 SMF 3 Executive Director; SMF 13 Chair of Nominations Committee; SMF 15 Chair of With-profits Committee; SMF 16 Compliance Oversight Function; SMF 17 Money Laundering Reporting Function; SMF18 Other Overall Responsibility Function; SMF 21 EEA Branch Senior Manager; SMF 22 Other Local Responsibility; SMF 23b Lloyd's Conduct Risk Oversight Function; SMF 27 Partner function. Under the overlap rule, if a candidate applies for an SMF requiring PRA approval, they may also perform SMF 3, SMF 13, SMF 15, or SMF 27 roles without needing separate approval, *FCA Handbook*, Supervision (SUP), 10C.9.

3. Elements of the SMCR

1.15 The SMCR encompasses several elements: the senior managers regime (SMR); the certification regime; regulatory references; and conduct rules. The applicability of these regimes depends on the role and (potential) impact of the individual on the institution's decision-making and risk. The SMR only applies to a small number of individuals, whereas the Certification Regime and Regulatory References apply to a broader set of individuals. Moreover, certain Conduct Rules only apply to Senior Managers whereas a different category applies to all employees of financial institutions.

(a) Senior Managers Regime

1.16 The SMR applies to individuals occupying roles classified as SMFs, which are responsible for managing one or more critical aspects of the affairs of an institution.[88] These roles carry a risk of serious consequences for the institution or business or other interests in the United Kingdom.[89] Both the PRA and the FCA have their respective lists of SMFs. The PRA's list includes six executive functions – CEO, CFO, CRO, Head of Internal Audit, Head of Key Business Area and Group Entity Senior Manager – and five non-executive roles, including board chairmen and the chairs of the audit, remuneration and risk committees, as well as senior independent directors.[90] The FCA's list is more extensive and includes functions such as compliance oversight and money laundering reporting, as well as the chair of the board's nominations committee.[91] For solo-regulated institutions the SMFs vary by institution type. For instance, 17 SMFs are required for enhanced firms, 6 for core firms, and 3 for limited scope firms.[92] Among the SMFs, specific prescribed responsibilities (PRs) must be allocated to ensure critical functions corresponding with regulatory objectives are covered.[93] These include inter alia prescribed responsibilities for culture[94] or compliance with the elements of the SMCR,[95]

88 See the FSBRA 2013, Explanatory Notes, para 174.

89 Section 59ZA FSMA 2000 inserted by the FSBRA 2013 (c. 33), ss. 19, 148(5); S.I. 2014/1819, art. 2(1)(a).

90 Cf. *PRA Rulebook*, Senior Management Functions. For credit unions there is only the credit union senior management function, 6.1–6.3.

91 *FCA Handbook*, SUP, 10C.4.4.

92 Cf. *FCA Handbook*, SUP, 10C Annex 1, 5.2; 6.2; 7.4.

93 *PRA Rulebook*, Allocation of Responsibilities, 4; FCA Handbook, SYSC, 24.2.

94 *PRA Rulebook*, Allocation of Responsibilities, 4.1 PRs I and H.

95 *PRA Rulebook*, Allocation of Responsibilities, 4.1 PRs A, B, C, U, G, H; *FCA Handbook*, SYSC, 24.2.6 PRs (a), (b), (d), (b-1), (f), (g), (j), (k).

but also other regulatory responsibilities such as risk management and stress-testing[96] or recovery and resolution planning.[97]

Institutions must submit an application for regulatory approval before appointing an individual to a SMF to ensure the candidate is fit and proper for the role.[98] This assessment considers the individual's good repute, integrity, knowledge, experience, qualifications, competence, capability and financial soundness, including a criminal record check.[99] Once approved, institutions are required to reassess the fitness and propriety of senior managers annually and notify the regulator if there are any grounds that could warrant a withdrawal of approval.[100] Furthermore, the regulators may approve a candidate for a SMF with specific conditions or for a limited period, which may also be imposed or modified after initial approval.[101] The regulatory approval process is subject to a statutory three-month deadline within which the regulators must reach a determination.[102] **1.17**

The FCA imposes fines and prohibition orders on SMF holders who fail to meet standards of fitness and propriety, often due to findings of a lack of integrity. This lack of integrity may stem from personal conduct unrelated to the SMF holder's actions within the institution where the individual holds the SMF. For example, in February 2024, Nicholas Andrew McNeil, an executive director and SMF holder, received a fine and prohibition order from the FCA due to a criminal conviction for possessing a false instrument, indicating a lack of honesty and integrity.[103] Similarly, the Upper Tribunal upheld an FCA's older decision to deny Thomas Llewellyn Kalaris authorisation to perform SMFs for Saranac Partners Ltd, citing dishonesty in enforcement interviews related to a different institution several years prior as grounds for his lack of **1.18**

96 *PRA Rulebook*, Allocation of Responsibilities, 4.1 PR S; *FCA Handbook*, SYSC, 24.2.6 PR (aa), (s).

97 *PRA Rulebook*, Allocation of Responsibilities, 4.1 PR R.

98 *PRA Rulebook*, Fitness and Propriety, 2.1; *FCA Handbook*, SUP, 10C.10.14G; Section 60A FSMA 2000 inserted by the FSBRA 2013, ss. 21, 148(5); S.I. 2015/490, art. 2(1)(c) and 61(1) FSMA 2000 substituted by the FSBRA 2013 (c. 33), ss. 23(2), 148(5); S.I. 2015/490, art. 2(1)(c).

99 *PRA Rulebook*, Fitness and Propriety, 2.6; FCA Handbook, SUP, 10C.10.14G; Sections 60A (2)(a)–(d) FSMA 2000 inserted by the FSBRA 2013, ss. 21, 148(5); S.I. 2015/490, art. 2(1)(c).

100 *FCA Handbook*, SUP 10C.14.18R to SUP 10C.14.25G; Section 63(2A) FSMA 2000 inserted by the FSBRA 2013 (c. 33), ss. 25, 148(5); S.I. 2015/490, art. 2(1)(c).

101 Section 63ZD and 63ZE FSMA 2000 inserted by the FSBRA 2013, ss. 27, 148(5); S.I. 2014/1819, art. 2(1)(b).

102 Section 61(3A)(ii) FSMA 2000 inserted by Financial Services Act 2012 (c. 21), s. 122(3), Sch. 5 para. 5(6) (with Sch. 20); S.I. 2013/423, art. 3, Sch.

103 FCA, 'Final Notice – Nicholas Andrew McNeil' (8 February 2024) https://www.fca.org.uk/publication/final-notices/nicholas-andrew-mcneil-2024.pdf.

integrity, honesty and transparency.[104] A lack of integrity may also be related to an SMF holder's approval or lack of preventing an institution's infringement of regulatory requirements. For example, in February 2024, the FCA imposed a fine and prohibition order on Floris Jakobus Huisamen, director of London Capital and Finance plc (LCF), for approving LCF's misleading financial promotions, deeming him a risk to consumers and the UK financial system's integrity.[105] These sanctions followed an FCA notice against LCF in October 2023, citing violations of the *FCA Handbook*'s fair, clear and not misleading rule.[106]

1.19 In addition to fitness and propriety requirements, institutions are required to prepare and submit a Statement of Responsibilities (SoR) to regulators outlining the specific responsibilities of each SMF.[107] For dual-regulated and enhanced solo-regulated institutions, there is also a requirement to maintain a Management Responsibilities Map (MRM).[108] These tools provide a clear view of senior managers' specific responsibilities and the institution's governance structure, ensuring that accountability is not inhibited by lack of clear allocation of responsibility. However, defining and documenting responsibilities in line with regulatory requirements is complicated by the dynamism of individual governance structures including overlapping, evolving and delegated roles. Moreover, this must remain up to date and be accompanied by related documents, such as job descriptions and contracts or partnership agreements on an ongoing basis.

(b) Certification regime

1.20 The Certification Regime applies to employees who do not occupy SMFs but hold roles that significantly impact the institution's risk profile or pose risks to customers (significant-harm functions).[109] Unlike SMFs, individuals

---

104 *Saranac Partner Ltd v The Financial Conduct Authority* [2024] UKUT 00254 (TCC); FCA, 'Decision Notice – Saranac Partners Limited and Thomas Llewellyn Kalaris' (17 November 2022) https://www.fca.org.uk/publication/decision-notices/saranac-partners-limited-2022.pdf.

105 FCA, 'Final Notice – Floris Jakobus Huisamen' (13 February 2024) https://www.fca.org.uk/publication/final-notices/final-notice-floris-jakobus-huisamen-2024.pdf.

106 FCA, 'Final Notice – London Capital & Finance plc' (11 October 2023) https://www.fca.org.uk/publication/final-notices/london-capital-and-finance-plc-2023.pdf; *FCA Handbook*, COBS, 4.2.1.

107 Sections 60 (2A)–(2C) FSMA 2000 inserted by the FSBRA 2013, ss. 20(2), 148(5); S.I. 2014/1819, art. 2(3); S.I. 2015/490, art. 2(1)(b); *PRA Rulebook*, Allocation of Responsibilities, 2; *FCA Handbook*, SUP, 10C.11. If the functions of a senior manager change significantly, institutions have to submit to the regulator a revised statement of responsibilities, Section 62A FSMA 2000 inserted by the FSBRA 2013, ss. 24, 148(5); S.I. 2015/490, art. 2(1)(c).

108 *PRA Rulebook*, Allocation of Responsibilities, 7; *FCA Handbook*, SYSC, 25.

109 Section 63E(5) FSMA 2000 inserted by the FSBRA 2013 (c. 33), ss. 29, 148(5); S.I. 2014/1819, art. 2(2)(b); S.I. 2015/490, art. 2(1)(a)(2). See also *PRA Rulebook*, Certification; *FCA Handbook*, SYSC, 27.

under the Certification Regime do not require regulatory approval. However, institutions are required to assess and certify that these employees are fit and proper for their roles both upon appointment and annually thereafter and issue certificates that specify the aspects of the affairs of the institution that the employee will be involved with.[110]

(c) Regulatory references

To substantiate decisions on appointing individuals to senior manager or certification functions, institutions must obtain regulatory references for applicants to Senior Manager, Certification and non-executive director roles from all employers within the past six years.[111] These references must detail any breaches of conduct rules and other pertinent information on the individual's fitness and propriety.[112] Institutions must also provide such references to other institutions within six weeks upon request, using a standard template.[113] Institutions are, however, only required to take reasonable steps to obtain regulatory references and, if unsuccessful, may simply document the steps taken to acquire them.[114] Beyond serving as a tool to support institutions and regulators in assessing individuals' fitness and propriety, regulatory references preemptively promote good conduct and compliance, as individuals are likely to consider the impact of their conduct on future references and their chances of holding managerial functions.[115] **1.21**

(d) Conduct rules

The SMCR also imposes conduct rules,[116] which the PRA and FCA are empowered to enforce and sanction in cases of breaches.[117] These rules extend beyond those prescribed by company law, with Individual Conduct Rules applicable to all staff and Senior Manager Conduct Rules applicable to those **1.22**

110 Section 63E and 63F FSMA 2000 inserted by the FSBRA 2013, ss. 29, 148(5); S.I. 2014/1819, art. 2(2)(b); S.I. 2015/490, art. 2(1)(a)(2).

111 *PRA Rulebook*, Fitness and Propriety, 2.7; *FCA Handbook*, SYSC, 22.2.

112 Ibid.

113 *PRA Rulebook*, Fitness and Propriety, 7.1; *FCA Handbook*, SYSC 22 Annex 1 Template.

114 *PRA Rulebook*, Fitness and Propriety, 2.7; *FCA Handbook*, SYSC, 22.7.4.

115 Cf. UK Finance, 'SMCR – Evolution and Reform' (September 2019) 19 https://www.ukfinance.org.uk/system/files/SMCR%20-%20Evolution%20and%20Reform.pdf.

116 Ss. 64A, 64B inserted by the FSBRA 2013, ss. 30(3), 148(5); S.I. 2014/1819, art. 2(2)(c); S.I. 2015/490, art. 2(1)(d). Cf. *PRA Rulebook*, Conduct Rules; *FCA Handbook*, Code of Conduct sourcebook (COCON).

117 Sections 66–67 FSMA 2000 as amended by the (7.3.2016) by the FSBRA 2013, s. 148(5), Sch. 3 para. 5(6)(a); S.I. 2015/490, art. 2(1)(b).

occupying SMFs. These rules are designed to promote minimum standards of behaviour across the financial sector.[118]

1.23 The Individual Conduct Rules outline the fundamental standards of behaviour expected of all employees. Staff must act with integrity; apply due skill, care and diligence in their roles; and cooperate openly with regulators.[119] Employees are also required to consider the interests of customers, treat them fairly and adhere to proper market conduct standards.[120] Additionally, they must contribute to delivering good outcomes for retail customers through their actions.[121] Senior Manager Conduct Rules impose the duty to ensure that an institution's business is effectively controlled and compliant with regulatory requirements. Moreover, any delegation of responsibilities must entrust suitably qualified individuals and ensure proper oversight.[122] They are also obligated to act with integrity, due skill, care and diligence, and must disclose any information that the FCA or PRA would reasonably expect to be notified about.[123]

1.24 Under the Duty of Responsibility, which operates alongside the Conduct Rules, senior managers may face regulatory action if the regulator demonstrates a failure to meet regulatory requirements in the manager's institution, that the senior manager was responsible for the area in which the failure occurred and that they did not take reasonable steps to prevent it.[124] The concept of 'reasonable steps' is however deliberately flexible and non-prescriptive. Whilst the FCA provides examples of breaches,[125] such as failing to appropriately apportion responsibilities within a manager's control,[126] and offers a non-exhaustive list of considerations for assessing reasonable steps, its interpretation depends on context and case-specific facts.[127] Nevertheless, the interpretation of 'reasonable steps' remains subjective, posing challenges for institutions. Even

118 FCA, 'Conduct Rules' (27 March 2023) https://www.fca.org.uk/firms/senior-managers-and-certification-regime/conduct-rules.

119 *PRA Rulebook*, Conduct Rules, 2.1–2.3; *FCA Handbook*, COCON, 2.1.1–2.1.3.

120 FCA Handbook, COCON, 2.1.4–2.1.6.

121 Cf. Section D of this chapter on the Consumer Duty.

122 *PRA Rulebook*, Conduct Rules, 3.1 and 3.3; *FCA Handbook*, COCON, 2.2.1 and 2.2.3.

123 *PRA Rulebook*, Conduct Rules, 3.2 and 3.4; *FCA Handbook*, COCON, 2.2.2 and 2.2.4.

124 Section 67 FSMA 2000 last amended by the FSBRA 2013 (c. 33), s. 148(5), Sch. 3 para. 6; S.I. 2015/490, art. 2(1)(b). See also Sections 66A(5) and 66B(5) FSMA 2000 substituted by the Bank of England and Financial Services Act 2016 (c. 14), s. 41(3), Sch. 4 para. 16(4); S.I. 2018/990, reg. 2(1)(2)(3) (with regs. 3–6); S.I. 2019/1136, reg. 2(2)(3)(4)(5) (with regs. 3–5, 7). See also *FCA Handbook*, DEPP, 6.2.9A.

125 *FCA Handbook*, COCON, 4.2.10. Cf. also for the other Senior Manager Conduct Rules *FCA Handbook*, COCON, 4.2.16 and 4.2.23.

126 FCA Handbook, COCON, 4.2.10.1.

127 FCA Handbook, Decision Procedure and Penalties Manual (DEPP), 6.2.9-E.

though the burden of proof to justify enforcement action rests with the regulator, institutions must thoroughly document and evidence their actions to be able to potentially rebut the regulator's claims.

Examples for enforcement action under the duty of responsibility include a case in 2018 where the FCA and PRA each imposed fines on the CEO of Barclays for breach of regulatory requirements after he attempted to uncover the identity of an anonymous whistle-blower who had raised concerns about Barclays' hiring strategy. The CEO was found to have breached Individual Conduct Rule 2, which requires acting with due skill, care and diligence.[128] More recently, in April 2023, the PRA fined the Chief Information Officer (CIO) of TSB Bank for breaching Conduct Rule 2 (compliance with regulatory requirements). This action was related to an institution's service disruptions, where the CIO, responsible for IT and outsourcing, failed to verify assurances from an outsourced provider regarding the readiness of an IT migration and compromised the institution's operational resilience. In its decision, the PRA emphasised the importance of senior managers providing governance bodies with well-substantiated assurances and maintaining active oversight of outsourced providers and their management of subcontractors to ensure effective risk management and maintain operational resilience.[129] Similarly, recent enforcement action by the PRA involved a senior manager holding various SMFs of Wyelands Bank, which had breached risk concentration limits, failed to identify connected party exposures and did not meet record-keeping obligations. The senior manager also provided inadequately verified statements to the PRA regarding the institution's exposure controls and the role of an external compliance adviser linked to a connected party. As a result, he was found to be in violation of Individual Conduct Rule 2 requiring skill, care and diligence and Senior Manager Conduct Rules 1, effective control, and 2, compliance.[130] A breach of Conduct Rules can also result in the refusal of an application for approval to perform senior manager functions. This was recently illustrated in an FCA decision, upheld by the Upper Tribunal, where regulatory approval **1.25**

128 FCA, 'Final Notice – James Edward Staley' (11 May 2018) https://www.fca.org.uk/publication/final-notices/mr-james-edward-staley-2018.pdf; PRA, 'Final Notice' (11 May 2018) https://www.bankofengland.co.uk/-/media/boe/files/prudential-regulation/regulatory-action/final-notice-from-pra-to-mr-staley.pdf.

129 PRA, 'Final Notice – Carlos Abarca' (2023) https://www.bankofengland.co.uk/-/media/boe/files/prudential-regulation/regulatory-action/final-notice-from-pra-to-former-tsb-bank-plc-cio.pdf.

130 PRA, 'Final Notice - Iain Mark Hunter' (10 January 2024) https://www.bankofengland.co.uk/-/media/boe/files/prudential-regulation/regulatory-action/final-notice-from-pra-to-iain-mark-hunter.pdf.

was denied because the applicant had been dishonest during two prior enforcement interviews in connection with FCA investigations.[131]

4. Enforcement

1.26 As indicated above, in the event of breaches under the SMCR, both the FCA and PRA are empowered to investigate and, where necessary, take action, which may include fines, sanctions or prohibiting individuals from holding (future) SMFs.[132] Additionally, Senior Managers can face criminal liability if their actions result in the failure of an institution.[133] Moreover, enforcement action against institutions can be tied to the SMCR if the institution lacks responsible and effective oversight through a senior manager. For example, in January 2024, the PRA fined HSBC for breaching the Depositor Protection Rules. HSBC was found to have breached Fundamental Rule 6, which mandates responsible and effective organisation and control of affairs, due to the absence of a SMCR senior manager to oversee these processes.[134] Decisions of the FCA and PRA under the SMCR are subject to appeal. The Upper Tribunal can review the substance of PRA or FCA decisions[135] and further appeals on points of law can be made to the Court of Appeal.[136]

(a) Regulatory sanctions

1.27 The FCA and PRA have the authority to impose a wide range of sanctions, including public censure, financial penalties and the suspension or limitation of an individual's approval.[137] If a senior manager is found not to be fit and proper, regulators may withdraw their approval[138] or issue a prohibition order.[139] Nevertheless, there has been little enforcement by the FCA and PRA

---

131 FCA, 'Final Notice – Saranac Partners Ltd' (6 September 2024) https://www.fca.org.uk/publication/final-notices/thomas-llewellyn-kalaris-saranac-partners-limited-2024.pdf; *Saranac Partners Limited v The Financial Conduct Authority* [2024] UKUT 00254 (TCC).

132 Sections 63A, 66, 66A, 66B and 67 FSMA 2000.

133 Section 37(2)–(6) FSBRA 2013.

134 PRA, 'Final Notice – HSBC' (29 January 2024) https://www.bankofengland.co.uk/-/media/boe/files/prudential-regulation/regulatory-action/final-notice-from-pra-to-hsbc.pdf.

135 Sections 62(4), 63(5), 67(7) FSMA 2000. The proceedings before the Tribunal are regulated by FSMA 2000, sections 133–133B. Given the availability of the special dispute resolution process provided for by FSMA 2000, judicial review of a PRA decision is not available save in the most exceptional circumstances. See *R (on the application of Davies) v Financial Services Authority* [2003] EWCA Civ 1128; and *R (on the application of Christopher Willford) v Financial Services Authority* [2013] All ER (D) 114.

136 Section 13 Tribunals, Courts and Enforcement Act 2007.

137 Sections 66, 66A, 66B and 67 FSMA 2000.

138 Section 63 FSMA 2000 last amended by the Bank of England and Financial Services Act 2016 (c. 14), s. 41(3), Sch. 4 para. 8; S.I. 2018/990, reg. 2(1)(2)(3) (with regs. 3–6); S.I. 2019/1136, reg. 2(2)(3)(4)(5) (with regs. 3–5, 7).

139 Section 56 FSMA 2000 last amended by the FSMA 2023 (c. 29), s. 86(1)(e), Sch. 10 para. 3.

under the SMCR,[140] especially given that one of its primary objectives was to increase accountability through enforcement to remedy the shortcomings of the previous Approved Persons Regime.[141] While the FCA has opened a number of investigations, it only imposed a few actual sanctions[142] and the PRA only imposed its first ever fine for breach of the Senior Manager Conduct Rules in April 2023.[143] Moreover, both regulators have been criticised for significant delays in their regulatory action.[144] This has prompted responses by both regulators.

The FCA published a Consultation Paper on its Enforcement Approach outlining its strategy to expedite enforcement cases and increase transparency.[145] In this vein, the FCA intends to prioritise a targeted set of cases aligned with its strategic priorities and close cases lacking achievable outcomes more swiftly.[146] **1.28**

To aid effective enforcement, the PRA has introduced the Early Account Scheme,[147] a voluntary initiative requiring investigation subjects to conduct the initial fact-finding phase and submit their findings, accompanied by a Senior Manager attestation (Account). In this Account, the Senior Manager must attest to the integrity of the fact-finding process, their oversight, the accuracy **1.29**

140 Keller and Kokkinis (n 73) 326 et seq. Eleanore Hickman, 'Is the Senior Managers and Certification Regime Changing Banking for Good?' (2022) 85 *The Modern Law Review* 1440; Nicholas Ryder and others, 'Review of the Senior Managers & Certification Regime' (2023) 2 *Journal of Economic Criminology* 100029.

141 PCBS, 'Changing Banking for Good' (2013) HL Paper 27-II, HC 175-II para. 136.

142 From 2016 to 2022 a total of 71 cases were opened by the FCA against senior managers, of which 24 were closed, with only one leading to enforcement action; 49 investigations were opened against non-SMF individuals, of which 33 were closed, however without enforcement action: FCA, 'Information on Investigations Opened under the Senior Managers' Regime – June 2022' (2022) https://www.fca.org.uk/freedom-information/information-investigations-opened-under-senior-managers-regime-june-2022. Since 2013, FCA fines and prohibition orders against individuals have declined markedly, with 84 per cent of individual penalties targeting SME directors rather than senior executives in large firms. Spotlight on Corruption, 'Power Without Responsibility' (February 2024) 47 https://www.spotlightcorruption.org/wp-content/uploads/2024/02/Spotlight-Power-Without-Responsibility-full.pdf.

143 PRA, 'Final Notice – Carlos Abarca' (13 April 2023) https://www.bankofengland.co.uk/-/media/boe/files/prudential-regulation/regulatory-action/final-notice-from-pra-to-former-tsb-bank-plc-cio.pdf.

144 National Audit Office, 'FCA: Financial services regulation: Adapting to change' (Session 2023-24, 8 December 2023, HC 313) https://www.nao.org.uk/wp-content/uploads/2023/12/Financial-services-regulation-Adapting-to-change.pdf.

145 FCA, 'Consultation Paper CP24/2: Our Enforcement Guide and publicising enforcement investigations – a new approach' (February 2024) https://www.fca.org.uk/publication/consultation/cp24-2.pdf.

146 FCA, 'Consultation Paper CP24/2: Our Enforcement Guide and publicising enforcement investigations – a new approach' (February 2024) 3–4 https://www.fca.org.uk/publication/consultation/cp24-2.pdf.

147 PRA, 'Policy Statement PS1/24 – The Bank of England's approach to enforcement' (January 2024) paras 2.7 et seq. https://www.bankofengland.co.uk/prudential-regulation/publication/2024/january/the-bank-of-england-approach-to-enforcement-policy-statement.

of findings and the absence of any undisclosed relevant information.[148] The SMCR has indeed increased the use of internal investigations by institutions, often conducted to pre-empt regulatory action. Institutions may be motivated to share these findings with regulators to persuade them against launching formal investigations or to limit their scope. However, this can create inherent conflicts of interest, as the institution conducting the investigation may itself be liable. Additionally, conflicts may arise between institutions and individual senior managers, as regulatory investigations by the FCA or PRA can target both entities and individuals.[149] Moreover, the reliance on internal investigation reports by regulators has also faced criticism. In a recent case involving the integrity of two former Julius Baer employees, the Upper Tribunal criticised regulators for excessively relying on internal investigation reports commissioned by the institution, rather than conducting their own independent investigations.[150] The Tribunal criticised the FCA for accepting the version of events from an individual whose credibility it later questioned. According to the Tribunal, the FCA '*swallowed [this] hook, line and sinker*' and anchored this in its initial assessment, displaying confirmation bias and failing to objectively reconsider its allegations when new evidence emerged.[151]

(b) Criminal liability

1.30 Senior managers can face criminal liability for reckless banking if their decisions cause the failure of a financial institution.[152] This offence carries penalties of up to seven years in prison and/or an unlimited fine.[153] To establish liability, six elements must be demonstrated under the criminal standard of proof: (1) the institution must have failed; (2) the failure is linked to a specific decision; (3) the individual was a senior manager at the time; (4) the senior manager agreed to or did not prevent the decision (5) and was aware of the risk that the decision could cause failure; and (6) this conduct fell significantly below the standards expected of a person in their position.[154] However, demonstrating these elements under the criminal standard of proof presents

148 PRA, 'Policy Statement PS1/24 – The Bank of England's approach to enforcement' (January 2024) paras 2.29 et seq. https://www.bankofengland.co.uk/prudential-regulation/publication/2024/january/the-bank-of-england-approach-to-enforcement-policy-statement.

149 Keller and Kokkinis (n 73) 326 et seq.

150 *Thomas Seiler, Louise Whitestone, Gustavo Raitzin v The Financial Conduct Authority* [2023] UKUT 00133 (TCC).

151 See inter alia ibid para. 928.

152 Section 37(2)–(6) FSBRA 2013. On the criminal law interpretation of 'senior manager', see Section 37(7)–(8) FSBRA 2013.

153 Section 36(4) FSBRA 2013.

154 Section 36(1)(c) FSBRA 2013.

significant challenges. First, establishing causation between a single decision and the failure of a financial institution is difficult under the criminal standard of proof.[155] This is due to the fact that such failures often result from a series of missteps rather than a single event, complicating the but-for test of causation.[156] Second, proving that a senior manager was aware of the risks associated with a particular decision is complex, given the intricacies of financial institutions and their risk management systems. Third, demonstrating that a senior manager did not take all reasonable steps to prevent a harmful decision is complicated by the shared responsibilities among various management bodies in large institutions.[157] Finally, the requirement to prove gross negligence adds another layer of difficulty.[158]

5. Recent FCA Review and Reflections

In 2023, as part of the Edinburgh Reforms,[159] HM Treasury, the FCA and the PRA initiated a comprehensive review of the effectiveness of the SMCR.[160] This follows inter alia the 2019/2020 evaluation of the SMCR by the FCA[161] and PRA[162] as well as annual surveys reflecting employees' perceptions of their organisational cultures and senior managers' responsibility.[163] The review focuses on several key concerns, including institutions' experiences with specific elements of the regime, such as the lengthy authorisation process for senior managers. It also examines challenges faced by institutions operating across multiple jurisdictions. The review seeks to balance maintaining high regulatory standards with reducing compliance burden and explores **1.31**

---

155 Kokkinis (n 77) 245.

156 *R v White* [1910] 2 KB 124. Cf. ibid 245.

157 Cf. Lowry John and Edmunds Rod, 'Directors Duties and Liabilities: Disqualifying "Unfit" Directors at Banks? Political Rhetoric and the Directors' Disqualification Regime' in Iris H-Y Chiu (ed), *The Law on Corporate Governance in Banks* (Edward Elgar Publishing 2015), 96.

158 Andreas Kokkinis (n 77) 245.

159 HM Treasury, 'Financial Services: The Edinburgh Reforms' (9 December 2022) https://www.gov.uk/government/collections/financial-services-the-edinburgh-reforms.

160 PRA and FCA, 'Joint Discussion Paper: Review of the Senior Managers and Certification Regime' (30 March 2023) (DP1/23) https://www.bankofengland.co.uk/prudential-regulation/publication/2023/march/review-of-the-senior-managers-and-certification-regime; HM Treasury, 'Senior Managers & Certification Regime: A Call for Evidence' (30 March 2023) https://www.gov.uk/government/calls-for-evidence/senior-managers-certification-regime-a-call-for-evidence.

161 FCA, 'Senior Managers and Certification Regime Banking Stocktake Report' (5 August 2019) https://www.fca.org.uk/publications/multi-firm-reviews/senior-managers-and-certification-regime-banking-stocktake-report.

162 PRA, 'Evaluation of the Senior Managers and Certification Regime (SM&CR)' (16 December 2020) https://www.bankofengland.co.uk/prudential-regulation/publication/2020/evaluation-of-the-senior-managers-and-certification-regime.

163 Financial Services Culture Board, 'Assessment Results 2022' (2022) https://financialservicescultureboard.org.uk/assessment-results-2022/.

opportunities to enhance the UK's attractiveness for financial institutions, aligning with the competitiveness and growth objective introduced by the FSMA 2023. The FCA and PRA's discussion paper assesses the effectiveness of the SMCR examining whether the regime meets its objectives of making it easier to hold individuals to account and improving safety and soundness and conduct in a proportionate manner that still enhances competition or international competitiveness.[164] It also investigates the individual elements of the SMCR, focusing on whether its objectives, mechanisms and enforcement approach are effective in relation to the internal processes and realities of financial institutions, with the aim of identifying areas for improvement.[165]

1.32 The Review of the SMCR is a welcome development considering criticisms about the FCA's practice and enforcement.[166] Stark criticism of the FCA's regulatory and enforcement practices has also been expressed by the Upper Tribunal. The Tribunal has repeatedly condemned delays in the FCA's investigation process[167] and deficiencies in its disclosure practices.[168] In response, the FCA has acknowledged these issues and committed itself to improvements in relation to both disclosure practice[169] and the speed of its investigations.[170] However, the FCA has been less receptive to criticism regarding the requirements to establish a lack of integrity. In the *Markou* case,[171] the Tribunal found the FCA had failed to adequately demonstrate the lack of integrity required to meet the 'fit and proper' standard for a SMF holder. Rather than revising its

---

164 DP1/23 chapter 3.

165 DP1/23 para. 3.7 and chapter 4.

166 Cf. ibid Section B.4.(a). See also APPG, 'Report on the Call for Evidence about the Financial Conduct Authority (26 November 2024) https://www.appgifffs.org/wp-content/uploads/2024/11/FINAL-Call-for-Evidence-Report-PUBLIC.pdf which reveals the negative perception and criticism of the practice of the FCA as expressed by stakeholders, victims of financial crime, whistleblowers and former FCA employees.

167 The Tribunal was particularly adamant about this in its decision in the Julius Baer Case, *Thomas Seiler, Louise Whitestone, Gustavo Raitzin v The Financial Conduct Authority* [2023] UKUT 00133 (TCC). Here the FCA stated that the 'lapse of time … between the events in question and the hearing […] was obviously unsatisfactory' (para. 59). The Tribunal referred to a glacial pace of the progress of the investigation entirely attributable to the Authority (para. 117) and that this was 'on any view unacceptable' (para. 119), and advised the FCA that 'when such a situation arises, it is for the Authority to give serious consideration as to whether it is appropriate to continue with an investigation which it does not have the resources to complete within a reasonable period of time and where it has decided that its priorities for limited resource lie elsewhere' (para. 119).

168 Cf. *Thomas Seiler, Louise Whitestone, Gustavo Raitzin v The Financial Conduct Authority* [2023] UKUT 00133 (TCC).

169 FCA, 'Consultation Paper CP24/2: Our Enforcement Guide and publicising enforcement investigations – a new approach' (February 2024) https://www.fca.org.uk/publication/consultation/cp24-2.pdf.

170 FCA, 'Enforcement regulatory disclosure review: outcome' (November 2024) https://www.fca.org.uk/news/statements/enforcement-regulatory-disclosure-review-outcome.

171 Cf. *Markou v The Financial Conduct Authority* [2023] [2023] UKUT 00101 (TCC).

approach, the FCA publicly rejected the Tribunal's decision as 'incorrect and irrational'[172] and has appealed the case.[173]

In terms of the scope of misconduct relevant to a lack of integrity, the FCA has gradually broadened its focus. Initially concentrating on financial misconduct as explicitly indicated in its guidance,[174] the FCA has gradually expanded to a broader scope of misconduct including misconduct related to regulatory proceedings[175] and non-financial misconduct.[176] Recent proposals include expanding the definition of misconduct relevant to fitness and propriety, regulatory references and suitability threshold conditions to encompass bullying, harassment and offences related to characteristics such as sex or race, both within and beyond the institution. The expansion of relevant misconduct accompanied by guidance is to be welcomed in the interest of clarity and the promotion a purposeful culture within financial institutions. Nevertheless, this must remain appropriate and respect the judicially established criteria, such as the required link between the misconduct and the individual's professional practice or the profession's standing.[177] **1.33**

D. EXECUTIVE REMUNERATION

A key aspect of prudential regulation with broader implications for financial institutions' culture is the regulation of executive remuneration, which also gained prominence after the GFC. Performance-based remuneration schemes that prioritise short-term financial gains can misalign the incentives of senior management with regulatory objectives posing risks for financial stability. In contrast, remuneration frameworks that incorporate non-financial performance metrics – such as compliance, customer satisfaction and team dynamics **1.34**

172 FCA, 'Upper Tribunal decision in Mr Markos Markou vs FCA' (April 2023) https://www.fca.org.uk/news/statements/upper-tribunal-decision-markou.

173 *Markou v The Financial Conduct Authority*, CA-2023-001229.

174 *FCA Handbook*, FIT, 2.1.

175 Here Kalaris had been dishonest in an unrelated regulatory interview several years prior. FCA, 'Final Notice – Saranac Partners Ltd' (6 September 2024) https://www.fca.org.uk/publication/final-notices/thomas-llewellyn-kalaris-saranac-partners-limited-2024.pdf; *Saranac Partners Limited v The Financial Conduct Authority* [2024] UKUT 00254 (TCC).

176 Cf. ibid Section E.3.(c); FCA, 'Culture and non-financial misconduct survey – findings' (October 2024) https://www.fca.org.uk/data/culture-non-financial-misconduct-survey-findings. The FCA also refers to its Consultation Paper CP23/20, Diversity and Inclusion in the Financial Sector, where it proposes integrating non-financial misconduct into staff fitness and propriety assessments, Conduct Rules and Threshold Conditions, aiming to clarify expectations and empower firms to act decisively against such misconduct. Cf. ibid Section E.

177 This was held in *Ryan Beckwith v SRA* [2020] EWHC 3231, [54] regarding solicitors. The Upper Tribunal drew from this case in *Jon Frensham v The Financial Conduct Authority* [2021] UKUT 0222 (TCC).

– can help foster a more sustainable and purposeful culture. This section outlines the applicable legal frameworks for remuneration in listed companies in general, as well as the specific frameworks for financial institutions. It then addresses the policy reasons for the removal of the bonus cap as well as its impact on remuneration practices.

1. Legal Framework on Remuneration for Listed Companies

1.35 The Code recommends that listed companies across all sectors establish remuneration committees to ensure executive directors do not set their own pay.[178] Moreover, under the Companies Act 2006, listed companies are required to prepare an annual directors' remuneration report, detailing the pay of individual directors, and a remuneration policy outlining the principles and criteria for setting executive remuneration.[179] Executive remuneration typically has fixed and variable components. Fixed remuneration includes salary, fixed pay allowances, benefits in kind and pension contributions, while variable remuneration is performance-based and includes bonuses, performance shares and share options.[180] To strengthen shareholder control, listed companies must hold an annual advisory vote on the remuneration report and a binding vote every three years on the remuneration policy.[181] Although a rejection in the advisory vote does not invalidate payments, it can cause reputational damage and trigger shareholder dissent, often pressuring companies to reduce pay.[182] In contrast, changes to the remuneration policy without shareholder approval are void. Such shareholder approval is also mandatory for director service contracts exceeding two years[183] and for payments related to loss of office or retirement, with full disclosure of such payments required.[184]

2. Framework for Remuneration in Financial Institutions

1.36 Beyond the general rules on remuneration for listed companies, specific rules on remuneration apply to financial institutions. The Walker Review recommended broadening the remit of remuneration committees to cover group-level

---

178 Provision 32 et seq. of the 2024 Code.

179 Sections 420–422A Companies Act 2006.

180 For a detailed discussion of the various components of senior executive remuneration, see Marc Moore, 'Design and Control of Remuneration in UK Banks' in Iris H.-Y. Chiu, *The Law on Corporate Governance in Banks* (Edward Elgar Publishing 2015) 134–139.

181 Section 439 Companies Act 2006.

182 Kokkinis (n 77) 235.

183 Section 188 Companies Act 2006.

184 Sections 215–217 Companies Act 2006.

policies[185] and the compensation of high-end employees.[186] It also proposed that half of variable remuneration be vested in long-term schemes, with half vesting after three years and the other half after five years.[187] Additionally, bonuses were to be paid over three years, and senior employees and executive directors were encouraged to maintain shareholdings proportional to their remuneration to align interests with long-term performance.[188] The Financial Services Act 2010 then granted regulators the authority to enforce remuneration policies that align with sound risk management and to prohibit non-compliant compensation.[189] Further reforms introduced by the CRD IV targeted excessive risk-taking and imposed stringent rules on executive remuneration for senior management, risk takers and employees in control functions.[190] These rules are now anchored in the *PRA Rulebook* and *FCA Handbook*.

The PRA expects institutions' remuneration and incentive structures to promote careful and prudent management, ensuring appropriate controls to minimise excessive risk-taking by senior management while aligning incentives with the institution's long-term interests.[191] These expectations are codified in the Remuneration Part of the *PRA Rulebook* and are applicable to CRR firms. To a large degree, they still transpose the CRD IV and are supplemented by a PRA Supervisory Statement, which outlines regulatory expectations for the application of the Remuneration Part as well as further guidance. Regarding executive remuneration, the *PRA Rulebook* mandates the establishment of remuneration committees composed of non-executive directors.[192] Fixed remuneration must be substantial enough to allow institutions to withhold variable pay when performance is poor.[193] Additionally, at least 50 per cent of variable remuneration must be paid in shares or capital instruments,[194] with **1.37**

185 Walker Review para. 7.7.

186 Walker Review para 7.10.

187 Walker Review para 7.34.

188 Walker Review para 7.35.

189 Section 139A FSMA 2000.

190 Recital 53 and Art. 92(2) CRD IV. For an academic critique of the mismatch between bank executive remuneration and long-term performance, see Lucian Bebchuk, Alma Cohen and Holger Spamann, 'The Wages of Failure: Executive Compensation at Bear Sterns and Lehman 2000–2008' (2010) 27 *Yale Journal on Regulation* 257.

191 PRA, 'Supervisory Statement SS2/17: Remuneration' (December 2023) 1.3 (SS2/17) https://www.bankofengland.co.uk/-/media/boe/files/prudential-regulation/supervisory-statement/2023/ss217-december-2023.pdf.

192 *PRA Rulebook*, CRR Firms, Remuneration, 7.4; Cf. Art. 95 CRD IV.

193 *PRA Rulebook*, CRR Firms, Remuneration, 15.9(2); Cf. Art. 94(1)(f) CRD IV.

194 *PRA Rulebook*, CRR Firms, Remuneration, 15.15; Cf. Art. 94(1)(l) CRD IV.

60 per cent deferred for at least seven years for senior managers.[195] Institutions must also implement malus and clawback provisions, allowing the reduction of unvested deferred remuneration or recovery of vested variable remuneration in cases of misconduct or significant risk management failures.[196] The PRA further requires that financial institutions adjust metrics used to assess senior management performance to align with sound risk management.[197] As a result, financial institutions now include non-profit-related metrics, such as capital strength, liquidity and customer satisfaction, in performance assessments.

1.38 Similarly, the FCA's Remuneration Codes aim to promote effective long-term risk management, support positive behaviours, foster healthy cultures and discourage misconduct and poor customer outcomes.[198] These codes are primarily found in the FCA's Senior Management Arrangements, Systems, and Controls (SYSC) sourcebook which includes five chapters, each containing a remuneration code applicable to different types of institutions.[199] Other modules of the *FCA Handbook* include further rules on remuneration, compensation and incentives tied to specific products, services and arrangements.[200] For dual-regulated institutions, the FCA provides its own Remuneration Code (SYSC 19D).[201] The Dual-regulated Firms' Remuneration Code operates alongside the UK CRR and rules in the *PRA Rulebook* and guidance. It requires that institutions establish, implement and maintain remuneration policies consistent with sound and effective risk management.[202] To support this, it outlines principles covering areas such as risk management, alignment with the institution's strategy and long-term interests, governance, control functions and risk-adjusted remuneration.[203]

195 *PRA Rulebook*, CRR Firms, Remuneration, 15.17 and 15.18. All CRD IV regulated institutions are expected to defer 40 per cent of variable remuneration of all material risk takers. However, in the case of payments over 500,000 euros and payments to directors of significant institutions, 60 per cent of remuneration must be deferred.

196 *PRA Rulebook*, CRR Firms, Remuneration 15.22 and 15.23 respectively.

197 *PRA Rulebook*, CRR Firms, Remuneration, 11.2–11.6.

198 FCA, 'Remuneration' (3 July 2023) https://www.fca.org.uk/firms/remuneration.

199 FCA Handbook, SYSC 19B, 19D, 19E, 19F and 19G which include Remuneration Codes for AIFMs, dual-regulated firms, UCITS, MIFIDPRU and on remuneration and performance management for sales staff.

200 These include chapters 6 and 19 of the Conduct of Business sourcebook (COBS), chapter 2A.1 of the Mortgages and Home Finance: Conduct of business sourcebook (MCOB) and chapter 2.11 of the Consumer Credit sourcebook (CONC).

201 Further guidance can be found in FCA guidance on proportionality (FG23/5), ex-post risk adjustment for variable remuneration (FG23/6), and FAQs on the Remuneration Code (FG23/4).

202 FCA, SYSC, 19D.2.1.

203 FCA, SYSC, 19D.3.

The FCA also regularly sends letters to the chairs of remuneration committees highlighting key areas for institutions to consider when shaping their remuneration policies. In its most recent 2023 letter the FCA addressed the removal of the bonus cap, the Consumer Duty, culture and accountability, diversity and inclusion and sustainability in finance, expecting chairs to integrate these principles into their remuneration strategies.[204] **1.39**

The PRA and FCA have the authority to establish rules prohibiting specific individuals from being remunerated in certain ways.[205] Additionally, HM Treasury can direct the PRA and FCA to issue such prohibitions following consultation.[206] Any agreement that violates these prohibitions may be deemed void, and any payments or property transferred under such agreements can be recovered.[207] The PRA Remuneration Part and the FCA's Codes contain provisions to prevent avoidance of the rules and ensure compliance. If an institution breaches these rules, it must notify the regulators and provide details of any recovery actions taken.[208] Sanctions for non-compliance can range from private warnings and public censure to financial penalties. In more severe cases, non-compliance could result in the cancellation or variation of an institution's authorisation.[209] **1.40**

3. Removal of the Bonus Cap

The removal of the bonus cap effective 31 October 2023 represents a significant shift away from EU financial regulation post-Brexit.[210] This followed a consultation by the PRA and FCA[211] and a government commitment in **1.41**

---

204 FCA, 'Dear Chair of the Remuneration Committee Letter 2023' (30 October 2023) https://www.fca.org.uk/publication/correspondence/dear-chair-remuneration-committee-2023.pdf.

205 Section 137H(1) FSMA 2000 inserted by the Financial Services Act 2012 (c. 21), ss. 24(1), 122(3).

206 Section 137I FSMA 2000 inserted by the Financial Services Act 2012 (c. 21), ss. 24(1), 122(3).

207 Section 137H(1) FSMA 2000 inserted by Financial Services Act 2012 (c. 21), ss. 24(1), 122(3) (with Sch. 20); S.I. 2013/113, art. 2(1)(c), Sch. Pt. 3; S.I. 2013/423, art. 3, Sch.

208 *PRA Rulebook*, Notifications, 2.4; *FCA Handbook*, SUP, 15.3.11.

209 Section 206(1) FSMA as amended by Financial Services Act 2012 (c. 21), s. 122(3), Sch. 9 para. 12(2)(b) (with Sch. 20); S.I. 2013/423, art. 3, Sch.

210 PRA and FCA, 'Joint Policy Statement Remuneration: Ratio between Fixed and Variable Components of Total Remuneration ("Bonus Cap")' (PRA policy statement 9/23; FCA policy statement 23/15 PS9/23/PS23/15) https://www.bankofengland.co.uk/prudential-regulation/publication/2023/october/remuneration-ratio-between-fixed-and-variable-components-of-total-remuneration%20. (Bonus Cap Joint Policy Statement) The bonus cap requirements were removed through amendments to the *PRA Rulebook*'s Remuneration and Disclosure (CRR) Parts, as well as to SYSC 19D and updates to the PRA's Supervisory Statement (SS)2/17. The FCA did not immediately update references to the bonus cap in para. 4.4 of Finalised Guidance (FG)20/5, opting to review this guidance at a later stage.

211 PRA and FCA, 'Joint Consultation Paper CP15/22 – Remuneration: Ratio between Fixed and Variable Components of Total Remuneration ("Bonus Cap")' (19 December 2022) https://www.bankofengland.co.uk/prudential-regulation/publication/2022/december/remuneration (CP15/22).

2022.[212] The bonus cap had been introduced under EU law and faced regulatory resistance in the UK since its inception (a). Its removal, decided in late 2023, was justified on policy grounds related to enhancing financial stability and boosting the competitiveness of the UK financial sector (b). This section also examines the impact of the removal on remuneration practices within financial institutions (c).

(a) Introduction of the bonus cap and regulatory resistance

1.42 The CRD IV introduced a cap on variable remuneration for CRR firms' executive directors and senior managers, with the purpose of reducing excessive risk-taking by aligning executive pay with long-term stability.[213] The cap applied to Material Risk Takers (MRTs) who significantly impact the institution's risk profile and includes directors, senior managers, and those overseeing key business units or control functions. The cap limited variable remuneration to 100 per cent of fixed remuneration, or 200 per cent with shareholder approval of the maximum variable remuneration opportunity.[214] The majority of financial institutions obtained shareholder approval to extend variable remuneration to 200 per cent of fixed pay.[215] Moreover, financial institutions responded to the cap by introducing fixed pay- or role-based allowances in shares to offset the impact on variable remuneration.[216] The bonus cap was met with criticism, particularly from the PRA, which warned that increasing fixed remuneration could reduce flexibility during financial crises.[217] HM Treasury then challenged the cap before the European Court of Justice, arguing that the EU lacked competence, but was unsuccessful, and the cap remained part of the UK's regulatory framework.[218] Arguably, more effective means of regulating

212 HM Treasury, 'The Growth Plan 2000 – CP 743' (September 2022) para 4.9 https://assets.publishing.service.gov.uk/government/uploads/system/uploads/attachment_data/file/1105989/CCS207_CCS0822746402-001_SECURE_HMT_Autumn_Statement_2022_BOOK_Web_Accessible.pdf.

213 Recital 65 CRD IV.

214 Art. 94(1)(g) CRD IV.

215 CP15/22 para. 2.36.

216 This can be seen in the 2014, 2015 and 2016 Annual Reports and Accounts issued by Barclays, HSBC, Lloyds Banking Group, the Royal Bank of Scotland and Standard Chartered. For a detailed analysis of the way in which the remuneration practices of major UK banks changed due to the implementation of the bonus cap, see Andreas Kokkinis, 'Exploring the Effects of the "Bonus Cap" Rule: The Impact of Remuneration Structure on Risk-Taking by Bank Managers' (2019) 19 *Journal of Corporate Law Studies* 167.

217 PRA, 'Strengthening Capital Standards: Implementing CRD IV – Policy Statement 3/14; Policy Statement 7/13; Consultation Paper 5/13' (30 April 2014) para 4.7 https://www.bankofengland.co.uk/prudential-regulation/publication/2013/strengthening-capital-standards-implementing-crd-4.

218 Case C-507/13 *United Kingdom v Parliament and Council* [2013] was removed from the register on 4 May 2015.

variable remuneration exist to promote risk management than a bonus cap.[219] The bonus cap provoked unintended consequences, such as undermining malus and clawback provisions,[220] and was easily circumvented through fixed pay allowances in shares.[221] Through that, the prudential aim of the bonus did not materialise, as a risk-taking incentive was retained through circumventive mechanisms introduced by institutions in the form role-based allowances, classified as fixed pay, which allowed them to increase remuneration without raising salaries directly.[222] The academic support in spite of this largely referred to concerns over distributive justice and curbing excessive executive pay.[223]

(b) Decision to remove the bonus cap

The FCA and PRA justified the removal of the bonus cap on grounds of financial stability concerns and promoting the UK financial sector's competitiveness and growth.[224] The PRA and FCA argue that removing the bonus cap increases institutions' flexibility to restructure pay, which can enhance financial stability by allowing institutions to share risks with employees and adjust remuneration in response to losses, poor performance or misconduct.[225] By linking more remuneration to an institution's performance, the regulators seek to better align the incentives of material risk takers with long-term value creation and shareholder interests. This increases the proportion of 'at risk' compensation, ensuring that senior decision-makers have a larger share of their pay tied to long-term institution performance and risk management.[226] The regulators also noted that while the bonus cap curbed variable remuneration, there was a lack of evidence that it reduced excessive risk-taking due to the use of circumventive mechanisms.[227] This raised concerns because role-based allowances and fixed salaries could still reward risk-taking, while simultaneously increasing fixed costs, reducing institutions' ability to absorb losses during downturns.[228] Additionally, the bonus cap limited the amount of variable **1.43**

219 John Thanassoulis, 'The Case for Intervening in Bankers' Pay' (2012) 67 *The Journal of Finance* 849.

220 Kevin J Murphy, 'Regulating Banking Bonuses in the European Union: A Case Study in Unintended Consequences' (2013) 19 *European Financial Management* 631.

221 Kokkinis (n 216) 186.

222 CP15/22 paras. 2.3 et seq.; Ieva Sakalauskaite and Qun Harris, 'Measuring the effects of bank remuneration rules: evidence from the UK' (2022) PRA Staff Working Paper No 1008.

223 See Marc T Moore, 'Corporate Governance, Pay Equity, and the Limitations of Agency Theory' (2015) 68 *Current Legal Problems* 431, 438–441 and Alan Dignam, 'Remuneration and Riots: Rethinking Corporate Governance in the Age of Entitlement' (2013) 66 *Current Legal Problems* 401.

224 CP15/22 para. 3.16.

225 Bonus Cap Joint Policy Statement paras. 1.13-1.16; CP15/22 para. 2.43.

226 CP15/22 para. 2.29.

227 CP15/22 para. 2.17.

228 CP15/22 para. 2.40.

pay subject to regulatory tools aimed at promoting effective risk management, such as performance scorecards, deferral and risk adjustment.[229] In their view, removing the cap extends the potential effect of such mechanisms to deter short-term excessive risk-taking.[230] Finally, eliminating the cap aligns dual-regulated institutions' remuneration frameworks with other types of institutions' remuneration codes that do not impose a bonus cap.[231] The regulators also justified the removal of the bonus cap in the context of the new secondary objective focused on promoting the UK's international competitiveness and long-term growth.[232] The removal of the bonus cap will allow institutions to adopt remuneration structures adaptable to market conditions, facilitating better business opportunities.[233] It is also expected to improve institutions' ability to attract skilled staff, increase labour mobility[234] and allow UK institutions to better compete globally with markets where no bonus cap applies.[235]

(c) The effect of the bonus cap removal

1.44 Since the publication of the Joint Policy Statement in late 2023, institutions are permitted to disregard the bonus cap. This allows institutions to change their remuneration policies subject to shareholder approval. Following the removal of the cap, major UK financial institutions have adjusted their remuneration policies to allow variable pay between 10 and 25 times fixed remuneration. Some institutions opted to lower base salaries, leveraging the increased flexibility in variable compensation, while others chose to maintain their existing base salary levels.[236] Despite the removal of the cap, institutions are still required to set appropriate ratios between fixed and variable pay, reflecting an individual's role and potential for excessive risk-taking.[237] Whether, alongside its other goals, removing the cap will enhance competitiveness and promote labour mobility to the UK is however yet to be seen.[238]

---

229 CP15/22 para. 2.12, 2.7, 2.8.

230 CP15/22 para. 2.44.

231 CP15/22 para. 2.9.

232 Bonus Cap Joint Policy Statement paras. 1.13 et seq.

233 CP15/22 para. 2.45.

234 CP15/22 para. 2.46.

235 CP15/22 para. 2.47.

236 Goldman Sachs opted to lower base pay while increasing the bonus ratio to 25 times income, whereas employees at JP Morgan will now be able to earn up to 10 times their base salary in bonuses while fixed pay will remain the same. Barclays, Citigroup, Morgan Stanley and HSBC are also among the institutions that have removed their caps. Ortenca Aliaj, 'JPMorgan Follows Goldman in Lifting UK Bonus Cap' (19 June 2024) https://www.ft.com/content/0b60b642-51a4-484a-a785-a2f679616a7b.

237 See updated regulatory guidance: the PRA added paragraphs 3.18A–3.18C to SS2/17 and the FCA amended SYSC 19D.3.48A.

238 For a critical perspective see John Kong Shan Ho, 'Removing Bankers' Bonus Cap: Will This Enhance the Competitiveness of the UK Financial Market?' (2023) 18 *Capital Markets Law Journal* 556.

From the perspective of remuneration as a tool to incentivise prudent risk-taking and foster a culture geared toward positive outcomes, the cap on the ratio of variable to fixed remuneration is just one factor influencing managers' decision-making.[239] While the bonus cap was designed to limit excessive risk-taking, pay-performance sensitivity of remuneration – rather than the ratio of variable to fixed remuneration – is crucial. The ratio itself is not a reliable proxy for aligning managers' incentives with prudent decision-making. Instead, variable remuneration, when coupled with deferral and clawback requirements, can incentivise managers to prioritise long-term stability and positive outcomes.[240] As directors are rarely removed unless a company is significantly underperforming,[241] remuneration serves as a crucial mechanism for guiding senior management's decision-making. Consequently, following the removal of the cap, regulators should focus on the criteria for awarding variable remuneration, both financial and non-financial, to ensure that decisions increasing risk or failing to align with positive outcomes for consumers and diversity and inclusion do not lead to higher remuneration. 1.45

This is also reflected in requirements relating to the Consumer Duty,[242] as well as diversity and inclusion considerations.[243] The FCA's guidance on Consumer Duty emphasises that institutions should not structure staff incentives, performance management, or remuneration in ways that conflict with their Consumer Duty obligations.[244] These guidelines caution that such structures, if misaligned, could harm retail customers. It is important to adhere to the cross-cutting rule that institutions must act in good faith and ensure that remuneration frameworks promote positive customer outcomes rather than create conditions for customer detriment.[245] Similarly, the regulatory focus on diversity and inclusion has highlighted that accountability for progress towards strengthened diversity and inclusion within an institution should be reinforced 1.46

239 For an in-depth discussion of the bonus cap see Kokkinis (n 216).

240 Ibid 3 et seq.

241 For a discussion of UK shareholders' voting powers and the practical limitations to their use, see Marc T Moore, *Corporate Governance in the Shadow of the State* (Hart 2013), 208–212. A broader discussion of the balance of powers between directors and shareholders can be found in JG Hill, 'The Rising Tension between Shareholder and Director Power in the Common Law World' (2010) 18 *Corporate Governance: An International Review* 344.

242 See in more detail on the Consumer Duty in Section D of this chapter.

243 See in more detail on Diversity and Inclusion in Section E of this chapter.

244 FCA Handbook, PRIN 2A.8.2.

245 FCA, 'FG22/5 Final non-Handbook Guidance for firms on the Consumer Duty' (July 2022) (FG22/5) para. 5.10 https://www.fca.org.uk/publication/finalised-guidance/fg22-5.pdf.

through variable remuneration linked to diversity and inclusion goals.[246] By holding senior managers accountable for removing barriers to diversity and inclusion, institutions are more likely to meet their diversity and inclusion objectives while fostering behaviours that contribute positively to the institution's risk culture, safety and soundness.[247]

E. FCA CONSUMER DUTY

1.47 As indicated in the previous section, the Consumer Duty introduces higher-level standards on financial institutions' governance and culture.[248] The Consumer Duty aims to enhance consumer protection in retail markets through a consumer principle (to act to deliver good outcomes for retail customers), along with cross-cutting rules and guidance that financial institutions must adhere to.[249] This requires consumer protection to be ingrained in an institution's culture and behaviour, with explicit attention to consumer behavioural biases and vulnerabilities.[250] The introduction of the Consumer Duty aligns with a pro-consumer narrative pursued by the FCA in recent years[251] that acknowledges the power imbalance between institutions and consumers, in particular vulnerable consumers.[252] This section examines the nature of the requirements under the Consumer Duty and its scope. It then outlines and

246 FCA, PRA, and BoE, 'Joint discussion paper: DP21/2 – Diversity and Inclusion in the Financial Sector: Working Together to Drive Change' (07 July 2021) (DP21/2) https://www.bankofengland.co.uk/prudential-regulation/publication/2021/july/diversity-and-inclusion-in-the-financial-sector.

247 PRA, 'Consultation paper 18/23: Diversity and inclusion in PRA-regulated firms' (25 September 2023) (CP18/23) https://www.bankofengland.co.uk/prudential-regulation/publication/2023/september/diversity-and-inclusion-in-pra-regulated-firms.

248 The Consumer Duty came into force in July 2023 for products and services still available for sale or renewal and since July 2024 for closed products and services. It applies on a forward-looking basis to existing products or services still being sold to customers, as well as closed products or services that are no longer marketed but still allow existing customers to continue payments under the original terms see above. Cf. FG22/5 chapter 3 on guidance for closed products and services. This was supported by a number of sector specific FCA 'Dear CEO letters' published on 16 May 2024 https://www.fca.org.uk/firms/consumer-duty/resources#section-dear-ceo-letters-closed-products-and-services.

249 FCA, 'Consumer Duty' (15 September 2022) https://www.fca.org.uk/firms/consumer-duty.

250 Cf. in particular FCA Handbook, PRIN, 2A.2.25 and 2A.7.4. Cf. also FCA, 'Guidance for Firms on the Fair Treatment of Vulnerable Customers' (19 July 2021) https://www.fca.org.uk/publications/finalised-guidance/guidance-firms-fair-treatment-vulnerable-customers.

251 Cf. Anat Keller, 'The Public Role of Banks: A New Narrative Born?' (2022) Journal of International Banking Law Review 6.

252 See, for instance, John Y Campbell, 'Restoring Rational Choice: The Challenge of Consumer Financial Regulation' (2016) 106(5) American Economic Review: Papers and Proceedings 1; O Ben-Shahar, 'The Myth of "Opportunity to Read" in Contract Law' (2009) 5 *European Review of Contract Law* 1, 2. On vulnerability see Diane Bugeja, *Reforming Corporate Retail Investor Protection* (Hart 2019) 13.

critically evaluates how the FCA expects the Consumer Duty to be embedded within a financial firm, as well as the FCA's approach to enforcement.

1. Nature of the Requirements under the Consumer Duty

The Consumer Duty aims to improve consumer outcomes by addressing concerns that financial services markets often fail to offer products and services that meet consumer needs or deliver expected results, thereby causing harm.[253] The Duty sets clear expectations for institutions to prioritise consumer interests by delivering products that meet customer needs, provide fair value, and support financial objectives without causing harm. **1.48**

While the introduction of the Consumer Duty stems from section 29 of the Financial Services Act 2021, which required the FCA to consult on whether it should introduce rules imposing a statutory duty of care towards consumers,[254] the FCA decided against implementing a statutory duty of care and instead introduced a broader package of measures.[255] This package can be broken down into three elements: the Consumer Principle, cross-cutting rules and outcomes. **1.49**

The Consumer Principle, outlined in Principle 12 of the FCA's Handbook, requires institutions to 'act to deliver good outcomes for retail clients.' This principle encourages institutions to assess their practices by considering whether they are treating customers as they would expect to be treated and ensuring that their products deliver the anticipated outcomes.[256] It establishes a higher standard than Principle 6 (Customers' interests), which mandates that institutions pay due regard to customer interests and treat them fairly. Unlike Principle 6, the Consumer Principle adopts an outcomes-based approach, focusing not only on processes but also on the actual impact of institutions' actions on consumers. The enforceable rules associated with these outcomes provide the Consumer Principle with more authority than the earlier Treating **1.50**

---

253 FCA, 'Consumer Duty' (n 249).

254 FCA, 'Consultation Papers: A new Consumer Duty Feedback to CP21/13 and further consultation' (December 2021) https://www.fca.org.uk/publication/consultation/cp21-36.pdf.

255 FCA, 'Feedback Statement FS19/2: A duty of care and potential alternative approaches: summary of responses and next steps' (April 2019) https://www.fca.org.uk/publication/feedback/fs19-02.pdf. This followed the consultation (CP21/13) and a discussion paper published in July 2018, in which the FCA sought input on the merits of introducing a statutory duty of care. FCA, 'Discussion Paper: DP18/5: Discussion Paper on a duty of care and potential alternative approaches' (July 2018) https://www.fca.org.uk/publication/discussion/dp-18-05.pdf.

256 FG22/5 chapter 4.

Customers Fairly (TCF) guidance.[257] As a result of this shift, the FCA disapplies Principles 6 and 7 (Communications with clients) in areas where the Consumer Duty applies, although these Principles apply outside the scope of the Duty.[258] The Consumer Principle thereby emphasises proactively delivering good outcomes and requires institutions to ensure that consumers are able to make decisions in their own best interests, with products and services tailored to meet those needs effectively.

1.51 The Cross-Cutting Rules outline expectations for institutions' culture and behaviour under the Consumer Principle.[259] Institutions must act in good faith, ensuring honesty, fairness, consistency and transparency aligned with consumers' reasonable expectations.[260] They must also take proactive steps to avoid foreseeable harm from their conduct, products, or services, though they are not required to protect consumers from risks the consumers knowingly accepted.[261] Additionally, institutions must reasonably support customers in achieving their financial objectives.[262]

1.52 The Consumer Principle and Cross-Cutting Rules are supported by four outcomes that define the relationship between customers and institutions. These outcomes cover responsibilities within the distribution chain and product-related outcomes. They emphasise that products and services must be designed to meet consumers' needs and appropriately targeted,[263] offer fair value in pricing,[264] provide clear communication for informed decision-making[265] and deliver ongoing support to meet customer needs throughout their relationship with the institution.[266]

1.53 Unlike a statutory duty of care, the threefold Consumer Duty has a broader scope but is limited to regulatory enforcement, lacking a private right of action. The FCA thereby followed responses put forward on the question of whether a statutory duty should be introduced, stating that if consumers could pursue legal action for breaches, this would lead to increased complexity, delays, costs,

---

257 FCA, 'The FCA's Consumer Duty Will Lead to a Major Shift in Financial Services' (27 July 2022) https://www.fca.org.uk/news/press-releases/fca-consumer-duty-major-shift-financial-services.

258 However, related materials in the *FCA Handbook* and non-Handbook guidance continue to apply, FG22/5 para. 4.2.

259 FCA Handbook, PRIN, 2A.2; FG22/5 chapter 5.

260 FCA Handbook, PRIN, 2A.2.1-7; FG22/5 para. 5.2.

261 FCA Handbook, PRIN, 2A.2.8-13; FG22/5 para. 5.38.

262 FCA Handbook, PRIN, 2A.2.14-22; FG22/5 para. 5.37.

263 FCA Handbook, PRIN, 2A.3; FG22/5 paras. 6.18 et seq.

264 FCA Handbook, PRIN, 2A.4; FG22/5 chapter 7.

265 FCA Handbook, PRIN, 2A.5; Cf. also PRIN 7; FG22/5 chapter 8.

266 FCA Handbook, PRIN, 2A.6; FG22/5 chapter 9.

potential inconsistencies between court and FCA decisions and a risk of adversarial relationships between firms and consumers.[267] Although the FCA has opted against a statutory duty of care, it has left open the possibility of introducing a private right of action in the future,[268] suggesting that this deferral allows the industry time to integrate the Duty without the immediate pressure of litigation.[269] While private recourse litigation is not permitted under the Duty, related disputes may be resolved by the financial ombudsman,[270] whose decisions could indirectly shape common law. Furthermore, senior management is tasked with ensuring the Duty's effective implementation and may be held accountable under the SMCR.[271]

2. Scope

The Consumer Duty applies to all institutions conducting regulated activities under the FSMA, the Payment Services Regulations 2017 (PSRs) and the E-money Regulations 2011 (EMRs) for prospective and actual retail customers.[272] The definition of retail customers is sector-specific and aligned with regulatory scopes in the respective FCA sourcebooks. For example, in consumer credit, the Duty applies to all regulated credit-related activities, and in deposit-taking activities, it covers consumers, micro-enterprises and large charities, as well as trustees acting outside their professional capacity.[273] It also extends to SMEs, non-UK customers and high-net-worth individuals, provided that existing regulation and protections apply.[274] Conversely, the Consumer Duty does not apply to activities where an exclusion exists under FCA rules. 1.54

The Consumer Duty applies across the entire distribution chain, covering all institutions with material influence over customer outcomes tied to the creation, distribution, or post-sale management of products and services for retail 1.55

---

267 PRA, 'Feedback Statement FS19/2: A duty of care and potential alternative approaches: summary of responses and next steps' (April 2019) para. 1.15 et seq. https://www.fca.org.uk/publication/feedback/fs19-02.pdf.

268 PS22/9 chapter 11.

269 CP21/36 chapter 5.

270 On the Financial Ombudsman Service's position on the Consumer Duty see Abby Thomas, 'What Does the Consumer Duty Mean for Resolving Financial Complaints?' (Consumer Duty Implementation Summit, City & Financial Global, 20 June 2023) https://www.financial-ombudsman.org.uk/data-insight/blogs/consumer-duty-resolving-financial-complaints.

271 Summarised in FG22/5 para. 1.9. See below under ibid section C.

272 FG22/5 chapter 2 in particular para. 2.1.

273 This follows the definition of 'banking customer' in the in the Banking Conduct of Business Sourcebook (BCOBS), cf. FG22/5 para. 2.3.

274 FG22/5 para. 2.4.

customers.[275] The Consumer Duty operates under a standard of reasonableness which considers the nature and risk of the product or service, the financial capabilities and characteristics of retail customers and the institution's role in the distribution chain.[276]

1.56 Institutions cannot be deemed to have material influence when their role is confined to operating under another institution's mandate, such as a portfolio manager managing assets under the direction of an independent professional client, or IT providers.[277] Institutions conducting due diligence on other entities within the distribution chain must reasonably incorporate the Consumer Duty into their processes.[278] While institutions are primarily responsible for their own conduct, they are required to notify the FCA if another institution in the chain is not complying with the Duty. Additionally, they must inform other institutions if they believe harm has been caused to retail customers.[279] When outsourcing, institutions remain accountable for compliance under the SYSC, ensuring that outsourcing activities (e.g., customer service) do not negatively affect customers.[280] The FCA exempts certain wholesale activities, including those related to non-retail financial instruments for wholesale purposes.[281] However, this exclusion does not extend to activities where institutions are advising on, designing or distributing investment funds with high minimum investments aimed towards retail customers.[282]

3. Embedding the Consumer Duty in Governance and Culture

1.57 The three-layered approach of the Consumer Duty places a stronger emphasis on prioritising customer interests and outcomes, which must be embedded into an institution's processes and organisational structure. The FCA expects institutions to exercise greater judgment in evaluating how their behaviours, policies and processes throughout the entire product lifecycle contribute to achieving these outcomes.[283]

1.58 When applying for authorisation, institutions must demonstrate compliance with the Consumer Duty by providing a comprehensive analysis of their target

---

275 FG22/5 para. 2.12.
276 *FCA Handbook*, PRIN, 2A.7; FG22/5 paras. 2.14–2.16.
277 FG22/5 paras. 2.12 et seq.
278 FG22/5 paras. 2.21 et seq.
279 *FCA Handbook*, PRIN, 2A.9.17; FG22/5 para. 2.23.
280 FG22/5 para. 2.24.
281 FG22/5 para. 2.32.
282 FG22/5 para. 2.30.
283 FG22/5 para. 11.18.

market, fair value assessments and governance frameworks to monitor customer outcomes. Institutions must also provide details on customer support monitoring policies, supporting management information, and processes for identifying the root causes of customer complaints.[284] Additionally, institutions are required to continuously monitor, test, and adapt their practices and provide data demonstrating the results of these activities.[285] They should outline policies ensuring customer understanding, monitoring of customer outcomes and mechanisms to support and assess customer satisfaction. Additionally, institutions are expected to continuously monitor, test and refine their practices, backed by data on these efforts, including the root cause analysis of customer complaints.

(a) Guidance on governance and culture

Under the Consumer Duty, governance and culture are central areas of focus supported by specific rules and guidance.[286] The FCA expects institutions to embed a culture that prioritises good customer outcomes, ensuring all employees, including those in control and support roles, understand their part in achieving these goals. Institutions must empower staff to raise concerns and ensure those concerns are addressed. Governance structures should integrate the Consumer Duty into strategic and remuneration discussions and prioritise customer outcomes in risk and audit processes. Continuous assessment of external factors that could impact the ability to deliver good outcomes is required, along with the identification and mitigation of risks. Institutions should define clear short-, medium- and long-term outcomes to guide their practices, supported by ongoing analysis of customer data. If adverse outcomes are identified among specific consumer groups, institutions must investigate the causes, take steps to improve outcomes and assign accountability, with clear timelines for these improvements. Remuneration and incentives should be structured to drive positive customer outcomes effectively, ensuring that the institution's culture aligns with the goals of the Consumer Duty.[287] **1.59**

It is evident that these are more akin to high-level standards rather than precise rules. The FCA's own 2024 consultation document confirms that the introduction of the new statutory objectives of international competitiveness and **1.60**

284 FCA, 'Consumer Duty' (n 249).
285 *FCA Handbook*, PRIN 2A.9; FG22/5 chapter 11.
286 *FCA Handbook*, PRIN 2A.8; FG22/5 chapter 10.
287 FG22/5 para. 10.7.

growth[288] has led to the FCA mitigating any anti-business effects of its theoretically stringent consumer duty by adopting a principles-based approach.[289] There is the risk, however, that this approach will lead to *de facto* self-regulation by financial firms and limit the effectiveness of the Consumer Duty. This critique is evident in the response provided by the FCA Consumer Panel to question 5 of the aforementioned consultation, which emphasises that prescriptive rules have their own advantages and envisages a hybrid approach with prescriptive rules setting clear minimum standards that are complemented by high-level principles.[290] Prescriptive rules can be of particular value for consumers as they promote standardisation and facilitate comparability and informed choice – thus making the retail markets more competitive. Another major benefit of prescriptive rules identified by the Panel is their potential to empower the Financial Ombudsman Services to decide complaints to the benefit of consumers. This is because, although the Consumer Duty does not give rise to a right to private action at the moment, the FOS decides complaints based on what is fair and reasonable[291] rather than solely on the basis of the law, and therefore prescriptive rules could guide the FOS in the exercise of its discretion. In the same vein, debt advisers and consumer charities would benefit from prescriptive rules in being able to identify contexts in which consumers are likely to bring a successful complaint. These problems highlight the tensions between international competitiveness and consumer protection due to the inevitable trade-offs between, on the one hand, innovation and economic growth, and on the other, enabling consumers to meaningfully engage with, and benefit from, financial services. As the saying goes: 'You can't ride two horses at the same time.'

(b) Responsibility of senior management

1.61 The Consumer Duty is closely linked to the SMCR, as the FCA expects senior managers to ensure compliance with the Duty in their respective business areas. This is reflected in the amended SMCR individual conduct rules, which require senior managers to act to deliver good outcomes for retail customers.[292]

288 FSMA 2000, s 1B(4A), inserted by FSMA 2023, s 25. Regarding the challenges of introducing the new objectives, see E Ferran, 'International Competitiveness and Financial Regulators' Mandates: Coming Around Again in the UK' (2023) 9(1) *Journal of Financial Regulation* 30.

289 Call for Input Review of FCA requirements following the introduction of the Consumer Duty (July 2024).

290 Financial Services Consumer Panel, Response to CFI: Review of FCA requirements following the introduction of the Consumer Duty (October 2024) https://www.fca.org.uk/panels/consumer-panel/publication/20241031_final_fscp_response_to_cfi_on_fca_handbook_review.pdf.

291 *FCA Handbook* Disp. 3.6.

292 FG22/5 paras. 10.16 et seq; *FCA Handbook*, COCON, 6.

SMF holders are also obligated to notify the FCA of breaches related to the Duty, whether by their own institution or other institutions.[293] Additionally, the FCA recommends appointing a 'Consumer Duty Champion' at the board level, alongside the chair and CEO, to ensure ongoing discussion and monitoring of the Duty.[294] Ideally, this role should be taken on by an independent non-executive director. While not a prescribed SMCR responsibility, this role focuses on ensuring the board actively engages with and challenges the institution's approach to the Duty.[295] The institution's board must annually review and approve an assessment of whether the institution is delivering good outcomes in line with the Duty.[296] Before approval, the board should agree on actions to address any identified risks, customer harm or necessary adjustments to the institution's strategy to improve outcomes.[297]

4. Breaches and Enforcement Action

The FCA identifies several harmful practices by institutions that lead to consumer harm. These include practices that hinder consumers from making informed decisions, such as providing misleading or overly complex information, or offering products and services that are not fit for purpose, fail to meet consumer expectations or are inappropriate for the target market. Additionally, products that do not offer fair value and poor customer service that impedes consumers' ability to manage their financial affairs constitute harmful practices.[298] Practices that create barriers, such as difficulty in exiting products, or exploit consumer vulnerabilities, biases or information asymmetries, may also constitute breaches of the Duty.[299] **1.62**

The FCA's enforcement action against HSBC relating to behaviour prior to the Consumer Duty's entry into force provides insights into potential enforcement actions related to the fair treatment of vulnerable customers. Here, the FCA identified failings in HSBC's treatment of customers in financial difficulty, particularly vulnerable individuals, breaching Principles 3 (responsible organisation and control) and 6 (fair treatment of customers), alongside breaches of **1.63**

293 *FCA Handbook*, COCON, 4.2.31
294 FG22/5 para. 10.10.
295 FG22/5 para. 10.19; *FCA Handbook*, COCON, 6.
296 *FCA Handboo*k, PRIN, 2A.8.4.
297 *FCA Handbook*, PRIN, 2A.8.5.
298 See in this regard FCA, 'Price and Value Outcome: Good and Poor Practice update' (September 2024) www.fca.org.uk/publications/good-and-poor-practice/price-value-outcome-good-poor-practice-update.
299 FG22/5 para. 9.57.

CONC and MCOB rules, resulting in a fine of more than £6 million.[300] The FCA found several issues which relate to the inadequate consideration of individual circumstances, such as through inconsistent application of forbearance and affordability assessments and automated systems issuing default notices. These failings were linked to inadequate policies, insufficient staff training and a lack of governance oversight.[301] In its final notice, the FCA issued guidance closely aligned with Consumer Duty expectations, emphasising the need for thorough staff training, ensuring that automated systems take proportionate actions, generating outcomes-focused management information and establishing clear forbearance policies to reduce the risks associated with personal discretion.[302]

F. DIVERSITY AND INCLUSION (D&I)

1.64 As part of the regulatory focus on financial institutions' governance and culture, diversity and inclusion (D&I) considerations affect various areas of financial regulation described in this chapter such as board structure, senior management, remuneration and the Consumer Duty. This section outlines regulatory aims directed towards an understanding of D&I and sheds light on current standards and related regulatory proposals. It is recommended that regulators move beyond a strictly instrumental view of diversity and inclusion as a vehicle to promoting core regulatory objectives and instead conceptualise D&I as an independent value.

1. Regulatory Aims Related to D&I

1.65 Regulators believe that greater D&I in the financial sector enhances governance, decision-making and innovation, helping institutions better meet consumer needs and support regulatory objectives. For the FCA, D&I is a central component of its ESG priorities.[303] Similarly, the PRA views D&I as integral to good corporate culture and effective risk management, aligning with its goal of ensuring the safety, soundness and resilience of the financial sector.[304]

300 FCA, 'FCA Fines HSBC £6.2 Million over Treatment of Customers in Financial Difficulty' (23 May 2024) https://www.fca.org.uk/news/press-releases/fca-fines-hsbc-6-million-over-treatment-customers-financial-difficulty.

301 FCA, 'Final Notice – HSBC' (23 May 2024) https://www.fca.org.uk/publication/final-notices/hsbc-uk-bank-hsbc-bank-marks-and-spencer-financial-services-2024.pdf.

302 Ibid.

303 FCA, 'Our Strategy 2022–2025' https://www.fca.org.uk/publication/corporate/our-strategy-2022-25.pdf.

304 CP18/23 para. 1.3.

Both regulators see D&I as crucial to fostering a positive culture and managing risks in regulated entities.

A lack of diversity can lead to groupthink, a phenomenon where group cohesion and the pressure to conform lead to irrational or suboptimal decisions.[305] Groupthink, as noted in the Walker Review, was a key factor that led to a lack of appropriate challenge on boards and contributed to the GFC.[306] Additionally, research suggests that diverse teams make better decisions as they are more likely to re-examine facts and remain objective.[307] Greater diversity allows organisations to incorporate a wide range of perspectives during decision-making processes, improving innovation and outcomes.[308] Moreover, poor D&I can also expose institutions to operational and reputational risks.[309] Thus, the avoidance of groupthink through D&I is seen as a major factor to mitigate systemic risk and prevent consumer harm. **1.66**

The concern in taking such an instrumentalist approach is that it is contingent on factual evidence that 'diverse' directors and senior managers behave differently from their 'non-diverse' counterparts. This is problematic on two levels. First, commitment to diversity is at risk of being weakened if evidence does not in fact support the assumed correlation between demographic characteristics and decision making. Second, by making the facile assumption that simply because a senior manager is a woman or belongs to an ethnic minority or comes from a working-class background they will necessarily behave differently and reduce groupthink, regulators support the perpetuation of harmful stereotypes and the erasure of the individual personhood of those belonging to disadvantaged groups. **1.67**

2. Regulatory Understanding of D&I

In view of the above-mentioned objectives, the PRA defines three key types of diversity: demographic diversity, diversity of experience and cognitive **1.68**

---

305 Paul 't Hart, 'Irving L. Janis' Victims of Groupthink' (1991) 12(2) *Political Psychology* 247–78.

306 Walker Review para. 4.3. See also on the influence of lack of female representation in leadership Julie A Nelson, 'Would Women Leaders Have Prevented the Global Financial Crisis? Implications for Teaching about Gender, Behavior, and Economics' (2012) Global Development and Environment Institute Working Paper No 11-03.

307 David Rock and Heidi Grant, 'Why Diverse Teams Are Smarter' (*Harvard Business Review*, 4 November 2016) https://hbr.org/2016/11/why-diverse-teams-are-smarter.

308 Erik Larson, 'New Research: Diversity + Inclusion = Better Decision Making At Work' (10 December 2021) https://www.forbes.com/sites/eriklarson/2017/09/21/new-research-diversity-inclusion-better-decision-making-at-work/?sh=5d88170a4cbf%20.

309 CP18/23 para. 9.9.

diversity.[310] Cognitive diversity involves incorporating varied perspectives, knowledge, and approaches to problem-solving. The PRA emphasises that a combination of demographic diversity and diversity of experience is likely to foster cognitive diversity, helping to mitigate the risk of groupthink.[311] According to the regulators, cognitive diversity is shaped by various factors, including both visible and non-visible demographic characteristics such as gender, age, ethnicity, disability, sexual orientation and education. Beyond the nine protected characteristics defined in the Equality Act 2010, additional factors – such as socio-economic diversity, gender identity and cultural background – also contribute to diverse perspectives and life outcomes.[312] Gender diversity has been a key focus, beginning with the Women in Finance inquiry, which reported in June 2018.[313] This report outlined the benefits and barriers to gender diversity. In July 2023, the Sexism in the City inquiry followed, addressing issues such as barriers for women, gender pay gaps in financial services and sexual harassment.[314] While there have been improvements in gender diversity,[315] diversity in terms of ethnicity[316] and socio-economic background[317] is far behind, with only little progress. However, with regard to diversity of thought, these are also crucial factors to avoid groupthink and foster an inclusive culture.

---

310 CP18/23 para. 1.4.

311 CP18/23 para. 1.4.

312 PRA; FCA, 'Discussion Paper DP21/2: Diversity and inclusion in the financial sector – working together to drive change' (July 2021) para. 1.15 https://www.fca.org.uk/publication/discussion/dp21-2.pdf.

313 Treasury Committee, 'Women in finance: Fifteenth Report of Session 2017–19' HC 477 (6 June 2018) https://publications.parliament.uk/pa/cm201719/cmselect/cmtreasy/477/477.pdf.

314 House of Commons Treasury Committee, 'Sexism in the City: Sixth Report of Session 2023–24' (March 2024) https://committees.parliament.uk/publications/43731/documents/217019/default.

315 See for example with regard to signatories to HM Treasury's Women in Finance Charter, which has risen from 27 per cent to 35 per cent since its launch in 2016. HM Treasury, 'HM Treasury Women in Finance Charter: Annual Review 2023' (March 2024) 10 https://assets.publishing.service.gov.uk/media/65fb084d9316f5001164c432/HMT_WIFC_Review_2023.pdf.

316 Less than 10 per cent of management positions in financial services are held by individuals from Black, Asian, or other ethnic minority backgrounds. Ranstad, 'Paying attention: A guide to salaries within the financial services sector in 2018' (2018) https://www.randstad.co.uk/s3fs-media/uk/public/2019-10/fs-salary-survey-paying-attention-2018.pdf. See also Reboot 'Race to Equality: UK Financial Services Report Addressing underrepresentation of ethnic minorities in the financial services sector' (October 2021) https://fticommunications.com/wp-content/uploads/2021/10/Reboot-Race-to-Equality-UK-Financial-Services-Report-2021.pdf.

317 A study of eight financial firms, including regulatory bodies, revealed that individuals from higher socio-economic backgrounds occupy 89 per cent of senior positions. Bridge Group, 'Who gets ahead and how? Socio-economic background and career progression in financial services: a study of eight organisations' (2020) https://static1.squarespace.com/static/5c18e090b40b9d6b43b093d8/t/5fbc317e96e56f63b563d0f2/1606168962064/Socio-economic_report-Final.pdf.

Inclusion is understood as creating a culture where individuals feel psychologically safe, supported and empowered to contribute fully. This includes encouraging employees to challenge peers and senior management and to speak up without fear of repercussions, particularly in cases of potential misconduct. The PRA stresses that diversity without inclusion is insufficient, as diverse perspectives only add value when individuals feel comfortable expressing them and are taken seriously.[318] **1.69**

Boards and senior management hold the responsibility for fostering a safe and inclusive environment, ensuring that a broad range of voices is heard. Both the FCA and PRA highlight the importance of an inclusive tone from the top to embed these values across an institution. Regulators also link inclusion directly to effective risk management, noting that the ability to speak up, including through whistleblowing channels, is essential for identifying and mitigating risks. The PRA also underscores the importance of risk and control functions having systems in place to support these inclusive practices, ensuring institutions are both diverse and inclusive in their operations and governance.[319] **1.70**

3. Current Rules on D&I

Whilst the current regulatory framework contains some rules embedding D&I considerations into the regulatory framework, the PRA and FCA are set on expanding related requirements. **1.71**

(a) Board diversity

Currently, the General Organisational Requirements[320] and Conditions Governing Business[321] mandate a board diversity policy. Specifically, institutions with a nomination committee must set gender diversity targets for their boards.[322] Institutions must also consider a wide range of qualities when recruiting board members and are required to publicly explain their board diversity policies on their websites.[323] Moreover, boards are expected to promote a culture of risk awareness and ethical behaviour throughout the institutions.[324] The PRA highlights that without sufficient diversity of thought, skills **1.72**

318 CP18/23 para. 1.6.
319 CP18/23 para. 2.11.
320 *PRA Rulebook*, General Organisational Requirements, 6.2–6.4.
321 *PRA Rulebook*, Conditions Governing Business, 2.7–2.9.
322 *PRA Rulebook*, General Organisational Requirements, 6.2(4).
323 *PRA Rulebook*, General Organisational Requirements, 6.2(1), 6.3, and 6.4.
324 PRA, 'Supervisory Statement 5/16: Corporate governance: Board responsibilities' (31 March 2016) https://www.bankofengland.co.uk/prudential-regulation/publication/2016/corporate-governance-board-responsibilities-ss (SS5/16).

and experience, boards may overlook or underestimate significant risks in their strategic decisions, which could undermine the effectiveness of risk management and decision-making processes.[325]

(b) Responsibility for D&I

1.73 As mentioned above, the *PRA Rulebook* establishes Prescribed Responsibilities for promoting culture in the day-to-day management of the firm (PR H) and leading the development of the firm's culture by the governing body as a whole (PR I).[326] Assigning SMFs with responsibility for D&I fosters accountability for achieving these goals, contributing to the PRA's primary objective.[327] This is supported by research that suggests that establishing clear accountability for diversity progress can lead to the most significant improvements in managerial diversity within institutions.[328]

(c) Non-financial misconduct

1.74 Non-financial misconduct is an important concern for the culture of financial institutions and may play a role in the assessment of managers' fitness and propriety. Financial institutions are required to ensure that individuals performing regulated functions are deemed fit and proper on an ongoing basis. Non-workplace misconduct, such as criminal behaviour, may affect an individual's suitability for a regulatory role. For example, a financial adviser was judged unfit after being convicted of voyeurism against his tenant.[329] While regulators have attempted to take a more expansive approach, the Upper Tribunal has ruled that under the current rules, regulators must demonstrate the direct relevance of the misconduct or conviction to the individual's professional responsibilities in financial services to justify prohibition.[330] This ruling concerned a case in which the FCA sought to impose a prohibition order on a financial adviser based on a criminal conviction due to his conviction for

325 SS5/16, paras. 2.3 and 3.1.

326 *PRA Rulebook*, Prescribed Responsibilities I and H, 4.1(6) and 4.1(14). The PRA further expects institutions foster a culture supporting prudent management, with a focus on embedding safety and soundness principles throughout the organisation, PRA, 'Supervisory Statement 28/15: Strengthening individual accountability in banking' (December 2021) https://www.bankofengland.co.uk/-/media/boe/files/prudential-regulation/supervisory-statement/2021/ss2815-december-2021.pdf (SS28/15).

327 CP 18/23 para. 9.29.

328 Alexandra Kalev and others, 'Best Practices or Best Guesses? Assessing the Efficacy of Corporate Affirmative Action and Diversity Policies' (2006) 2 *American Sociological Review* 588.

329 FCA, 'Final Notice – Mark Horsey' (3 November 2020) https://www.fca.org.uk/publication/final-notices/mark-horsey-2020.pdf.

330 *Jon Frensham v The Financial Conduct Authority* [2021] UKUT 0222 (TCC).

attempting to meet a child following sexual grooming.[331] While the Tribunal acknowledged that the FCA's decision fell within a 'range of reasonable decisions', the Tribunal disagreed with the FCA's view that the conviction alone was sufficient to deem the individual unfit to practice, emphasising that non-financial misconduct outside the workplace must be qualitatively relevant to the individual's role in financial services.[332]

4. Proposals for a New Framework for D&I

Following a joint discussion paper[333] published by the PRA, the FCA and the Bank of England in 2021, both the FCA[334] and PRA[335] launched consultations proposing a new regulatory framework for D&I in the financial sector in September 2023. The FCA's proposed framework for D&I in the financial sector aims to promote healthier cultures, reduce groupthink, unlock new talent and better address diverse consumer needs.[336] The proposals set minimum D&I standards, focusing on the express inclusion of non-financial misconduct in conduct rules, fit and proper assessments and suitability threshold conditions.[337] The FCA proposes additional requirements for large institutions relating to explicit D&I strategies,[338] additional data reporting[339] and disclosure, setting targets[340] and risk and governance.[341] The FCA also introduces new glossary terms, such as 'discriminatory practices' and 'diversity **1.75**

331 FCA, 'Final Notice – Jon Frensham' (17 September 2021) https://www.fca.org.uk/publication/final-notices/jon-frensham-formerly-known-jonathan-james-hunt-2021.pdf.

332 The courts' current approach holds that private conduct damages concepts such as integrity and trust in a profession only when it directly relates to the individual's professional practice or the profession's standing. This was held in *Ryan Beckwith v SRA* [2020] EWHC 3231, [54] regarding solicitors. The Upper Tribunal drew from this case in *Jon Frensham v The Financial Conduct Authority* [2021] UKUT 0222 (TCC) and noted that Frensham's offence, was unrelated to his professional role and lacking financial dishonesty (para 176). However, the Tribunal upheld the FCA's position that the offence impacted public trust and the FCA's integrity objective, as public knowledge of the offence damaged both Frensham's reputation and that of the industry (para 185).

333 PRA, FCA, PRA and BoE, 'Joint discussion paper: DP21/2 – Diversity and Inclusion in the Financial Sector: Working Together to Drive Change' (07 July 2021) (DP21/2) https://www.bankofengland.co.uk/prudential-regulation/publication/2021/july/diversity-and-inclusion-in-the-financial-sector.

334 FCA, 'Consultation Paper 23/20: Diversity and inclusion in the financial sector – working together to drive change' (September 2023) https://www.fca.org.uk/publication/consultation/cp23-20.pdf (CP23/20).

335 PRA, 'Consultation paper 18/23: Diversity and inclusion in PRA-regulated firms' (25 September 2023) https://www.bankofengland.co.uk/prudential-regulation/publication/2023/september/diversity-and-inclusion-in-pra-regulated-firms (CP18/23).

336 CP23/20 paras. 2.2. et seq.

337 CP23/20 paras. 4.2. et seq.

338 CP23/20 paras. 5.6 et seq.

339 CP23/20 paras. 5.39–5.65.

340 CP23/20 paras. 5.20 et seq.

341 CP23/20 paras. 5.89 et seq.

and inclusion employee number', to promote clarity.[342] Furthermore, the FCA proposes guidance that recognises lacking D&I as a non-financial risk that should be managed within governance structures. Institutions are encouraged to engage in various functions, including risk management, to mitigate risks associated with a lack of D&I, such as groupthink and poor decision-making, which could harm consumer and market outcomes.[343]

1.76 The PRA's proposals focus on embedding D&I into institutions' culture strategies through governance, monitoring and accountability.[344] The PRA expects the new requirements to support both financial stability and institution-specific benefits, fostering innovation and expanding the talent pool in the financial services industry.[345] The PRA proposes that large institutions[346] implement and publish institution-wide D&I strategies with risk and control functions supporting these initiatives,[347] and set diversity targets, including mandatory minimums for gender and ethnic representation where underrepresentation is evident.[348] Additionally, the FCA is proposing to introduce a requirement for institutions to publish board-level D&I strategies, with clear expectations for succession planning and board accountability.[349] The PRA emphasises that SMFs responsible for culture should oversee D&I strategies, and their performance objectives and remuneration should align with this responsibility.[350] It also suggests clarifying that behaviours such as bullying, discrimination and harassment may impact fitness and propriety assessments, as they can undermine an institution's safety and soundness.[351] Moreover, the PRA calls for internal monitoring of D&I efforts[352] and proposes regulatory reporting of D&I targets and data for large institutions, contributing to an industry-wide benchmarking.[353]

---

342 CP23/20 paras. 3.33 et seq.

343 CP23/20 paras. 5.89 et seq.

344 CP18/23 para. 1.18. To achieve this, the PRA proposes changes to its Rulebook and supervisory statements, alongside a new supervisory statement on D&I designed to guide institutions in applying these D&I rules holistically (Cf. Draft version in Appendix 6 to CP18/23).

345 CP18/23 paras. 9.47–9.50.

346 CP18/23 para. 1.21.

347 CP18/23 chapter 2.

348 CP18/23 chapter 3.

349 CP18/23 chapter 4. The PRA also proposes to update SS5/16. Cf. Draft amendments to SS5/16 in Appendix 2 to CP18/23.

350 CP18/23 paras 5.4–5.7.

351 CP 18/23 para. 5.11 which proposes amending SS28/15.

352 CP18/23 chapter 6.

353 CP18/23 chapters 7 and 8.

G. CONCLUSION

The legal and regulatory frameworks governing financial institutions play a critical role in shaping their culture, purpose, leadership, people and governance. These frameworks include structural governance requirements, the SMCR, executive remuneration rules, the Consumer Duty and D&I considerations. Developed in response to lessons from the GFC, these rules and standards aim to manage risks to institutional safety and soundness and ensure financial system stability. Despite the extensive proliferation of binding and soft standards around corporate governance and culture, the analysis in this chapter reveals that enforcement remains a constant weakness mostly due to limitations on the effectiveness of the relevant supervisory authorities, especially the FCA. More fundamentally, at the level of the design of the applicable rules and standards, it is evident that there is a degree of ambivalence on the part of policymakers. This can be evidenced by the removal of the bonus cap without any simultaneous strengthening of other aspects of remuneration regulation such as the rules on malus, clawback and deferral of variable remuneration. Further, the reliance on high-level standards in the implementation of the Consumer Duty reveals an ambivalence between stronger consumer protection and enhancing international competitiveness and growth. At the same time, the incremental development of policy with piling layers of rules, regimes and rationales that mix financial stability, consumer protection and broader social justice objectives has led to mixed messages and haphazard outcomes, even though all those objectives are worthy of pursuit. A more holistic approach through viewing culture as an overarching mechanism, and a simpler and more coherent regulatory framework, would perhaps both reduce compliance cost for firms and contribute towards greater achievement of policy objectives. **1.77**

2

BOARDS AND REGULATORS – SHAPING AND ASSESSING ORGANISATIONAL CULTURE

Alan Brener

A. INTRODUCTION

The boards of highly regulated financial services firms are in the spotlight – particularly when anything goes wrong.[1] This includes both regulatory and, often, media scrutiny. This is particularly an issue for non-executive directors (NEDs), who will not have the same amount of time and level of engagement as those with executive responsibilities within the firm. This chapter suggests a number of practical measures which can be applied to help all board members in their onerous task of oversight and setting the strategy for the organisation. 2.1

At the organisation's core will be the business's culture. It is unlikely that there will be only one culture. In a large, complex organisation there will be many cultures operating in the various functional 'silos' and team structures. A poor culture will undermine all the good management intentions and guidance. It may jeopardise compliance and in a significant area, threaten the existence of the firm. Nothing will work as intended. Each day the business will spin the revolver's chambers, pull the trigger and await the potential explosion. It is possible that the board will be in blissful ignorance of the risks being run until the crash occurs. 2.2

The same issues may apply to the regulators who fail to focus their attention on the firm's culture. 2.3

Both boards and regulators should start by trying to find out more about the many cultures operating within the regulated organisation. There are a number of means available to assess these various cultures. This chapter focuses on key measures including staff engagement and the process and practice for raising concerns. Done to the right standards, these approaches are likely to help the board understand the culture to a high level of detail and to act with precision. 2.4

Boards and senior executives need to understand these cultures. This is largely done by *measuring* and, if necessary, taken action if the cultures revealed are unacceptable. A number of methods can be utilised, including: 2.5

- *attracting, recruiting and inducting* people who exhibit the right culture;
- encouraging a culture of *trust and accountability*. This will include *setting the measures* and the achievements of the organisation congruent with the right culture and ensuring that stakeholders in the organisation, who are *celebrated and promoted*, demonstrate the culture sought by the board;

---

1 All weblinks were last accessed 25 December 2024.

- *removing obstacles to personal accountability* such as the prevalent so-called three lines of defence model (explained in more detail below in section 5) and the widespread use of non-disclosure agreements (see section 7.7 for more details);
- encouraging all stakeholders in the organisation to *raise concerns*, and ensuring that these are listened to and acted upon and that no vindictive action is taken against those that speak up. This forms part of the two-way communication within the organisation and the trust that should ensue;
- a continual focus on *training*, including that of the board and senior executives. This will include ensuring that those with power in the firm understand the extent of their influence on those around them and that they are always being watched and the responsibility and accountability that results.

B. MEASURING CULTURE WITHIN AN ORGANISATION USING STAFF OPINION SURVEYS

2.6 Providing the board and senior management with considerable detail on how a firm undertakes its staff surveys including the response rates can itself indicate the culture of the business. It can also be an indicator to those outside the organisation (e.g. regulators) of how the board sees its role and how seriously it takes its obligations. The approach to undertaking these surveys is crucial.[2]

2.7 The surveys need to cover all the main business areas and locations; have a high level of granularity (probably down to the smallest unit); include 'engagement' type questions (e.g. 'does the firm turns a blind eye to unethical behaviour?'); and have all of the answers categorised as red, amber and green so that it is possible to compose 'dashboards' for each section within the organisation to help to identify potential troubling areas at a glance. It should be undertaken at least annually and be supported by an effective communications plan including support by local management. Many of the key questions should aim to assess staff engagement with the firm and its management and their perception of the organisation. This information can give a striking view of the culture in each area including the level of 'fear' in the organisation and the extent to which staff view their ability to challenge the actions and views of their bosses, and how the firm reacts to ethical issues in the workplace.

2.8 It is useful, if possible, for surveys to be supported by randomised, structured staff interviews and focus group meetings. Although it may be costly to

---

2 Alan Brener, *Strategies for Compliance: Tools, Techniques and Challenges in Financial Services* (Routledge 2021).

undertake these, it will provide the board and senior executives with a deeper understanding of any potential issues.

These surveys and focus groups may also indicate managerial problems within the bowels of the organisation. For example, low response rates to the survey may be a sign of broader management issues. The views expressed in these focus group meetings and interviews may, for example, puncture board-level complacency. **2.9**

Moreover, the results of these surveys should be presented with disaggregated data. This latter point is important since, in most organisations, problem areas are usually masked by the more positive attitudes of the majority of employees. Antony Salz, in his review of Barclays, including its culture, found that **2.10**

> some of the more qualitative information that could have alerted the Board to fundamental indications of cultural issues was not discussed...Most of the time, the Board was given aggregated scores which showed that employee satisfaction was increasing year-on-year across the Group. But the Board reports did not consistently include granular data indicating, for example, wide-ranging concerns about escalating ethical issues.[3]

All stakeholders in an organisation, including employees, contractors and suppliers, want to be valued and appreciated. While monetary reward is important, it is not sufficient. The respect paid by the board and senior executives to these stakeholders appears to be strongly linked to organisational culture. This was clearly explained in the seminal report by Sir Robert Francis into the scandal at the Mid Staffordshire NHS Foundation Trust. **2.11**

'The overwhelming majority of people respond positively to being appreciated for what they do'.[4] However, normally as a result of poor leadership and management, their morale will fall, sickness absences will rise and 'more stress is placed on the diminishing number of well-motivated staff'.[5] It requires 'the leadership of organisations to ensure that their workforce do not feel taken for granted'.[6] **2.12**

---

3 Anthony Salz and Russell Collins, 'Salz Review: An Independent Review of Barclays' Business Practices' (April 2013) 91 https://online.wsj.com/public/resources/documents/SalzReview04032013.pdf.

4 Robert Francis, 'Report of the Mid Staffordshire NHS Foundation Trust Public Inquiry ('Robert Francis's Report')' (HMSO, London 2013), HC 898-III, Vol 3, 1381 https://webarchive.nationalarchives.gov.uk/20150407084231/http://www.midstaffspublicinquiry.com/report.

5 Ibid 1381.

6 Ibid.

C. ENCOURAGING TRUST AND ACCOUNTABILITY

2.13 At its heart, an organisation's culture is based on trust and accountability. It includes both behaviours and competence.[7] A saintly organisation which fails to deliver for its customers is almost as useless as one with vampiric tendencies.

2.14 Customers and employees are clearly important but there are other critical stakeholders, such as the firm's suppliers. The failure to take sufficient account of the latter may have a detrimental effect on the perception of an organisation's culture. For example, it is reported that

> Rolls-Royce recently told several longtime suppliers that it was cutting expected orders at short notice. The news stunned the companies involved. Plants that had been set aside for Rolls-Royce would now lie idle. While the orders had not been contractually agreed, such a drastic reduction in the so-called schedule – used by suppliers to plan capacity – was unusual and potentially 'devastating for the supply chain', according to two industry executives familiar with the situation. 'It was catastrophic,' said one. 'The supply chain does not trust them anymore.' The move comes after Rolls-Royce was suspended this year from the government's prompt payment code for failing to pay 95 per cent of its supplier invoices within 60 days ... Several people interviewed by the FT say that senior management is out of touch with events on the ground, in particular at the group's main UK site in Derby. 'The levers being turned are not working. Unions are not the problem. It is something in management, or culture,' said one company veteran.[8]

D. ATTRACTING, RECRUITING, INDUCTING AND RETAINING STAFF

1. Attraction and Recruitment

2.15 Recruitment itself is central to a firm's culture.[9] There are several stages to ensuring that firms attract, recruit and induct individuals with the highest standards. It is important how an organisation positions itself to attract new recruits with the right culture. This includes recruitment marketing on social media and with agencies. It needs to make certain that what it says to attract new recruits reflects its culture. Draft text and images need to be tested before they are made public to see who they appeal to and how the firm's image is interpreted.

---

7 Richard Lambert, 'Banking Standards Review' (19 May 2014), 2 https://financialservicescultureboard.org.uk/pdf/banking-standards-review.pdf.

8 Peggy Hollinger, 'Rolls-Royce Chief Battles with Turnround as Engine Woes Persist' *Financial Times* (17 December 2019) https://www.ft.com/content/8c56cd9c-1b92-11ea-9186-7348c2f183af.

9 Alan Brener, 'The Golden Threads of Compliance' (1995) (4) *Journal of Financial Regulation and Compliance* 344–9.

Board and senior executives should look at the recruitment process within their business: what briefs are given to recruitment agencies; the types of recruitment adverts used; how these are positioned on, for example, social media and jobs platforms; the guidance given to recruiters; how recruitment actually works; who is appointed and why; and who is rejected against what criteria. Equally important is the induction and initial training process. What does this tell you about the firm? Who leaves during this process and why, and who leaves within the first year and why? **2.16**

The approach and quality of the induction process can often indicate the culture of the firm. At the extreme is that portrayed in the film *Boiler Room*, which displayed a poisonous process for selecting and inducting new recruits to a bond brokerage.[10] **2.17**

2. Who and What Gets Celebrated

It is possible to ascertain the culture of a firm by looking at both who and what gets celebrated by the business. This includes the allocation of financial rewards, various types of accolade and promotions. At the other end, there is the ritual humiliation of those perceived as failing. **2.18**

It is worth looking at whether bonuses are given to those who are commended by customers as providing the highest level of service and not just those with the highest sales scores. Are back-office staff perceived as 'second class' (or lower) employees? There are likely to be numerous large and small measures of recognition. For example, who gets the best offices and desk spaces and IT equipment? Who do senior managers speak to when they do walk-about? Who do non-executive directors seek out when they want to understand the business better? Employees will minutely note these small but important degrees of prestige and act accordingly. **2.19**

It is also important to see who gets humiliated by the business. That this may occur at all is a symptom of a problematic culture. Such practices need to be identified and the management responsible rooted out. For example, it has **2.20**

10 The film was issued in 2000 and produced by Jennifer and Suzanne Todd. It was apparently based on the recruitment and induction process operated by Sterling Foster & Co. 'In February 1997, the SEC filed a civil complaint charging Sterling Foster, a registered broker-dealer, and four individuals, including the firm's president, with illegally obtaining $75 million from investors by using boiler room sales practices and other fraudulent conduct in connection with the sale of six companies.' Securities Exchange Commission (SEC), 'Sterling Foster & Co.' (20 February 2003) https://www.sec.gov/divisions/enforce/claims/sterlingf.htm.

been reported that a Halifax bank branch held a weekly 'cash or cabbages day'[11] and that

> Employees who exceeded their sales were publicly rewarded cash. Those who missed their bonuses were given cabbages ... Two tellers at branches of the bank in Glasgow and Paisley had the vegetables placed on their desks within full public view. In the first case, an 18-year-old male teller was said to be deeply upset by the cabbage put on his desk. In the second case ... a 24-year-old had a cauliflower placed on her desk. She was apparently told she could only pass it on when someone opened an account.[12]

2.21 Another independent report produced for the independent directors of the board of Wells Fargo Bank in the US recorded the 'diseased culture' of the bank and gave as an example an event for bank staff in one region where district managers had to 'run the gauntlet':[13] staff were required to dress in outlandish costumes on a common theme and were formed into a gauntlet, and each manager had to 'run down the line to a whiteboard and report the number of sales they achieved'.[14]

3. 'Casting a Shadow' and Corporate Culture

2.22 Originally developed by Goldman Sachs, the Leadership Shadow Model is simple and practical.[15] Staff and other stakeholders such as contractors will look at what the management do every day, hour by hour. This pattern will go to the very top of the organisation, including the board. The 'watchers' will take their lead from the management while the latter need to understand the shadow they cast. This includes:

- what they say;
- how they act;
- what they prioritise;
- what they measure and reward.

2.23 What board members and managers do will percolate through the firm and help set the cultural tone. The senior members of the business need to

---

11 André Spicer, 'A Report on the Culture of British Retail Banking' (2014) New City Agenda and Cass Business School (now known as Bayes Business School) 21–2).

12 Kirsty Scott, 'Cabbage Lands Bank in the Soup' *The Guardian* (17 August 2005) https://www.theguardian.com/money/2005/aug/17/business.accounts.

13 Independent Directors of the Board of Wells Fargo, 'Sales Practices Investigation Report' (April 2017) 22 https://lowellmilkeninstitute.law.ucla.edu/wp-content/uploads/2018/01/WF-Board-Report.pdf.

14 Ibid 23.

15 There are a number of sources that consider this aspect of management. For example, Anthony Kasozi, 'The Leadership Shadow – What it is and Why it Matters?' (01 October 2015) *Anthony Kasozi* 8 https://anthonykasozi.info/thought_pieces/3/the_leadership_shadow_what_it_is_and_why_it_matters.

appreciate this and understand that they are always being watched and their behaviour is likely to be emulated. Employees want to know how to do well and to learn what behaviours and attributes will help them succeed. They will look to sources of authority to get a sense of how the organisation works. They also want to be appreciated and to be recognised for what they can contribute. It can be as simple as asking their opinion and taking these views seriously and thanking them. The basic premise is inclusivity. No one is left out. Everyone has value and should be recognised.

4. Cultural Memory

As well as recruiting new staff, it is important to reduce staff turnover and to reduce stress and sickness levels. This is, in itself, a big area, and one which has been the subject of extensive research.[16] **2.24**

The board and senior management also need to appreciate that organisations often retain 'cultural memories'. These can be positive or negative and they may well thwart change. Any changes in a firm which are, for example, complex to understand or not properly explained may result in staff working as before as they strive to adapt the two procedures. The older practices may re-emerge often when new IT arrangements are introduced. Staff will merge the old and new arrangements and develop sub-routines or 'work-arounds'. Similar results may be produced when senior management tries to introduce new cultures, for example, following a corporate takeover. **2.25**

E. THE ROLE OF THE BOARD IN REMOVING OBSTACLES TO GOOD ORGANISATIONAL CULTURE

1. The 'Three Lines of Defence' Delusion

Strategies to deflect proper board and senior management accountability may harm organisations developing and maintaining a good culture. It has been fashionable in regulated firms for boards and the senior management to employ the 'three lines of defence' model. However, among other things it may undermine a good culture within an organisation by obfuscating accountabilities and creating complacency in the board and among senior executives. **2.26**

16 For example, Tanja Braun and others, 'Better Health at Work? An Evaluation of the Effects and Cost–Benefits of a Structured Workplace Health Improvement Programme in Reducing Sickness Absence' (2015) 37(1) *Journal of Public Health* 138.

2.27 In outline, the 'three lines of defence' divide the roles of ensuring control of risks and compliance into three, with the front-line business functions taking primary responsibility for risk management and regulatory compliance; a second line of control functions, such as the compliance department, checking and reporting on the effectiveness of the first line; and the firm's internal audit function as a third and final line of defence.

2.28 While this approach sounds conceptually attractive, it is difficult to operate successfully. It comes as no surprise that this approach has been described by the Parliamentary Commission on Banking Standards (PCBS) as providing 'a wholly misplaced sense of security ... responsibilities have been blurred, accountability diluted, and officers in risk, compliance and internal audit have lacked the status to challenge front-line staff effectively. Much of the system became a box-ticking exercise whereby processes were followed, but judgement was absent.'[17] The same report stated that the 'three lines of defence' model also promoted the use of an 'accountability firewall' which seems to have developed 'to prevent those in senior positions having a strong sense of personal engagement with and responsibility for failings and misconduct within their line of management'.[18] The report described the model as the 'Maginot line of defence'.[19]

2.29 The 'three lines of defence' model has been described as being at the 'heart of the dysfunctionality of risk and compliance' since it reinforces misjudgments and over-complexity.[20] It may also induce a false sense of security. Those operating the compliance function in the first line of defence may be confused as to their role and suffer conflicts of interest since they are part of the business and report to managers and at the same time are required to be independent with oversight of what is happening and their own local management. They are very much part of the line business unit with local reporting lines. This may provide some advantages, since they are closer to the issues and may understand both the regulatory issues specifically relating to that business with a high level of knowledge and expertise and in greater depth than a more centralised function. On the other hand, they may identify too closely with the business and not approach problems with sufficient criticality and objectivity of mind.

---

17 Parliamentary Commission on Banking Standards, 'Changing Banking for Good' (2013) HL Paper 27-II HC 175-II, Vol. I, 18.

18 Ibid Vol. II 283.

19 Ibid 138. See also Peter Bonisch, 'Excuse Me, How Many Lines of Defence? The New Financial Maginot Lines', *Paradigm Risk* (18 March 2013), https://paradigmrisk.wordpress.com/2013/03/18/excuse-me-how-many-lines-of-defence-the-new-financial-maginot-lines/.

20 Atul Shah, *The Politics of Financial Risk, Audit and Regulation: A Case Study of HBOS* (Routledge 2017) 39.

2.30 Paul Moore, the former Head of Group Regulatory Risk at Halifax Bank of Scotland (HBOS), who was fired by the HBOS CEO who was himself subsequently disgraced, considered that 'the "three lines of defence" governance model (designed by consultants with little or no practitioner experience) which is commonly in use in large organisations does not work and is dysfunctional'.[21]

2.31 Oversight by the so-called second line may work on a consultant's diagram but it may also, among other things, simply encourage excessive proceduralism. The PCBS report remarked that witnesses to the Commission 'described adherence to procedure with little regard to judgement throughout the three lines system'.[22] Generally, judgement is lacking, and this was acknowledged by Paul Lawrence, Group Head of Internal Audit at HSBC, who said it 'is actually very difficult for an audit unit, based on the skill sets it had and where it traditionally was in the organisation, to pass an opinion on judgments or issues of strategy'.[23]

2.32 There are many examples of confusion and failure to operate the 'three lines of defence' model. For example, Mike Walters, then Group Head of Compliance, Barclays Bank, provided oral evidence to the PCBS and described the compliance function in the second line of defence signing off new business products. When challenged by a MP on the Commission, Walters stated:

> we [Compliance] are the second line of defence, and we are very clear that we are. The tension, of course, is: what is the best way to operate? One could pull back from having anything to do with the first line of defence and simply seek to quasi-audit them after the event ... we are much better off and more likely to be successful as a compliance function and to protect Barclays if we have the ability to put our hand up and to ask our questions when that debate is happening. It is a somewhat sterile exercise and, therefore, has some inherent risks if you seek to do that on a cold review basis after the event.[24]

2.33 Another example was highlighted in the independent report by the law firm Slaughter and May in 2019 on the catastrophic IT systems transfer failure at TSB Bank. The report recorded that the 'three lines of defence' model was employed both as business as usual for risk management and specifically for

21 Parliamentary Commission on Banking Standards, 'Paul Moore written evidence' (13 May 2013) 3.5 https://publications.parliament.uk/pa/jt201314/jtselect/jtpcbs/27/27v_we94.htm.

22 Parliamentary Commission on Banking Standards, 'Changing Banking for Good' (n 17) Vol. II 141.

23 Ibid.

24 Parliamentary Commission on Banking Standards, 'PCBS hearing 28 November 2012 – Minutes of Evidence Session 2013–14' (28 November 2012) HL Paper 27-VIII/HC 175-VIII DQ652 https://publications.parliament.uk/pa/jt201213/jtselect/jtpcbs/c706-v/c70601.htm.

this major project.[25] Unfortunately, the first line failed to identify a number of key risks and failed during the course of the programme to update the risks log sufficiently to reflect the recognition of important changes and risks to the successful execution of the programme.[26] The second and third lines were no better at identifying the significant risks which caused the project to fail, with the subsequent resignation of the CEO and a number of other senior staff.[27]

2.34 The effectiveness of internal audit which forms the third line of defence continues to be questioned in the light of each financial disaster: 'however independent it might be, is often perceived as intervening too late to be useful in preventing risks crystallising.'[28]

2.35 While the 'three lines of defence' model may be attractive to boards, the culture that seeks to insulate the board from being held accountable is pernicious. One of the key themes in this chapter is the importance of boards directly engaging with key issues, whether this be staff culture, problem identification and escalation to the board or, as considered later, the ability of even the most junior individual to speak up and be heard. These are not just emblematic of a good culture; they are part of its foundations.

2. The 'Directed Telescope'

2.36 A major issue, as already mentioned, is the challenge faced by the board and senior executives in finding out what is going on. The larger and more complex the organisation, the more difficult the task. This may be exacerbated by managers operating with a culture of defensiveness and secrecy, as discussed in section 7 below. The Prussian general staff, in the second half of the 19th century, encountered a similar problem. The various armies were commanded by princes of the blood who saw little reason to inform the general staff of what they were up to. To counter this, the latter employed what is known as a 'directed telescope' strategy.[29] This involved posting keen young officers to the various armies and corps with orders to keep tabs on what was happening and

---

25 Slaughter and May, 'Independent Review of TSB's 2018 Migration to a New IT Platform' (December 2019) 210 https://www.slaughterandmay.com/news/slaughter-and-may-s-independent-review-of-tsb-s-2018-migration-to-a-new-it-platform/.

26 Ibid 211.

27 'TSB Loses 16,000 Customers after IT Meltdown' *BBC* (24 October 2018) https://www.bbc.co.uk/news/business-45952283.

28 Howard Davies and Maria Zhivitskaya, 'Three Lines of Defence: A Robust Organising Framework, or just Lines in the Sand?' (June 2018) 9 (Supplement 1) *Global Policy* 40 https://onlinelibrary.wiley.com/doi/pdf/10.1111/1758-5899.12568.

29 Martin van Creveld, *Command in War* (Harvard University Press 1985) 142.

to report directly back to the general staff, by-passing the local commanders. Thus, the former were able to see directly into the remote unit. The same could operate, and has operated, in modern business.[30]

3. Avoiding Setting the 'Wrong' Targets

Setting the wrong targets can easily undermine an organisation's culture. The 'wrong' targets are those that incentivise poor outcomes for patients, customers, suppliers and other key stakeholders in the organisation. The targets indicate to everyone what the organisation sees as important. The views expressed by the board and senior executives may sound fine and supportive, but the targets may proclaim a truer picture. The failure to meet targets may instil fear throughout the organisation. For example, at the Mid Staffordshire NHS Foundation Trust inquiry one witness mentioned that a 'high priority was placed on the achievement of targets, and particularly the A&E waiting time target. The pressure to meet this generated a fear, whether justified or not, that failure to meet targets could lead to the sack.'[31] There will be more on this important report later. **2.37**

Similar issues were found at Credit Suisse (CS) following the Archegos debacle. The report to the board of CS emphasised that '[s]enior management, supported by the Board, should set a "tone at the top" that stresses the importance of risk and related controls. CS should encourage employees to proactively confront issues as they arise, and should provide clear paths for escalation.'[32] The same report recommended that the bank instil 'a culture of responsibility, accountability, and respect for controls'.[33] **2.38**

F. THE IMPORTANCE OF A CULTURE OF 'SPEAKING UP'

1. Speaking Up Freely

The importance in an organisation of even the most junior member of staff being able, freely, to raise concerns and to be listened to, and the issues acted **2.39**

---

30 Alan Brener, 'The Golden Threads of Compliance' (1995) 3(4) *Journal of Financial Regulation and Compliance* 344–349, 348 and 349.

31 Robert Francis, 'Independent Inquiry into Care Provided by Mid Staffordshire NHS Foundation Trust' (January 2005–March 2009) HC375-I, Vol 1, 168 https://assets.publishing.service.gov.uk/government/uploads/system/uploads/attachment_data/file/279109/0375_i.pdf.

32 Credit Suisse Group Special Committee of the Board of Directors, 'Report on Archegos Capital Management' (29 July 2021) 164 https://www.sec.gov/Archives/edgar/data/1159510/000137036821000064/a210729-ex992.htm.

33 Ibid.

upon, cannot be overstated. It is possible that staff who raise concerns are the most powerful 'tool' available to the board since they provide valuable information on what may be happening in the depths of the organisation. It requires a culture of being able to 'speak up' without fear of retribution. Issues of significance raised need to be escalated rapidly and brought to the attention of the board. Effective action must be taken and be seen to be taken.

2.40 Employees, contractors and other stakeholders working in, or with, a firm need to understand that they have 'permission' to raise concerns. This has been a particular issue in very hierarchical institutions such as hospitals. For example, the Royal College of Nursing (RCN) has actively campaigned to encourage nurses to raise concerns. The College's training and leaflets make it clear that in the UK's National Health Service (NHS) staff must not 'wait for a problem to develop. If you see poor care or feel you are being prevented from providing safe, compassionate care, you should raise your concern as soon as you can. All NHS employees have a contractual right and a duty to raise concerns with their employer that they consider to be in the public interest – including malpractice, patient safety, financial impropriety, or any other serious risks.'[34]

2.41 The same standards should apply in financial services, and in other industries, with all staff encouraged to speak up freely. The benefits of this open culture are immense. Besides helping to protect customers and employees it safeguards the organisation as a whole. It is a key purpose of the board to help ensure this culture of free dialogue and openness. The existence of a culture of 'speaking up' and its actual operation can also provide valuable information to regulators both about issues within the firm but also about its culture and whether it can be trusted. It may give an indication of the culture and ethics of a business and in particular, how receptive an organisation is to internal criticism, whether it listens and takes action and the extent to which managers adopt a more vindictive approach seeking out the person who has raised their concerns.

2. Organisations in a State of Denial Exhibit a Poor Culture

2.42 It is not clear which way causation runs but it is certain that it is a sign of a poor culture where an organisation suppresses issues and denies the existence or the full extent of a problem. Organisations will often demonstrate a range of responses to criticism, ranging from denying responsibility and avoiding accountability to deflecting issues and attacking the person raising the concern.

---

34 'Raising Concerns: Guidance for RCN Members' *Royal College of Nursing* (RCN) https://www.rcn.org.uk/employment-and-pay/raising-concerns/guidance-for-rcn-members.

There is always a risk that individuals in organisations may react defensively to concerns raised. As a result, problematic issues may be dismissed or simply explained away without proper investigation. Again, such reactions are all evidence of a poor corporate culture. Poor quality organisations often demonstrate similar problematic issues. These include poor staff morale, high levels of denial that there are any issues, that they are personally not responsibly for any issues and that the problems are the fault of the complainants.[35] **2.43**

3. Someone Is Always Aware Where Something Is Not Right

Whenever there was a problem within an organisation it is likely that there was someone who knew or suspected that something was wrong. Often these individuals were in relatively junior roles. Besides understanding that there was something awry they may not have appreciated the full seriousness of the issues. They may have tried to raise their concerns but their concerns were dismissed or they were simply told not to worry further. They may have been too scared to speak-up, or worried about informing on a colleague or because of some mis-placed loyalty to the company. Working in 'silos' they viewed the actions in another section as 'none of their business' and consequently, a problem for someone else. It may be simply the desire to avoid being made to look foolish if their concern turns out to lack foundation. **2.44**

It is thus important to understand how people in the organisation can be encouraged to provide this information to the highest levels, including the board. It is like gold dust for board members and it should be fundamental to a regulatory view of the firm. Unfortunately, it is not evident that regulators pay much, if any, attention to these areas. **2.45**

4. An Open Culture Is Critical to Communications

This culture of open communication is critical to the board undertaking its oversight role. Some of the concerns may be the result of misunderstandings or in very few cases, malicious intent but the vast majority of those that speak up will be doing so because they are troubled by what they have seen or experienced and these views need to be welcomed and taken seriously. **2.46**

---

35 An example of this can be seen in the Wirecard AG scandal. Bernd Ziesemer, 'Why was Frankfurt So Blind for So Long about Wirecard?' Financial Times (21 June 2020) https://www.ft.com/content/f04793df-43a2-4d69-a39f-e04dac36ce8e 'The case raises a disturbing question for Frankfurt's financial community. Why did so many institutions fail to take into account what the Financial Times had reported might be going on there? One reason sticks out. Many saw the reports as an invented, or at least co-sponsored, by shady Anglo-Saxon speculators and "locusts".'

2.47 A good culture will demonstrate that:

- there is a process for handling concerns raised within the firm including protecting the individual from retribution;
- these arrangements need to include a member of the senior management to oversee the policies and their implementation;
- there also needs to be a non-executive director who carries out the same role but at a board level;
- all staff, including contractors, need to be aware of these processes, the protections they afford and who to contact, and how best to do this;
- all concerns are followed up appropriately, and those that spoke up kept informed and protected;
- other senior management, control functions, the board and the regulators are informed and updated.

5. Guidance on Raising Concerns

2.48 The Public Interest Disclosure Act 1998 provides protection for someone if they are harmed or dismissed as a result of 'blowing the whistle' (known as making a disclosure) about a firm or individual'.[36] More broadly, the Department of Business, Innovation and Skills, as it was in 2015, issued 'Whistleblowing: Guidance for Employers' which is short, clearly written and should form the basis for producing guidance for all levels of staff within a bank, and more widely. For example, 'recognising workers are valuable ears and eyes: workers are often the first people to witness any type of wrongdoing within an organisation. The information that workers may uncover could prevent wrongdoing, which may damage an organisation's reputation and/or performance, and could even save people from harm or death'.[37]

6. Culture and Organisational Hierarchies

2.49 Based on my own experience, the more organisational 'layers' in an organisation the more difficult it will be for the board and senior team to influence its culture. Informational flows will get longer and slower and messages are likely to be distorted. Further, those raising concerns are likely to want to avoid their issues going direct to their line boss because the latter is often part of the problem. Therefore, having a safe and trusted parallel reporting system will help instil trust and speed reporting of issues with the least distortions.

---

36 FCA, 'Whistleblowing' https://www.fca.org.uk/firms/whistleblowing.

37 Department of Business, Innovation and Skills, 'Whistleblowing, Guidance for Employers and Code of Practice' (2015) 3 https://assets.publishing.service.gov.uk/government/uploads/system/uploads/attachment_data/file/415175/bis-15-200-whistleblowing-guidance-for-employers-and-code-of-practice.pdf.

Ideally it is best to have a 'flat' organisational structure with the smallest hierarchy possible but this is a matter for the firm's management. Another method is to focus on a 'procedural approach' and have, for example, open-ended questions in regular reports from staff (e.g. 'is there anything concerning you that senior management should know about?').[38] However, this alone is unlikely to work. **2.50**

In part, managers are often tempted to suppress bad information including taking action against those that raise concerns. Additionally, it is also likely that reports, of all types, will be collated and aggregated and be summarised as they proceed up the management chain. From my own experience, any report that is distilled up through more than two layers of management becomes 'sanitised' to such an extent that it is probably not worth having. In addition, any adverse comments are usually, quickly and easily rationalised away (eg 'sour grapes', 'it is a personal grievance' and 'result of a personality clash'). **2.51**

7. A Parallel Reporting Process

As already mentioned, a parallel reporting process for reporting concerns outside the normal line management system is important. However, it only works with the right cultural approach. This includes using independent investigators who have no position to defend and who will not be fobbed-off with management platitudes and facile rationalisations. Further, a parallel reporting process only works if it is supplemented by an investigative mind and supported by those with the power and authority to take clear and effective action. Training on these processes and the various responsibilities is important. It forms part of the foundations of a firm's culture. It may encourage staff to speak up about their concerns and give them confidence that they will be listened to and not victimised. **2.52**

The need to focus on culture as well as process is noted by the Financial Conduct Authority FCA.[39] This increased regulatory attention is evident following the Prudential Regulatory Authority's (PRA) legal action against **2.53**

38 Michael Davis, 'Avoiding the Tragedy of Whistleblowing' (Winter 1989) 8(4) *Business and Professional Ethics Journal* 3–19.

39 FCA, 'Retail and Wholesale Banking: Review of Firms' Whistleblowing Arrangements' (14 November 2018) https://www.fca.org.uk/publications/multi-firm-reviews/retail-and-wholesale-banking-review-firms-whistleblowing-arrangements.

Lloyds of London (Lloyds) following the latter's failure to operate an adequate whistleblowing system.[40]

2.54 The PRA had concerns about Lloyds' whistleblowing systems and controls following its disclosure to the PRA on 15 February 2019 that the 'only anonymous whistleblowing channel provided for Corporation Staff (as opposed to people working in the Lloyd's market more generally) had not been operational since 1 October 2017'.[41] The firm had advance notice that this channel would cease to work but failed to put in place a suitable alternative anonymous channel until the end of February 2019 (i.e. some 16 months later). Lloyds voluntarily disclosed this information to the PRA. However, the situation was exacerbated when, in response to a question from the regulator, the firm confirmed to the PRA that it had not, as required by the rules, produced an annual whistleblowers report for its board.[42] Subsequently, the PRA took the highly unusual steps of formally intervening and Lloyds had to report annually direct to the PRA. These reports need to include information on, for example, staff whistleblower training, whistleblower reports received and actions taken as a result, third-party checks that the notifications systems are working properly and 'the results of any surveys of staff or third party assurance reviews carried out during the preceding year to verify that the [whistleblower] channels remained in operation'.[43] In addition, using the format of an 'attestation letter', the PRA took the unusual step of making a senior executive of Lloyds personally responsible for the adequacy of this reporting process until 2022.[44]

2.55 Particular concerns existed about the staff culture at Lloyds. There were 'allegations that sexual harassment was rife at the [Lloyds] market, a lack of diversity and an enduring reputation for 'laddishness' [which] have made Lloyd's appear out of step with much of the rest of the City. A survey published in September found almost 500 people at the market, equivalent to one in 12 of the respondents, had witnessed sexual harassment in the previous 12 months'.[45]

40 PRA, 'Written Notice: Application for Imposition of New Requirements pursuant to s55M(5) of FSMA 2000' (23 December 2019) https://www.bankofengland.co.uk/-/media/boe/files/prudential-regulation/regulatory-action/written-notice-from-the-pra-to-the-society-of-lloyds.pdf?la=en&hash=825F21DB1C8FB24BD5854BB8E374E0DFF63C5E3C.

41 Ibid 6.

42 Ibid 7.

43 Ibid 2–3.

44 Ibid 8.

45 'Lloyd's Lapse Draws Tighter BoE Scrutiny of Whistleblower Systems' *Financial Times* (23 December 2019) https://www.ft.com/content/8eabd3fe-2578-11ea-9305-4234e74b0ef3.

8. Instilling a Culture of Listening

It is important that those who raise concerns are heard and taken seriously, and their issues understood. As mentioned earlier, they also need to be kept informed of what is being done as a result of their actions. In some circumstances, it may be possible to consult them on what is proposed, since they are likely to have a high level of expertise on the issues. **2.56**

An example of this was highlighted by the official enquiry and report on the Herald of Free Enterprise Zeebrugge disaster in 1987, in which almost two hundred people lost their lives.[46] The ferry sailed out of the harbour with her bow doors still open and seawater flowed in and capsized the vessel. The doors were not closed due to errors by several of the crew and also the failure by the ferry's captain 'to issue and enforce clear orders. But a full investigation into the circumstances of the disaster leads inexorably to the conclusion that the underlying or cardinal faults lay higher up in the Company. The Board of Directors did not appreciate their responsibility for the safe management of their ships … the directors did not have any proper comprehension of what their duties were.'[47] Additionally, the ferry captain, on the ship's bridge, could not see the ferry's doors and had no way of knowing whether they were open or closed since there was no alarm or other indicator of the state of the bow doors on the bridge. **2.57**

Moreover, the investigating judge found that the company's management 'took very little notice of what they were told by their' ship captains. Specifically, the senior managers rarely met the captains and 'did not listen to the complaints or suggestions or wishes of their' captains, whose collective voice 'fell on deaf ears' regarding their 'complaints that ships proceeded to sea carrying passengers in excess of the permitted number' and their 'wish to have lights fitted on the bridge to indicate whether the bow and stern doors were open or closed'.[48] **2.58**

This failure to understand and to listen is indicative of a malaise and cultural lacuna. **2.59**

46 Justice Sheen, Wreck Commissioner, 'Herald of Free Enterprise Report of Court No. 8074 Formal Investigation' (1987) HMSO 1 https://assets.publishing.service.gov.uk/media/54c1704ce5274a15b6000025/FormalInvestigation_HeraldofFreeEnterprise-MSA1894.pdf.

47 Ibid 14.

48 Ibid 17.

G. THE POTENTIAL CULTURAL OBSTACLES WHICH OFTEN PREVENT BOARDS AND SENIOR EXECUTIVES FINDING OUT WHAT IS GOING ON

2.60 There are many potential cultural barriers which may prevent the board and others finding out what is going on in the organisation. Some of these key issues are set out below.

1. Fear of 'Disloyal' Insiders Who Tell the Truth

2.61 Whistle blowing tends to invite swift retaliation as 'much organizational wrongdoing is visible only by people on the inside who are in a position to document it'.[49] As a consequence, 'organizations are afraid of men and women who remember that they are first of all citizens who belong to an entity larger than the organization'.[50] If an organisation has the wrong culture it will seek to ensure that 'every act, practice, and ritual' promotes loyalty in 'an attempt to persuade its members to think of themselves as first and foremost citizens of the organization'.[51] This type of culture is a strong warning indicator for boards and others.

2. The Psychological Fear of Taking Action

2.62 Often, an individual may not have raised their voice due to a psychological fear of taking action. The FCA has published its own guidance on the 'psychological safety' of staff at regulated firms.[52] In particular, the FCA is concerned that managers may not understand how all-powerful they appear to staff. Their status, and the 'shadow they cast', may intimidate employees sufficiently to deter them from speaking up. A key part of a manager's role is to create 'psychological safety' which encourages staff to say what they think.[53]

3. Poor Culture, Inwardly Focused Organisation, and with a Spirit of Omertà

2.63 Organisations with a poor culture will often be highly secretive, and the management inwardly focused. Between 2008 and 2013, as mentioned earlier, a

---

49 Charles Frederick Alford, 'What Makes Whistleblowers So Threatening? Comment on 'Cultures of silence and cultures of voice: the role of whistleblowing in healthcare organisations' (2015) 5(1) *International Journal of Health Policy and Management* 71–73 https://www.ncbi.nlm.nih.gov/pmc/articles/PMC4676977/pdf/IJHPM-5-71.pdf.

50 Ibid 72.

51 Ibid 72.

52 FCA, 'Psychological Safety' (18 February 2019) https://www.fca.org.uk/culture-and-governance/psychological-safety.

53 Ibid.

formal review into the Mid Staffordshire NHS Foundation Trust provided many examples of a very poor culture which emanated from the top of the organisation. This resulted in a high number of patient deaths and inadequate patient care. It is claimed that, for example, some patients were left to drink water from flower vases and 'hospital receptionists [were] assessing emergency cases', while 'patients needing pain relief either got it late or not at all, leaving them crying out for help, and there were cases where food and drinks were left out of reach'.[54] The hospital trust used non-disclosure agreements (NDAs) to silence dissent and one of those who raised concerns, Julie Bailey, a former nurse, was ostracised.[55]

Secrecy and keeping failings hidden were central to the management culture **2.64**
at the hospital trust. For example, a senior manager at the Mid Staffordshire NHS Foundation Trust gave evidence to the public inquiry of the 'gap that existed then between management and staff 'the executive team at that time was very much inward looking. I mean, it was a small cabal who ran things but didn't get out and about much and meet the people … there was a feeling that management held everybody at arm's length'.[56] The boards and senior management of all organisations, including those in the financial services sector, need to engage directly with the stakeholders and employees. There are a range of methods for this. They include regular and frequent focus groups, open engagement forums both in person and online and briefing and listening sessions across the organisation. The number of levels within the organisation from top to bottom should be kept as small as possible. This has many management advantages, not least increasing the likelihood of knowledge and understanding of the problems and concerns of stakeholders.

54 James Gallagher 'Mid Staffs: Helene Donnelly and Julie Bailey Honoured' *BBC News* (30 December 2013) https://www.bbc.co.uk/news/health-25549054.

55 Tim Adams, 'Mid Staffs Whistleblower Julie Bailey: "I don't go out here on my own any more"' *The Guardian* (27 October 2013) https://www.theguardian.com/society/2013/oct/27/julie-bailey-mid-staffordshire-nhs-whistleblower. 'She faced threats, abuse and her mother's grave was vandalised, forcing her to leave her home. But the Mid Staffs whistleblower who exposed neglect at the town's hospital is determined to continue her campaign for a better NHS.' Sarah Calkin, 'Whistleblowing Mid Staffs Nurse Too Scared to Walk to Car after Shift' *Nursing Times* (17 October 2011) https://www.nursingtimes.net/clinical-archive/accident-and-emergency/whistleblowing-mid-staffs-nurse-too-scared-to-walk-to-car-after-shift-17-10-2011/. 'A whistleblowing nurse from Mid Staffordshire Foundation Trust has told how she was physically threatened by colleagues after raising concerns about standards in the accident and emergency department.'

56 Robert Francis, 'Independent Inquiry into Care Provided by Mid Staffordshire NHS Foundation Trust' (n 31) 168.

4. Poor Culture and Denial

2.65 Denial can take the form of rejecting the evidence that there is an issue by claiming either that the information is wrong or that the conclusions drawn are incorrect. These approaches are not mutually exclusive.[57] For example, noted in the Francis Report is that any criticism of surgical procedures was deflected by denying there was an issue. 'One of the things I learnt through ten-plus years of dealing with people who didn't like what we were telling them about their heart surgery results is your first response is to say, "The data's wrong". Your second response is to say, "Okay, the data's right but your analysis is wrong".'[58]

2.66 Denial can also take the form of rejecting any responsibility. This is particularly true where the organisational culture rejects ownership of issues and this 'can result in all problems be blamed on outsiders and the 'other' – things that cannot be controlled. This may result in 'numbing' staff into believing nothing can ever be done and lapsing into 'fatalistic acquiescence'. It may also involve the excuse of 'acting on orders'.[59] In the Mid Staffordshire NHS Foundation Trust Inquiry the former chair of the Trust gave evidence saying that the bad publicity attracted by the public inquiry exaggerated the problem and that there was, in fact, no serious issue.[60] 'The reality is that once a trust is publicised as having killed up to 1,200 people, however mistakenly, then that ... stigma advertises it so much that all sorts of things start to surface which wouldn't in a normal hospital ... I am genuinely, not defending bad care. I am really not ... It could be that we are worse than most. I seriously hope that is not the case but it could be. But there are often two sides to quite a lot of stories.'[61] The Inquiry Report commented: 'regrettably the impression left by [the former chair's] evidence is that, while she genuinely regrets that such incidents of poor care have occurred, she has been unable to accept the enormity of the problems that engulfed the hospital and ... did not appear to accept the Board's responsibility for what went wrong. Such a position, held in the teeth of external adverse opinion, suggests an entrenched attitude of denial and dissociation from the issues that beset the hospital and its patients.'[62]

---

57 Anelia Larsen and others, 'Psychopathology, Defence Mechanisms, and the Psychosocial Work Environment' (2010) 56(6) *International Journal of Social Psychiatry* 563–577.

58 'Robert Francis's Report' (n 4) 1362.

59 'Robert Francis's Report' (n 4) 1369.

60 Robert Francis, 'Independent Inquiry into Care Provided by Mid Staffordshire NHS Foundation Trust' (n 30) 181.

61 Ibid.

62 Ibid 182.

Another senior manager who gave evidence to the Inquiry describes that first there was 'an overwhelming sense of denial in the organisation, characterised by "It's not our fault, it is somebody else's", it is the PCT [Primary Care Trust] or the department or the Healthcare Commission or whoever else was around that you could blame for how awful it is. Then the second overwhelming impression that everywhere else is probably the same but they just have never been caught.'[63] The Trust's new medical director attended a board meeting in 2009 as an observer since he had yet to start in his new role and described an organisation in denial. There 'was the overwhelming feeling of denial, that there wasn't [an] acknowledgement that things were going wrong … clinical matters were left right at the end, like a serious event that was discussed right at the end of a three and a half hour meeting and all the other agenda items were nothing to do with patient care.'[64] This reinforces the importance of senior management and boards adopting an outward-facing culture and engaging with all stakeholders. **2.67**

5. A Culture that Attacks Those Who Raise Concerns

All too often, those who raise concerns expose themselves to vindictive action by managers. This clearly demonstrates a poisonous culture within the organisation. The Francis Report on the Mid Staffordshire Foundation Trust illustrates this in one of the quotes from its enquiry. Nurses at a mental health hospital, when challenged about their poor care of patients, responded in writing that they were 'defenceless against, and wide open to, unfair criticism from people who are inexperienced in the care of subnormal people, and who are also hypersensitive and prone to exaggeration'.[65] This type of reaction provides a flashing alarm of deep-seated cultural problems. **2.68**

6. The Risk of Approaching Concerns from a Legalistic Perspective

Boards and senior executives often pass the handling of whistleblower concerns to their lawyers to address. The risk is that the process becomes the solution. How the process is perceived and operated, and the results, may be seen as secondary. There is a tendency for policies covering raising concerns to be written by lawyers. Public Concern at Work (now called 'Protect'), a charity to support whistleblowers, has stated that in the course of its work it sees 'a great number of whistleblowing policies … many policies are too legalistic [and] **2.69**

63 Ibid.

64 Ibid.

65 'Robert Francis's Report' (n 3) 1369.

complicated … do not provide adequate (or any) assurances to the individual, [and] place the duty of fidelity above all else, and contain contradictory and/or poor reassurances on confidentiality'.[66] As Martin Woods has said, 'ultimately it is all about culture, a culture which promotes the rights morals and values'.[67]

7. The Widespread Use of Non-disclosure Agreements

2.70 Non-disclosure agreements (NDAs) may be useful but there is a strong temptation to misuse them 'to silence and remove a problem from an organization ... NDAs effectively use contractual arrangements to prevent employees and others speaking up. While there are good reasons to use NDAs all too often lawyers, both in-house and in professional firms, go along with their abusive use out of [a] mis-placed loyalty to their "client". In this way, NDAs can be seen as a means of stifling proper governance and scrutiny of those organisations.'[68] The abuse of NDAs can be a sign of an organisation with an insular culture. The senior management and board may be worried about what may be revealed and instead of genuine interest in protecting their commercial interest, wish to suppress bad news. They may wish to ignore trouble by denying its existence and preferring a state of moral blindness. These firms live in permanent denial, often dominated by a culture of fear and secretiveness. They will frequently employ NDAs to hide the truth.

H. TRAINING, THE BOARD AND CORPORATE CULTURE

1. Training as Evidence of Good Culture

2.71 Many of the problems created by firms are a consequence of incompetence rather than simply greed. Additionally, a lack of adequate training may be an indicator of a poor business culture and lack of professionalism. This can have the consequence of failing to 'anchor' the actions and judgements of those working in the business. Good-quality training also provides each individual with a benchmark against which to make their own judgements and for each

---

66 Public Concern at Work, 'Written Evidence from Public Concern at Work to the Parliamentary Banking Commission of Banking Standards' (24 June 2013) para 10 https://publications.parliament.uk/pa/jt201314/jtselect/jtpcbs/27/27v_we27.htm.

67 Martin Woods, 'Written Evidence of Martin Woods to the Parliamentary Banking Commission of Banking Standards' (14 February 2013) para 93 https://publications.parliament.uk/pa/jt201314/jtselect/jtpcbs/27/27v_we107.htm.

68 Richard Moorhead, 'Ethics and NDAs' (April 2018) UCL Centre for Ethics and Law 6–7 https://www.ucl.ac.uk/laws/sites/laws/files/ethics_and_ndas.pdf.

to make their own independent assessments. It can form a key component of the firm's culture.

An adequate programme of training for all staff, properly delivered and reinforced, is an indicator of the firm's culture. It demonstrates a commitment to helping to ensure the organisation's future coupled with a desire to develop the full potential of its staff. The need for properly trained staff whose knowledge and skills are continually improved and updated needs to be seen as part of a broad development of the professionalism of the business and its employees and management. It forms a key element demonstrating the organisation's commitment to its staff and it can help set high standards in competence and judgement. **2.72**

Some may be surprised that in the UK, besides requiring specific training and assessment for some very highly specialised roles, the regulators have placed little focus on the need for high levels of training since the early 2000s.[69] The regulations regarding the need for competence and training for other staff are limited.[70] Nevertheless, the UK's financial services legislation requires that certain individuals covered by the Senior Managers & Certified Persons Regime (SM&CR), considered below, are trained and competent.[71] **2.73**

2. Board and Senior Executive Training and Culture

Most firms will provide some level of training and briefings for new board directors, and some updates for existing members of the executive and board. This is an area worth developing further since even experienced directors, new to the organisation, may not understand all aspects of the firm and its risks, and, in many instances, any formal training they had may have been undertaken some time ago and would merit refreshing and updating. Competent and skilled directors will appreciate their own knowledge weaknesses and not view the need for more training as a personal reflection on their competence. **2.74**

---

69 FCA, Handbook TC App 1.1, 'Activities and Products/Sectors to which TC Applies Subject' https://www.handbook.fca.org.uk/handbook/TC/App/1/1.html and TC TP 3 Regulated Mortgage Contracts: Assessments of Competence under the Mortgage Code Compliance Board Rules, https://www.handbook.fca.org.uk/handbook/TC/TP/3/3.html.

70 For example, para 24 of the Money Laundering, Terrorist Financing and Transfer of Funds (Information on the Payer) Regulations 2017.

71 '[T]he authorised person must have regard, in particular, to whether the candidate, or any person who may perform a function on the candidate's behalf – has obtained a qualification, has undergone, or is undergoing, training, possesses a level of competence, or has the personal characteristics, required by general rules made by the regulator in relation to persons performing functions of the kind to which the application relates', s60A Financial Services and Markets Act 2000 inserted (7.3.2016) by Financial Services (Banking Reform) Act 2013 (c. 33), ss. 21, 148(5); S.I. 2015/490, art. 2(1)(c).

These are all indicators of a good culture within a firm. Undertaking training at board level is a signal to both the rest of the firm and regulators of how seriously the firm takes a culture of continuous learning and improvement.

2.75 There are a number of steps boards could take, supported by the business. For example, the Irish Institute of Banking, a professional body for bankers, has a course designed for bank board directors: the Certified Bank Director programme.[72] It is a ten-day programme, divided into two blocks aimed at providing both non-executive and executive directors with a 'comprehensive understanding of the unique governance issues associated with banks arising from the inherent complexity of banking business models and their risk profile. It will provide a practical understanding of the duties and responsibilities of directors and the behaviours required from them and from well-functioning boards.'[73]

2.76 The course is assessed by each director keeping a 'learning journal' covering each module of the course. 'A learning journal is a reflective log that records a participant's learning experience of a particular topic/module. It allows participants to reflect on how their study and learning has developed during each module, what they are learning and the relevance or application of this learning to their own experiences in a work setting.'[74] Generally, boards of many organisations would benefit from increased professionalism, with copious time devoted to understanding the firm and the business and regulatory environment it operates within. This approach will go a long way towards achieving the goal of having a good culture within the organisation.

I. REGULATORY ACTIONS TO IMPROVE CULTURE IN REGULATED FIRMS

1. The UK's Senior Managers & Certified Persons Regime (SM&CR)

2.77 The failure to hold almost anyone in the UK to account following the Global Financial Crisis of 2007–9 understandably resulted in great public anger. Based on a series of recommendations from PCBS, in 2013 the regulators set out new rules on public responsibility and accountability known as the SM&CR. The latter was introduced in the UK in 2016, initially, for banks and

72 'Certified Bank Director Course', Irish Institute of Banking https://iob.ie/programme/certified-bank-director.

73 Ibid.

74 Ibid.

insurance companies.[75] The SM&CR 'aims to reduce harm to consumers and strengthen market integrity by making individuals more accountable for their conduct and competence'.[76] These regulations were extended to all regulated financial services firms and individuals in 2019.[77]

The aim of the new regulations is to ensure 'that senior management and other staff who are in a position to do significant harm to financial firms and their customers will, in future, each have their own documented areas of individual responsibility and will be held accountable, and hence liable to sanction, for regulatory failures within those areas'.[78] Compliance should have an important role in making certain that all the individuals are identified and understand their individual roles and responsibilities, and that the certification process is effective and meets the expectations of the board and the regulators. **2.78**

The regulators have taken almost no enforcement action against individuals under the requirements of the SM&CR and it is difficult to say whether the regime has produced any real improvements in business culture.[79] However, there is anecdotal information that there may be too much focus on the technical elements of delivering and operating this new regime within firms. There is a danger, as identified in a different context by the PCBS, that compliance pursues 'a box-ticking approach to compliance, adhering only to the specifics of their interpretation of the regulator's detailed rules'.[80] It is possible that the SM&CR has largely become a matter of process and 'defensive' documentation. **2.79**

75 FCA, 'CP15/22: Strengthening Accountability in Banking: Final Rules (including feedback on CP14/31 and CP15/5' (July 2015) https://www.fca.org.uk/publication/consultation/cp15-22.pdf.

76 FCA 'Senior Managers and Certification Regime' (last updated 30 March 2023) https://www.fca.org.uk/firms/senior-managers-certification-regime.

77 FCA, 'Policy Statement PS18/14: Extending the Senior Managers & Certification Regime to FCA Firms' (July 2018) <https://www.fca.org.uk/publication/policy/ps18-14.pdf.

78 Alan Brener, 'Developing the Senior Managers Regime' in Costanza Russo, Rosa Lastra and William Blair (eds), *Research Handbook on Law and Ethics in Banking and Finance* (Edward Elgar Publishing 2019) 274.

79 Allen and Overy, 'FCA and PRA Enforcement Themes and Trends 2023' (20 February 2024) https://www.allenovery.com/en-gb/global/news-and-insights/publications/fca-and-pra-enforcement-themes-and-trends-2023-a-shake-up. 'At the end of 2023, only two senior managers have faced enforcement action since the introduction of the SMCR. The first was in 2017 and the second was announced in April 2023 [...] A third enforcement case against a senior manager is being challenged before the Upper Tribunal [...] [T]he regulators have fewer open cases against senior managers and certified persons in 2023 than they did in 2021, indicating a more cautious approach to opening enforcement investigations in this area than anticipated.'

80 Parliamentary Commission on Banking Standards, 'Changing banking for Good' (2013) (n 17) Vol. II 94.

2. Regulatory Focus

2.80 The vast majority of regulated firms will have little or no engagement with the regulators. The latter rely on regulated firms to act properly in accordance with both the spirit and the letter of the rules and principles. Known as 'meta-regulation', regulated firms are expected to effectively regulate themselves with the regulator 'steering rather than rowing'.[81] The foundation of regulation is trust and the basis of this trust rests on the business having a good culture. Without this, the edifice is built on sand and all the rules and regulations in the world will be as naught.

2.81 Based on anecdotal discussions with senior executives of these businesses and some former senior regulators, it is clear that the regulatory assessment of the culture operating in firms is very limited. There are a number of reasons for this, including the much greater regulatory focus on process and formal controls; regulators see culture as too nuanced and this presents them with difficulties in systematising any assessment of culture, and it is problematic to formulate any cultural remedial programme within a satisfactory regulatory timetable. It is indicative that the latest FCA Business Plan contains no mention of business culture.[82]

2.82 Regulators will rightly focus on hard data such as numbers. These lend themselves to reporting and analysis and the regulators can compare one firm with another and produce hard, factual information. The regulators will also examine processes. In any organisation of some size the rules are broken down into a number of steps for implementation by employees. This mass-production effect means that processes can be mapped and tested and this is reflected in the regulations and regulatory enforcement actions. Taking regulatory action based on 'outcomes' is bothersome. There is often too much judgement required and proving causation may be difficult. It is much easier to wield the regulatory stick where a process is so badly designed or implemented that it puts the right outcomes at risk – whether or not poor outcomes actually result.

2.83 Regulatory resources are severely limited so a key issue for the regulator is knowing where to look. In most cases it will simply be a case of rounding up the usual suspects (i.e. the largest firms). For smaller businesses it is likely to

---

81 Peter Grabosky, 'Meta-Regulation' in Peter Drahos (ed) *Regulatory Theory: Foundations and Applications* (Australian National University Press 2017) 149–162, 153.

82 FCA, 'Business Plan 2024/5' (9 April 2024) https://www.fca.org.uk/publications/business-plans/2024-25#lf-chapter-id-commitments-4-13.

simply be a matter of chance whether they come to the attention of the regulator or not.

A focus on the culture of a firm may well provide a clear clue to risk. Based on anecdotal information it is likely, however, that regulators spend little time considering 'culture' as part of their supervision of firms. A speech in 2023 by Emily Shepperd, Chief Operating Officer and Executive Director of Authorisations, highlighted a miscellany of regulatory points which were gathered together under the broad heading of 'cultural evolution'.[83] These included regulatory 'sandboxes, diversity and inclusion, firm's assessing and reporting adverse information on staff, the FCA's own whistleblower processes, the FCA's 'consumer duty' and climate change reporting. This is all somewhat scattergun in its approach. **2.84**

A much more rigorous and precise approach might help the regulators. By looking at some of the factors highlighted in this chapter, properly trained supervisors should be able to ascertain the culture of a firm very quickly. It is necessary to look at the information used by the firm's board and senior management, combined with talking to some stakeholders, including employees. The same approach can be applied to sections of larger businesses. **2.85**

As mentioned earlier, the aim is to indicate whether a regulated firm can be sufficiently trusted to apply the rules properly itself or whether it merits much closer supervisory inspection and intervention. **2.86**

J. CONCLUSION

All the indications are that there is only a limited focus by the regulators on culture and ethics within regulated firms. This needs to be increased significantly. This lack of regulatory focus provides a signal to the boards of regulated firms that culture is secondary to satisfying the facsimile of regulatory compliance. **2.87**

However, as this chapter hopefully shows, culture can be measured and there are many positive steps which boards can take to understand and improve **2.88**

83 Emily Sheppard, 'Cultural Evolution: How Culture Must Change to Meet Expectations' (26 June 2023) speech at Westminster Business Forum https://www.fca.org.uk/news/speeches/cultural-evolution-how-culture-must-change-meet-expectations.

the cultures of their organisations. These include attracting, recruiting and inducting the right people; celebrating and promoting those evidencing the right culture; avoiding targets and structures that may undermine a good culture; encouraging all stakeholders to speak up; and training everyone, including all board members, to a high standard.

3

DIVERSITY AND CULTURE IN UK FINANCIAL SERVICES

Eleanore Hickman

A. INTRODUCTION

You might be forgiven for feeling inundated by research relating to gender diversity in corporations.[1] It has been a subject of much research and debate which has led to considerable change over the past few decades. However, much of the work in this area has focused on the top level – the board. It has also focused on corporations more generally, not specifically within financial services. Very little research has been conducted into diversity across all levels of seniority.[2] While the importance of diverse leadership is acknowledged for a multitude of reasons that include improved performance, role modelling, 3.1

1 All weblinks were last accessed on 23 December 2024.

2 Karen Croxson, Daniel Mittendorf, Cherryl Ng and Helena Robertson, 'FCA Research Note: Gender Diversity in UK Financial Services' (November 2019) https://www.fca.org.uk/publication/research/research-note-gender-diversity-in-uk-financial-services.pdf.

and representation within decision making, boardroom diversity is only part of the picture. It is important to also understand how women are represented across the workforce to provide a more complete picture of the respective roles and opportunities available. Taking an industry-wide perspective offers a more holistic view of pinch points and front runners in diversity terms. This allows us to learn from and develop best practices to address remaining gender imbalances where necessary. As such, this chapter looks at gender diversity across the whole company, not just the board, at both an organisational and an industry level.

3.2 The interplay between diversity and corporate culture is a further distinct approach to this chapter. Culture in financial services has come under significant and deserved scrutiny following numerous major scandals and crises. The rhetoric of 'hypermasculinity' has frequently been used in relation to the financial crisis.[3] In this and other respects, diversity and culture are intertwined. What diversity means for culture in this industry is one of the key questions considered in this research.

3.3 It is important to note that diversity issues, research and initiatives go beyond gender. Ethnicity, identity, disability, sexuality and religion are all factors that need to be considered when seeking to understand the human side of corporations and their role in society, but they remain under-researched.[4] Ethnicity and gender intersect in many ways that can amplify disadvantages beyond any consideration of characteristics considered on their own. While the scope of this chapter is limited to gender, it is acknowledged that for a complete understanding of diversity in financial services, research concerning other personal characteristics should be taken into account.

---

3 For example, Linda McDowell, 'Capital Culture Revisited: Sex, Testosterone and the City' (2010) 34 International Journal of Urban and Regional Research 652; Mary Dejevsky, 'Testosterone to Blame for Banking Crash, Say Tory MPs' *The Independent* (3 September 2011) https://www.independent.co.uk/news/uk/politics/testosterone-to-blame-for-banking-crash-say-tory-mps-2348912.html.

4 See Angela P Harris, 'Race and Essentialism in Feminist Legal Theory' (1990) 42 *Stanford Law Review* 581; Mike Noon, 'The Fatal Flaws of Diversity and the Business Case for Ethnic Minorities' (2007) 21 *Work, Employment & Society* 773; Kimberle Crenshaw, 'Demarginalizing the Intersection of Race and Sex: A Black Feminist Critique of Antidiscrimination Doctrine, Feminist Theory and Antiracist Politics' (1989) 1 *University of Chicago Legal Forum* 31; Engage, 'Engage Survey Reveals Boardroom Ethnicity Gap' (18 July 2016).

B. WHAT DOES GENDER DIVERSITY IN FINANCIAL SERVICES LOOK LIKE?

Gender remains an issue across the financial sector at all levels of the firm. In the sub-sections that follow I break this down and look at the picture at senior levels, at wider workforce level and, more holistically, at industry level. 3.4

1. Senior Management and the Women in Finance Charter

To begin on a positive note, the level of diversity at senior levels within the financial industry has improved in recent years. Actions taken, including the Women in Finance Charter[5] (the 'Charter'), appear to have had a positive impact. The Charter is a pledge to improve gender balance across financial services firms and was initiated in 2015 in response to a government-commissioned review into the representation of women in senior management roles in financial services.[6] Firms that sign up to the Charter pledge to dedicate a senior executive to be accountable for gender diversity, set gender diversity targets and publish progress against the diversity targets, and 'intend' to link executive pay to the delivery of these diversity targets.[7] 3.5

In 2015 there were only 10 signatories to the Charter, but as of April 2025 there were more than 420.[8] On an annual basis, a report is published detailing how the signatories are faring against their pledges. The seventh of these reports concerned 20 and, with a focus on senior management, shows average female representation at 35 per cent for all financial services sectors.[9] This mirrors the picture across the FTSE100, which has 35.2 per cent women in leadership positions, and the FTSE250, where women account for 33.9 per cent.[10] Signatories to the Charter can select their own targets and these range from 35 per cent to 50 per cent, with an average target of 38 per cent.[11] In 2023, 64 per cent of signatories still had not met their self-selected target but 3.6

5 HM Treasury and Baroness Penn, 'Women in Finance Charter' (22 March 2016) https://assets.publishing.service.gov.uk/media/5a7f44e9ed915d74e62296df/women_in_finance_charter.pdf.

6 Ibid.

7 Ibid.

8 HM Treasury, 'Signatories to the Women in Finance Charter' (April 2025) https://www.gov.uk/government/publications/women-in-finance-charter/women-in-finance-charter-list-of-signatories-april-2025.

9 Yasmine Chinwala, Jennifer Barrow and Sheenam Singhal, 'HM Treasury Women in Finance Annual Review 2023' (March 2024) https://assets.publishing.service.gov.uk/media/65fb084d9316f5001164c432/HMT_WIFC_Review_2023.pdf.

10 FTSE Women Leaders, 'FTSE Women Leaders Review' (February 2024) 8 https://ftsewomenleaders.com/wp-content/uploads/2024/04/ftse-women-leaders-report-final-april-2024.pdf.

11 Chinwala, Barrow and Singhal (n 9) 7.

84 per cent of those claimed they were on track to meet it.[12] However, caution is needed before taking these claims at face value because they are based on the signatories' own estimates and 66 per cent of those who claim to be on track are actually below their annualised rate for an increase in female representation, from which it is increasingly hard to recover.[13]

3.7 Focusing on the board, in financial services, the gender split of board members was 43 per cent women in 2022.[14] This is similar to the FTSE350, where women account for 42.1 per cent of all board positions.[15] The higher representation of women on boards compared to senior management in the finance sector, and across corporations more broadly, is likely the result of decades of gender diversity targets and pressure on boards. This began in earnest with the 2011 Davies Report, which set a target of 25 per cent women on boards, driving significant progress in board-level diversity.[16] This target has been superseded twice as it continues to be met. It is only relatively recently that attention has been turned to *what* roles women are filling (largely non-executive roles) and the importance of shifting focus from the board to also include senior leadership. Making change among the executive and senior leadership is proving more difficult, perhaps because incumbents in these positions of power are harder to displace.[17]

3.8 The Financial Conduct Authority (FCA) is cautious about the level of progress indicated by Charter signatories for two reasons. First, the data presented may not always be comparable, as signatories can choose the populations for which they track and publicise diversity.[18] Second, there is the issue of self-selection. Those institutions who sign up to the Charter are likely to be those who are more confident in their diversity progress.[19] Signatories are typically large and not representative of smaller institutions.[20] There are also concerns regarding the authenticity of the changes that have been made. In particular, a number

---

12 Ibid 11.

13 Ibid.

14 EY, 'UK Financial Boardrooms Lead Europe in Acceleration of Female and Sustainability Appointments' (January 2023) https://www.ey.com/en_uk/newsroom/2023/01/uk-financial-boardrooms-lead-europe-in-acceleration-of-female-and-sustainability-appointments.

15 FTSE Women Leaders (n 10).

16 Lord Davies of Abersoch, 'Women on Boards' (February 2011) https://assets.publishing.service.gov.uk/media/5a78c710e5274a277e68f637/11-745-women-on-boards.pdf.

17 For more on this issue see Eleanore Hickman, *Diversity, Merit and Power in the C-Suite* (Hart Publishing 2023).

18 Karen Croxson, Daniel Mittendorf, Cherryl Ng and Helena Robertson, 'FCA Research Note: Gender Diversity in UK Financial Services' (n 1).

19 Ibid.

20 Ibid.

of firms have elevated support roles – such as human resources and communications – to the executive committee.[21] These roles are often filled by women and therefore provide a quick win in terms of diversity statistics, but whether it changes the substance of the role, and therefore the proportion of women in positions of power, is questionable.

Within the finance sector, there is sub-sector variance in the level of gender diversity. Looking at the industry as a whole, the pace of change suggests gender parity would be reached in 2038,[22] but research suggests that for hedge funds gender parity will only be reached by 2109 and for fintechs 2212.[23] According to Baroness Helena Morrissey, 'still only 12% of named fund managers [...] are women today. That has hardly changed in the whole 36 years since I have been in the City.'[24] The reason these sectors are especially male-dominated and resistant to change is likely to be sector-specific. For hedge funds, it is thought that those running hedge funds have inordinate power and control that allows them to dictate their own terms and pay little attention to external pressures to change.[25] From a fintech perspective, it is clear that there is a lack of funding for female entrepreneurs which will clearly impact the number of companies with women at the helm.[26] **3.9**

On balance, in relation to senior positions, progress in gender diversity has been made in recent years. However, as is so often the case, a closer look at the details (sector variances and diversity by role) reveals the journey is by no means near completion and optimistic reports of progress need to be considered with appropriate caution. **3.10**

2. Wider Corporation

Despite being relevant to a substantially larger proportion of society, research into diversity at organisational level is relatively sparse. Finance is no exception. This difference in attention is also reflected in the work finance firms **3.11**

21 Yasmine Chinwala, Jennifer Barrow and Panagiotis Asimakopoulos, 'HM Treasury Women in Finance Charter: Five Year Review' (July 2021) https://assets.publishing.service.gov.uk/media/60f6a01fe90e0764cb10be0e/2021.07_WIFC_-_Five_year_review_.pdf.

22 Yasmine Chinwala, Jennifer Barrow and Sheenam Singhal, 'HM Treasury Women in Finance Annual Review 2023' (n 9) 10.

23 Yasmine Chinwala, Jennifer Barrow and Panagiotis Asimakopoulos, 'HM Treasury Women in Finance Charter: Five Year Review' (n 21).

24 House of Commons Treasury Committee, 'Sexism in the City – Sixth Report of Session 2023–24' (8 March 2024) 8.

25 Megan Neely, *Hedged Out: Inequality and Insecurity on Wall Street* (University of California Press 2022).

26 Jim Eckenrode, 'Achieving Gender Equity in the Fintech Community' (Deloitte Insights, 1 October 2020) https://www2.deloitte.com/us/en/insights/industry/financial-services/women-in-fintech.html.

do for gender representation, with most firms focusing on senior leadership levels.[27] This may be a consequence of the external targets and continued media attention surrounding boardroom diversity. The comparative inattention on the wider workforce is not because diversity isn't an issue. Research into gender diversity in UK financial services in 2019 found that only 17 per cent of individuals approved to work in managerial roles in financial services were women.[28] Furthermore, in an analysis of financial service firm diversity data, the number of women falls most rapidly when moving from junior to mid-level roles.[29]

3.12 The UK is not alone in finding gender diversity problematic in the financial industry. US research finds that there is a gender gap in promotions in the financial industry.[30] Looking specifically at loan officers, they found that male officers were 15 per cent more likely to be promoted than females, after controlling for sales performance, experience and other observable characteristics.[31] They label this the 'Broken Rung' issue that women face at the start of their career in finance.[32] Alongside research suggesting there is a glass ceiling forestalling the progress of women's careers,[33] a sticky floor holding women and minorities back from progressing at the same rate as men[34] and a glass cliff whereby women are promoted to precarious positions,[35] the barriers to progression and consequent disincentives mount up. According to the Broken Rung study, the suspected cause of the variation in promotion levels was the stereotyped perception of female versus male ability. It is suggested that similar stereotypes have been in operation in the UK.[36] Given the differences in

---

27 Financial Conduct Authority, 'Understanding Approaches to D&I in Financial Services' (1 December 2022) https://www.fca.org.uk/publications/multi-firm-reviews/understanding-approaches-diversity-inclusion-financial-services.

28 Karen Croxson, Daniel Mittendorf, Cherryl Ng and Helena Robertson, 'FCA Research Note: Gender Diversity in UK Financial Services' (n 1).

29 Financial Conduct Authority, 'Consultation Paper 23/20: Diversity and Inclusion in the Financial Sector – Working Together to Drive Change' (September 2023) https://www.fca.org.uk/publication/consultation/cp23-20.pdf.

30 Ruidi Huang, Erik J Mayer and Darius P Miller, 'Gender Bias in Promotions: Evidence from Financial Institutions' (2024) 37 *The Review of Financial Studies* 1685.

31 Ibid.

32 Ibid.

33 Roberto M Fernandez and Mabel Abraham, 'Glass Ceilings and Glass Doors? Internal and External Hiring in an Organizational Hierarchy' (2011) MIT Sloan Research Paper No 4895-11.

34 Margaret Yap and Alison M Konrad, 'Gender and Racial Differentials in Promotions: Is There a Sticky Floor, a Mid-Level Bottleneck, or a Glass Ceiling?' [2009] *Journal of Industrial Relations* 593.

35 Michelle K Ryan and S Alexander Haslam, 'The Glass Cliff: Evidence That Women Are Over-represented in Precarious Leadership Positions' (2005) 16 *British Journal of Management* 81.

36 Madeline E Heilman, Francesca Manzi and Susanne Braun, 'Presumed Incompetent: Perceived Lack of Fit and Gender Bias in Recruitment and Selection' in Adelina M Broadbridge and Sandra L Fielden (eds),

gender representation in UK financial services, it is not unreasonable to suspect a similar issue at play here, though research would be needed to verify this.

Just as in relation to senior leadership diversity, sub-sectors of finance have different gender balances and associated antecedents and effects. In investment banking, research by Adams et al shows that funds run exclusively by women account for 1.9 per cent of the industry's assets whereas those run exclusively by men account for 74 per cent.[37] Only one in five members of the Chartered Financial Analyst Institute (CFAI) are women, and this is changing very slowly, with an increase of only 1.5 per cent since 2013.[38] This data is global in nature as the CFAI runs an accreditation programme across more than 160 markets and has more than 190,000 members.[39] However, the data does not reflect the proportion of women charterholders in the UK, according to a 2016 report.[40] For UK Fintech, a 2023 report detailed the employee base in the industry to be 72 per cent male and only 17 per cent of the non executive directors are female.[41] In comparison, in the insurance industry there is a more balanced proportion of men and women, but this begins to drop steeply from senior management level and upwards.[42] The difference in seniority is a story that is supported by the gender pay gap within the financial industry. In 2023, the gender pay gap was largest in the financial and insurance sector.[43] The size of this gap has narrowed in recent years, from 40 per cent in 1997 to 27.9 per cent as it currently stands.[44] 3.13

When looking at the workforce, the ability to understand the distribution of gender by role is essential to a full understanding of the authenticity of 3.14

Handbook of Gendered Careers in Management (Edward Elgar Publishing 2015).

37 Renee B Adams, Brad M Barber and Terrance Odean, 'Family, Values, and Women in Finance' (2016) https://ssrn.com/abstract=2827952.

38 Gavin Anthony, 'Gender Diversity in Investment Management. The Challenge and a Solution' (*CFA Institute Research and Policy Center*, 18 June 2024) https://rpc.cfainstitute.org/research/reports/2024/gender-diversity-in-investment-management.

39 Chartered Financial Analyst Institute, 'Membership' https://www.cfainstitute.org/en/membership.

40 Rebecca Fender, Renée B Adams, Brad M Barber and Terrance Odean, 'Gender Diversity in Investment Management: New Research for Practitioners on How to Close the Gender Gap' (*CFA Institute Research and Policy Center*, 1 September 2016) https://rpc.cfainstitute.org/research/foundation/2016/gender-diversity-in-investment-management.

41 EY, 'Changing the Face of UK Fintech' (2023) https://www.ey.com/content/dam/ey-unified-site/ey-com/en-uk/insights/banking-capital-markets/documents/changing-the-face-of-uk-fintech.pdf.

42 KPMG, 'Reshaping DEI in Insurance – KPMG UK' (KPMG, 31 May 2024) https://kpmg.com/uk/en/home/insights/2023/02/reshaping-dei-in-insurance.html.

43 Statista, 'UK Gender Pay Gap by Sector 2023' (*Statista*, 11 December 2024) https://www.statista.com/statistics/760342/gender-pay-gap-uk-by-sector/.

44 Spyridon Lagaras, Maria-Teresa Marchica, Elena Smintzi and Margarita Tsoutsoura, 'Women in the Financial Sector' (2022) https://ssrn.com/abstract=4098229.

diversity. Such data is hard to come by. Workforce data from the US in 2013 show the proportion of men to be much higher than women in managerial and sales roles, whilst the proportion of women in office and clerical worker roles was around 30 per cent higher than the proportion of men.[45] The nuance of role-based segregation is masked when the data is aggregated so that role type is disregarded, making gender diversity across the workforce appear much more balanced.

3.15 According to qualitative research among women in the finance industry, there are several factors that make it less likely women will continue in the finance services, including it being 'easier to survive as a man because they fit the social norm of what a worker in financial and professional services looks like'.[46] The creation of a perception of what a worker in finance looks like is a broad issue encompassing a multitude of factors over time. Some of these will be considered in the following section.

C. PUBLIC DIVERSITY IN FINANCE

3.16 It could be argued that from a sociological perspective, finance and money-related subjects are perceived as the domain of men.[47] This is a view that has been widely promoted by the media and in popular culture. Examples of movies in which finance is depicted as a masculine domain include *Wall Street* (1987), *The Big Short* (2015), *The Wolf of Wall Street* (2013), *It's a Wonderful Life* (1946), *Margin Call* (2011), *The Other Guys* (2010) and *Trading Places* (1983), to name a few.[48] Maclean describes how 'hyper-masculinity of the financial industries' is propagated by popular culture and calls for this cultural construction to be challenged in order to better understand the cause of the 'exclusion of femininity from finance'.[49]

3.17 It continues to be the case that there are fewer women studying economics than there are men, and the gender mix of public finance roles continues to lack diversity.[50] At the time of writing all of the Central Bank Governors of the G7 countries were male and Chrystia Freeland (Canada) and Janet Yellen

---

45 Sandra K Miller and James J Tucker III, 'Diversity Trends, Practices, and Challenges in the Financial Services Industry' (2013) 67 *Journal of Financial Service Professionals* 46, 53.

46 Grace Lordan, 'The Good Finance Framework Report' (2021) *Women in Banking & Finance* 21.

47 Gillian Tett, 'Why Economics Is Still a Man's World' *Financial Times* (London, 8 December 2017).

48 For a discussion of masculinity in finance as depicted in movies see Kate Maclean, 'Gender, Risk and the Wall Street Alpha Male' (2016) 25 *Journal of Gender Studies* 427.

49 Ibid 23.

50 Gillian Tett, 'Why Economics Is Still a Man's World' (n 47).

(USA) were the only female finance ministers. According to research by the Official Monetary and Financial Institutions Forum, as of 2019, 'out of 173 central banks globally, only 14 are headed by women'.[51]

Promotion is another thorny matter. The European Central Bank (ECB) commissioned research which indicated that women were less likely to be promoted than men. This spurred the ECB to put in place policies to rectify the imbalance and, since implementation, those differences have been reduced.[52] However, despite improvement in the promotion of women when compared to men, there remains a gap in the number of women applying for promotion, as compared to men. The implication the authors of the ECB report draw from this is that there is a difference between men and women in their appetite for competition.[53] The research claims to 'lend support to supply-side explanations for the existence of remaining gender differences in promotion outcomes'.[54] One could also argue that abstaining from processes in which women are competing against men is a social behaviour that has been learnt over a long time and that will take longer to change than implementing policies regarding promotion decisions. **3.18**

D. DIVERSITY AND CULTURE

Having detailed the gender diversity environment within financial services in the sections above, the following will consider how this is shaped by and in turn shapes the culture within firms in the industry. **3.19**

1. What Is Meant by Culture?

Corporate culture has been a hot topic for the past several decades. Business literature has promoted corporate culture as a managerial tool that can help increase employee productivity and ultimately promote financial success.[55] Thakor refers to a strong culture in banking as a form of 'off-balance-sheet capital'.[56] Though an effective corporate culture is widely promoted as the key **3.20**

51 James Fitzgerald, 'Gender Balance Index 2019' OMFIF https://www.omfif.org/gender-balance-index-2019/.

52 Laura Hospido, Luc Laeven and Ana Lamo, 'The Gender Promotion Gap: What Holds Back Female Economists from Making a Career in Central Banking?' (2022) 104(5) *Review of Economics and Statistics* 981–96.

53 Ibid.

54 Ibid.

55 Tristin K Green, 'Work Culture and Discrimination' (2005) 93 *California Law Review* 623, 627.

56 Anjan V Thakor, 'Corporate Culture in Banking' (2016) 22(1) *Economic Policy Review* 5.

to a successful business, there is much less agreement about what corporate culture means. In a corporate context, culture has been described as 'a form of impression management' whereby people act in a way that seeks to impress upon others that they conform to certain values.[57] Almost exactly opposing this view is that expressed by Bob Diamond, former CEO of Barclays, who described culture as 'how people behave when no-one is watching'.[58] Taking a more granular approach to culture, the UK Banking Standards Board identifies the characteristics of culture as honesty, competence, reliability, responsiveness, personal/organisational resilience, accountability, openness, respect and shared purpose.[59]

3.21 I adhere to the view that culture is an 'empty vessel'[60] and it is for the organisation to create the cultural infrastructure (how culture is disseminated and shaped). [61] In contrast, the cultural character of an organisation is a product of the values of the corporation and its people, manifested in their behaviours. Cultural character is harder to shape than the infrastructure, but it does and can change. This understanding of culture incorporates both Diamond's idea (above) that culture is the way things get done (infrastructure) and the Banking Standards Board's list of characteristics (character). According to this understanding, a corporation's cultural character could as easily be greed, competition and personal gain as it could be honesty, respect and shared purpose. Viewing culture in this way allows a more responsive understanding of what corporate culture might be in practice.

3.22 Corporations are at pains to present a positive picture of their cultural characteristics, often described as core values. Table 3.1 below sets out the core values of the ten largest publicly listed financial institutions in the UK, by market capitalisation. This shows a substantial amount of overlap in what are considered to be appropriate core values for institutions in finance. Common to the core values are themes of respect, accountability and integrity. Though it may be the intention for the corporation's culture to be based on those values, the extent to which that is true will depend on whether employees assimilate

57 J Gregg Robinson and Judith S McIlwee, 'Men, Women, and the Culture of Engineering' (1991) 32 *The Sociological Quarterly* 403.

58 Anon, 'Culture Shocks', *Financial Times* (London, 17 July 2012).

59 Banking Standards Board, 'Worthy of Trust? Law, Ethics and Culture in Banking' (2017) https://financialservicescultureboard.org.uk/wp-content/uploads/2017/12/Worthy-of-trust-Nov17.pdf.

60 Dan Awrey and David Kershaw, 'Toward a More Ethical Culture in Finance: Regulatory and Governance Strategies' in Nicholas Morris and David Vines (eds), *Capital Failure: Rebuilding Trust in Financial Services* (Oxford University Press 2014).

61 Eleanore Hickman, 'Is the Senior Managers and Certification Regime Changing Banking for Good?' (2022) 85(6) *The Modern Law Review* 1440.

Table 3.1 Core values of the 10 largest UK public financial institutions

Financial Institution[1]	**Core values in Code of Conduct**	**Diversity as a core value?**
HSBC Holdings plc	We value difference. We succeed together. We take responsibility. We get it done.[2]	Yes
Banco Santander SA	Think customer, embrace change, act now, move together, speak up[3]	No. However, the 'Code in practice' says 'when making decisions, be objective, tolerant and promote diversity'
London Stock Exchange Group plc	Integrity, Partnership, Excellence, and Change[4]	Yes. Excellence is described as including embracing diverse perspectives.
Banco Bilbao Vizcaya Argentaria SA	Customer comes first; We think big; We are one team.	No public code of conduct found.
Lloyds Banking Group plc	People first. Bold. Inclusive. Sustainable. Trust[5]	Yes.
Barclays plc	Respect, integrity, service, excellence and stewardship[6]	Yes. A behaviour associated with respect is to embrace and increase diversity.
3i Group plc	Ambition, rigour and energy, accountability, integrity. No public code of conduct found.	n/a
Natwest Group plc	Inclusive, curious, robust, sustainable, ambitious[7]	Yes
Standard Chartered plc	Do the right thing. Never settle. Better together[8]	No. However, diversity is listed as one of the behaviours associated with the values.
Prudential plc	Our customer is our compass. We pursue our entrepreneurial spirit. We succeed together. We respect and care for one another.	No. However, 'Embracing diversity' is part of the policies to implement the values.

[1] *Largest UK financial institutions by market capitalisation, according to data from the London Stock Exchange, as of 3 Sept 2024. See FTSE 100, 'FTSE overview' London Stock Exchange https://*www.londonstockexchange.com/indices/ftse-100?trkcode=lsehomeftse.
[2] *HSBC Holdings plc, 'Statement of Business Principles and Code of Conduct' (2024) https://*www.hsbc.com/-/files/hsbc/our-approach/risk-and-responsibility/pdfs/241014-statement-of-business-principles-and-code-of-conduct.pdf.
[3] *Santander, 'General Code of Conduct' (July 2024) https://*www.santander.com/content/dam/santander-com/en/contenido-paginas/accionistas-e-inversores/gobierno-corporativo/c%C3%B3digo-de-conducta/do-General code of conduct.pdf.
[4] *London Stock Exchange Group, 'LSEG Code of Conduct' (2023) https://*www.lseg.com/content/dam/lseg/en_us/documents/policies/lseg-code-of-conduct.pdf.
[5] *Lloyds Banking Group, 'Code of Ethics and Responsibility' (2022) https://*www.lloydsbankinggroup.com/assets/pdfs/who-we-are/responsible-business/downloads/group-codes-and-policies/2022-lbg-code-of-ethics-and-responsibility.pdf.
[6] *Barclays, 'The Barclays Way:* How we do business' (July 2018) https://www.barclays.it/content/dam/barclays-it/modello231/TheBarclaysWay.pdf.
[7] *Natwest, 'Our Code' (February 2024) https://*www.natwestgroup.com/content/dam/natwestgroup_com/natwestgroup/pdf/20240202-Our-Code-English-Global-External.pdf.
[8] *Standard Chartered, 'Code of Conduct and Ethics' (October 2023) https://*av.sc.com/corp-en/nr/content/docs/code-of-conduct-and-ethics.pdf.

and manifest them in their behaviours. This aligns with the UK Parliament's view that 'Poor standards in banking are not the consequence of absent or deficient company value statements. Nor are they the result of the inadequate deployment of the latest management jargon to promulgate concepts of shared values. They are, at least in part, a reflection of the flagrant disregard for the numerous sensible codes that already existed.'[62] In many respects, the core values presented by corporations can only be viewed as aspirational. However, given the identification of the sector as one in which culture is problematic, improvement in adherence to core values should be a priority.[63] Achieving this is complicated, particularly as there are often pockets of different cultures throughout an organisation, with variations across roles and hierarchies, in which the corporate values are adhered to differently.[64]

2. How Does Culture Relate to Diversity?

3.23 Listing diversity within corporate annual reports as a core value does not necessarily translate into organizational behaviour. Diversity initiatives within the financial services industry have recently been described as 'box-ticking' exercises and 'virtue-signalling'.[65] Translating diversity values on paper into genuine organisational values goes deeper than developing initiatives and requires adoption within culture. As can be seen in the table above, when looking into the codes of conduct associated with the core values of the ten largest financial institutions by market capitalisation, diversity is commonly referred to although only described as 'core' in 50 per cent of these. US research shows that references to diversity, equity and inclusion increased 658 per cent in earnings calls for the S&P500 between 2018 and 2022.[66]

3.24 Culture has been described as 'the bridge between a company's purpose and its people'.[67] If a company's purpose forms the foundation of its values, the manifestation of those values in human behaviour could be viewed as the

---

62 Parliamentary Commission on Banking Standards, 'Changing Banking for Good' (2013) HL Paper 27-II, HC 175-II 44.

63 Ibid.

64 Green, 'Work Culture and Discrimination' (n 55) 633.

65 House of Commons Treasury Committee, 'Sexism in the City – Sixth Report of Session 2023–24' (n 24) 11.

66 Brian Kropp, Jessica Knight and Jonah Shepp, 'How Fair Is Your Workplace?' (2022) *Harvard Business Review* https://hbr.org/2022/07/how-fair-is-your-workplace.

67 Deloitte, 'Annual Report Insights 2020: Surveying FTSE Reporting' (2020) 14, https://www.deloitte.com/content/dam/assets-zone2/uk/en/docs/industries/life-sciences-health-care/2023/deloitte-uk-annual-report-insights-2020.pdf as referenced in Akshaya Kamalnath, *The Corporate Diversity Jigsaw* (Cambridge University Press 2022) 144.

physical articulation of that purpose. The demographic characteristics of individuals will impact upon their beliefs and values, driving at least some of their behaviours and thereby feeding into that culture and articulation of corporate purpose. Other drivers of behaviour will derive from colleagues and team members and therefore demography comes into play for a second time. According to Green, there is a human 'predisposition to categorise and stereotype along racial and gender lines' and a tendency to use group membership, favouritism, positions of power and a desire for social dominance to bolster a person's view of themselves.[68] This helps create and maintain traditional demographic divides. Culture can be used as a tool to combat these in/out groups and divides, or it can perpetuate them. To be a positive tool for diversity, it is critical that the culture overtly and authentically supports diversity. It is also a mutually dependent relationship in that without diversity the corporate culture will be negatively impacted, and without a strong corporate culture there will likely be less diversity.

Ways in which a culture can support diversity include through effective cultural infrastructure. A key aspect of a company's cultural infrastructure is accountability channels or the ability for employees to speak up about issues or concerns. Where people do not feel they can speak out, issues can go unchecked. Where only some people feel they can speak out, discriminatory issues develop. Effective line managers are crucial to developing an environment in which people feel like they can speak up and that it is worthwhile to do so.[69] An example of how a culture in which accountability is absent can be seen in the example of Crispin Odey, owner and manager of one of Europe's largest hedge funds, who was accused of sexual harassment of thirteen women over a period spanning more than 20 years.[70] According to the Financial Times, senior executives were aware of his behaviour but only launched an investigation after 16 years, during which time he dismissed the executive committee that attempted to remove him.[71] 3.25

---

68 Green (n 55) 647.

69 Amy Huntley, 'How Leaders Can Be Better Listeners – The Importance of Leadership Listening in Creating a Speak-up Culture' (Financial Services Culture Board, 3 May 2023) https://financialservicescultureboard.org.uk/how-leaders-can-be-better-listeners-the-importance-of-leadership-listening-in-creating-a-speak-up-culture/.

70 Madison Marriage, Antonia Cundy and Paul Caruana Galizia, 'How Crispin Odey Evaded Sexual Assault Allegations for Decades' *Financial Times* (London, 8 June 2023) https://www.ft.com/content/e5d14398-e866-44b3-8ecb-4e6371167c6d.

71 Ibid.

3.26 In terms of cultural characteristics, fairness, respect and integrity are key to supporting diversity. However, there is a lack of fairness in organisational cultures in which one gender is paid more than and promoted in advance of another. Fairness also relates to whether employees are considered for opportunities, are supported by their manager or team, and whether their contributions are recognised. How this translates into the behaviours of the employees within that culture is an open question. One suggestion is that a perception of fair treatment can increase employee performance by 26 per cent.[72] In contrast, a perception of unfairness might create an underlying message that one gender or ethnicity is valued over another and this could lead to further preferential treatment in the provision of opportunities and the amplification (or otherwise) of voices. When speaking about access to workplace opportunities in the financial industry 38 out of 44 women spoke of a perceived lack of affinity being the biggest barrier to opportunities. Affinity bias and familiarity bias cause gatekeepers to be significantly more likely to give opportunities to 'people like them'.[73] As discussed in section 3, the unique reputation that finance has as being particularly masculine could serve to exacerbate the 'people like them/me' issue.

3.27 Another cultural characteristic – respect – is essential to teamwork, arguably especially within diverse teams. If members of a team feel they are not respected, they are unlikely to be able to offer their best work, speak out with their views or collaborate as effectively. They are also more likely to exit the company. According to Anne Richard, CEO of M&G Investments, management teams need help managing more diverse teams, because 'it is much easier to manage a bunch of people who are very like you'.[74] Research by Brennan suggests that 'corporate managers often fail to acknowledge how diversity can lead to conflict and fail to examine ways to overcome that conflict. They often engage in counterproductive training programmes which can increase mutual distrust and suspicion.'[75] On this basis, it is crucial to find effective ways to foster respect amongst colleagues.

3.28 Respect can be undermined in more egregious ways in cultures where women are or feel unsafe. Research into the impact of sexual harassment on women

---

72 Brian Kropp, Jessica Knight and Jonah Shepp, 'How Fair Is Your Workplace?' (n 74).

73 Grace Lordan, 'The Good Finance Framework Report' (n 46) 14.

74 House of Commons Treasury Committee, 'Women in Finance', Fifteenth Report of Session 2017–19 (13 June 2018) 20.

75 Jason Brennan, 'Diversity for Justice vs. Diversity for Performance: Philosophical and Empirical Tensions' (2023) 187 *Journal of Business Ethics* 433, 444.

in the investment professions demonstrates empirically the negative effect on female performance, and goes on to suggest that this might explain the under-representation of women in the profession.[76] Sexual harassment and worse are not uncommon. In interview research looking at 'the headwinds and tailwinds that women experience when working in financial services', although not specifically asked, 5 out of the 44 women interviewed described situations of clear sexual harassment and a further 10 revealed undoubted sexism.[77] The HM Treasury Report 'Sexism in the City' reported 'receiv[ing] a large amount of evidence relating to sexual harassment in financial services [...]. The evidence we took was shocking, especially the extent of misogyny, sexual harassment and bullying, up to and including sexual assault and rape'.[78] The prevalence of such behaviour undermines reporting on 'respect' as a corporate value and goes a long way to explaining why women are underrepresented in the industry. The issue is further discussed below.

3. Are Financial Services a Special Case?

Much of the preceding discussion about corporate culture is general in nature but there are important questions to ask about whether there are specificities about the finance sector that make the culture and diversity environment unique. Reasons for lack of diversity in corporations, most specifically corporate boardrooms, have been abundant. They often boil down to issues such as pipeline of talent, role models and bias, much of which interrelates strongly with corporate culture. If these are the issues that cause a lack of diversity in corporations more generally, there is nothing to suggest those issues don't also apply in finance. However, there is research suggesting certain issues are more extreme or more prevalent in financial services. One such issue, already touched upon, is sexual harassment and bullying.[79] At a general level this is a problem that is beginning to be addressed via movements such as the #MeToo movement and the Workplace Protection Act (discussed in section 5). That the issue is particularly problematic in finance is a likely cause of the disparity in gender levels across the industry, as large numbers of women feel unsafe or, at best, uncomfortable. Until women feel safe in the industry, many will stay away. **3.29**

---

76 Gjergji Cici and others, '#MeToo Meets the Mutual Fund Industry: Productivity Effects of Sexual Harassment' (2021) 40 *Finance Research Letters* 101687.

77 Grace Lordan, 'The Good Finance Framework Report' (n 46) 25.

78 House of Commons Treasury Committee, 'Sexism in the City – Sixth Report of Session 2023–24' (n 24) 29.

79 Ibid.

3.30 There is a substantial strand of research that looks at the importance of banking culture in the context of financial stability and risk.[80] This is beyond the scope of this chapter. Broader culture research in the finance sector is rare but Kelly et al. show that, within financial services firms, there is a stronger focus on employees than in corporations more generally.[81] The research showed that 88 per cent of financial services companies made a commitment to employees within their corporate values, compared to 68 per cent among all corporations.[82] One might expect that a greater focus on employees would have a positive impact on culture. However, given the reports about the prevalence of bullying, harassment and sexism in the financial sector, it is possible that this apparently heightened commitment to employees is not sincere.

3.31 In relation to diversity more specifically, the aforementioned rhetoric of 'hypermasculinity' and whether there was or is reason to associate that with the finance sector deserves interrogating. In 2009 the Equalities and Human Rights Commission conducted a report into sex discrimination and gender pay within financial services and found workplace cultures that excluded or demeaned women within the sector.[83] In 2013, the UK Parliament Report 'Changing Banking for Good' honed in on culture as one of the areas which required significant improvement, and from a diversity perspective found that 'the culture on the trading floor is overwhelmingly male'.[84] A push for greater diversity at the senior level was made following the crisis with some justifications based on a perceived difference in risk appetite between men and women.[85] More recently, in the aforementioned 'Sexism in the City' report, Baroness Helena Morrissey states: 'I'm afraid that the big problem remains culture.'[86]

80 See for example Anjan V Thakor, 'Corporate Culture in Banking' (n 56); Dan Awrey and David Kershaw, 'Toward a More Ethical Culture in Finance: Regulatory and Governance Strategies' (n 60); Alain Cohn, Ernst Fehr and Michel André Maréchal, 'Business Culture and Dishonesty in the Banking Industry' (2014) 516 Nature 86.

81 Chris Kelly, Paul Kocourek, Nancy McGaw and Judith Samuelson, 'Deriving Value from Corporate Values' (2003) The Aspen Institute 4.

82 Ibid.

83 Equalities and Human Rights Commission, 'Financial Services Inquiry. Sex Discrimination and Gender Pay Gap Report of the Equality and Human Rights Commission' (2009) 7 https://www.equalityhumanrights.com/sites/default/files/financial_services_inquiry_report_0.pdf.

84 Parliamentary Commission on Banking Standards, 'Changing Banking for Good' (n 62).

85 Ajay Palvia, Emilia Vähämaa and Sami Vähämaa, 'Are Female CEOs and Chairwomen More Conservative and Risk Averse? Evidence from the Banking Industry During the Financial Crisis' (2015) 131 *Journal of Business Ethics* 577.

86 House of Commons Treasury Committee, 'Sexism in the City – Sixth Report of Session 2023–24' (n 24) 9.

There is evidence that the approach to diversity and culture is evolving within financial services. The FCA has conducted research into the diversity and inclusion initiatives of 12 large financial services firms, finding that all of them were developing diversity and inclusion initiatives, though most of these only started in earnest between 2019 and 2020.[87] However, while efforts are being made, their effectiveness is questioned. The FCA found an overreliance 'on measures such as training, network group and allyship, which although important, will not bring about the kind of systemic change needed'.[88] In the recent HM Treasury inquiry, respondents described firms making diversity initiatives aimed at 'chang[ing] women to fit the culture better, rather than chang[ing] the culture to fit women better'.[89] **3.32**

It is perhaps the case that the perception that finance is a male domain is exacerbating common cultural issues such as respect and fairness. Considered at a high level, there are similar proportions of men and women in large financial services firms as there are in large corporations, but a closer look at the detail in the sector reveals specific areas of concern including role segregation, gender pay and sexual harassment. **3.33**

E. ADDRESSING CULTURE AND DIVERSITY IN FINANCIAL SERVICES

In Europe, the recent Women on Boards Directive requires listed companies to have at least 40 per cent of the underrepresented gender on their board.[90] Several jurisdictions to which this directive applies already had mandatory quotas in place, but the change seeks to bring a greater level of consistency of boardroom diversity across Europe. It does not apply in the UK and there are no mandatory quotas in place. Despite this, the UK is one of the leading European countries for boardroom diversity. UK progress in relation to boardroom diversity is attributable, at least in part, to non-binding targets and the pressure imposed by the voluntary UK Corporate Governance Code. There is little in the way of laws and regulations relating to workforce diversity in the broad context of corporations, apart from the gender pay gap legislation. In relation to financial firms, the Senior Managers and Certification regime attempts to regulate culture, though with no specific input on diversity. **3.34**

87 Financial Conduct Authority, 'Understanding Approaches to D&I in Financial Services' (n 27).

88 Ibid.

89 House of Commons Treasury Committee, 'Sexism in the City – Sixth Report of Session 2023–24' (n 24) 9.

90 Eleanore Hickman, 'The EU Directive on Women on Boards' (2023) 20(4) *European Company Law* 84.

However, this relative lack of regulatory input is subject to change as a consultation to impose new diversity requirements for financial services firms was in progress at the time of writing. Each of these regulations, codes and plans is discussed in turn below.

1. UK Corporate Governance Code

3.35 Companies that are listed on the main market of the London Stock Exchange are required to comply with the UK Corporate Governance Code, which requires that boards make appointments based on merit and objective criteria and promote diversity, inclusion and equal opportunity.[91] This should be annually evaluated[92] and the annual report should detail the gender balance of the senior management and the policy and initiatives on diversity and inclusion.[93] In relation to culture, the foreword to the Code (2024) aligns good corporate culture with all of the values discussed in section 4 above. It states that successful and sustainable businesses are built of relationships that are 'based on respect, trust and mutual benefit. Accordingly, a company's culture should promote integrity and openness, value diversity and be responsive to the views of shareholders and wider stakeholders.'[94] There is a clear emphasis on wider stakeholders, which goes beyond a company's employees but applies to them. One of the provisions of the Code, supporting the principle of culture, purpose and value alignment, is that boards need to monitor the business culture and take action when it lacks that alignment.[95]

3.36 The Code applies to listed corporations whether or not they are in the financial services industry. They set out the standard by which large companies should be governed and the value placed on diversity and culture therein evidences the recognition that these are crucial aspects of good corporate governance across industries. Nevertheless, the Code lacks teeth on these issues in part because of its nature as a form of soft law, and in part because the issues of diversity and culture are difficult to define and/or control. In that respect, short of making drastic changes to the Code, we cannot expect it to make significant further inroads into the issue.

91 UK Corporate Governance Code 2024, Principle J.
92 Ibid Principle L.
93 Ibid Provision 23.
94 Ibid.
95 Ibid provision 2.

2. Gender Pay Gap Legislation

The finance sector has the highest gender pay gap per hour, which, in 2023, was 27.9 per cent – more than 10 per cent higher than the average across industries, which was 14.3 per cent.[96] The average bonus gap in banks between men and women in 2018 was more than 50 per cent.[97] These issues are at risk of being heightened following the removal of the bonus cap which took effect in October 2023.[98] As the bonus gap presents a much starker gap between genders, the removal of the cap has the potential to exacerbate the overall differences in pay. **3.37**

In 2017, the Gender Pay Gap Information Regulation came into force, requiring firms with more than 250 employees to report on a variety of metrics relating to the gender pay gap within their organisations. Firms are also encouraged to provide an action plan on how they plan to address their pay gap, but this aspect of the regulations is voluntary. The regulations apply to all organisations in the UK of the appropriate size, not just those in the financial sector. Firms that do not report on their pay gap have to follow action taken by the Equality and Human Rights Commission ('EHRC') that consists of a letter and the potential to bring a court order.[99] Those who do not report their gender pay gap are listed on the EHRC website. In 2023 there were no finance firms who did not report their gender pay gap.[100] **3.38**

Addressing disparities in pay would go some way to improving a culture of fairness in financial institutions as well as speaking directly to diversity. However, there is a dispute as to the effectiveness of the regulations because there are ways in which firms can present their data or structure their reporting so that the gender pay gap is mitigated. This has allowed firms to 'circumvent [...] the spirit of the legislation'.[101] Furthermore, there is a view that within finance, the disparities in pay have lost their shock factor and, although uncomfortable, **3.39**

96 Statista, 'UK Gender Pay Gap by Sector 2023' (n 43).

97 House of Commons Treasury Committee, 'Women in Finance – Fifteenth Report of Session' (n 82) 27.

98 PRA and FCA, 'PRA policy statement 9/23 | FCA policy statement 23/15 PS9/23/PS23/15: Joint Policy Statement Remuneration: Ratio between Fixed and Variable Components of Total Remuneration ("Bonus Cap")' (24 October 2023) https://www.bankofengland.co.uk/prudential-regulation/publication/2023/october/remuneration-ratio-between-fixed-and-variable-components-of-total-remuneration%20.

99 Equality and Human Rights Commission, 'Gender Pay Gap: Our Enforcement Action' (*EHRC*, 1 August 2024) https://www.equalityhumanrights.com/our-work/gender-pay-gap-our-enforcement-action.

100 Ibid.

101 House of Commons Treasury Committee, 'Women in Finance – Fifteenth Report of Session' (n 82) 34.

are seen as an industry-wide phenomenon. Consequent to this apparent apathy, the drive to change has lessened.[102]

3.40 In order for the gender pay gap legislation to have a more significant impact on diversity in the industry, work needs to be done to reduce the opportunities to manipulate firm data for appearance purposes alongside a renewed sense of injustice at a societal level, when faced with the data.

3. Senior Managers and Certification Regime

3.41 The Senior Managers and Certification Regime (SMCR) is a relatively new form of regulation that seeks to improve corporate culture via an increase in the level of accountability among senior management.[103] One of the ways it does this is by requiring a list of prescribed responsibilities to be individually allocated to specific members of senior management who are then accountable for that. The idea is that by increasing individual responsibility, and therefore overall accountability, culture within banking will improve as people take personal ownership of specific areas of management.

3.42 There are no prescribed responsibilities within the SMCR that relate to diversity. In contrast, Ireland has brought out similar regulation, called the Senior Executive Accountability Regime (SEAR) under which one of the prescribed responsibilities[104] is 'responsibility for leading the development of the firm's culture, including on matters relating to diversity and inclusion, by the Board'.[105] Another member of senior management must be responsible for 'overseeing the adoption of the firm's culture, including on matters relating to diversity and inclusion, by the Board'.[106]

3.43 One of the recommendations of the Women in Finance Charter (discussed in section 2) was that a member of the executive committee be nominated to take charge of progressing diversity targets. Where this has been adopted, 70 per cent have nominated the CEO.[107] One could question the value of heaping

102 House of Commons Treasury Committee, 'Sexism in the City – Sixth Report of Session 2023–24' (n 24) 24.

103 For more on this see Eleanore Hickman, 'Is the Senior Managers and Certification Regime Changing Banking for Good?' (n 61).

104 Irish Central Bank (Supervision and Enforcement) Act 2013 (Section 48(1)) (Senior Executive Accountability Regime)) Regulations 2024, s 6(2).

105 Irish Central Bank (Supervision and Enforcement) Act 2013 (Section 48(1)) (Senior Executive Accountability Regime)) Regulations 2024, Schedule 2 PR5.

106 Irish Central Bank (Supervision and Enforcement) Act 2013 (Section 48(1)) (Senior Executive Accountability Regime)) Regulations 2024, Schedule 2 PR6.

107 House of Commons Treasury Committee, 'Women in Finance – Fifteenth Report of Session' (n 82) 19.

this further responsibility on the CEO who, at least theoretically, is ultimately responsible for their firm's progress against targets (including diversity) in any event. It is likely that, when the CEO is considering how to prioritise which targets to move forward, those directly impacting the bottom line are going to take precedence. Unfortunately, there is a perception that diversity initiatives are '"special interest", rather than core to business strategy'.[108] Under SEAR this issue would be mitigated because of the requirement that a senior manager to be allocated the single prescribed responsibility of diversity. For this reason (and its mandatory nature), SEAR is likely to be more impactful than its comparable provision in the Charter.

It is too early to tell whether the innovative diversity provisions of SEAR are effective in improving diversity and culture in financial services firms. However, it is a very promising approach for at least two reasons. First, by attributing individual responsibility at a senior level it is more likely that progress will be made because the individual in charge will not be able to hide behind group decision making which can allow ideas and plans to stagnate. Second, according to research by the Women in Banking and Finance membership network, in order to improve gender diversity within financial services it is important to 'move beyond interventions that are compliance based (e.g. transparency of pay, targets and quotas) which firms 'have to do' and towards real cultural change'.[109] Ascribing responsibility for the progress of diversity to a senior individual is not compliance-based and does not require any boxes to be ticked. If the idea is that 'real culture change will only happen when enough inclusive leaders with diversity mindsets are within organisations giving equal opportunities, voice and visibility to all talent, including women',[110] then identifying leaders as inclusive leaders in the manner of SEAR appears to be a step in the right direction. I would therefore advocate for a similar prescribed responsibility in the SMCR. **3.44**

4. Worker Protection Act

The Worker Protection (Amendment of Equality Act 2010) Act 2023 came into effect in October 2024 and introduces a duty on employers to take **3.45**

108 House of Commons Treasury Committee, 'Women in Finance – Fifteenth Report of Session' (n 82) 20.

109 Jasmine Virhia, Yolanda Blavo and Grace Lordan, '100 Diverse Voices: A Framework for the Future of Work in Financial and Professional Services' (2022) Women in Banking and Finance 11 https://www.wibf.org.uk/wp-content/uploads/2023/01/WIBF-ACT-100-Diverse-Voices.pdf.

110 Ibid.

reasonable steps to prevent sexual harassment.[111] Where a court finds that the employer did not take reasonable steps, they may be required to pay the victim an uplift of the compensation awarded, of up to an additional 25 per cent.[112] It is not specific to the financial industry but, given the major concerns around sexual harassment within the sector, it could be considered a welcome change. The question is whether it goes far enough. One of the more obvious criticisms is that determining what amounts to 'reasonable steps' is subjective and is likely to lead to inconsistency of approach. Also, in the context of large financial institutions, an additional 25 per cent on top of a compensation award may not prove to be a sufficiently incentivising sum of money, especially considering that only a small proportion of sexual harassment claims are taken to tribunal.[113]

5. Proposed Regulation

3.46 The PRA and FCA are consulting on a proposal to increase the reporting of firms' diversity and inclusion data to the regulator.[114] The proposals will require regulated firms to provide specific data on their employees, the extent of which will depend on size and regulated status. For most large firms that are not dual regulated, this will include the number of employees and demographic information of age, gender, disability, ethnicity and sexual orientation. Other data, such as parental responsibilities, gender identity and socio-economic status, would be provided on a voluntary basis.

3.47 At the time of writing, there has been no formal response to the proposals. However, several financial institutions have made their responses publicly available. Blackrock expresses concern that the additional reporting requirements will 'cause inefficiency or increase costs for larger global organisations', in part because of the lack of alignment between the proposals and existing diversity reporting such as what is (voluntarily) required by the Charter.[115] It also expresses concern that for demographic data to become useful, employees

111 Equality Act 2010 section 40A inserted (26.10.2024) by Worker Protection (Amendment of Equality Act 2010) Act 2023 (c. 51), ss. 1, 5(3).

112 Equality Act 2010 section 124A inserted (26.10.2024) by Worker Protection (Amendment of Equality Act 2010) Act 2023 (c. 51), ss. 3, 5(3).

113 House of Commons Treasury Committee, 'Sexism in the City – Sixth Report of Session 2023–24' (n 24).

114 Financial Conduct Authority, 'Consultation Paper 23/20: Diversity and Inclusion in the Financial Sector – Working Together to Drive Change' (n 29).

115 Blackrock, 'Response to FCA CP23/20 and PRA CP23/18 on Diversity and Inclusion' (Blackrock, 18 December 2023) https://www.blackrock.com/corporate/literature/publication/fca-pra-diversity-and-inclusion-121823.pdf.

need to engage and consent to providing the relevant information.[116] This reflects concerns raised in 2022 that those least likely to provide demographic information may also be the people who are more often discriminated against.[117] UK Finance, a body representing more than 300 banking and finance firms in the UK, states that there is 'significant debate' over the proposal for diversity data collection, noting that 'some firms do not agree with mandating the collection of any diversity data characteristics and believe that efforts are better spent focusing on culture and initiatives that deliver sustainable long term progress'.[118] The specifics of what diversity data should be collected are common areas of concern even when responses cite general support for the proposals.[119]

3.48 In his response to the consultations, Edmans argues that securing demographic data from firms is unhelpful, comparing it to 'the proverbial drunk who looks under the lamppost for his keys, because that is where the light is, rather than in the bushes where he dropped them'.[120] This is an important point – it is not necessarily the case that a change in numbers equates to an improvement in the inclusivity of an organisation. This is in part why it is so important to look at the culture of an organisation. Similarly, in the recent HM Treasury Report 'Sexism in the City' one of the recommendations is that 'regulators drop their plans for extensive data reporting and target setting', arguing that 'a lack of diversity is a problem that the market itself should be able to solve'.[121] I agree that, in circumstances where it is possible for employees to not engage with the data collection, it has limited usefulness. Certainly, when you are looking at culture and diversity holistically, demographic data requirements appear to be a blunt tool for a complex problem. Nevertheless, it is hard to deny that public data about firms' diversity is likely to make many firms more aware of how

---

116 Ibid.

117 Rosie Almond and Olivia Olivarius, 'Exploring Diversity Data Sharing in Financial Services' (*Financial Services Culture Board*, 13 December 2022) https://financialservicescultureboard.org.uk/exploring-diversity-data-sharing-in-financial-services/.

118 UK Finance, 'UK Finance Response to FCA's CP23/20 and PRA's CP 8/23' (UK Finance, 19 December 2023) https://www.ukfinance.org.uk/policy-and-guidance/consultation-responses/uk-finance-response-fcas-cp-2320-and-pras-cp-1823.

119 UKGI, 'FCA Practitioner Panel Response to the FCA – CP23/20: "Diversity and Inclusion in the Financial Sector – Working Together to Drive Change" | UKGI – Aviva' (12 January 2024) https://abc.ukgigroup.com/fca-practitioner-panel-response-to-the-fca-cp23-20-diversity-and-inclusion-in-the-financial-sector-working-together-to-drive-change/.

120 Alex Edmans, 'Response to FCA Consultation Paper CP23/20. Diversity and Inclusion in the Financial Sector – Working Together to Drive Change' (17 November 2023) https://alexedmans.com/wp-content/uploads/2023/11/FCA-Diversity-2023-Final.pdf.

121 House of Commons Treasury Committee, 'Sexism in the City – Sixth Report of Session 2023–24' (n 24) 16.

that data looks and this may incentivize them to take action. In this respect, the FCA proposals should form part of a suite of efforts that together make up a more complete approach. What might be needed is a rethink about the number and type of data characteristics required. This is particularly the case in the context of a political environment which is seeing companies begin to roll back their DEI initiatives.[122] Overall, the promise of more demographic data, much of which employees will be able to opt out of providing, seems like an unlikely solution.

6. Other Proposals

3.49 Finding ways in which management can have some skin in the diversity game is increasingly frequently proposed as a way to improve gender and ethnicity balance in corporations. It is another of the Women in Finance Charter pledges and the one which signatories report they find the most challenging to adhere to.[123] On top of this, out of the four pledges of the Charter, linking diversity and pay is also the pledge that signatories find least impactful.[124] It is thought that this is because remuneration at a senior level in large companies is 'opaque and highly confidential'.[125] The resistance to linking diversity and pay has lessened over time and the number of signatories who have implemented a link to pay increased from 15 in 2020 to 165 in 2023.[126] This increase is large, but the number of signatories has also increased dramatically and 165 forms less than half the total number of signatories. Despite these doubts about the effectiveness of linking diversity and remuneration, the Sexism in the City report recommends that this aspect of the Charter is hardened into a 'comply-or-explain' requirement.[127]

3.50 Linking incentives to achievement against targets can be seen in other jurisdictions, often voluntarily implemented. For example, executives at Starbucks Corp. were reportedly to be awarded more shares if diversity of the company's managerial positions was increased by 2024.[128] More broadly, several large

122 Lee Harris, 'Three Things to Know about Corporate DEI Rollbacks' *Financial Times* (London, 9 September 2024).

123 Yasmine Chinwala, Jennifer Barrow and Panagiotis Asimakopoulos, 'HM Treasury Women in Finance Charter: Five Year Review' (n 21).

124 Ibid 16.

125 Ibid.

126 Yasmine Chinwala, Jennifer Barrow and Sheenam Singhal, 'HM Treasury Women in Finance Annual Review 2023' (n 9) 23.

127 House of Commons Treasury Committee, 'Sexism in the City – Sixth Report of Session 2023–24' (n 24) 15.

128 Akshaya Kamalnath, *The Corporate Diversity Jigsaw* (n 75) 162.

companies have linked bonuses to ESG goals. Apple, for instance, 'introduced a modifier to executive bonus payouts, adjusting them by up to 10% based on performance with respect to 'Apple Values'" which included diversity and inclusion.[129] However, getting the balance right when measuring progress against a multitude of goals is challenging. There is a danger that there are too many factors to measure against and, like the problem of too many masters, executives are not accountable to any of them. Also, linking ESG goals which include diversity to executive pay relies on the assumption that 'people tend to make better decisions when the stakes are high'.[130] However, if a lack of diversity is (at least in part) a consequence of cognitive biases, such as affinity bias, then there is reason to question the impact of financial incentives. In empirical research by Gneezy et al, it was found that 'cognitive biases are largely and almost entirely unresponsive to stakes'.[131] On that basis, trying to change biases associated with gender stereotypes by recourse to financial incentives will be ineffective. Encouraging diversity via remuneration does not deal with the cultural aspects of diversity.

One suggestion which could help to tackle sexual harassment in the workplace is for a tightening up of the use of non-disclosure agreements (NDA). There is evidence that NDAs are increasingly used to cover up scandals around sexual abuse and discrimination.[132] The report 'Sexism in the City' suggests the FCA monitor the use of NDAs and, in the longer term, the government ban their use in harassment.[133] Without the potential protection of NDAs, would-be perpetrators of harassment would be forced to be more cognisant and consequentially appropriate in their behaviour. This would likely help make workplaces feel safer for women. 3.51

Taking a more practical course, it has been suggested that tech could help track and monitor culture issues including harassment and workplace incidents.[134] 3.52

129 Phillippa O'Connor, Lawrence Harris and Tom Gosling, 'Linking Executive Pay to ESG Goals' (2021) PWC Study 5 https://www.pwc.com/gx/en/issues/reinventing-the-future/take-on-tomorrow/download/Linking-exec-pay-ESG.pdf.

130 Richard H Thaler, 'The Psychology and Economics Conference Handbook: Comments on Simon, on Einhorn and Hogarth, and on Tversky and Kahneman' (1986) 59 *The Journal of Business* 279.

131 Benjamin Enke, Uri Gneezy, Brian Hall, David Martin, Vadim Nelidov, Theo Offerman and Jeroen Van deVen, 'Cognitive Biases: Mistakes or Missing Stakes?' (2023) 105 *The Review of Economics and Statistics* 818.

132 'Can't Buy My Silence Factsheet' https://static1.squarespace.com/static/655b3a3bb4003741a06e1b82/t/6731f15ea519b13bd9663d70/1731326302647/NDA+Fact+Sheet+-+Latest+UK+Version+%281%29.pdf.

133 House of Commons Treasury Committee, 'Sexism in the City – Sixth Report of Session 2023–24' (n 24) 38.

134 Akshaya Kamalnath, *The Corporate Diversity Jigsaw* (n 75) 72.

Setting up a system in which incidents can be reported easily and perhaps anonymously would help to uncover issues that form a pattern of behaviour, which could then be appropriately addressed. Kalmanath reports that such an app has been developed and is in use, including a feature which allows colleagues to see whether their particular issue is also faced by others in the organisation.[135] Any process facilitating employee ability to speak up would form an important part of the cultural infrastructure of an organisation. An app such as that described could also enable the workforce to participate in culture monitoring and could form an effective way to raise awareness and address behaviours which may adversely impact women or marginalised groups. The downside of employing such a device is the possibility for it to be misused or manipulated to the detriment of individuals or groups of individuals. There is also the possibility that such a process or device could work against the effective culture of an organisation by creating conflict or a fear of working together. As important as culture is, we have already noted how difficult it is to define. We can see it is also difficult to analyse and understand. It is important that measures intended to impact upon culture do not have unintended consequences. The development of whistleblowing processes should consider and seek to address these potential negative outcomes.

F. CONCLUSION

3.53 The gender diversity picture in financial services, as in other areas of business, is not as stark as it once was. We are seeing more women in boardrooms and a more balanced proportion of women in financial organisations. However, as is so often the case, the devil is in the detail. While there are more women on boards, those women are often in non-executive positions which hold less decision-making power than the executive. Further, while there are more women in management, the proportion remains significantly lower than the more high-profile board positions. Across the organisation, while there is a high-level balance between the number of women and men in the organisation, a look at the segregation of roles reveals that women are more often found in supporting functions and the gender pay gap between women and men in finance is nearly double the average gap across the other industries. As such, much remains to be done for gender diversity in the financial sector.

135 Ibid.

The relevance of diversity to culture in financial services is outwardly unique, given society's historic perception of finance as a largely male domain. Inwardly, however, there is little evidence that the type of culture-based diversity issues in financial services is different from those found in other organisations. Though there are some high-profile instances of problematic cultures in financial services, including differential treatment and sexual harassment, the same is true of many industries. The issue is not that the problems are different in financial services, but that some of them are worse. Core cultural characteristics which are particularly pertinent to diversity are values such as respect, fairness and integrity. Key cultural infrastructures that support diversity include the ability to speak up. It is argued that to better foster diversity in financial services, work needs to be done to develop these aspects of culture. 3.54

There are several current or proposed initiatives that speak to diversity and/or culture in financial services and corporations more generally. Where these initiatives become more mandatory in nature, such as in relation to disclosure or linking diversity with remuneration, there is a clear distancing from the interaction between diversity and culture. Though useful to a degree, in important respects, these initiatives miss the point because they work against developing the culture in financial services. In contrast, initiatives that support the cultural infrastructure within organisations can provide a more holistic solution to the problem. A greater attention to corporate culture will foster diversity naturally; in turn, increased levels of diversity would likely help perpetuate an inclusive culture. Attributing responsibility for diversity, as is demonstrated by Ireland's Senior Managers and Accountability Regime, should imbue an individual with the personal drive to ensure the appropriate infrastructure is in place so that individuals can speak up about the issues that concern them and context-specific responses can be developed. 3.55

Though many of the initiatives discussed relate specifically to finance, they do not have unique attributes which means they can or should only apply to financial services. There is a particular drive to tackle diversity in financial services because of the rhetoric of the masculinity of the finance domain. Given that this rhetoric emanates from social discourses that do not wholly originate from within financial services, it is important to think about ways in which the narrative can be shifted so that those within and outside financial services start to believe that finance is open to all. 3.56

4

EXECUTIVE REMUNERATION IN FINANCIAL FIRMS – DRIVING BEHAVIOUR AND SHAPING CULTURE

Longjie Lu

A. INTRODUCTION

4.1 The intended role of executive remuneration in the financial sector has become increasingly complex, having evolved from a corporate governance tool for shareholder value maximisation to a quasi-regulatory mechanism for achieving broader economic and societal goals.[1] This evolution has been particularly pushed forward by regulatory and market forces at two turning points in the financial markets: the first is the Global Financial Crisis (GFC), following which financial regulators started to intervene in remuneration practices in order to curb excessive risk-taking and urge financial institutions to prioritise financial stability; the second is the ongoing systematic transformation towards sustainable finance and corporate governance, amidst which both private and regulatory initiatives are emphasising the imperative of linking executive remuneration with sustainability goals.

1 All weblinks were last accessed on 20 December 2024.

Regulators and market forces place emphasis on executive remuneration because it is the primary incentive mechanism in modern companies for motivating executives to deliver the best performance.[2] By setting up certain economic or societal goals as performance targets that are determinative of executives' rewards, remuneration is made a straightforward and powerful way to shape desirable managerial behaviours. These behaviours gradually evolve into the common norms and mindsets in a company, which are essential for reinforcing a benign organisational culture.[3] However, for the same reason, executive remuneration is always considered a major culprit for corporate failures and market breakdowns. Following these negative consequences, regulators and market forces try to find out which part of remuneration practices became distorted and initiate reforms of remuneration so as to reorient executives' behaviours and reframe corporate cultures. 4.2

This chapter examines whether executive remuneration in financial institutions can lead the process of behavioural changes at the individual level and cultural shifts at the organisational level towards desirable economic and societal goals. It will focus primarily on the changing landscapes of executive remuneration following the two turning points mentioned above, namely, the post-GFC remuneration arrangements which have been substantially reformed by regulation and the increasing trend of incorporating environmental, social and governance (ESG) factors into remuneration incentives. These changes indicate that executive remuneration is deviating from its original objective – motivating executives to maximise shareholder value and becoming an instrument for regulators to reorient business practices and implement their policies and objectives. 4.3

Contemporary executive remuneration is based on agency theory and designed to align the interests of executives and shareholders.[4] However, remuneration arrangements such as stock options and short-term financial targets exacerbated managerial short-termism and excessive risk-taking, which were particularly severe in the financial sector.[5] The risky activities driven by shareholder 4.4

2 Michael Armstrong and Helen Murlis, *Reward Management: A Handbook of Employee Reward Management and Practice* (5th edn, Kogan Page 2007) 58.

3 Ibid, xi; Ruth Bender, 'Onwards and Upwards: Why Companies Change Their Executive Remuneration Schemes, And Why This Leads to Increases in Pay' (2007) 15(5) *Corporate Governance: An International Review* 709, 716–17.

4 Michael C. Jensen and Kevin J. Murphy, 'Performance Pay and Top-Management Incentives' (1990) 98(2) *Journal of Political Economy* 225, 225–7.

5 Lucian A. Bebchuk and Holger Spamman, 'Regulating Bankers' Pay' (2010) 98(2) Georgetown Law Journal 247, 250; Lucian A. Bebchuk et al., 'The Wages of Failure: Executive Compensation at Bear Stearns and Lehman 2000–2008' (2010) 27(2) *Yale Journal on Regulation* 257, 259.

value-oriented remuneration externalised substantial social costs,[6] which justified the post-GFC regulatory intervention aimed at reshaping executive remuneration to serve the purpose of financial stability. In terms of the effects of remuneration regulation, academic views are controversial. On the one hand, there is evidence that financial institutions subject to remuneration regulation have been much more attentive to long-term performance and prudential risk-taking; however, on the other hand, it is found that remuneration regulation has resulted in increased total remuneration, reduced pay-to-performance sensitivity and higher CEO turnovers.[7]

4.5 This chapter argues that in essence, the regulation-led reform of executive remuneration is to align executives' personal economic interests with broader economic and social interests, not only shareholder interest. However, it means that executives will need to achieve more performance targets to realise their remuneration and bear a higher level of uncertainty. When a reformed remuneration system creates stricter conditions for performance rewards, it will only work when executives do not have other methods to achieve the same level of remuneration as before, or if there are other methods but the additional efforts required are not in excess of the costs of shifting to other methods. In fact, the aforementioned unintended consequences are just 'other methods' that are not only available but also economically efficient from the perspective of executives. A hypothetical example is: when regulation requires remuneration to be determined by additional social targets, executives can simply manipulate their boards to increase the threshold of total remuneration; executives would not consider this method if doing so incurs legal liabilities or reputational damages and the economic consequences to themselves are severe, such as losing their jobs.

4.6 A deep-seated reason for this deadlock is the inherent conflict between the culture of responsibility that regulators expect to foster and the culture of calculation and self-interest in which contemporary executive remuneration is rooted. The effects of executive remuneration in driving behavioural changes and cultural shifts away from calculation and self-interest are doomed to be limited. It is crucial but also very difficult to establish a robust and reliable alignment between executives' interests and the objectives regulators intend to achieve. In addition to financial stability, both regulators and market forces are trying to encourage companies to further align executive remuneration

6 Andrew Johnston, 'Exploring Post-crisis Trajectories of European Corporate Governance' (2014) 41(1) *Journal of Law and Society* 6, 7.

7 See Section D.

with sustainability goals. Compared to shareholder value and financial stability, it is much more difficult to establish a robust and reliable alignment between executives' interests and a wide range of stakeholder interests because of the unmeasurable and multi-faceted characters of many ESG issues and the absence of standardised ESG metrics.[8] Furthermore, with ESG incentives, executives need to make even more efforts, making other methods which allow them to circumvent these tough conditions more appealing.

The possibility that executives are powerful enough to harness remuneration arrangements to serve their own interests and window-dress the relevant incentives and behaviours as legitimate challenges the assumption that remuneration can fundamentally shape executives' incentives and direct their behaviours. It further warns regulators that reorienting business behaviours to account for broader social and social welfare through interventions in remuneration incentives may be ineffective or even counterproductive. **4.7**

The remainder of this chapter proceeds as follows. Section B reviews shareholder value-oriented remuneration and how it stimulated excessive risk-taking in the financial sector. Section C elaborates on the post-GFC regulatory measures aimed at reorienting executive remuneration in financial institutions towards prudential risk-taking and financial stability. Section D analyses the empirical findings and arguments about both the positive effects and unintended consequences of remuneration regulation, as well as the essential reasons for unintended consequences. Section E discusses the increasing trend of ESG-based remuneration and critically elucidates its incompetence in fostering sustainability-oriented behaviours and cultural norms. Section F concludes. **4.8**

B. EXECUTIVE REMUNERATION AND THE RISK-TAKING CULTURE IN FINANCIAL INSTITUTIONS

In the shareholder-oriented corporate world, executive remuneration is grounded on the agency theory narratives of the relationship between shareholders and executives. Interest alignment between executives and shareholders provides the general solution to mitigating the agency problem arising from executives utilising their decision-making power to pursue self-interest. **4.9**

8 See Section E.

Due to its pecuniary nature, executive remuneration is naturally a very useful tool for interest alignment.[9]

4.10 Contemporary executive remuneration is primarily about the design of appropriate incentives for executives to maximise shareholder value. However, if incentives are designed with flaws or function distortedly in practice, remuneration would counterproductively facilitate executives to exploit corporate and shareholder interest, which is described as 'rewards for failure' or 'pay without performance'.[10] More seriously, extensive debates continuously make the criticism that shareholder value maximisation has led to shareholder expropriation of other stakeholders and businesses behaving irresponsibly for the wider economy and society,[11] which also fundamentally challenges the acknowledged objective of executive remuneration. A perfect illustration of the compounded effects of both problems is the remuneration practices in large financial institutions prior to the GFC, which contributed to the disastrous consequences for not only these institutions but also the global financial system.

4.11 The objective of shareholder value maximisation is embedded in executive remuneration mainly through two mechanisms: first, equity-based components, usually in the form of stock options or restricted shares, by which the actual level of executive remuneration is directly determined by stock price performance;[12] second, performance-based (variable) remuneration, which is conditional on the achievement of pre-designated financial indicators of shareholder value, such as total shareholder return and earning per share.[13]

---

9 Jensen and Murphy, 'Performance Pay and Top-Management Incentives' (n 4) 242; Geoffrey S. Rehnert, 'The Executive Compensation Contract: Creating Incentives to Reduce Agency Costs' (1985) 37(4) *Stanford Law Review* 1147, 1156–7; Michael C. Jensen et al., 'Remuneration: Where We've Been, How We Got to Here, What Are the Problems, and How to Fix Them' (2004) ECGI – Finance Working Paper No. 44/2004 https://papers.ssrn.com/sol3/papers.cfm?abstract_id=561305.

10 House of Commons, 'Rewards for Failure Sixteenth Report of Session 2002–03' (2002) HC 914 https://publications.parliament.uk/pa/cm200203/cmselect/cmtrdind/914/914.pdf; Lucian Bebchuk and Jesse Fried, *Pay without Performance: The Unfulfilled Promise of Executive Compensation* (Harvard University Press 2004).

11 Dorothy S. Lund, 'Enlightened Shareholder Value, Stakeholderism, and the Quest for Managerial Accountability' in Elizabeth Pollman and Robert B. Thompson (eds), *Research Handbook on Corporate Purpose and Personhood* (Edward Elgar Publishing 2021) 92; Ian B. Lee, 'Corporate Law, Profit Maximization, and the Responsible Shareholder' (2005) 10(2) *Stanford Journal of Law, Business & Finance* 31, 33–5.

12 Brian J. Hall and Kevin J. Murphy, 'The Trouble with Stock Options' (2003) 17(3) *Journal of Economic Perspectives* 49, 49; Philipp Geiler and Luc Renneboog, 'Managerial Compensation: Agency Solution or Problem?' (2011) 11(1) *Journal of Corporate Law Studies* 99, 101–2 and 111; Jensen et al., 'Remuneration: Where We've Been, How We Got to Here, What Are the Problems, and How to Fix Them' (n 9) 56–7.

13 Longjie Lu, *Market or State: The Regulation and Practice of Bankers' Remuneration in the UK and China* (CUP 2022) 12.

To maximise their rewards, executives will contrive to concentrate efforts and corporate resources on realising these performance targets. The efficacy of these two mechanisms is premised on the assumption that stock price and financial indicators are unbiased estimates of corporate fundamental value, which, as proven by financial studies, is very often untrue.[14]

Managerial short-termism, which describes the tendency of executives to engage in activities that can boost stock price performance or earnings in the short run at the expense of the company's long-term value, is a pervasive problem in corporate governance.[15] Arrangements for the timeframe of performance assessment and payment are one of the significant contributors. Traditional stock options for executives, if not conditional on performance, will become exercisable after the pre-set vesting period.[16] Usually, at least a portion of the granted options becomes vested after approximately one year;[17] it is also possible for executives to initiate early vesting.[18] Annual bonuses are short-term incentives, which focus only on a single year's performance.[19] Long-term incentive plans (LTIPs) were invented as a solution to managerial short-termism; nevertheless, the standard period for performance assessment in an LTIP is three years. [20] In the pre-GFC era, the evolution of executive remuneration in financial instructions was on the same path as that in all other 4.12

14 Bengt Holmström and Jean Tirole, 'Market Liquidity and Performance Monitoring' (1993) 101(4) *Journal of Political Economy* 678; José A. Scheinkman and Wei Xiong, 'Overconfidence and Speculative Bubbles' (2003) 111 *Journal of Political Economy* 1183; Maosen Zhong et al., 'Do US Stock Prices Deviate from Their Fundamental Values? Some New Evidence' (2003) 27(4) *Journal of Banking & Finance* 673; Victor L. Bernard and Jacob K. Thomas, 'Evidence that Stock Prices Do Not Fully Reflect the Implications of Current Earnings for Future Earnings' (1990) 13(4) *Journal of Accounting and Economics* 305; Jesse M. Fried et al., 'Stock Investors' Returns are Exaggerated' (2021) European Corporate Governance Institute – Law Working Paper No. 618/2021 https://papers.ssrn.com/sol3/papers.cfm?abstract_id=3964177.

15 Lynne L. Dallas, 'Short-Termism, the Financial Crisis, and Corporate Governance' (2012) 37(2) *Journal of Corporation Law* 265, 268; Razeen Sappideen, 'Focusing on Corporate Short-termism' (2011) *Singapore Journal of Legal Studies* 412, 413; Mark J. Roe, 'Corporate Short-Termism – In the Boardroom and in the Courtroom' (2013) 68(4) *The Business Lawyer* 977, 981.

16 Robert Dean Ellis, 'Equity Derivatives, Executive Compensation, and Agency Costs' (1998) 35(2) *Houston Law Review* 399, 401–2; Jensen et al., 'Remuneration: Where We've Been, How We Got to Here, What Are the Problems, and How to Fix Them' (n 9) 57.

17 Stacey Kole, 'The Complexity of Compensation Contracts' (1997) 43 *Journal of Financial Economics* 79, 85; Brian D. Cadman et al., 'Stock Option Grant Vesting Terms: Economic and Financial Reporting Determinants' (2013) 18 *Review of Accounting Studies* 1159, 1161.

18 Neil Brisley, 'Executive Stock Options: Early Exercise Provisions and Risk-taking Incentives' (2006) 61(5) *Journal of Finance* 2487, 2489.

19 Alistair Bruce et al., 'Executive Bonus and Firm Performance in the UK' (2007) 40 *Long Range Planning* 280, 281.

20 Alexander Pepper et al., 'Are Long-term Incentive Plans an Effective and Efficient Way of Motivating Senior Executives?' (2013) 23(1) *Human Resource Management Journal* 36, 36; Sanjai Bhagat and Roberta Romano, 'Reforming Executive Compensation: Focusing and Committing to the Long-Term' (2009) 26(2) *Yale Journal on Regulation* 359, 364.

publicly traded companies.[21] Their arrangements were therefore highly identical to these common practices.

4.13 Executives' horizon is limited to the period during which their performance is assessed and their remuneration is pending. They are inclined to trade off future corporate value for current performance.[22] As evidenced, executives holding stock options with shorter vesting periods undertake more short-term speculation.[23] They behave more myopically when running up to the end of an assessment period, even if the activities are value-destroying for the company.[24]

4.14 Regardless of the timeframe, equity-based remuneration *per se* is a cause of short-termism. Executives accumulate large shareholdings from exercised options and vested shares, which they expect to unwind not only at a high price but also immediately.[25] In this sense, executives have the same mindset as short-term shareholders. When short-term shareholders are dominant in a company, executives are under greater pressure to invest in speculative projects which can produce a 'bump' in stock price.[26] The lessons of Bear Stearns and Lehman Brothers show that holding large amounts of disposable shares and options gave their executives strong incentives to 'place significant weight on the effect of their decisions on short-term stock prices'.[27] Therefore, equity-based remuneration in fact served for aligning the interests between executives and short-term shareholders.[28]

4.15 Short-termism fuels excessive risk-taking.[29] This problem is particularly serious in financial institutions, especially banks. Commercial banks and investment banks are highly leveraged, namely, running on borrowed money. For banks organised with a corporate structure, their shareholders owe limited

---

21 Lu, *Market or State: The Regulation and Practice of Bankers' Remuneration in the UK and China* (n 13) 30.

22 Lin Peng and Ailsa Roell, 'Managerial Incentives and Stock Price Manipulation' (2013) 69(2) *The Journal of Finance* 487, 488–9.

23 Patrick Bolton et al., 'Executive Compensation and Short-Termist Behaviour in Speculative Markets' (2006) 73(3) *The Review of Economic Studies* 577, 581.

24 Jensen et al., 'Remuneration: Where We've Been, How We Got to Here, What Are the Problems, and How to Fix Them' (n 9) 71.

25 Qiang Cheng and Terry Warfield, 'Equity Incentives and Earnings Management' (2005) 80(2) *The Accounting Review* 441, 442; Bebchuk et al., 'The Wages of Failure: Executive Compensation at Bear Stearns and Lehman 2000–2008' (n 5) 265–9.

26 Robert Anderson, 'The Long and Short of Corporate Governance' (2015) 23(1) *George Mason Law Review* 19, 20.

27 Ing-Haw Cheng et al., 'Yesterday's Heroes: Compensation and Risk at Financial Firms' (2015) 70(2) *The Journal of Finance* 839, 840.

28 Bolton et al., 'Executive Compensation and Short-Termist Behaviour in Speculative Markets' (n 23) 597.

29 Sappideen, 'Focusing on Corporate Short-termism' (n 14) 413; Cheng et al., 'Yesterday's Heroes: Compensation and Risk at Financial Firms' (n 26) 840.

liabilities for bank debt, while being entitled to all the residual value.[30] From shareholders' perspective, the riskiness of a project which has the potential to cause huge losses beyond a company's equity capital will be underestimated.[31]

The risk appetite of banks' shareholders is exacerbated by the high leverage as their equity is a very small fraction of banks' total assets.[32] Banks invested borrowed money in the assets in speculative markets, regardless of their hidden risks.[33] Since the prices of these assets inflated rapidly, banks were further motivated to take more debt for expansion, resulting in a vicious circle between leveraging and risk-taking. The decade proceeding the GFC observed the surge in the leverage ratios of investment banks.[34] As well known, during this period, investment banks largely shifted their businesses from traditional investment banking and asset management to the trading of structured financial products, such as mortgage-backed securities, collateralised debt obligations and credit derivatives.[35] It was exactly the exposure to risks in these assets that caused several top investment banks to collapse.[36] **4.16**

In addition, to meet the increasing demand for funds, banks would choose to take riskier debt, exposing themselves to more risks in the financial system.[37] For instance, both Northern Rock and RBS – two large British banks – relied heavily on short-term wholesale borrowings and were severely hit due to the runs in wholesale markets in 2008.[38] **4.17**

The rise of transient institutional investors who pursue short-term returns through momentum trading strategies and therefore exhibit high turnovers is **4.18**

---

30 Larry E. Ribstein, 'Limited Liability and Theories of the Corporation' (1991) 50 *Maryland Law Review* 80, 109.

31 Ciril Bosch-Rosa et al., 'Risk Taking Under Limited Liability and Moral Hazard: Quantifying the Role of Motivated Beliefs' (2024) 71(2) *Management Science* 976–91.

32 Bebchuk and Spamman, 'Regulating Bankers' Pay' (n 5) 256–61.

33 Dallas, 'Short-Termism, the Financial Crisis, and Corporate Governance' (n 15) 268.

34 Ibid, 294; Robert J. Rhee, 'The Decline of Investment Banking: Preliminary Thoughts on the Evolution of the Industry 1996–2008' (2010) 5 *Journal of Business and Technology Law* 75, 82.

35 Rhee, 'The Decline of Investment Banking: Preliminary Thoughts on the Evolution of the Industry 1996–2008' (ibid) 83.

36 For a detailed analysis, see Viral V. Acharya and Matthew Richardson, 'Causes of the Financial Crisis' (2009) 21(2–3) *A Journal of Politics and Society* 195.

37 Rocco Huang and Lev Ratnovski, 'The Dark Side of Bank Wholesale Funding' (2010) Working Paper Series No. 1223, 7 https://www.ecb.europa.eu/pub/pdf/scpwps/ecbwp1223.pdf.

38 Financial Services Authority (FSA), 'The Failure of the Royal Bank of Scotland' (2011) 21 https://www.fca.org.uk/publication/corporate/fsa-rbs.pdf; House of Commons Treasury Committee, 'The Run on the Rock' (2008) Fifth Report of Session 2007–08, 5 https://publications.parliament.uk/pa/cm200708/cmselect/cmtreasy/56/56i.pdf.

also considered a main contributor to excessive risk-taking.[39] In addition to the direct pressure imposed on corporate directors to escalate current earnings, they cultivated the speculative environment through their overoptimistic and reckless attitudes towards risk-taking as well as their assessment of performance which was focused solely on profit.[40] Competition also played a main role. First of all, traditional commercial and investment banks were under the pressure brought by the novel financial products and investment strategies operated by unregulated financial firms; to ensure survival and overall profitability, they largely engaged in similar activities.[41] Second, banks and other financial firms competing for funds from the same investors, such as pension funds, would increasingly converge on their investment goals; as a result, adopting aggressive strategies to boost short-term returns became prevalent.[42] To a large extent, these investment goals were operationalised as the performance metrics of remuneration. At the firm level, excessive risk-taking was buttressed by driving managers to focus on efficiency, profit-making skills and self-interest.[43]

4.19 More importantly, excessive risk-taking and organisational risk cultures were mutually reinforced, resulting in excessive risk-taking, as both a pursuit and a practice, deeply permeating into every aspect of operation. Before major crises, the great payoffs from risky projects created a strong desire to win and a false sense of success and security, which reformulated executives' mindsets, beliefs and attitudes towards risk.[44] Their psychological and cognitive risk perceptions then transformed into the expressed or implicit norms and values of their firm through its top-down decision-making and managerial process.[45] As reported,

39 Shane S. Dikolli et al., 'Transient Institutional Ownership and CEO Contracting' (2009) 84(3) The Accounting Review 737, 740; Brian J. Bushee, 'Do Institutional Investors Prefer Near-Term Earnings over Long-Run Value?' (2001) 18(2) *Contemporary Accounting Research* 207, 213.

40 Dallas, 'Short-Termism, the Financial Crisis, and Corporate Governance' (n 15) 316.

41 Raphaële Chappe et al., 'Booms, Busts and the Culture of Risk' in Bob Jessop et al. (eds), *Financial Cultures and Crisis Dynamics* (Routledge 2014) 128.

42 Dallas, 'Short-Termism, the Financial Crisis, and Corporate Governance' (n 15) 295.

43 Ibid, 316.

44 Michael Power et al., 'Risk Culture in Financial Organisations: A Research Report' (2013) 12–14 https://www.lse.ac.uk/accounting/assets/CARR/documents/Risk-Culture-in-Financial-Organisations/Final-Risk-Culture-Report.pdf; Donald C. Langevoort, 'Chasing the Greased Pig Down Wall Street: A Gatekeeper's Guide to the Psychology, Culture, and Ethics of Financial Risk Taking' (2011) 96(5) *Cornell Law Review* 1209, 1219–20.

45 Donald C. Langevoort, 'Chasing the Greased Pig Down Wall Street: A Gatekeeper's Guide to the Psychology, Culture, and Ethics of Financial Risk Taking' (ibid) 1222–3.

in major UK banks, there was a systematic underestimation of risks and downplay of risk assessment by bank personnel across different divisions.[46]

Although excessive risk-taking can be influenced by multiple factors, such as financial innovation which provides a range of products for banks to shift and hedge risks, changes in the organisational and legal forms of businesses, and the cyclical tendency of investment during market upturns,[47] there are many aspects of it that 'could be analysed strictly from a microeconomic perspective in terms of the incentive structures in place'.[48] In this sense, reforming remuneration incentives is necessary for addressing excessive risk-taking. Nevertheless, since excessive risk-taking has already been at the heart of the organisational cultures of financial institutions, for any reform to be effective overall it needs to be a powerful driver of cultural shift, which means that it should focus on not only the setting of incentives but also individual and collective values, beliefs and mindsets. The following sections will try to answer whether this is achievable through the implemented and proposed remuneration reforms. **4.20**

C. REGULATION OF EXECUTIVE REMUNERATION IN FINANCIAL INSTITUTIONS

During the GFC, the crisis of subprime mortgage-backed securities cascaded rapidly throughout the entire global financial system, which brought the severity of systemic risk to the forefront of regulators' awareness. Systemic risk arises from a single institution or a segment in the market and results in system-wide losses. The social costs of excessive risk-taking activities by financial institutions were eventually externalised to the entire social economy.[49] Therefore, risk management in financial institutions, especially those deeply connected to other parts of the financial system, is of crucial importance. In 2011, the Financial Stability Board (FSB) introduced the concept of globally systematically important financial institutions (G-SIFIs) and started to **4.21**

---

46 'Salz Review: An Independent Review of Barclays' Business Practices' (2013) 6–7 https://www.wsj.com/public/resources/documents/SalzReview04032013.pdf; Parliamentary Commission on Banking Standards, 'An Accident Waiting to Happen: The Failure of HBOS Fourth Report of Session 2012–13' (HL Paper 144; HC 705) 8 https://publications.parliament.uk/pa/jt201213/jtselect/jtpcbs/144/144.pdf.

47 For a comprehensive analysis of how these factors had driven excessive risk-taking, see Dallas, 'Short-Termism, the Financial Crisis, and Corporate Governance' (n 15); see also Chappe et al., 'Booms, Busts and the Culture of Risk' (n 41) 123.

48 Chappe et al., 'Booms, Busts and the Culture of Risk' (n 41) 130.

49 John Armour and Jeffrey N. Gordon, 'Systemic Harms and Shareholder Value' (2014) 6(1) *Journal of Legal Analysis* 35, 37–8.

operate a recognition system.[50] Accordingly, major economies have established their systems to regulate national SIFIs. The post-GFC overhaul of financial regulation primarily includes measures aimed at promoting prudential risk-taking in these institutions as well as their resilience to crisis.[51]

4.22 Prudential risk-taking and sound risk management rely on effective behavioural changes at the individual level and cultural shifts at the organisational level.[52] Given that cultural shifts are long-term whereas the existing risk-taking culture is still influential, spurring behavioural changes through the use of appropriate incentives is not only the best way to start but also promising for nurturing and maintaining a culture of prudence and responsibility in the future.[53]

4.23 The regulation of executive remuneration in financial institutions is an important part of prudential regulation and closely correlates with risk management. By requiring financial institutions to integrate prudential goals into their remuneration arrangements, regulators aim to enhance compliance with prudential regulatory requirements, such as capital and liquidity requirements. Compared to these direct measures, remuneration regulation, which is 'softer', has its advantages in terms of enabling financial institutions to tailor firm-specific steps and policies under the generic regulatory framework. This section will elucidate the post-GFC approach to regulating executive remuneration in financial institutions by taking the UK's regime as an example, with necessary reference to the EU regulatory framework.[54] In terms of the objective, regulatory measures can be divided into those aimed at (1) promoting long-term managerial views in decision-making, (2) enhancing the sensitivity of remuneration to risks, and (3) directly mitigating incentives. Their impacts on executives' behaviours and the risk-taking culture are also different. The measure to directly mitigate incentives refers particularly to the cap on performance-based remuneration, also known as the 'bankers' bonus cap'. A detailed

---

50 FSB, 'Policy Measures to Address Systemically Important Financial Institutions' (2011) https://www.fsb.org/wp-content/uploads/r_111104bb.pdf?page_moved=1.

51 Daniel K. Tarullo, 'Financial Regulation: Still Unsettled a Decade After the Crisis' (2019) 33(1) *Journal of Economic Perspectives* 61, 62.

52 Frank Elderson, 'Treading Softly Yet Boldly: How Culture Drives Risk in Banks and What Supervisors Can Do About It' (19 September 2023) Speech at the 10th Conference on the Banking Union, Frankfurt https://www.bankingsupervision.europa.eu/press/speeches/date/2023/html/ssm.sp230919~589c61455b.en.html.

53 Bank of England, 'The Prudential Regulation Authority's Approach to Banking Supervision' (2023) 20 https://www.bankofengland.co.uk/-/media/boe/files/prudential-regulation/approach/banking-approach-2023.pdf.

54 To a large extent, the UK regulation has been compliant with the EU framework set in CRD IV.

analysis of this measure is provided in the overview chapter of this book. Thus, this chapter will only introduce the detailed rules falling into the first two categories, while still making reference to all of these measures to analyse the effects of remuneration regulation.

To provide a brief evolution of remuneration regulation, in 2009 the FSB issued the Principles for Sound Compensation Practices, emphasising the alignment of remuneration with prudential risk-taking. In the same year, the HM Treasury published the Walker Review, in which it made 39 recommendations for bank corporate governance reforms.[55] Many of the recommendations related to executive remuneration laid the foundation for the formal regulation set in the Financial Conduct Authority (FCA) Handbook. The Remuneration Code in SYSC 19D of the Handbook applies to dual-regulated firms (DRFs),[56] including large, systematically important financial institutions. Meanwhile, the EU authority started to draft the guidelines on remuneration policies and practices and finally enacted the mandatory regulation of executive remuneration in the Capital Requirements Directive (CRD) IV in 2013, which was later implemented by the FCA domestically. The FCA also implemented the revised rules set in the CRD V in 2019. **4.24**

1. Long-term Incentives

(a) Deferral

Orienting executives towards the long-term development of their institutions and the financial system at large requires incentives to be based on long-term performance assessment. First of all, the regulation has substantially extended the vesting period of variable remuneration through mandatory deferral. As a general principle, the deferral period of variable remuneration should be consistent with an institution's business cycle and risks as well as the specific risk-taking functions undertaken by each executive.[57] **4.25**

55 HM Treasury, 'A Review of Corporate Governance in UK Banks and Other Financial Industry Entities' (2009) (hereafter the 'Walker Review') https://www.iod.com/app/uploads/2022/02/The-Walker-Review-A-review-of-corporate-governance-in-UK-banks-and-other-financial-industry-entities-7c12bf7b56071cb103fdd7c0a84f28d9.pdf.

56 Dual-regulated firms refer to those regulated by both the FCA and the PRA.

57 FSA, 'The Turner Review: A Regulatory Response to the Global Banking Crisis' (2009) 80 http://news.bbc.co.uk/1/shared/bsp/hi/pdfs/18_03_09_turner_review.pdf.

4.26 As suggested in the Walker Review, 50 per cent of LTIPs should vest after three years, and the remainder should vest after five years.[58] Short-term bonus schemes should also be deferred for no less than three years.[59]

4.27 According to CRD IV, no less than 40 per cent of variable remuneration shall be deferred for at least three to five years, and the deferred remuneration shall not be vested faster than a pro-rata basis.[60] In addition, the minimum deferral ratio applied to executives whose variable remuneration is 'particularly high' was 60 per cent.[61] In its Remuneration Code, the FCA defined 'particularly high variable remuneration' as 'above GBP 500,000' or 'payable to a director of a significant firm that is significant in terms of its size, internal organisation and the nature, scope and complexity'.[62]

4.28 In 2015, the FCA and the Prudential Regulation Authority (PRA) initiated a new reform of executive remuneration in DRFs.[63] Prior to this reform, it was criticised that a deferral period of up to five years was still short relative to many financial activities and investments.[64] The recommendation made by the UK Parliamentary Commission on Banking Standards was to extend the deferral period to ten years.[65] The FCA and the PRA eventually took a relatively moderate position. For staff in DRFs who carry out a PRA-designated senior management function (SMF), such as chairmen, chief executives, executive directors, and senior managers,[66] a seven-year deferral would apply to their variable remuneration, and vesting should only start after three years since the allocation of variable remuneration.[67]

---

58 HM Treasury, 'The Walker Review' (n 53) Chapter 7, 98.

59 Ibid.

60 Directive 2013/36/EU of the European Parliament and of the Council of 26 June 2013 on access to the activity of credit institutions and the prudential supervision of credit institutions and investment firms, amending Directive 2002/87/EC and repealing Directives 2006/48/EC and 2006/49/EC, OJ L 176, 27.6.2013, p. 338–436 (hereinafter 'CRD IV'), Article 94(m). For instance, the deferral period is three years; by the end of the first year, the vested portion should be no more than one-third of the entire deferred package.

61 CRD IV, Article 94(m).

62 *FCA Handbook* (2014), SYSC 19A (3), (4) and (6).

63 FCA and PRA, 'Strengthening the Alignment of Risk and Reward: New Remuneration Rules' PRA PS12/15 and FCA PS 15/16 (2015) 7–9 https://www.fca.org.uk/publications/policy-statements/ps15-16-strengthening-alignment-risk-and-reward-new-remuneration.

64 Iris H-Y Chiu, *Regulating (From) the Inside: The Legal Framework for Internal Control in Banks and Financial Institutions* (Hart Publishing 2015) 224.

65 The Parliamentary Commission on Banking Standards, 'Changing Banking for Good' (First Report of Session 2013-14, HL Paper 27-II/HC 175-II) 399 https://www.parliament.uk/globalassets/documents/banking-commission/Banking-final-report-vol-ii.pdf.

66 *PRA Rulebook*, Senior Management Functions, Article 1.2.

67 *FCA Handbook*, SYSC 19D.3.59(1). This requirement is much stricter than that in Directive (EU) 2019/878 of the European Parliament and of the Council of 20 May 2019 amending Directive 2013/36/

In 2020, the FCA tailored the deferral policy applied to staff undertaking different levels of risk-taking. The seven-year deferral applies to 'higher paid material risk takers' (HPMRTs) whose total remuneration exceeds GBP 500,000 and variable remuneration exceeds one-third of the total.[68] The remuneration of staff in DRFs who are recognised as 'ordinary' material risk takers (MRTs) only needs to be delayed for five years. Considering that in most circumstances top executives still fall into the category of HPMRTs, this minor revision has limited impact on their remuneration. **4.29**

Strictly speaking, a deferral period is different from a performance assessment period. For example, annual bonuses are still based on the performance in a single year; if 80 per cent of the performance targets have been met, a corresponding size of bonuses are awarded; a portion of the awarded bonuses is subject to deferral, whereas the remainder becomes immediately disposable. Since the majority of bonuses and LTIPs are options and stocks, executives are encouraged to take care of the impact of their actions made during the performance assessment period on stock price in the future. In this sense, deferral can be considered an extension of performance assessment, which, however, weakly and indirectly aligns part of executive remuneration with the longer-term effects of performance. **4.30**

(b) Malus and clawback

Malus is an arrangement by which a financial institution can prevent the vesting of all or part of an executive's deferred remuneration. Clawback allows the institution to require its employees to return relevant paid cash, stocks or other forms of remuneration.[69] Both arrangements will only be triggered under pre-specified circumstances where executives' actions and decisions have caused negative consequences to their institutions, such as significant strategic failures or serious misconduct.[70] In so doing, executives' performance is continuously monitored over a longer period so that any variable remuneration should be **4.31**

EU as regards exempted entities, financial holding companies, mixed financial holding companies, remuneration, supervisory measures and powers and capital conservation measures, OJ L 150, 7.6.2019, p. 253–295 (hereinafter 'CRD V'), which has extended the minimum deferral period from three to four years, see CRD IV, Article 94(m).

68 *FCA Handbook*, SYSC 19D.3.59(2).

69 Lu, *Market or State: The Regulation and Practice of Bankers' Remuneration in the UK and China* (n 13) 57; Richard Leipe, *Conduct and Pay in the Financial Services Industry* (Routledge 2017) 298.

70 Chiu, *Regulating (From) the Inside: The Legal Framework for Internal Control in Banks and Financial Institutions* (n 64) 226.

awarded in accordance with the general principle that 'it is sustainable according to the financial situation of the firm as a whole'.[71]

4.32 During the GFC, without these two arrangements, top executives in failed financial institutions were able to realise vast net cash proceeds from their bonuses right before the failures, and no one was required by their institutions to return any of the 'ill-gotten wealth'.[72] As a result, the costs of executives' excessive risk-taking driven by self-interest maximisation were substantially externalised. By imposing *ex post* punishments, malus and clawback act effectively as cost internalisation strategies so that executives will behave more responsibly.[73]

4.33 Based on CRD V,[74] all variable remuneration should be subject to malus and clawback.[75] Upon the occurrence of a specific triggering event, the two arrangements will respectively take effect on the vested and unvested variable remuneration of any executive or senior employee who participated in related problematic activities or was responsible for the outcomes.[76] The FCA further specifies that the triggering events include a material failure of risk management in an institution's entire business, reasonably evidenced misbehaviour or material error, and a material downturn of financial performance.[77]

4.34 Malus applies to the unvested or unpaid portions of variable remuneration which are still under deferral. Therefore, it is consistent with the deferral period of an executive's remuneration. For clawback which applies to paid bonuses and vested shares, in 2015 the FCA stipulated that the minimum period of clawback was seven years; in addition, for staff performing a PRA-designated SMF, the minimum period would be extended to ten years in a situation where a regulatory authority has started an investigation into facts or events that could potentially lead to application of clawback.[78] In 2020, the FCA made minor changes to relax clawback rules and increase the flexibility

---

71 *FCA Handbook*, SYSC 19D.3.61.

72 Bebchuk et al., 'The Wages of Failure: Executive Compensation at Bear Stearns and Lehman 2000–2008' (n 5) 268; Deloitte, 'Senior Managers Regime: Individual Accountability and Reasonable Steps' (2016) 5 https://www.deloitte.com/uk/en/Industries/financial-services/research/senior-managers-regime.html.

73 Jesse Fried and Nitzan Shilon, 'Excess-pay Clawbacks' (2011) 36(4) *Journal of Corporation Law* 722, 727.

74 Malus and clawback provisions in CRD IV remain unchanged.

75 CRD IV, Article 94(n).

76 CRD IV, Article 94(n).

77 *FCA Handbook*, SYSC 19D.3.63 and 3.64. A material downturn of financial performance only applies to malus, which means that even if the downturn is not caused by executives' wrong decisions, when the institution suffers systematic instability or deterioration, executives should not be allowed to receive excessive pay.

78 FCA and PRA, 'Strengthening the Alignment of Risk and Reward: New Remuneration Rules' (n 63) 8.

of its application: clawback of the remuneration of staff who are not recognised as HPMRTs is reduced to six years,[79] whereas the seven-year requirement and the extension to ten years still apply to HPMRTs.[80]

According to financial firms' feedback on the FCA's proposal for this multi-layer clawback scheme, most of them considered the existing clawback period was too long. Some have also been concerned about the complexity in practice because employees may shift between HPMRTs and other MRTs and therefore their total remuneration changes, which will cause confusion about which clawback period should apply.[81] **4.35**

2. Risk-adjusted and Stability-based Performance Metrics

Performance assessment based on stock price and the financial indicators of short-term shareholder value ignored the hidden risks threatening both institutions and the financial system. The aim of direct regulatory interventions in performance metrics is to reorient executives' decision-making from firm-level short-term profits to system-wide stability. Regulatory measures in this regard include applying risk adjustment to financial indicators and introducing stability-based indicators. **4.36**

Financial institutions are required to ensure that any measurement adopted to calculate variable remuneration is adjusted to all types of current and future risks, including both financial and non-financial risks, as well as to take into account the cost and quantity of capital and liquidity.[82] In addition, risk adjustment needs to be carried out both *ex ante* for the intrinsic risks in business and *ex post* for the crystallisation of specific risk events.[83] The adoption of specific techniques and methodologies for risk adjustment is at the discretion of financial institutions, with the FCA monitoring the formulae being used and the exercise of discretion.[84] **4.37**

79 *FCA Handbook*, SYSC 19D.3.61(3A).

80 *FCA Handbook*, SYSC 19D.3.61(3)(4).

81 FCA, 'Updating the Dual-regulated Firms Remuneration Code to Reflect CRD V: Feedback to CP20/14 and Final Rules' PS 20/16 (2020) 16 https://www.fca.org.uk/publication/consultation/cp20-14.pdf.

82 *FCA Handbook*, SYSC 19D.3.23(1)(a), (2), and 3.24(3).

83 *FCA Handbook*, SYSC 19D.3.29(1). Ex post adjustments, following the occurrence of pre-designated events, will lead to the application of malus or clawback. The FCA has provided detailed, non-handbook guidance on ex post adjustments. See FCA and PRA, 'Strengthening the Alignment of Risk and Reward: New Remuneration Rules' (n 63).

84 *FCA Handbook*, SYSC 19D.3.24(4).

4.38 Those simple profit-based financial indicators adopted in remuneration before the GFC are considered not suitable for assessing long-term risks.[85] A major reason is that they are all determined in line with the fair value accounting model.[86] Fair value is the present value of future cash flows. Financial institutions used to incorporate it into their current earnings, without adjusting to the risks in future cash flows.[87] In a situation where a risk materialises, the realisable cash flows are lower than the recorded fair value. The remuneration paid for overestimated achievements does not reflect the genuine performance of executives. However, it is usually very difficult to ascertain the true value of cash flows that will occur in the future. The FCA requires financial institutions to take into account 'the need for consistency with the timing and likelihood of the firm receiving potential future revenues incorporated into current earnings'.[88] The specific method is to deduct a prudent valuation adjustment figure[89] from the fair value accounting figure.[90] Accordingly, financial indicators of shareholder value become risk-adjusted, such as return on equity being replaced by risk-adjusted return on equity.

4.39 The FCA also stipulates that both financial and non-financial performance should be taken into consideration for variable remuneration.[91] In practice, non-financial performance indicators have been increasingly adopted by large public companies since the 1990s, which was based on the Balanced Scorecard Model (BSM) developed by Kaplan and Norton.[92] The traditional form of this model is still grounded on shareholder value maximisation. It advocates the use of non-financial indicators as supplements to financial indicators in order to more comprehensively assess executives' performance by referring not

85 *FCA Handbook*, SYSC 19D.3.40(2).

86 This model is most frequently applied to financial assets and liabilities. For instance, the fair value of investments in securities, bonds and commodity is measured by current market price.

87 FCA and PRA, 'Strengthening the Alignment of Risk and Reward: New Remuneration Rules (Consultation Paper)' PRA CP15/14 and FCA CP14/14 (2014) 11 https://www.fca.org.uk/publications/consultation-papers/cp14-14-strengthening-alignment-risk-and-reward-new-remuneration.

88 *FCA Handbook*, SYSC 19D.3.23(1)(b).

89 The European Banking Authority (EBA) has published a guidance about how to make prudential valuation on profits and returns. The detailed methods are out of the cover of this book. If interested, please refer to EBA, *Final Draft Regulatory Technical Standards on Prudent Valuation under Article 105(14) of Regulation (EU) No 575/2013 (CRR)* (EBA/RTS/2014/06/rev1, January 2015).

90 Since 2012, UK financial firms have been required to submit quarterly reports which show the differences between prudent valuation and the fair valuation used in relevant firms' financial statements. Risk adjustment for determining remuneration packages should be informed by these figures. See FCA and PRA, 'Strengthening the Alignment of Risk and Reward: New Remuneration Rules' (n 63) 10.

91 SYSC 19D.3.39(1)(b).

92 Robert S. Kaplan and David P. Norton, 'The Balanced Scorecard – Measures that Drive Performance' (1992) January–February Harvard Business Review 71.

only to outcomes but also to the specific actions leading to these outcomes.[93] Therefore, most non-financial indicators are related to business operations.

Differently, the FCA emphasises that the assessment of non-financial performance is to detect and mitigate poor risk management and other poor behaviours that can generate significant risks. Indicators for this purpose should be appropriate for reflecting the institution's resilience and its impact on financial stability. If necessary, institutions should also allocate more weight to non-financial metrics than financial metrics.[94] The FCA's approach makes a fundamental shift in the role of BSM from an instrument for profit-making to a micro-level mechanism for prudential regulation. The effectiveness of this refined model in prudential risk-taking depends on the use of reliable and appropriate indicators of financial stability. The Basel III framework has reinforced the standards of capital adequacy, leverage and liquidity and made calibrations and methodologies uniform so that banks can directly apply these indicators as performance metrics. In particular, the FCA emphasises that regulatory compliance should also be part of the non-financial performance assessment.[95] In contrast, as will be discussed in Section V, in a situation where consistent ESG standards are absent, using non-financial indicators to incentivise executives to achieve sustainability goals is of substantial uncertainty. **4.40**

D. EFFECTS OF REMUNERATION REGULATION ON RISK-TAKING

It has been 15 years since the FSB issued the international principles and standards for executive remuneration in financial institutions. Remuneration regulation has also been implemented in Europe for ten years. Considering that the regulatory rules are prescriptive and mandatory, it is reasonable to assume that the reform of remuneration has been bold. **4.41**

Descriptive statistical results demonstrate that remuneration arrangements in regulated institutions have been substantially changed. Investigations into the remuneration policies of major financial institutions demonstrate full compliance.[96] There is also anecdotal evidence indicating that beyond **4.42**

93 Robert S. Kaplan and David P. Norton, *The Balanced Scorecard: Translating Strategy into Action* (Harvard Business School Press 1996) 18.

94 *FCA Handbook*, SYSC 19D.3.41(1).

95 *FCA Handbook*, SYSC 19D.3.40(1)(a).

96 Lu, *Market or State: The Regulation and Practice of Bankers' Remuneration in the UK and China* (n 13) 67–80; Anna (Ania) Zalewska, 'Bankers' Remuneration Reforms and New Challenges' (2023) 31 *Corporate Governance: An International Review* 161; Pablo de Andrés et al., 'European Banks' Executive Remuneration under the New European Union Regulation' (2019) 22(3) *Journal of Economic Policy Reform*

regulation, banks have taken initiatives to enhance long-term incentives and prudential risk-taking.

4.43 It is manifested that the proportion of LTIPs relative to annual bonuses has been substantially increasing,[97] and some institutions stopped paying annual bonuses.[98] Mandatory deferral policies apply to both LTIPs and annual bonuses; if institutions prefer shorter vesting periods they would choose to increase the proportion of annual bonuses; therefore, this observation demonstrates that institutions have placed more emphasis on long-term incentives.

4.44 Large financial institutions have deferred executives' variable remuneration in excess of the minimum requirements in regulation. Nevertheless, since the FCA tightened deferral requirements in 2016, institutions' voluntary extension of deferral has diminished.[99] This demonstrates that financial institutions have taken into their particular business cycle future risks and corporate governance needs, and tailored firm-specific deferral arrangements.

4.45 A number of academic studies recommend the use of debt-based remuneration, based on the assumption that debt incentives help counteract executives' risk appetite.[100] The best form is publicly traded debt since its price is sensitive to the riskiness of business, and for financial institutions, contingent convertible bonds, which are in nature subordinated debt, may further disincentivise executives from excessive risk-taking.[101] Worldwide, regulators have not yet taken on board debt-based remuneration, and in the financial industry, debt-based remuneration has not been adopted systematically. So far, a number of

---

208; Anya Kleymenova and İrem Tuna, 'Regulation of Compensation and Systemic Risk: Evidence from the UK' (2021) 59(3) *Journal of Accounting Research* 1123.

97 Lu, *Market or State: The Regulation and Practice of Bankers' Remuneration in the UK and China* (n 13) 67–80.

98 Kleymenova and Tuna, 'Regulation of Compensation and Systemic Risk: Evidence from the UK' (n 96) 1135.

99 Ieva Sakalauskaite and Qun Harris, 'Measuring the Effects of Bank Remuneration Rules: Evidence from the UK' Bank of England Staff Working Paper No. 1 008 (2022) 6 https://www.bankofengland.co.uk/-/media/boe/files/working-paper/2022/measuring-the-effects-of-bank-remuneration-rules-evidence-from-the-uk.pdf.

100 Frederick Tung, 'Pay for Banker Performance: Structuring Executive Compensation for Risk Regulation' (2011) 105(3) *Northwestern University Law Review* 1205, 1227; Seiler Moritz and Fischer Damian, '"Bonus Bonds" for Bankers: A New Type of Debt-Based Remuneration in the Financial Industry' (2015) 12(3) *European Company and Financial Law Review* 425, 430.

101 Alex Edmans, 'Executive Compensation: Practical Insights from Large-Scale Research' (2023) 23 https://alexedmans.com/wp-content/uploads/2023/08/Executive-Compensation-Alex-Edmans.pdf.

Swiss banks have used notional bonds as variable remuneration.[102] In the UK, Lloyds Bank has paid its bankers notes and bonds as annual bonuses.[103]

Empirical studies in the literature of finance also try to examine the effects of remuneration regulation and post-GFC remuneration practices on risk-taking in financial institutions. However, empirical findings remain inconclusive. 4.46

Several studies have reported positive outcomes. Cerasi et al. find that in jurisdictions where national regulations have been based on the FSB framework, variable remuneration in commercial banks has been less correlated with short-term profitability and more correlated with bank risks.[104] The authors also find that the effects on banks with a poorer risk management system before the GFC have been more significant.[105] This conclusion is compelling evidence of the effectiveness of remuneration regulation in reorienting bankers' risk-taking activities. Kleymenova and Tuna find that the contribution and sensitivity of UK banks to systemic risk relative to those of non-financial UK firms have been lower since the introduction of the FCA's Remuneration Code in 2010.[106] Given that non-financial firms are not subject to the same regulation, this finding reflects its positive effects on the mitigation of systemic risk in the banking sector. There are also studies applying experimental studies which attempt to provide evidence of the positive effects of deferral, malus and claw-back on mitigating executives' risk-taking propensity.[107] However, as will be discussed shortly, some of these studies also have concerns that under certain circumstances, these measures may become counterproductive. 4.47

102 Moritz and Damian, '"Bonus Bonds" for Bankers: A New Type of Debt-Based Remuneration in the Financial Industry' (n 100) 457–8.

103 See Lloyds Annual Report 2013, 103. https://www.lloydsbankinggroup.com/assets/pdfs/investors/annual-report/2013-download-links/2013_lbg_annual_report.pdf.

104 Vittoria Cerasi et al., 'How Post-crisis Regulation has Affected Bank CEO Compensation' BIS Working Papers No 630 (2017) 19 https://www.bis.org/publ/work630.pdf.

105 Ibid 17.

106 Kleymenova and Tuna, 'Regulation of Compensation and Systemic Risk: Evidence from the UK' (n 96) 1126.

107 Frank Hartmann and Sergeja Slapničar, 'An Experimental Study of the Effects of Negative, Capped and Deferred Bonuses on Risk Taking in a Multi-period Setting' (2015) 19 *Journal of Management & Governance* 875; Qun Harris et al., 'How Do Bonus Cap and Clawback Affect Risk and Effort Choice? Insight from a Lab Experiment' (2017) Bank of England Working Paper No. 736 https://www.bankofengland.co.uk/-/media/boe/files/working-paper/2018/how-do-bonus-cap-and-malus-affect-risk-and-effort-choice-insight-from-a-lab-experiment.pdf; John Thanassoulis and Misa Tanaka, 'Bankers' Pay and Excessive Risk' (2015) Bank of England Staff Working Paper No. 558 https://www.bankofengland.co.uk/-/media/boe/files/working-paper/2015/bankers-pay-and-excessive-risk.pdf; Florian Hoffmann et al., 'The Economics of Deferral and Clawback Regulation' (2022) 77(4) *The Journal of Finance* 2423.

4.48 Empirical findings of the positive effects of remuneration regulation on risk-taking have an insurmountable drawback: large financial institutions subject to remuneration regulation should also comply with the stringent post-GFC prudential regulation, therefore, it is difficult to decouple the impact of remuneration regulation from that of other mandatory rules. On the contrary, many other studies find the opposite – remuneration regulation may exacerbate excessive risk-taking and bring about unintended consequences. Based on these findings, it has to be concluded that without remuneration regulation as a countervailing power, other regulatory measures acting directly on prudential risk-taking would have been more effective.

4.49 The counterproductivity of bankers' bonus cap has been analysed in the overview chapter, which is also supported by empirical findings.[108] The UK regulators contrived to remove this rule and pin hopes on other regulatory measures. However, it is also possible for institutions to circumvent them.

4.50 Hoffmann et al. theorise that very stringent deferral and clawback rules will backfire as financial institutions have to increase the size of the entire remuneration package to compensate for the lost time value of money and the lower probability of being awarded.[109] Sakalauskaite and Harris provide empirical evidence to support this proposition; they find that the total remuneration of MRTs in UK financial institutions who are affected by the enhanced deferral rules enacted in 2016 increased more than that of non-affected MRTs.[110] This countermeasure against the negative impact of mandatory deferral on executives' actual incomes not only increases the operational costs of financial institutions but also undermines pay-to-performance sensitivity and reversely incentivises risk-taking. Assuming that the amounts of fixed pay and non-deferred variable remuneration in increased packages meet executives' personal expectations of 'secure' payments, they have the propensity to reduce their efforts on long-term risk management.

4.51 In the same way, this tactic can also undermine the risk mitigation and long-term incentive effects of malus and clawback. The model created by Thanassoulis and Tanaka demonstrates that clawback can effectively deliver

108 Stefano Colonnello et al., 'Compensation Regulation in Banking: Executive Director Behaviour and Bank Performance after the EU Bonus Cap' (2023) 76(1) *Journal of Accounting and Economics*; Harris et al., 'How Do Bonus Cap and Clawback Affect Risk and Effort Choice? Insight from a Lab Experiment' (ibid); Lu, *Market or State: The Regulation and Practice of Bankers' Remuneration in the UK and China* (n 13).

109 Hoffmann et al., 'The Economics of Deferral and Clawback Regulation' (n 107) 2424–5.

110 Sakalauskaite and Harris, 'Measuring the Effects of Bank Remuneration Rules: Evidence from the UK' (n 99) 4.

socially optimal risk choices only if appropriate restrictions are inflicted on the curvature of pay with respect to a firm's market value.[111] They have summarised that 'offering the bank executives pay that is convex in the bank's market value can easily restore their risk-taking incentives.'[112] That is, their model warns the regulators of two possible ways for banks to circumvent the risk-mitigating effects of clawback, namely, to compensate executives for the potential losses incurred by clawback if they take risky actions: one is similar to the theory of Hoffmann et al. that banks may increase the total level of remuneration; the second is that banks can try to increase their stock prices to top up the total value of equity-based remuneration.[113]

Moreover, Kleymenova and Tuna find that the introduction of the Remuneration Code has significantly escalated CEO turnover in the UK banking sector. Rather than shifting within the UK banking sector, most CEOs moved to foreign markets or other sectors where executive remuneration is less regulated.[114] This finding corroborates that financial institutions' countervailing measures are forced by the fear of losing top employees. **4.52**

Financial institutions face the trade-off between the two objectives remuneration is meant to serve – prudential risk-taking and the retention of top employees. Imbalance towards either side will lead to the failure of an institution. Although it is rational for financial institutions to consider the trade-off, their balancing strategies hinder the function of remuneration in fostering behavioural changes and cultural shifts. **4.53**

Essentially, regulators intervene in remuneration practices with the aim of nurturing a culture of responsibility in financial markets, as opposed to the prolonged, dominant culture of calculation and self-interest. However, contemporary executive remuneration is exactly a product of economic self-interest, and its incentive mechanism which bases performance on quantitative financial indicators, has ingrained a calculative mode of thinking and decision-making. A thorough cultural shift in financial institutions through accumulative behavioural changes needs to be underpinned by correct governance philosophy and **4.54**

111 John Thanassoulis and Misa Tanaka, 'Optimal Pay Regulation for Too-big-to-fail Banks' (2018) 33 *Journal of Financial Intermediation* 83, 85.

112 Harris et al., 'How Do Bonus Cap and Clawback Affect Risk and Effort Choice? Insight from a Lab Experiment' (n 107) 3.

113 John Thanassoulis and Misa Tanaka, 'Optimal Pay Regulation for Too-big-to-fail Banks' (n 111) 93.

114 Kleymenova and Tuna, 'Regulation of Compensation and Systemic Risk: Evidence from the UK' (n 96) 1161.

norms as well as collective mindsets and attitudes.[115] Although other regulatory measures and policies may aim to reframe these factors, remuneration regulation inherently lacks this capacity as it only tries to frame prudential and responsibility goals into the existing cultural system without changing its fundamental settings, the nature of which is still interest alignment. Rigid and demanding regulatory rules add more conditions for executives to realise their interests in remuneration; accordingly, the efforts to improve prudential risk-taking and sound risk management are encrypted in executives' economic calculation of self-interest.

4.55 In terms of the driver of executives' irresponsible and reckless behaviours, an alternative narrative to shareholder value maximisation is the well-known 'managerial power approach' which argues that executives have incentives to control the pay-setting process and manipulate performance outcomes to pursue self-interest more efficiently.[116] In other words, executives attempt to achieve the same level of self-interest at lower effort, regardless of whether doing so is at the expense of others' interests. Remuneration regulation imposed on financial institutions focuses mainly on how to align executives' interests with broader economic and societal interests, instead of solely with shareholder interest. However, it has been taken for granted that the 'alignment' is robust and reliable. If under the traditional remuneration model executives can scarify shareholder interest for self-interest, under the regulated model they can still scarify the economic and societal interests of others for the same purpose. In particular, since performance assessment has become harsher and more complex, more effort is required if executives want to maintain their remuneration as before. The relative costs of other approaches to achieving the same outcomes become lower. In this sense, moving to other markets or industries or requiring a larger remuneration package is a more economically efficient option for executives.

E. THE ESG TREND IN EXECUTIVE REMUNERATION

4.56 There have been increasing calls for businesses, especially large corporations, to behave responsibly in order to support the sustainable development of human

115 European Central Bank, 'Draft Guide on Governance and Risk Culture' (2024) 2 https://www.bankingsupervision.europa.eu/legalframework/publiccons/pdf/ssm.pubcon202407_draftguide.lv.pdf.

116 The 'managerial power approach' is established in Bebchuk and Fried, *Pay without Performance: The Unfulfilled Promise of Executive Compensation* (n 10).

society.[117] In recent years, national authorities have doubled down in this regard: one channel targets directly corporations to push forward its business model transitions and corporate governance reforms; the other channel targets indirectly corporations' financiers, namely sustainable finance. Financial institutions are the targets in both channels. Their own business models and corporate governance systems are the key determinants of their investment strategies and activities, which then are determinative of the way they mobilise money in the social economy.

The EU and the UK are leading the trend towards establishing a regulatory framework for sustainable finance. In the past few years, the two jurisdictions have introduced the Sustainable Finance Disclosure Regulation[118] and the Sustainability Disclosure Requirements[119] respectively, both of which stipulate the responsibility of financial institutions to make disclosures about their sustainable financial products and activities. In 2019, the PRA issued its Supervisory Statement on 'Enhancing Banks' and Insurers' Approaches to Managing the Financial Risks from Climate Change',[120] which requires banks and insurance companies to integrate climate risks into their risk management systems. Accordingly, under the current remuneration regulation, financial institutions need to give necessary considerations to climate risks when designing remuneration incentives. **4.57**

The EU and the UK have also been ambitious to cultivate sustainability-oriented corporate cultures through regulations. Mandatory disclosures are still a primary tool: since 2023, large and listed companies in the EU have been required to report comprehensively on sustainability issues in compliance with the Corporate Sustainability Reporting Directive; in the UK, recommendations of the Task Force on Climate-related Financial Disclosure (TCFD) have been implemented as mandatory requirements for large companies;[121] the UK authority has also been working on an overarching framework of Sustainability Reporting Standards to keep pace with the standards of the International Sustainability Standards Board. On the one hand, information **4.58**

117 Christopher M. Bruner, 'Corporate Governance Reform and the Sustainability Imperative' (2022) 131(4) *Yale Law Journal* 1217, 1221.

118 Regulation (EU) 2019/2088 of the European Parliament and of the Council of 27 November 2019 on sustainability-related disclosures in the financial services sector, OJ L 317, 9.12.2019, p. 1–16.

119 FCA, 'Sustainability Disclosure Requirements (SDR) and Investment Labels' PS23/16 (2023) https://www.fca.org.uk/publication/policy/ps23-16.pdf.

120 PRA, 'Enhancing Banks' and Insurers' Approaches to Managing the Financial Risks from Climate Change' SS3/19 (2019) https://www.bankofengland.co.uk/-/media/boe/files/prudential-regulation/supervisory-statement/2019/ss319.

121 The FCA has also updated its handbook accordingly, see *FCA Handbook*, ESG.2.

is at the core of sustainable finance; these mandatory corporate disclosures on sustainability are aimed at providing financial institutions with more extensive and comparable information to reorient their investment strategies.[122] On the other hand, disclosures are also expected to play a transformative role:[123] the enhanced transparency of corporate activities and the consequential reallocation of finance pressure companies to formulate sustainability strategies and practices,[124] which then gradually institutionalise sustainability norms in corporate governance.

4.59 These intensive regulatory initiatives apply widely to businesses and financial market players, with the purpose of driving the systematic transformation towards sustainability. To a large extent, the systematic transformation still counts on behavioural changes in corporate decision-making and governance. Undoubtedly, the potential of executive remuneration in driving behavioural changes has been increasingly endorsed. The UN Principles of Responsible Investment is a leading advocate for the integration of ESG factors in executive remuneration.[125] Both the EU Shareholder Rights Directive II and the UK Corporate Governance Code require executive remuneration to be aligned with corporate sustainability.[126] In a recent discussion paper, the FCA emphasised that remuneration incentives should be linked to a firm's sustainability commitments; it is also considering setting regulatory expectations or guidance on firm-level behavioural changes and cultural shifts.[127] As a matter of fact, institutional investors are currently the main force pushing forward the use of ESG incentives in their portfolio companies.[128]

---

122 Sebastian Steuer et al., 'The Role of Disclosure in Green Finance' (2022) 8(1) *Journal of Financial Regulation* 1, 1.

123 Julia Black, 'Reconceiving Financial Markets – From the Economic to the Social' (2013) 13(2) *Journal of Corporate Law Studies* 401, 409.

124 Shane Leong and James Hazelton, 'Under What Conditions is Mandatory Disclosure Most Likely to Cause Organisational Change?' (2019) 32(3) *Accounting, Auditing & Accountability Journal* 811, 813; David Hess, 'Social Reporting and New Governance Regulation: The Prospects of Achieving Corporate Accountability Through Transparency' (2007) 17(3) *Business Ethics Quarterly* 453, 468.

125 UN Principles of Responsible Investment, 'ESG-linked Pay: Recommendations for Investors' (17 June 2021) https://www.unpri.org/executive-pay/esg-linked-pay-recommendations-for-investors/7864.article.

126 Directive (EU) 2017/828 of the European Parliament and the Council of 17 May 2017 amending Directive 2007/36/EC as regards the encouragement of long-term shareholder engagement, OJ L 132, 20.5.2017, p. 1–25, art. 29; Financial Reporting Council, Corporate Governance Code 2024, Principle P.

127 FCA, 'Finance for Positive Sustainable Change: Governance, Incentives and Competence in Regulated Firms' DP23/1 (2023) https://www.fca.org.uk/publications/discussion-papers/dp23-1-finance-positive-sustainable-change.

128 Joe Marsh, 'ESG-Linked Pay: Investors Push for More Robust Targets' *Capitalmonitor* (26 April 2022) https://www.capitalmonitor.ai/analysis/esg-linked-pay-investors-push-for-targets/; pwc, 'ESG-driven Remuneration: Enhancing Sustainability in the Asset and Wealth Management Industry' (2024) https://www.pwc.com/sg/en/publications/assets/page/esg-driven-remuneration.pdf.

Embedding ESG factors into executive remuneration has become a market-wide trend. Either due to the motivation for better sustainable performance or pressure from investors, peers and the public, large financial institutions have been actively taking on board the idea of ESG-based remuneration. For instance, all British banks in FTSE 350 have attached a substantial portion of variable remuneration to ESG performance.[129] 4.60

Despite the widespread embrace of ESG-based remuneration, its rationale and purpose are unexplored. Investors' sustainability considerations may be motivated by different purposes. Sustainable investments following a financial logic still aim at returns maximisation, for which sustainability issues that may undermine the value of underlying assets are integrated into investing decisions from a risk adjustment perspective. Alternatively, sustainable investments following a common good logic aim at social or environmental welfare enhancement, for which financial returns can be sacrificed.[130] ESG-based remuneration serving different purposes will be arranged differently. 4.61

Remuneration regulation has directed executive remuneration in financial institutions away from a pure shareholder value approach. Nevertheless, the main purpose of regulated remuneration is limited to financial stability. In a broader sense, financial stability is also a sustainability goal. Nevertheless, the top concerns the government hopes to address through sustainable finance such as climate change are mostly non-financial. Financial stability and other major sustainability goals may converge in some situations while conflicting in others. 4.62

In principle, sustainability risks which may evolve into firm-level or system-wide financial risks should be integrated into performance assessment. However, existing arrangements for long-term incentives and risk adjustment may not be practicable. One conundrum is how to ascertain the performance assessment period. For many sustainability risks, the time horizons of risk materialisation are much longer than the horizons of conventional business cycles and risk management.[131] As is widely known, the materialisation of a 4.63

---

129 Longjie Lu, 'ESG-based Remuneration in the Wave of Sustainability' (2023) 23(1) *Journal of Corporate Law Studies* 297. The appendix to this article provides hand-collected data of ESG-based remuneration in FTSE 350 companies in the year of 2022.

130 Shipeng Yan et al., 'The Rise of Socially Responsible Investment Funds: The Paradoxical Role of the Financial Logic' (2019) 64(2) *Administrative Science Quarterly* 466, 466; Paul Brest et al., 'How Investors Can (and Can't) Create Social Value' 44 (2018) *Journal of Corporation Law* 205, 208.

131 Hugues Chenet, 'Climate Change and Financial Risk' in Constantin Zopounidis et al. (eds), *Financial Risk Management and Modeling* (Springer 2021) 402.

climate risk may take decades. Under the current remuneration regulation, the longest scenario of performance assessment is 22 years, including 5 years of an LTIP, 7 years of deferral and malus, and 10 years of clawback. However, this scenario will not be the usual case in reality because: (1) five-year LTIPs are uncommon; (2) clawback will only be extended to 10 years in exceptional circumstances; (3) the strictest requirements of deferral, malus and clawback only apply to a portion of the variable remuneration of a very small number of top executives who are identified as HPMRTs. Given that the existing regulatory requirements have already provoked backlash, regulatory mandates to further tighten these requirements will unlikely be effective. Given the time dimension, matching remuneration incentives with the measurement of long-term sustainability risks is therefore hard to achieve. For a sustainability risk which may materialise in a nearer period, it is still difficult to ascertain whether the institution's exposure to this risk was due to a decision of its executives. Unlike traditional financial risks or systemic risks which are endogenous, some sustainability challenges, such as climate change and zoonotic diseases, are intersystemic, which means that their effects cascade across various systems.[132] For a financial institution, the causes of these risk exposures are exogenous factors, its connection with which may be weak, indirect or unidentifiable. However, to reasonably apply malus and clawback, there needs to be a solid ground that executives are accountable for pre-defined triggering events.

4.64 Alternatively, sustainability can be aligned with remuneration incentives by using ESG targets and metrics. This is exactly the most common approach adopted by companies in practice. The use of ESG targets and metrics can be justified from either a financial logic or a common good logic – the principal difference in the setting of targets and metrics is whether they should be financially material. For financial institutions, under the existing regulation, which follows a financial stability logic, ESG targets and metrics are justified only if they are instrumental for financial stability; as mentioned above, the FCA has emphasised the use of non-financial metrics which are relevant to effective risk management. Differently, if an institution's financial activities are to serve the common good on a concessive basis, ESG targets and metrics should be reflective of the goals of social or environmental welfare. However, here comes the dilemma for both institutions and regulators. Whenever there is a trade-off between financial stability and other sustainability goals, the current remuneration regulation impedes the integration of other goals into

132 Veerle Heyvaert, 'Governing Intersystemic Systemic Risks: Lessons from Covid and Climate Change' (2022) 85(4) *Modern Law Review* 938, 945.

remuneration incentives. Even if the pursuit of a sustainability goal is uncorrelated to financial stability, it is still uncertain whether the current regulation allows such an arrangement which is irrelevant to its stated purpose. Undoubtedly, the financial regulator can simply extend the regulatory purpose of executive remuneration to other sustainability goals, which, however, will trap financial institutions in a dilemma where they cannot fully achieve either financial stability or other sustainability goals.

In addition, designing reliable ESG targets and metrics and correctly measuring the actual performance are challenging. An increasing number of corporate governance studies have pointed out the main obstacles,[133] which can boil down to three aspects. First, it is common for a sustainability issue to be qualitative and multi-faceted in nature, whereas a quantified and simplified metric may be a biased indicator. Second, due to the absence of uniform ESG standards, companies usually adopt self-defined and self-measured targets and metrics and provide vague calibrations and interpretations, in which context external investors and stakeholders are unable to assess their reliability and the authenticity of relevant performance outcomes. Third, as mentioned, there are trade-offs between sustainability goals and financial goals as well as between different sustainability goals; a diverse range of conflicting targets and metrics may confuse executives and lead to distorted decision-making. **4.65**

With these realistic difficulties, the idea of harnessing remuneration incentives to spur managerial behavioural changes in decision-making and daily governance and thereby foster the systematic transformation towards a sustainable culture remains unfeasible at this moment. Even if regulators and financial markets are able to create reliable ESG targets and metrics and precisely assess the long-term impact of sustainability risks, the problem discussed in Section D that contemporary executive remuneration is a product of the culture of calculation and self-interest in financial markets remains. In addition to financial performance and prudential risk-taking, incorporating more sustainability goals into executive remuneration will make the conditions for remuneration rewards more demanding; as a result, executives have more incentives to choose other approaches to realise the same level of self-interest. **4.66**

---

133 Lucian A. Bebchuk and Roberto Tallarita, 'The Perils and Questionable Promise of ESG-Based Compensation' (2022) 48(1) The Journal of Corporation Law 38; Lu, 'ESG-based Remuneration in the Wave of Sustainability' (n 129); Marco Dell'Erba and Suren Gomtsyan, 'Regulatory and Investor Demands to Use ESG Performance Metrics in Executive Compensation: Right Instrument, Wrong Method' (2024) Journal of Corporate Law Studies https://www-tandfonline-com.eux.idm.oclc.org/doi/full/10.1080/14735970.2024.2350139.

This argument is supported by ample evidence that in practice, companies adopt undemanding or symbolic sustainability targets which enable executives to unduly extract self-interest without meaningful contributions to sustainability. To illustrate, some companies define mandatory regulatory obligations such as TCFD-based disclosures as performance targets; others may pay their executives for setting up a sustainability goal, which is procedural, rather than achieving it, which is substantive; in the absence of standardisation, companies largely use self-defined metrics and subjective assessments, which are prone to manipulation and hard to verify.[134] In a situation where ESG-based remuneration is distorted, it will counterproductively reinforce executives' calculative and self-interest mindsets as opposed to the desire for a more responsible corporate culture.

F. CONCLUSION

4.67 Executive remuneration is the primary incentive mechanism by which a company can align executives' personal economic interests with the interests it pursues. An effective remuneration system provides executives with strong motivations to deliver the best performance. Along with the evolutionary understanding of whose interests companies should care about and what constitutes 'best performance', the role of executive remuneration is in a transitional process from a corporate governance tool for shareholder value maximisation to a quasi-regulatory mechanism for achieving broader economic and societal goals.

4.68 The transition first started in the financial sector, which was impelled by the mandatory regulation of executive remuneration in financial institutions. By redefining 'best performance' as prudential risk-taking and sound risk management, financial regulators hoped to harness remuneration arrangements to drive behavioural changes in firm-level decision-making and eventually nurture a culture of responsibility in the financial system.

4.69 Remuneration regulation focuses on changing the interests that are aligned with executive remuneration. However, what has been ignored is how to establish and maintain a robust and reliable alignment, which is an insurmountable problem in contemporary executive remuneration. When others' interests are defined as performance targets for remuneration purposes, they are brought into executives' calculation of self-interest maximisation. Executives will

134 Lu, 'ESG-based Remuneration in the Wave of Sustainability' (n 129) 319–26.

only pursue the designated performance targets when it is the only available way or the cheapest way for them to maximise remuneration. The observable unintended consequences of remuneration regulation, such as increased total remuneration, reduced pay-to-performance sensitivity and higher CEO turnover, all demonstrate that in reality there are alternative and cheaper ways for executives to attain the same outcomes. Although remuneration has the potential to orient executives' behaviours, it is also true that executives can often exert influence on remuneration practices in their favour. Any regulatory intervention in remuneration that ignores and fails to restrict their influence may become unavailing.

Essentially, since executive remuneration is a product of the culture of calculation and self-interest, which has inherent conflicts with the culture of responsibility that regulators are trying to foster, its role in driving behavioural changes and cultural shifts is limited to the extent that the efforts required for behavioural changes will not impede executives from maximising their remuneration. However, it does not mean that executives only care about remuneration. They may be motivated by other factors to make socially desirable changes, including but not limited to values, experience, reputation and the influence of social and cultural norms. That is, remuneration itself may not be a powerful tool for cultural shifts; nevertheless, when cultural shifts are driven through other mechanisms, remuneration can be an accelerator. This is because executives will not count the efforts to make behavioural changes towards the costs of maximising their remuneration. **4.70**

This conclusion has implications for the increasingly prevalent practice of ESG-based remuneration and regulators' intention to mandate it. Currently, incorporating sustainability goals in executive remuneration means that executives will need to make more efforts to achieve the same level of remuneration, which will further lower the relative costs of shifting to 'other methods'. Moreover, many ESG factors are qualitative, unmeasurable and multi-faceted, without uniform definitions or standardised metrics; all these realistic problems stimulate executives to circumvent the additional sustainability requirements imposed on their remuneration packages and even create new opportunities for rent extraction from their companies. Therefore, regulators should be very cautious about the possible ineffectiveness or counterproductive **4.71** effects of ESG-based remuneration. To push forward the systematic transformation towards sustainable finance and corporate governance, regulators will have to apply a variety of mechanisms, among which executive remuneration, if the aforementioned problems can be overcome in the future, may serve as a supplement.

5

THE IRISH INDIVIDUAL ACCOUNTABILITY REGIME AND CULTURAL CHANGE

Blanaid Clarke

A. INTRODUCTION

The stimulus for Ireland's new individual accountability regime was a review undertaken by the regulator, the Central Bank of Ireland ('CBI'), into cultures and behaviours in the then five main retail banks in Ireland.[1][2] This review was ordered by the Minister for Finance in 2017 amid public outcry at the perceived failure of these banks to redress the wrongs inflicted on thousands of their customers who had been incorrectly denied a tracker mortgage product or put on an incorrect rate.[3] The review was undertaken with the assistance of the Dutch Central Bank, De Nederlandsche Bank, and utilised its behaviour 5.1

1 All weblinks were last accessed on 25 December 2024.

2 These were AIB Group, Bank of Ireland Group, Permanent TSB, Ulster Bank Ireland and KBC Bank Ireland.

3 Derville Rowland, 'Learning to Lead: Cultural Change, Ethical Behaviour and Consumer Protection' (19 October 2018) speech at the Institute of Banking https://www.centralbank.ie/news/article/learning-to-lead-cultural-change-ethical-behaviour-and-consumer-protection The CBI's Tracker Mortgage Examination commenced in December 2015 and required all lenders to review their loan book to ensure compliance with regulatory and contractual requirements in relation to tracker mortgages.

and culture methodology. It focused primarily on the five banks' executive leadership groups because of their importance in driving effective customer-focused cultures. In 2018, the CBI published a report, *Behaviour and Culture of the Irish Retail Banks,* setting out the outcome of its review, explaining the risks associated with poor cultures and behaviours and identifying the actions needed to ensure that customer interests would be prioritised in the future.[4] The report explained that effective culture is essential both because of the 'central role that the financial sector plays in the modern economy, supporting growth, employment and future prosperity' and because it is essential to 'the sustainability of financial services firms themselves, with growing evidence that the lack of a consumer-focused culture in firms erodes competitiveness and damages their long-term prospects'.[5] The CBI emphasised that regulators cannot prescribe culture for individual banks as this was a matter for the institutions themselves, but it noted that as the regulator, it was responsible for monitoring, assessing and influencing culture within firms 'in order to guard against conduct risk and drive better outcomes for consumers'.[6] The then Governor stated that the CBI shared the view of other regulators 'that culture could not be changed simply by introducing rules alone' and that 'there had to be a clear onus on senior management of firms to take responsibility for and drive cultural change from within'.[7] Somewhat ironically, he then proceeded to announce rules to ensure that senior management took this responsibility.

5.2 One of the key recommendations in the aforementioned report was that the CBI be given statutory power to introduce an enhanced Individual Accountability Framework ('IAF') applicable to banks and other regulated financial services providers. Such a framework should include: Conduct Standards; a Senior Executive Accountability Regime ('SEAR'); enhancements to the CBI's Fitness and Probity ('F&P') Regime; and a unified enforcement process[8] to apply to all contraventions by firms or individuals of financial services legislation. This chapter will focus on the first two aspects of the IAF. The Government accepted the CBI's recommendation, and following a rather lengthy drafting

4 Central Bank of Ireland, 'Behaviour and Culture of the Irish Retail Banks' (2018) www.centralbank.ie/docs/default-source/publications/corporate-reports/behaviour-and-culture-of-the-irish-retail-banks.pdf?sfvrsn=2.

5 Ibid 12, citing De Nederlandsche Bank 'Supervision of Behaviour and Culture: Foundations, Practice and Future Developments' (2015).

6 Ibid 13.

7 Ibid 10.

8 This included the removal of a 'participation link' under which individuals could be sanctioned only if the CBI had first proven that their firm had committed a breach and that the individual had participated in this breach.

process,[9] the Central Bank (Individual Accountability Framework) Act 2023 (the IAF Act) was signed into law on 9 March 2023. The IAF Act is supported by regulations including the Central Bank (Supervision and Enforcement) Act 2013 (Section 48(1)) (Senior Executive Accountability Regime)) Regulations 2024 ('SEAR Regulations')[10] and *Guidance on the Individual Accountability Framework*[11] ('IAF Guidance') issued by the CBI. The latter was produced following an extensive consultation[12] and, together with speeches and presentations from CBI representatives, it provides a window into the CBI's regulatory vision for effective culture in financial services firms. The CBI's proposed approach to the implementation of the IAF is described therein as 'founded in proportionality, predictability and reasonable expectations'.[13]

The IAF introduces two duties of responsibility imposing individual accountability on specified persons, one in the context of SEAR and one in the context of the Conduct Standards. Sections B and C of this chapter describe the key features of each regime, before the nature of the two duties is explored in Section D. These duties require individuals to take 'reasonable steps' and thus a clear and consistent understanding by both the regulator and the regulated as to what might be considered reasonable in the circumstances is essential. Sections E and F explore two of the main concerns identified in relation to the operation of the IAF: the potential contradiction between individual accountability and collective decision-making; and the application of SEAR to all non-executive directors. 5.3

9 See further Blanaid Clarke, 'Senior Executive Accountability and Responsibility in Financial Institutions' (2021) 66 *Irish Jurist* 74.

10 The Central Bank (Supervision and Enforcement) Act 2013 (Section 48(1)) (Senior Executive Accountability Regime)) Regulations 2024 (S.I. No. 147/2024. See also Central Bank Reform Act 2010 (Section 21(6)) Regulations 2024 (S.I. No. 2/2024); Central Bank Reform Act 2010 (Sections 20 and 22 Holding Companies) Regulations 2023 (S.I. No. 664/2023); and Central Bank Reform Act 2010 (Sections 20 and 22) Regulations 2011 (S.I. No. 437/2011) as amended.

11 Central Bank of Ireland, 'Guidance on the Individual Accountability Framework' (April 2024) https://www.centralbank.ie/docs/default-source/publications/consultation-papers/cp153/appendix-2-to-the-feedback-statement-to-cp153-guidance-on-the-iaf.pdf?sfvrsn=5fdf9d1d_5.

12 Central Bank of Ireland, 'Consultation Paper: Enhanced governance, performance and accountability in financial services (CP153) and Feedback Statement to CP153' https://www.centralbank.ie/publication/consultation-papers/consultation-paper-detail/cp153-enhanced-governance-performance-and-accountability-in-financial-services-regulation-and-guidance-under-the-central-bank.

13 IAF Guidance, para 1.12.

B. SEAR

5.4 Whereas the Conduct Standards and the enhancements to the F&P regime were introduced at the end of 2023 in respect of all regulated entities, SEAR has been introduced on a phased basis. It currently applies to: credit institutions (excluding credit unions); insurance undertakings (excluding reinsurance undertakings, captive (re)insurance undertakings and Insurance Special Purpose Vehicles); investment firms which underwrite on a firm commitment basis and/or deal on own account and/or are authorised to hold client monies/assets; and third country branches of the above. SEAR is based on the Senior Managers and Certification Regime ('SMCR') which itself was introduced in 2016 upon the recommendation of the UK's Parliamentary Commission on Banking Standards ('PCBS') which examined professional standards and culture in the UK banking sector in the wake of the LIBOR scandal.

1. Statements of Responsibilities

5.5 The PCBS recommended that all key responsibilities within a bank should be assigned to specific senior individuals and recorded in personalised statements.[14] By signing off on these statements, individuals would acknowledge their accountability for the functions and responsibilities set out therein. The granular governance details provided by this statement also allow 'a more targeted assessment' of the suitability of prospective and incumbent directors by allowing their competence and proposed time commitment to be measured against their allocated responsibilities.[15] Under SEAR, in-scope firms are required to prepare and maintain an up-to-date Statement of Responsibilities in respect of every person holding a prescribed Pre-Approval Controlled function ('PCF').[16] This should list their 'inherent responsibilities' and 'allocated responsibilities' (including both 'prescribed responsibilities' and 'other responsibilities') in a single document.[17] This allows all key conduct and prudential risks to be assigned to accountable individuals, thus reducing the possibility of gaps in the framework of overall responsibility. The PCFs include executive

---

14 PCBS, 'Changing Banking for Good' (2013) HL Paper 27-II, HC 175-II Vol II 83. www.parliament.uk/globalassets/documents/banking-commission/banking-final-report-vol-ii.pdf.

15 Prudential Regulation Authority, 'Supervisory Statement SS28/15: Strengthening individual accountability in banking' (December 2021) 16 https://www.bankofengland.co.uk/-/media/boe/files/prudential-regulation/supervisory-statement/2021/ss2815-december-2021.pdf.

16 Central Bank Reform Act 2010 (Sections 20 and 22) Regulations 2011 S.I. No. 437/2011 as amended most recently by the Central Bank Reform Act 2010 (Sections 20 and 22) (Amendment) Regulations 2023 S.I. No. 663/2023.

17 SEAR Regulations, reg 10(1).

and non-executive directors ('NEDs'),[18] executives reporting directly to the board and heads of critical business areas, all of whom are also subject to the CBI's F&P Regime.

PCF holders have 'inherent responsibilities' related to aspects of a firm's affairs set out in the Schedule to the SEAR Regulations and linked to the various PCFs.[19] For executive directors (PCF1s), this refers to 'directing the business of the firm and for NEDs (PCF2s) this refers to 'overseeing and monitoring the strategy and management of the firm'. Although executive directors possess management responsibilities, it is submitted that their role on the board also requires them to exercise an oversight and monitoring role and that this responsibility should be ascribed to executive directors too.[20] The Chairs of the board and the audit, risk, remuneration and nomination committees possess additional specified inherent responsibilities to chair meetings and to lead and oversee the performance of their board or committee. The CEO's inherent responsibility is 'overall responsibility for managing and steering the business activities of the firm'. **5.6**

A 'prescribed responsibility' is one prescribed by the CBI and listed in Schedule 2 of the SEAR Regulations, which a firm must allocate to a PCF holder, and these include both general and sector or circumstance specific responsibilities.[21] In the application of proportionality, 12 prescribed responsibilities are listed for low-impact investment firms, 13 for third country branches and 34 for all other firms. An important Prescribed Responsibility (PR1) is responsibility for the firm's performance of its obligations under SEAR. This applies to all firms and third country branches. The CBI has indicated that a Prescribed Responsibility should be allocated to 'the most senior individual, with the appropriate authority, responsible for that area taking into account the governance structures of the firm'.[22] While the PCF role holder is ultimately responsible for that role, the tasks required to discharge that responsibility may **5.7**

18 As discussed below, the CBI announced a delay in applying SEAR in respect of non-executive functions until 1 July 2025. Non-executive directors were however required to be listed in Management Responsibilities Maps from 1 July 2024.

19 SEAR Regulations, reg 4.

20 Macey describes how the dual role of directors creates a fundamental, inescapable conflict for directors who as monitors 'inevitably are required to monitor themselves'. Jonathan R Macey, *Corporate Governance: Promises Kept, Promises Broken* (Princeton University Press 2008) 54.

21 SEAR Regulations, reg 6(1). An exception is made for a low-impact investment firm or a third country branch (reg 6(2)). Prescribed responsibilities are allocated in accordance with reg 6(2), (4) or (6) as applicable.

22 IAF Guidance, para 2.4.10.

be delegated to staff once the delegation is appropriately arranged, managed and monitored.[23]

5.8 Relevant Prescribed Responsibilities must be allocated in full to a PCF role holder, with the exception of job sharing[24] and PCF roles consisting of more than one distinct business line.[25] It is also the case, of course, that by their nature certain PCF responsibilities may be held by different persons, such as PCF1 and PCF2A. The CBI has indicated that in such cases 'each individual would be holding a distinct role', with the scope of their responsibilities clearly defined in their Statement of Responsibilities and set out on the Management Responsibilities Map.[26] The third category of 'other responsibilities' refers to other material functions, business areas or projects not otherwise captured which the firm considers should be identified, allocated and listed on the Statements of Responsibilities to ensure that the firm's key risks are appropriately allocated to PCF role holders.[27]

5.9 Keller and Kokkinis identify as a common ground in the organisational culture literature 'the crucial role that leadership plays in shaping culture, promulgating values and goals, setting incentives, and providing examples of appropriate behaviour'.[28] Two key Prescribed Responsibilities with a specific focus on culture are PR4,[29] 'Responsibility for leading the development of the firm's culture, including on matters relating to diversity and inclusion, by the Board', and PR5, 'Responsibility for overseeing the adoption of the firm's culture, including on matters relating to diversity and inclusion, in the day to-day operation of the firm'. Although PR4 applies to all firms, PR5 does not apply to low-impact investment firms. An earlier draft of PR5 referred to 'adopting' the firm's culture rather than 'overseeing the adoption', and the amendment was made in response to valid criticism that adoption of a firm's culture in day-to-day operations is a responsibility of all staff and could not be allocated

---

23 See further IAF Guidance, ch 3.

24 Job-sharing is defined as 'an employment arrangement where two people are employed on a part-time or reduced-time basis to perform a job normally fulfilled by one person'. Each individual is considered fully accountable for all the responsibilities inherent in the PCF and responsibilities are required to be allocated jointly to all the individuals holding that PCF role (IAF Guidance Para 2.3.2).

25 IAF Guidance, para 2.3.2.

26 IAF Guidance, para 2.3.4.

27 Sear Regulations, reg 8.

28 Anat Keller and Andreas Kokkinis, 'The Senior Managers and Certification Regime in Financial Firms: An Organisational Culture Analysis' (2022) 22 *Journal of Corporate Law Studies* 299, 307.

29 An earlier draft of PR4 in the draft regulations circulated with CP153 (https://www.centralbank.ie/docs/default-source/publications/consultation-papers/cp153/annex-1-to-the-consultation-paper-153-draft-regulations.pdf?sfvrsn=502a991d_4) referred to culture and stated 'including conduct, by the Board as a whole including effectively managing any conflicts of interest in relation to consumer protection risk'.

to one individual.[30] PR4 is described as a non-executive responsibility[31] and, because of the leadership role, is likely to be assigned to the Chair.

2. Management Responsibilities Map

Each in-scope firm is required to prepare and maintain an up-to-date Management Responsibilities Map describing its management and governance arrangements in respect of each of its activities, business areas and management functions.[32] The map should provide a clear picture across an entire organisation as to how risks are being managed within that organisation and what further controls might be needed. The SEAR Regulations set out specific information which should be described, including: a description of each aspect of the firm's activities, business areas and management functions; how each aspect operates within the overall business of the firm and their reporting lines and lines of responsibility, including how decision making and governance operates; matters reserved for the board and how its subcommittees, and other senior level committees, contribute to board decisions; where CF1s[33] are identified in the map, information on their employment status in the firm or their status with or in relation to the firm and any responsibilities they may have in relation to other group entities; and each PCF holder's inherent responsibility, allocated responsibilities and reporting lines.[34] An organisational chart should also set out the group structure and arrangements.[35] **5.10**

When firms are seeking authorisation, they will be required to submit these maps to the CBI, and this will demonstrate at a glance that all the key responsibilities are being looked after by competent persons. This will make it clear to both the individuals themselves and the CBI which responsibilities are tasked to which individuals. Apart from that, the maps need only be available to the CBI on request. The Financial Services Union had suggested that in the interests of transparency, these maps should be shared with consumers, staff and regulators, suggesting the failure was 'a huge shortcoming in the regulations' which could lead to a disjointed approach and understanding **5.11**

30 Banking and Payments Federation of Ireland, 'Response to CP153' (13 June 2023) https://www.centralbank.ie/docs/default-source/publications/consultation-papers/cp153/banking-payments-federation-ireland-response-to-cp153.pdf?sfvrsn=e92a9d1d_2.

31 IAF Guidance para 2.4.10 Table 1.

32 Sear Regulations, reg 7(1) and 7(2).

33 CF1s are other individuals who may exercise significant influence on the conduct of a firm's affairs within the meaning of Schedule 1 to the Central Bank Reform Act, 2010 (Sections 20 and 22) Regulations, 2011 as amended.

34 Sear Regulations, reg 7(3).

35 Sear Regulations, reg 7(3)(c).

across the sector.[36] While this may be a valid argument, there are likely to be commercial and competitive sensitivities involved in the public disclosure of this information.

5.12 Firms in scope for SEAR will already be complying with one aspect of Directive 2024/1619 (CRD VI) which will introduce the concept of individual statements of all roles and duties and maps of duties across all Member States.[37] The former involves an up-to-date statement of the individual roles and duties of all members of the management body in its management function. The map of duties, which must also be kept up to date, includes details of the reporting lines, the lines of responsibility and the persons who are part of the governance arrangements of the institution, as well as their duties. Member States have been given the discretion to adopt or maintain stricter requirements for such tools.

C. CONDUCT STANDARDS

5.13 The IAF Act introduced a single set of standards of behaviour which apply to relevant individuals in all regulated firms.[38] These comprise Common Conduct Standards[39] which apply to all persons who perform a controlled function ('CF') and Additional Conduct Standards[40] for PCF role holders and CF1s. Section 53E of the Central Bank Reform Act 2010 ('the 2010 Act') as amended by the IAF Act lists the following basic standards of good behaviour: acting with honesty and integrity; acting with due skill, care and diligence; cooperating in good faith and without delay with the CBI and authorities in other jurisdictions performing comparable functions; acting in the best interest of customers and treating them fairly and professionally; and operating in compliance with standards of market conduct and trading venue rules and market codes. It sets out a non-exhaustive list of standards of behaviour under

36 Financial Services Union, 'Response to CP153' https://www.centralbank.ie/docs/default-source/publications/consultation-papers/cp153/financial-services-union-response-to-cp153.pdf?sfvrsn=902b9d1d_2.

37 Directive (EU) 2024/1619 of the European Parliament and of the Council of 31 May 2024 amending Directive 2013/36/EU as regards supervisory powers, sanctions, third-country branches, and environmental, social and governance risks, OJ L 2024/1619 (19.6.2024). Art. 1(29)(b) introduces a new art. 88(3) Directive 2013/36/EU of the European Parliament and of the Council of 26 June 2013 on access to the activity of credit institutions and the prudential supervision of credit institutions and investment firms, amending Directive 2002/87/EC and repealing Directives 2006/48/EC and 2006/49/EC, OJ L 176, 27.6.2013, p. 338–436.

38 Section 17A of the 2010 Act as amended by SEAR also introduces Business Standards for RFSPs.

39 2010 Act as amended, s 53E.

40 2010 Act as amended, s 53F.

each of these Standards. For example, acting with due skill, care and diligence includes monitoring the performance of any delegated tasks and ensuring that those tasks are appropriately performed.[41]

The CBI declined to provide specific guidance on each of the aforementioned listed behaviours on the basis they are 'generally self-explanatory and should be readily understood by those to whom they apply'.[42] It is submitted that, as the responses indicated, this is not always the case. For example, a question was raised about the lawfulness of assessing directors' conduct by reference to 'an ill-defined "consumer interest" test' on the basis that this might 'cut across the "bedrock principle" of "shareholder value" to which directors are subject pursuant to their statutory duties under the Companies Act'.[43] The example given related to a delay by a financial service provider to pass on a cost decrease to customers where 'that decision may enhance the business and improve shareholder value' but may not be consistent with 'an executive's new consumer interest obligation'. While section 228(1)(a) of the Companies Act 2014 requires directors to act in good faith in what they believe to be 'in the interests of the company', in interpreting this duty regard must be had to the corresponding common law rules and equitable principles.[44] Traditionally, the common law fiduciary duty to act in the interest of the company as a whole was interpreted as acting in the interests of the 'shareholders as a whole',[45] which included both current and future shareholders taking into account the long-term and short-term interests of the company.[46] This might be seen thus as a version of 'enlightened shareholder value'[47] which would allow a focus on customers only where this would be in the long-term interest of the shareholders. Quinn has opined that '[t]here is nothing in section 228(1)(a) which requires a shareholder value approach other than the courts' interpretation of this phrase' and he makes a strong argument that equating the interests of the company with the shareholders' interests is both legally flawed and is 'an 5.14

41 The IAF Guidance para 3.12.3 notes that doing this includes ensuring that delegates were made aware of the culture and the values of the firm.

42 IAF Guidance, para 5.1.4.

43 Law Society of Ireland, 'Submission on the Individual Accountability Framework (CP153)' (June 2023) https://www.centralbank.ie/docs/default-source/publications/consultation-papers/cp153/law-society-of-ireland-response-to-cp153.pdf?sfvrsn=432b9d1d_2.

44 Companies Act 2014, s 227(4).

45 *G&S Doherty Ltd v Doherty* [1969] High Court (Henchy J, 19 June 1969).

46 *Gaiman v National Association of Mental Health* [1971] Ch 317. See Brian Hutchinson, *Keane on Company Law* (5th edn Bloomsbury 2016) 427.

47 This term was coined by The Company Law Review Steering Group, *Modern Company Law for a Competitive Economy: The Strategic Framework* (Dept. of Trade and Industry 1999).

inferior approach when it comes to promoting company success'.[48] That said, until the Irish Courts provide guidance on this point, the steps expected of directors in managing a potential conflict remain uncertain.

5.15 The Additional Conduct Standards are: (a) 'that the business of the regulated financial service provider is controlled effectively'; (b) 'that the business of the regulated financial service provider is conducted in accordance with its obligations under financial services legislation'; (c) 'that any delegated tasks are assigned to an appropriate person with effective oversight' and (d) 'that any information of which the [CBI] would reasonably expect notice in respect of the business of the regulated financial service provider is disclosed promptly and appropriately to the [CBI] including information relevant to, or giving rise to a suspicion or expectation of, any of [a list of specified activities]'. The latter activities include the commission of an offence or a prescribed contravention or any other breach of obligations under financial services legislation by the regulated financial service provider or a person performing a CF in relation to it.

5.16 The CBI provides useful guidance on the distinction between executive directors and NEDs in the context of these Additional Conduct Standards.[49] It recognises that NEDs 'individually do not manage a firm's business in the same way as executive directors' and that the responsibilities for which they are accountable 'are more limited, relating to their role in respect of governance, oversight and challenge' and they are 'not expected to assume executive responsibilities'.[50] The standards thus to be met by these individuals in their role as NEDs and INEDs 'will relate purely to their non-executive, oversight functions and will be limited to what should reasonably be expected of individuals in that context'.[51] In the context of the aforementioned Standard that the business is 'controlled effectively', the CBI provides advice which repeats standard best practice in terms of the challenge expected from NEDS. It advises that directors and other PCF role holders 'in attending and contributing at meetings at which collective decisions are made, should ensure they have sufficient information and understanding of the matter(s) at hand to participate effectively in the collective decision making, commensurate with the

48 John Quinn, 'The Duty to Act in the Interests of the Company: Simply a Duty to Increase Shareholder Wealth?' UCD Working Papers in Law, Criminology & Socio-Legal Studies Research Paper No. 07/2015 14 http://dx.doi.org/10.2139/ssrn.2625982.

49 The same guidance is provided in relation to the duty of responsibility in section 53B(2) at para 2.8.7 of the IAF Guidance.

50 IAF Guidance, para 6.1.3.

51 Ibid.

parameters of their role including any broader responsibilities in the running of the business where relevant'.[52] This includes: taking steps to obtain sufficient information and understanding of the matters at hand and ensuring that they are 'appropriately informed, seeking further briefings and explanations to the extent necessary'; rationally challenging and debating the matters including reviewing any risks involved in the decision; and taking 'appropriate follow-up action where the outcome is not in the best interest of the firm and its related stakeholders, including its customers'.[53]

Given the wide range of individuals to whom the Common Conduct Standards apply, firms are advised to develop appropriate policies as to how the Standards will be 'incorporated into the firm's culture in order to drive the right behaviours and standards'.[54] The SEAR Regulations introduce a general Prescribed Responsibility which applies to all firms and third country branches (PR3), which is responsible for embedding the Conduct Standards throughout the firm. Firms are required to consider how failure to meet these Standards could be linked to performance reviews and promotions as a means of ensuring they are 'meaningfully embedded in the culture of the firm'.[55] The Financial Services Bar Association suggested that the term 'embedding' is too vague and imprecise to form the basis for a prescribed responsibility which could lead to enforcement or disciplinary action and that the guidance above does not provide the required clarity as it contains 'multiple layers of subjectivity'.[56] Firms' senior management and PR3 holders for firms in scope of SEAR must oversee and challenge firms' review of their control framework and their policies, incorporating the Conduct Standards into the firm's culture.[57] The firm itself is described in the IAF Guidance as playing a critical role in integrating the Conduct Standards in its culture for all individuals, including via notifying and the provision of training to individuals performing CF roles.[58] It must also establish, maintain and give effect to policies on how the Common Conduct Standards are integrated into the culture and conduct of the affairs of the firm.[59] **5.17**

52 IAF Guidance, para 6.2.2.

53 Ibid.

54 Para 4.34.

55 Para 4.35.

56 Financial Services Bar Association, 'Submission of the Financial Services Bar Association in response to CP153' 8 https://www.centralbank.ie/docs/default-source/publications/consultation-papers/cp153/financial-services-bar-association-response-to-cp153.pdf?sfvrsn=ba2b9d1d_2.

57 IAF Guidance para 4.36.

58 IAF Guidance para 4.26.

59 Ibid.

5.18 While the CBI acknowledges a conceptual overlap between its F&P Standards[60] and the Common Conduct Standards, it has pointed to their disparate purposes.[61] The former seek to set the standard that staff in CF roles must meet to ensure that 'they are sufficiently skilled and have the requisite integrity to be trusted in their roles'.[62] By contrast, the Conduct Standards govern the conduct of persons in CF roles, 'imposing positive, enforceable legal obligations' on them 'to act in accordance with a single set of standards of expected behaviour'.[63] While it may be that some minor breaches of Conduct Standards might not necessarily signify a failure to meet the F&P Standards, firms will have to make this assessment based on the particular facts and circumstances.

D. STATUTORY DUTIES OF RESPONSIBILITY

5.19 Section 53B(2) of the 2010 Act as amended by the IAF Act introduces a statutory duty of responsibility.[64] It provides that

> [a] person who has inherent or allocated responsibility for an aspect of the affairs of a regulated financial service provider shall take any steps that it is reasonable in the circumstances for the person to take to secure that, while the person has that responsibility, the aspect of the affairs of the regulated financial service provider is conducted so as to avoid contravention by it of its obligations under financial services legislation.

5.20 Avoiding contravention has been stated to include avoiding continuation of a contravention.[65]

5.21 A related duty set out in section 53C of the 2010 Act as amended is the statutory duty to take reasonable steps to meet Conduct Standards. The duty applies to all RFSPs and not just firms within-scope of SEAR. It provides:

> 1. A person who performs a [CF] in relation to a [RFSP] shall take any steps that it is reasonable in the circumstances for the person to take to ensure that the [Common Conduct Standards] are met.

---

60 Central Bank of Ireland, Fitness and Probity Standards (Code issued under Section 50 of the Central Bank Reform Act 2010) (December 2023) https://www.centralbank.ie/docs/default-source/regulation/how-we-regulate/fitness-probity/regulated-financial-service-providers/fitness-and-probity-standards.pdf?sfvrsn=b764da1d_6.

61 IAF Guidance paras 4.12 and 4.13.

62 Para 4.14.

63 Para 4.15.

64 This duty is similar to that imposed by section 66A(5) and 66B(5) of the Financial Services and Markets Act 2000.

65 2010 Act as amended, s 53B(3).

2. A person who performs a PCF in relation to a [RFSP] or any [CF1 holder] shall take any steps that it is reasonable in the circumstances for the person to take to ensure that [Additional Conduct Standards] are met.

1. Reasonable Steps

Section 53D of the 2010 Act as amended sets out a non-exhaustive list of the circumstances considered to be relevant for purposes of both sections 53B(2) and 53C(1) and (2). These are: the nature of the firm's business, including its scale and complexity; the functions of the person in relation to the firm and 'the level of knowledge and experience that a person with such functions could reasonably be expected to have'; the level of knowledge and experience of the person; the existence and application of 'appropriate and effective systems (including risk management systems, internal control mechanisms and governance arrangements)', 'effective oversight of any delegation of responsibilities and effective safeguards against any inappropriate delegation' and 'appropriate and effective procedures for identifying and remedying problems'; the extent to which these matters were within the person's control or influence; and in the case of section 53C, the CBI's guidelines on the Conduct Standards. 5.22

The CBI has emphasised that in implementing the duties, proportionality, predictability and reasonable expectations would be the foundations of its approach. Thus, individuals taking on senior or different roles for the first time will, 'subject to certain minimum expectations as to competence and capability', be recognised to be 'on a learning curve'.[66] Recognising that errors can occur, it has provided the important assurance that 'perfection is not the required standard'.[67] It has also confirmed that standards will not be applied 'retrospectively or with the benefit of hindsight'.[68] It noted that the concept of reasonable steps should be embedded already in CF role holders' day-to-day actions in managing their areas of responsibility.[69] While this is true in many cases, the potential breadth and scope of some of the Standards may test their understanding. One particular Common Conduct Standard often cited in this regard is the requirement to have 'appropriate knowledge of the legal and regulatory framework, including any legal obligation or standard imposed on the regulated financial services provider relevant to the controlled 5.23

66 IAF Guidance, para 3.10.2.
67 Para 3.5.
68 Ibid.
69 IAF Guidance, para 3.5.

function'.[70] A similarly broad-ranging Additional Conduct Standards relates to ensuring that firm's business is conducted 'in accordance with its obligations under financial services legislation'.[71] This has been explained in terms of 'ensuring the operational effectiveness of related systems and controls' rather than putting in place those systems or controls, unless that is within their role and responsibilities.[72] Individuals should ensure that 'compliance with relevant regulatory requirements is appropriately monitored and that all staff are aware of and understand the need for compliance' and that they themselves 'should promote the embedding of a culture of compliance, by visibly leading by example and setting a tone that supports and encourages the compliance of those in the relevant area'.[73] Meeting the requirement to identify, never mind understand, a complex, extensive and undefined 'legal and regulatory framework' or 'financial services legislation' will be a challenge. The Law Society, commenting on the lack of a definitive list of prescribed contraventions and rules violations which amount to sanctionable breaches, made the cogent observation that this lack of clarity 'makes it close to impossible to ensure compliance' and 'undermines legal certainty in a manner that is unfair to those affected, creating greater jeopardy for executives'.[74] Keller and Kokkinis have expressed concern that an overly draconian enforcement of an individual accountability regime might instil a 'fear-based' culture where employees are afraid to raise concerns or admit mistakes and their employers signal a low tolerance for such errors, encouraging concealment rather than reporting.[75] This problem could be exacerbated by an extensive and potentially unclear list of contraventions. Another Common Conduct Standard likely to prove difficult is the meaning of 'best interests of customers'[76] in certain grey areas such as a decision to delay passing on an interest rate reduction. The Financial Services Bar Association has asked that the CBI 'discuss and reflect this with reference to practical decisions and actions and discuss the tension between the best interests of a customer and the interests of a firm and the balancing which is required'.[77]

---

70 2010 Act as amended, s 53E(1)(b)(ii).

71 2010 Act as amended, s 53F(b).

72 IAF Guidance, para 6.3.2.

73 IAF Guidance, para 6.3.2.

74 In the context of such uncertainty, it also noted that the difficulty of compliance is compounded by the fact prescribed contraventions expressly include: an attempt to commit a prescribed contravention; aiding, abetting, procuring, inducing or attempting to induce, or conspiring to commit a contravention; and failure to report information giving rise to a suspicion of a prescribed contravention.

75 Anat Keller and Andreas Kokkinis, 'The Senior Managers and Certification Regime in Financial Firms: An Organisational Culture Analysis' (n 28) 321–322.

76 2010 Act as amended, s 53E(1)(d).

77 The Financial Services Bar Association, 'Submission of the Financial Services Bar Association in response to CP153' (n 55). See also the response of Financial Services Ireland: Financial Services Ireland, 'Re:

With overlapping responsibilities, it is possible that more than one PCF role holder will have contravened the section 53B duty 'where each of them fails to take reasonable steps to avoid the firm contravening its obligations in relation to that aspect'.[78] In such circumstances, the CBI has stated it will consider whether it is appropriate to take enforcement action 'against one, some or all such individuals', but it does not explain what criteria it will use in making this decision.[79] While one may assume that any person not found to have taken the necessary reasonable steps will be sanctioned, the principle of proportionality may suggest otherwise. Interestingly, the Law Society questions whether 'this ambiguity could seriously prejudice executives' rights of defence where the Central Bank uses leniency enticements to pit executives at different levels of the organisation, perhaps with overlapping liabilities, against each other'.[80] This would constitute a classic prisoner's dilemma. 5.24

Finally, it should be noted that there will be an increased emphasis on being able to prove that reasonable steps were taken and retaining records by way of evidence. The CBI noted that during its consultation exercise, the potential impact on the dynamic at the board or other key meetings was raised by certain respondents 'whereby minutes become very detailed in order to document the various exchanges that occurred rather than to capture key discussions and decisions'.[81] The CBI promised to consider this matter as part of its proposed three-year post implementation review.[82] One respondent suggested that demonstrating an individual's performance of reasonable steps would be easier for individuals with agreed Statements of Responsibility and suggested that individuals performing CFs should have such Statements, giving them 'the same level of comfort as PCF holders in assessing whether they are adequately discharging their obligations'.[83] 5.25

Consultation Paper on the Individual Accountability Framework' (13 June 2023) https://www.centralbank.ie/docs/default-source/publications/consultation-papers/cp153/financial-services-ireland-response-to-cp153.pdf?sfvrsn=af2b9d1d_2.

78 IAF Guidance, para 2.8.10.

79 Ibid para 2.8.11.

80 Law Society of Ireland, 'Submission on the Individual Accountability Framework (CP153)' (n 43).

81 Central Bank of Ireland, Feedback Statement: Enhanced governance, performance and accountability in financial services (CP153)' (November 2023) 22 https://www.centralbank.ie/docs/default-source/publications/consultation-papers/cp153/feedback-statement-to-cp153.pdf.

82 Ibid 24.

83 The Association for Financial Markets in Europe, 'Consultation Response' (13 June 2023) https://www.centralbank.ie/docs/default-source/publications/consultation-papers/cp153/association-for-financial-markets-in-europe-response-to-cp153.pdf?sfvrsn=822a9d1d_2.

2. Enforcement

5.26 The reporting obligations of regulated financial services firms and individuals is an area where additional clarity would be welcome. A number of respondents queried what disciplinary action taken by firms needs to be reported to the CBI and the manner in which breaches of duties or Conduct Standards should be reported and by whom.[84] There were also calls for more detailed guidance on the types of scenarios in which the CBI would expect an individual to make a report in respect of some of the very broadly drafted Conduct Standards. For example, one of the Additional Conduct Standards provides that 'any information of which the Bank would reasonably expect notice in respect of the business of the regulated financial service provider' should be reported promptly to the CBI.[85] The CBI's guidance that individuals '[b]y virtue of their position' are expected to 'have the expertise to recognise when this is something which the [CBI] would reasonably expect notice of'[86] will not always be sufficient or helpful. A similarly broad reporting requirement is introduced by section 38(2) of the Central Bank (Supervision and Enforcement) Act 2013 which requires PCFs to report information relating to, inter alia, 'prescribed contraventions' that may have been/are being committed, where the PCF believes that the information will be of material assistance to the CBI. Although the CBI does not provide a definitive list of such contraventions, a breach of the Common Conduct Standards and/or Additional Conduct Standards is expressly stated to be such a 'prescribed contravention' thus giving rise to a reporting requirement. Further guidance would help individuals understand what exactly is expected of them and would help avoid over- or under-reporting. The former, it has been pointed out, could expose the reporter to an action by their employer for breach of confidence or defamation and could raise questions as to breaches of GDPR.[87]

5.27 Despite describing its approach to the enforcement of the IAF as based upon principles of proportionality, predictability and reasonable expectations, there is a level of apprehension amongst some market participants as to the manner in which the IAR will be applied and enforced. During the consultation exercise, for example, the Institute of Directors made the stark statement that,

84 Central Bank of Ireland, 'Feedback Statement: Enhanced governance, performance and accountability in financial services (CP153)' (n 81) 8.

85 2010 Act, s 53F(d).

86 IAF Guidance para 111.

87 Mason Hayes & Curran, 'Response to Central Bank of Ireland Consultation Paper 153 on Individual Accountability Framework' (13 June 2023) https://www.centralbank.ie/docs/default-source/publications/consultation-papers/cp153/mason-hayes-curran-response-to-cp153.pdf?sfvrsn=b4349d1d_2.

based on its member research, 'there appears, as things stand, to be quite a low level of confidence within the financial services sector for certain of the CBI supervisory processes', citing PCF approval since the introduction of the F&P Regime. It opined that the CBI is 'considered by many to be unapproachable', which 'has not engendered confidence amongst industry participants that the IAF will be proportionate, fair, and sufficiently transparent.' This seems a harsh indictment, and not one that was one generally reflected in the other responses. What was a common statement, however, was the importance of having clarity on this approach, and in particular how the principle of proportionality would be applied in the implementation of the framework.[88] Respondents encouraged increased transparency by the CBI in order to build confidence and trust in the new framework, described as 'essential to its success'.[89] The decision of the Irish Financial Services Appeals Tribunal ('FSAT') in *AB v Central Bank of Ireland* will not have been encouraging in this regard. The FSAT, an independent body established to determine appeals from aggrieved parties, determined that a decision by the CBI that an individual was unfit to be a non-executive Chair of an authorised investment fund was flawed.[90] It determined that the individual was 'denied fair procedures at each stage of the process'. The CBI responded swiftly and well to this decision; it established an independent review of the F&P regime by Andrea Enria, the former Chair of the Supervisory Board of the European Central Bank, and it subsequently agreed to implement all the recommendations set out in the resulting report.[91]

The Law Society has expressed concern at the possibility of 'inequality of arms' in the context of the CBI's strong negotiating power in enforcement actions, pointing to the fact that it is empowered 'to make, interpret and enforce the rules'.[92] This argument is likely of course to be more persuasive in the case of small firms and individuals meeting their own legal expenses than for large financial services groups or individuals with legal or financial support from their associated firms. The Law Society also noted in this context that all the fines imposed by the CBI to date have stemmed from settlements. It identified the potential for unlawful 'conviction by settlement' in the absence of a public 5.28

88 Central Bank of Ireland, 'Feedback Statement: Enhanced governance, performance and accountability in financial services (CP153)' (n 80) 12.

89 Ibid.

90 Financial Services Appeals Tribunal (IFSAT), *AB v Central Bank of Ireland* (31 January 2024) https://ifsat.fusio.dev/app/uploads/2024/05/AB-v-The-Central-Bank-of-Ireland-Decision_15-03-24.pdf.

91 Andrea Enria, 'Fitness and Probity Review' (July 2024) Central Bank of Ireland 22 https://www.centralbank.ie/docs/default-source/regulation/how-we-regulate/fitness-probity/communications-publications/fitness-and-probity-review-by-andrea-enria.pdf?sfvrsn=ab7c611a_9.

92 Law Society of Ireland, 'Submission on the Individual Accountability Framework (CP153)' (n 43) 2–3.

hearing and where employees may make self-accusatory statements or confess to wrongdoing which have not been formally adjudicated on by the CBI or by a court.[93] The constitutional rights of an individual to earn a livelihood and to have a good name are obviously key rights to protect in this respect. A related concern was the conflict of interest that might arise where individuals at different levels within an organisation might be potentially liable for the same wrongdoing, giving the example of a CEO and a Chief Information Officer in the context of a potential IT breach.[94] This might also give rise to 'complex legal questions regarding the reliability and use of leniency and whistle-blower testimony by one executive against another'.[95] Particular attention will need to be paid in these circumstances, by both the firms and the CBI, to procedural fairness and the individual's fundamental rights. As the Law Society noted, this is likely to include the provision by the firm of independent legal advice and support throughout the process.[96] While constitutional rights are not of course unqualified, the aforementioned Enria review emphasised that the F&P regime must strike a balance 'between the fundamental rights of an individual including the right to a good name and the right to earn a livelihood' and 'the statutory obligations and duties of the Central Bank to protect consumers and financial services'.[97] The same delicate balancing act will apply to the other components of the IAF.

E. COLLECTIVE RESPONSIBILITY

5.29 One of the most contentious issues in relation to the operation of individual accountability frameworks, and in particular to the assignment of individual responsibility to individual directors, is the extent to which they may be inconsistent with the practice of collective decision-making and the principle of collective responsibility. There is concern that separately accountable individuals with individual mandates set out in their personalised statements of responsibility may act differently to a balanced Board with collective responsibility.[98]

93 Ibid.
94 Ibid 3.
95 Ibid.
96 Ibid.
97 Andrea Enria, 'Fitness and Probity Review' (n 91) 22.
98 Insurance Ireland, 'Insurance Ireland Submission to the Central Bank of Ireland (CBI) Consultation on Enhanced Governance performance and accountability in financial services: Regulation and Guidance under the Central Bank (Individual Accountability Framework) Act 2023' (13 June 2023) 6 https://www.centralbank.ie/docs/default-source/publications/consultation-papers/cp153/insurance-ireland-response-to-cp153.pdf?sfvrsn=db2b9d1d_2.

5.30 Decisions made at directors' meetings must be decided by a majority of votes[99] and the resulting board decision is considered to be a 'collective decision' of the entire board and not a series of individual decisions. Although it is correct thus to say that the board as an entity made the decision and is responsible for it, this does not necessarily mean that either the board as an entity or the directors individually will be held liable for that decision.[100] Directors are liable for breaches of their own individual duties in contract, tort or statute where they arise, and their failures to meet the requisite duty may include their failure to act as part of the board in meeting the board's responsibilities. Elsewhere, the author has examined the extent to which the concept of collective responsibility has a place in the current Irish regulatory environment.[101] The approach of the Irish Courts is evident in *Tralee Beef and Lamb Limited (In Liquidation)*,[102] where the Irish High Court cited with approval the decision of the England Court of Appeal in *Re Westmid Packing Services Ltd, Secretary of State for Trade and Industry v Griffiths*. In the latter case, Lord Woolf MR stated: 'the collegiate or collective responsibility of the board of directors must [...] be based on individual responsibility. Each individual director owes duties to the company to inform himself about its affairs and to join with his co-directors in supervising and controlling them.'[103]

5.31 Similarly, the eight 'fiduciary' duties of directors set out in section 228(1) of the Companies Act 2014 are described as the duties of each director.[104] These include the duties to act honestly and responsibly in relation to the conduct of the company's affairs and to exercise a prescribed standard of care, skill and diligence. While a director's actions or omissions during a board meeting in exercising poor oversight could amount to a breach of these duties by that individual director, it is noteworthy that section 228 is not generally viewed as inconsistent with the collective responsibility of the board. Rather, each director is deemed to be individually responsible for their part in the

99 Companies Act 2014, s 160(2) provides: 'Questions arising at any such meeting [of directors] shall be decided by a majority of votes and where there is an equality of votes, the chairperson shall have a second or casting vote.'

100 A useful discussion of the meaning of these the terms 'responsible' and 'liable' is available at Alan Brener, 'Developing the Senior Managers Regime', in Constanza A Russo, Rosa Lastra and William Blair (eds), *Research Handbook on Law and Ethics in Banking and Finance* (Edward Elgar Publishing 2019) 277.

101 Blanaid Clarke, 'Senior Executive Accountability and Responsibility in Financial Institutions' (n 9) 74–100.

102 *Tralee Beef and Lamb Limited (In Liquidation)*, High Court, Finlay Geoghegan J, 20 July 2004 (Unreported).

103 *Re Westmid Packing Services Ltd* (No 3) [1998] 2 BCLC 646, 653.

104 Section 227(1) Companies Act 2014 states that 'the duties' are owed by a director to the company and the company alone. There is no such provision in the IAF Act although the CBI is responsible for enforcing the duty.

collective decision. The same approach would apply to the IAF's Conduct Standards. Belcher has described the collective responsibility of directors thus as 'operationalised only by converting it into an individual responsibility and liability'.[105] Similarly, in the context of the IAF regime, the CBI's Guidance explains that 'collective decision-making [...] is dependent on the contributions of individual members of senior management'.[106] (It is clear for example that the inherent responsibility of a non-executive director 'overseeing and monitoring the strategy and management of the firm' is the responsibility of each and every non-executive director.) Thus, enhancing individual accountability should result in better collective decision-making, leading to 'a heightened awareness on the part of individuals of their own increased accountability for the discharge of their function, including with respect to their participation in collective decision-making'.[107] The logical conclusion thus is: the better the individual components of the collective decision, because of this heightened awareness, the better that decision will be. Rather than being inconsistent with collective responsibility, thus, 'the IAF is designed to reinforce the concept of collective responsibility as a core aspect of well-functioning firms'.[108]

5.32 This focus on the individual components of a decision can be viewed through the prism of process accountability. A distinction is made in the literature on accountability systems between process accountability, where individuals are held accountable for 'their efforts to achieve outcomes [...] with minimal regard for the accuracy or quality of those outcomes', and outcome accountability, where they are held accountable for their 'effectiveness in actually delivering outcomes [...] with minimal regard for the processes utilized to arrive at these outcomes'.[109] It would seem that the duty set out in section 53C could be described as process accountability and a similar view might be taken of the duty set out in section 53B(2).[110] However, one might also consider that

---

105 Alice Belcher, 'Metaphysical Spookiness: The Collective Responsibility of Company Directors' (2012) 21 *Griffith Law Review* 609.

106 IAF Guidance para 2.9.1.

107 Ed Sibley, 'Governance and Risk in a Time of Uncertainty and Change' (17 February 2021) speech to the Institute of Directors https://www.centralbank.ie/news/article/speech-governance-risk-uncertainty-change-ed-sibley-17-Feb-21.

108 Central Bank of Ireland, 'Feedback Statement: Enhanced governance, performance and accountability in financial services (CP153)' (n 81) 13.

109 Shefali V Patil, Ferdinand Vieider, and Philip E Tetlock, 'Process Versus Outcome Accountability' in Mark Bovens, Robert E Goodin, and Thomas Schillemans (eds), *The Oxford Handbook of Public Accountability* (Oxford University Press 2014) 1–2. See also Wieke Scholten and Joe McGrath, J. (2025). 'The under-explored effects of increased accountability: a normative evaluation of the cultural impact and challenges of individual accountability regimes in finance'. *Journal of Corporate Law Studies*, 1–24.

110 This was the view put forward by Financial Services Ireland in its response to CP153 Financial Services Ireland, 'Re: Consultation Paper on the Individual Accountability Framework' (n 77) 3–4. 'Based on

because the duty in section 53B(2) is rooted in the avoidance of a contravention by the in-scope firm of its obligations under financial services legislation, it could constitute a hybrid system that leans in the direction of process accountability but blends features of outcome accountability as appropriate to each new context.[111] Patil, Vieider and Tetlock explain that process accountability 'mitigates evaluation apprehension by reassuring decision-makers that they will be "socially safe" as long as they deploy defensible procedures' and encourages decision-makers to focus their attention 'on "how" to make sound decisions'.[112] They note that this reassurance is especially important for decision-makers 'who believe they live in a world of irreducible uncertainty'.[113] This research emphasises the importance of regulated entities and persons being confident that the reasonable steps will be interpreted by the CBI in a proportionate and fair manner.[114]

During the consultation exercise, respondents questioned the impact that the increased focus on individual responsibility and the reporting requirements would have on collective responsibility and the manner in which boards interact in practice.[115] The CBI was asked to acknowledge in the IAF Guidance that Inherent and Prescribed Responsibilities held by directors are 'discharged on the basis of collective decision-making, consistent with the Companies Act and the relevant Corporate Governance Codes and guidelines'.[116] Collective decision-making cannot of course constitute an excuse to allow one director to excuse their failure to meet their own responsibilities. Each individual is fully accountable for all the responsibilities inherent in their role and the responsibilities of the role will be discharged where they can demonstrate that they took reasonable steps to discharge the responsibility. Keller and Kokkinis have **5.33**

---

academic input we have received, we believe that accountability in [the context of the IAF] should be informed by the process that leads to a decision, rather than the outcome (which would be in the realm of collective responsibility of the Board.'

111 Shefali V Patil, Ferdinand Vieider, and Philip E Tetlock, 'Process Versus Outcome Accountability' (n 109) 12.

112 Ibid 3. The authors cite Karen Siegel-Jacobs and J Frank Yates, 'Effects of Procedural and Outcome Accountability on Judgment Quality' (1996) 65 *Organizational Behavior and Human Decision Processes* 1–17.

113 Ibid 3. The authors cite Kenneth R Hammond, *Human Judgment and Social Policy: Irreducible Uncertainty, Inevitable Error, Unavoidable Injustice* (Oxford University Press 1995).

114 The Financial Services Ireland submission concluded on this point by stating correctly that clarification on this would help to ensure the regime is 'adopted correctly, and applicable in a practical sense': Financial Services Ireland, 'Re: Consultation Paper on the Individual Accountability Framework' (n 77) 1.

115 See for example Association for Financial Markets in Europe, 'Consultation Response' (13 June 2023) 5 (n 83).

116 The Chartered Governance Institute UK & Ireland, 'Consultation Response' (13 June 2023) 2. https://www.centralbank.ie/docs/default-source/publications/consultation-papers/cp153/chartered-governance-institute-uk-ireland-response-to-cp153.pdf?sfvrsn=3c2a9d1d_2.

explained how the ethos of collective responsibility is 'underpinned by the company law principle that all directors owe a duty of care to the company and the corporate governance principle that independent directors must contribute to strategic leadership'.[117] Indeed, pursuant to the Common Conduct Standards, directors' obligation to act with due skill, care and diligence expressly includes 'acting appropriately' in collective decision-making and ensuring decisions are properly informed and exercising sound judgement.[118] By making this explicit, it is the CBI's hope that the IAF will 'reinforce the concept of collective responsibility as a core aspect of a well-functioning firm' and assist boards and directors in their respective roles in the governance of firms.[119]

5.34 Having reflected on the feedback from its consultation process, the CBI decided to defer by 12 months until July 2025 the application of SEAR to NEDs in order to provide a 'learning/implementation period [to enable firms] to better manage the perceived issues identified in reconciling the collective responsibility of boards with the new individual accountability regime'.[120] It noted the importance of 'ensuring that the role of collective responsibility and decision-making remains central to firms' and avoiding this being negatively impacted 'as a result of an increased focus on individual responsibilities in the new framework'.[121] It also stated that this additional time would afford it time to manage any such issues if they did materialise.[122]

5.35 Finally, it should be noted that concerns about the practical effect of individual accountability on board decision making is not solely a parochial concern. In the consultation process which preceded CRD VI, one of the issues explored by the European Commission was the extent to which the collective functioning of the board might be affected by the introduction of a system where individuals have defined sets of responsibilities. Respondents were asked to consider the possible effects on both individual conduct and the impact on the board's collective responsibility or the quality of its discussions.[123] The Banking & Payments Federation Ireland, the representative group for the

---

117 Anat Keller and Andreas Kokkinis, 'Consultation Response to Senior Managers & Certification Regime: A Call for Evidence' (31 May 2023) 8.

118 2010 Act as amended, s 53E(1)(b)(vi).

119 Central Bank of Ireland, 'Feedback Statement: Enhanced governance, performance and accountability in financial services (CP153)' (n 81) 23.

120 Ibid 6.

121 Ibid.

122 Ibid 23.

123 European Commission, 'Public Consultation Document Implementing the Final Basel III Reforms in the EU' (2019) https://finance.ec.europa.eu/system/files/2019-10/2019-basel-3-consultation-document_en.pdf.

banking and payments sector in Ireland, responded by acknowledging the potential for conflict between collective and individual responsibilities but emphasised the need for an individual accountability regime to recognise that 'once there is evidence of a clear and rational decision-making process, decisions made in this context can be reasonably and correctly made'.[124] Taking on board respondents' concerns, the requirement to introduce the statements and maps in Article 88(3) referred to above commences with the phrase 'Without prejudice to the overall collective responsibility of the management body'.

F. APPLICATION OF SEAR TO NON-EXECUTIVE DIRECTORS

One particularly controversial issue in relation to SEAR is the extent to which NEDs are included within scope.[125] They fall outside the individual accountability regime in Singapore but within the regimes in Hong Kong and Australia. In the UK, only the Chairman of the Board, the Audit Committee, the Risk Committee, the Remuneration Committee and the Senior Independent Director are within scope. The diversity of views across the sector is exemplified by the responses received by the CBI to the proposed inclusion of NEDS. Of the 19 respondents who provided detailed feedback on this issue, nine supported the approach, four noted some practical concerns and six were not supportive.[126] This indicates the need for further clarity and comfort on this issue in order to ensure industry-wide buy-in. 5.36

The arguments in favour of excluding NEDS from the scope of SEAR have been widely aired. The primary concern is that the application of the SEAR to NEDs would blur the distinction between executive and non-executive positions and involve NEDS in operational matters, rather than monitoring and strategy, which should be their primary focus. This involvement in day-to-day operational management might undermine their independence, a key part of their value to the firm. However, the CBI has described the responsibilities of NEDS as more limited and relating to their role in respect of governance, oversight and challenge without any expectation they assume executive responsibilities and it noted 'considerations in respect of reasonable steps will be limited to what should reasonably be expected of individuals in that 5.37

124 Banking & Payments Federation Ireland, 'BPFI Response to the European Union Public Consultation Document Implementing the Final Basel 3 Reforms in the EU' (December 2019) 17 https://bpfi.ie/wp-content/uploads/2021/02/BPFI_final_Response_EC_Basel3_.pdf.

125 As noted above, non-executive directors were not brought within scope in July 2025.

126 Central Bank of Ireland, 'Feedback Statement: Enhanced governance, performance and accountability in financial services (CP153)' (n 81) 21.

context'.[127] The list of non-executive prescribed responsibilities are framed in this way including PR4 referred to above.[128] Respondents generally seemed to welcome their inclusion where their responsibilities are in line with their oversight role. However, many of those who welcomed the inclusion of NEDs as appropriate sought further consideration and guidance in relation to the impact on collective responsibility. The Banking & Payments Federation for example described their inclusion as reasonable 'if applied proportionally, with collective decision making and separation of executive /nonexecutive powers clear'.[129] It might be argued that including only executive directors within SEAR might undermine the principle of collective responsibility, as all directors play a role in the decision. The Institute of Directors argued there was an inconsistency of understanding within the CBI and across the sector of what 'oversight' means in practice and an 'expectations gap' in respect of the proxies for NED effectiveness and contribution.[130] It suggested that these proxies are 'narrow and inaccurate', citing by way of example the 'level of detail (often managerial in nature) that management feel compelled to provide to boards and 'the CBI's emphasis on the level and depth of evidence of challenge in a set of board minutes'.[131]

5.38 It has been claimed that NEDs have limited influence and making them accountable is not appropriate. The UK's PCBS identified the options of a dissatisfied NED as being to 'make their point at board level, record dissent in the minutes, press their view to a formal vote, report their concerns to the regulator, or resign'.[132] This would appear to undervalue the role of the board as the key decision maker, discussed below. Although directors are likely to have delegated to executive managers, they must oversee the exercise of those delegated functions and actively participate in the board's decision-making process. A further concern is that the inclusion of NEDS may act as a disincentive to well-qualified individuals, reducing the potential calibre of the board and its diverse nature. The CBI's response on this point has been to acknowledge this risk but to note that its emphasis on proportionality, predictability and

127 IAF Guidance para 2.8.7.

128 IAF Guidance Table 1.

129 Banking & Payments Federation, 'Response to CP153' (13 June 2023) 20 https://www.centralbank.ie/docs/default-source/publications/consultation-papers/cp153/banking-payments-federation-ireland-response-to-cp153.pdf?sfvrsn=e92a9d1d_2.

130 Institute of Directors, 'Re: Consultation Paper 153 ("CP153")' (13 June 2023) 26 https://www.centralbank.ie/docs/default-source/publications/consultation-papers/cp153/institute-of-directors-in-ireland-response-to-cp153.pdf?sfvrsn=f62b9d1d_2.

131 Ibid 7. The Institute recommended further engagement with professional bodies such as itself to agree inter alia 'a common philosophy and understanding of the practical realities of being a [NED]'.

132 PCBS, 'Changing Banking for Good' (2013) HL Paper 27-II, HC 175-II Vol II 347.

reasonable expectations means that the framework is 'well designed, balanced, and unlikely to produce such effects'.[133] It also noted correctly that this 'chilling effect' has not been the experience in other jurisdictions but said that it will review this in its proposed three-year post implementation review.[134] A final concern to note related to the potential interaction between the responsibilities imposed under the IAF Regime and preexisting statutory duties. The CBI was asked to consider whether requiring independent NEDS to assume responsibilities prescribed by the CBI and the creation of 'corresponding direct personal exposure to the CBI is inappropriate and potentially inconsistent with their general duties under corporate law'. It was suggested that this could place directors in 'a position of conflict of duties' or even lead to a situation where on a day-to-day basis the director might perceive their 'responsibilities and exposures to the CBI as being more important than those owed to the company'.[135]

Notwithstanding the above, the decision to apply SEAR to NEDS was the correct one. First, excluding NEDS would have been inconsistent with the policy objectives of an individual accountability regime. The CBI opined that, having considered the concerns raised in the consultation process, it remained of the view that excluding NEDs from the framework 'would do a disservice to the significance of their role in the financial system'.[136] The Securities and Futures Commission in Hong Kong in justifying its inclusion of NEDS explained that the board is 'the ultimate decision-making body within the corporation' and all directors 'play an essential role in managing the licensed corporation's business and should therefore be regarded as part of senior management'.[137] In addition to monitoring, NEDs play a strategic advisory and leadership role and should be held responsible for the performance of these roles. Second, a distinction between the roles of executive and non-executive directors is not usually made in legislation. As noted above, section 228 of the Companies Act 2014 codifying directors' duties to the company makes no such distinction.[138] However, the duty of skill, care and diligence set out 5.39

133 Central Bank of Ireland, 'Feedback Statement: Enhanced governance, performance and accountability in financial services (CP153)' (n 81) 13.

134 Ibid.

135 Mason Hayes & Curran, 'Response to Central Bank of Ireland Consultation Paper 153 on Individual Accountability Framework' (n 87) 3.

136 Central Bank of Ireland, 'Feedback Statement: Enhanced governance, performance and accountability in financial services (CP153)' (n 81) 6.

137 Securities and Futures Commission, 'Measures for augmenting senior management accountability in licensed corporations' www.sfc.hk/en/faqs/intermediaries/licensing/Measures-for-augmenting-senior-management-accountability-in-licensed-corporations#CD0999C31D084FBAB2280D6DC5151C60.

138 This was a deliberate decision. See Company Law Review Group, *First Report 2000–2001* (2001) 242 https://www.clrg.org/media/ycilc5dz/1-clrg-first-report.pdf.

in section 228(1)(g) acknowledges that not all directors will possess the same knowledge and experience and the standard involves taking into account both '(i) the knowledge and experience that may reasonably be expected of a person in the same position as the director; and (ii) the knowledge and experience which the director has'. NEDs might thus expect to be evaluated against their peers and not the expectations of executive directors. This duty is based on certain common law rules and equitable principles[139] and the Irish Courts have had no difficulty applying these duties to NEDS as well as executive directors. In *Re Mitek Holdings Ltd; Grace v Kachkar*,[140] the Supreme Court explained that the nature and extent of directors' duties would be informed by the circumstances and that '[t]he [NED] will usually be dependent on the [executive director] for information about the affairs and of the finances of the company, a fact which will impose correspondingly larger duties on the [executive director]'. Finally, the exclusion of all NEDs from the application of SEAR would have involved a diminution in the current level of accountability. An administrative sanction prior to the IAF is instructive. In 2018, the CBI reached a settlement agreement with Mr Michael Walsh, former NED and Chairman of Irish Nationwide Building Society.[141] As part of the settlement, Mr Walsh admitted 'participating' in certain prescribed contraventions of financial services law and was fined €20,000 and given a three-year disqualification. The CBI noted that Mr Walsh was 'in a position to ensure that the Board received timely and relevant information from management and that the Board was addressing all relevant issues' and that while he had taken a variety of steps to address these issues, which had been flagged by various internal and external reports, he accepted responsibility as Chairman for the fact that these issues were not fully addressed.

G. CONCLUSION

5.40 The IAF is to be welcomed. It strengthens the accountability of senior executives and should encourage and facilitate good governance and positive culture within the relevant firms. This will come at a cost, as firms will need to devote resources to preparing statements of responsibilities and management responsibilities maps, renegotiating some employment contracts and monitoring conduct to ensure compliance with the F&P Regime and the Conduct Standards.

139 Section 227(4) Companies Act 2014.

140 *Re Mitek Holdings Ltd; Grace v Kachkar* [2010] I.R. 374.

141 'Settlement Agreement between the Central Bank of Ireland and Michael P. Walsh' (12 February 2018) www.centralbank.ie/news-media/legal-notices/enforcement-actions.

Particularly in the first couple of years, as evidenced in other jurisdictions, these costs are likely to be large. While it might be argued that firms will pass these compliance costs on to consumers, the market being oligopolistic, it is submitted that these costs should ultimately be outweighed by the benefits of the IAF to good governance, customer protection and financial stability more broadly.

The importance of clarity cannot be underestimated, both in terms of the responsibilities imposed by the IAF and the CBI's approach to enforcement. This will generate confidence and facilitate consistent and effective implementation. It is not surprising that many in the financial services industry have sought increasing levels of specificity, examples of good practice, case studies and scenarios particularly in the context of illustrating the 'reasonable steps' to be taken by individuals.[142] The Irish Banking Culture has recently introduced two case studies examining two Common Conduct standards with a view to providing further elucidation on how to gauge whether steps might be reasonable.[143] While the IAF Guidance is extremely useful and CBI staff regularly engage with stakeholders at industry and academic events, the challenge for individuals in seeking to ensure they have fulfilled their responsibilities and taken 'reasonable steps' can be great. This can be seen from the CBI's comment that while the IAF Guidance provides a non-exhaustive list of factors which we may take into consideration, these 'may not be relevant in every case and there may be other factors that are relevant'.[144] Of course, it is understandable too that the CBI is keen to ensure that 'there is the necessary flexibility to accommodate different governance structures, business models, and situations across firms'.[145] It is cautious that providing specific scenarios, roles and sectors could result in the Guidance becoming 'overly prescriptive' and a 'tick-box' exercise, which may diminish the ability of an individual, in their respective firms to fulfil their obligations'.[146] The CBI recognises that 'that regulatory expectations evolve'[147] and the guidance may in the future include 'further detail as to what constitutes reasonable steps and what 'good' looks like based on evidence and firm's experience of implementing the regime'. It seems thus 5.41

142 Central Bank of Ireland, 'Feedback Statement: Enhanced governance, performance and accountability in financial services (CP153)' (n 81) 30.

143 Irish Banking Culture Board, *IAF Case Study 1* (30 October 2024) https://www.irishbankingcultureboard.ie/publications/case-study-one-interest-rate-changes/ and *IAF Case Study 2* (30 October 2024) https://www.irishbankingcultureboard.ie/publications/case-study-two-ai-decision-making/.

144 Ibid 31.

145 Ibid 30.

146 Ibid 31.

147 Ibid 30.

that there is an opportunity for the CBI and industry to work together to ensure that as expectations develop and different scenarios emerge, regulated individuals are certain as to what they need to do to comply with the IAF Act. This could involve a type of IAF 'sandbox'.[148] This would not provide derogations or waivers from the IAF Act or the SEAR Regulations but would deliver 'deeper, clearer and more informed engagement'[149] and regulatory advice and support to firms and individuals. This would better inform the CBI's regulatory and enforcement approach and assist firms as they develop their own internal IAF programmes. The CBI has been keen to emphasise that the IAF is not just about enforcement and that it will support the existing supervisory relationship between the firms and the CBI by helping both parties understand how the firm is being run and how it is implementing its business model and managing its risks.[150] An IAF sandbox would provide an opportunity to do this.

148 This idea was presented by the author and Joe McGrath at the IBCB Behaviour and Culture Conference (17 October 2024) and is the subject of a working paper 'An Individual Accountability Sandbox' UCD Working Papers in Law, Criminology & Socio-Legal Studies Research Paper No. 01/2025, available at https://ssrn.com/abstract=5186507.

149 Central Bank of Ireland, 'Feedback Statement – Consultation Paper 156: Central Bank of Ireland approach to innovation engagement in financial services' (June 2024) https://www.centralbank.ie/docs/default-source/publications/consultation-papers/cp-156/cp156-central-bank-approach-to-innovation-engagement-in-financial-services.pdf?sfvrsn=fb359d1d_8.

150 Central Bank of Ireland, 'Feedback Statement: Enhanced governance, performance and accountability in financial services (CP153)' (n 81) 9.

6

PROFESSIONALISM, CORPORATE GOVERNANCE AND PURPOSEFUL CULTURE IN BANKING

Peter McCormack

A. INTRODUCTION

Professionalism is important for creating trust and is exhibited by the behaviour and conduct of the person providing the professional service and observed by the person receiving the service.[1] This professionalism (and the status that goes with it) has, for more than a century, increasingly been seen as underpinned by detailed educational requirements, such as in the legal profession and the accountancy profession, although for many years it was possible to learn these professions 'on the job' in the form of becoming an articled clerk.[2] 6.1

Banking has historically been learnt 'on the job', with early banking often being controlled and managed by families. Quaker families were particularly active in this field. Indeed, two of the United Kingdom's largest banks have 6.2

---

1 The views expressed in this chapter are the author's own and do not necessarily represent the views of the Chartered Banker Institute. All weblinks were last accessed 23 December 2024.

2 Edward Leslie Burgin, 'The Education and Training of the Solicitor's Articled Clerk' (1928) *Journal of the Society of Public Teachers of Law* 1; Mary E Murphy, 'Education and Training of English Accountants' (1938) (13)4 *The Accounting Review* 404–410.

Quaker foundations[3] – Barclays[4] and Lloyds Banking Group.[5] One can only surmise that their founders might not be that happy with the way they manage their customer relationships today.

6.3 In a recent line of attempts to get banks to support their customers, regulators have recently been focusing on 'purposeful culture'[6] and have supplemented their review of this area with a new consumer duty.[7] In addition to regulation and the role of the banks themselves, professional institutes have, and should have, a key role to play in supporting the development of purposeful cultures and restoring trust in the banking profession.[8]

6.4 The first Banking Institute was founded in London in 1851. Although it provided monthly meetings and was founded as an informal learning club, its failure to provide examinations, often seen as a hallmark of professionalism, was probably the cause of its demise in 1853.[9]

6.5 With the advent of the joint stock company,[10] and the increasing separation of owners and managers, recognition of the need for professional education increased. In 1875 the first professional institute for banking was founded as the Institute of Bankers in Scotland[11] (now the Chartered Banker Institute (CBI)),[12] with the English institute formed shortly after in 1879[13] (now the

---

3 Mike King, *Quakernomics: An Ethical Capitalism* (Anthem Press 2014).

4 Philip W Matthews and Anthony W Tuke, *History of Barclays Bank Limited* (Blades, East & Blades Ltd 1926).

5 Richard S Sayers, *Lloyds Bank in the History of English Banking* (Clarendon Press 1957).

6 Financial Conduct Authority, 'DP 20/1: Transforming culture in financial services – driving purposeful cultures' (2020) https://www.fca.org.uk/publications/discussion-papers/dp20-1-transforming-culture-financial-services-driving-purposeful-cultures.

7 Financial Conduct Authority, 'Policy Statement PS22/9: A new Consumer Duty, feedback to CP21/36 and final rules' (2022) https://www.fca.org.uk/publication/policy/ps22-9.pdf; FCA, *FCA Handbook* PRIN 2.1 Principle 12 https://www.handbook.fca.org.uk.

8 Peter McCormack and Jonathan Deacon, 'Can Trust Be Restored to High-Street Banking: A 20-Year Challenge?' (2017) 4(1) *Cogent Business & Management* 1366284 https://www.tandfonline.com/doi/full/10.1080/23311975.2017.1366284.

9 Edwin Green, *Debtors to Their Profession: A History of The Institute of Bankers 1879–1979* (Methuen & Co Ltd 1979) 25.

10 Lucy Ann Newton, 'Change and Continuity: The Development of Joint Stock Banking in the Early Nineteenth Century' (2007) University of Reading, Department of Economics https://www.researchgate.net/publication/24121111_Change_and_continuity_the_development_of_joint_stock_banking_in_the_early_nineteenth_century#:~:text=The%20article%20focuses%20on%20the%20bank%20notes%20that%20were%20issued.

11 Robert Noble Forbes, *The History of the Institute of Bankers in Scotland* (Institute of Bankers in Scotland 1975).

12 See Chartered Banker Institute https://www.charteredbanker.com.

13 Edwin Green, *Debtors to Their Profession: A History of The Institute of Bankers 1879–1979* (n 9).

London Institute of Banking and Finance (LIBF)).[14] These two institutes have taken different paths, with the LIBF having gone down the route of obtaining degree awarding powers and offering degrees and the CBI now the main provider of non-degree vocational education to the banking industry, although the CBI does support a Chartered Banker MBA via a partnership with Bangor University.[15]

The need for trained bankers was recognised in the 1840s[16] and although the first Institute did not focus on banking education, education was at the core of the Scottish Institute and the English Institute – and still is for both of the continuing bodies, the CBI and LIBF respectively. **6.6**

The Institute of Bankers in both countries has always been focused on providing banking education to those working in the commercial banking sector, that is, those banks supporting personal customers and small and medium-sized enterprises (SMEs). As noted, the English Institute diversified to cover wider financial services and became the Institute of Financial Services (IFS); latterly it has a focus on degree-awarding powers, offering a range of degrees under the LIBF banner. The CBI is the Institute with the main focus on vocational education. The focus of this chapter is on vocational education within the commercial banking sector. **6.7**

Restoring trust[17] is the challenge, with Edelman's 2023 Trust Barometer[18] noting the financial services sector as the second least trusted sector in the survey. A key component of restoring trust is establishing the right culture for commercial banking. This should be a purposeful culture that establishes/re-establishes the banker–customer relationship – a relationship of trust and confidence. Training has a key role to play here – ethical training to provide an underpinning for trust, and technical training to provide an underpinning for confidence. **6.8**

This chapter examines the role of history, structure, professionalism, corporate governance, demise of the branch and regulation in establishing a purposeful **6.9**

14 See London Institute of Banking and Finance https://www.libf.ac.uk/.

15 See Chartered Banker MBA at Bangor University https://www.bangor.ac.uk/courses/postgraduate-taught/mba-chartered-banker.

16 James W. Gilbart, 'Banking Profits and Expenditure' (1846) *Bankers Magazine* 27, cited in Edwin Green, *Debtors to Their Profession: A History of The Institute of Bankers 1879–1979* (n 9).

17 Peter McCormack and Jonathan Deacon, 'Can Trust Be Restored to High-Street Banking: A 20-Year Challenge?' (n 8) 6–8.

18 Edelman Smithfield, '2023 Edelman Trust Barometer' (2023) https://www.edelmansmithfield.com/2023-Edelman-Trust-Barometer-FS; 'In FS we (Mis)trust' (Spring 2023) *Chartered Banker Magazine* 32–34.

culture in banking. Understanding the history of the profession over the past 50 years, and that the provision of vocational education alone is unlikely to deliver better service to customers, may encourage policymakers and regulators to pay greater attention to issues that will boost the national economy and improve the well-being of citizens.

B. HISTORY

6.10 The educational reforms brought about in the late 19th century professionalised banking and contributed to the elevation of the banker to the position of 'pillar of the community' for much of the 20th century.[19] The banker was seen to be supporting the management of the financial affairs of both personal customers and SMEs in their community.

6.11 Although the head office of the bank was often in London, many of the banks operated regional head offices (supporting local branches) that maintained local expertise and a local feel. The vast majority of commercial bankers were not university educated and progressed in their role with on-the-job training and the support of professional training provided by their professional institutes.[20] In an era in which many employees stayed with one employer for most of their career, many commercial bankers became lifelong members of their professional Institutes, and guardians of the integrity of the profession.

6.12 Up until the 1960s banking had changed little, with the core financial instruments being the bill of exchange and the cheque (supported by underlying legislation[21]), and traditional activity that of deposits, current accounts, lending and taking security. The focus of banking regulation had been on regulating the instruments rather than the institutions, with the first piece of legislation regulating the institutions being the Banking Act 1979 – separating banks into Banks and Licenced Deposit Takers.[22] Banks also provided a range of ancillary services such as arranging insurance, arranging for the purchase, sale and safekeeping of securities, safety deposit facilities for key documents (e.g. insurance policies, share certificates and wills), and a range of trade services

---

19 Ian Peacock, *Bankers: From Pillars to Pariahs* (Novum Publishing 2018).

20 See Robert Noble Forbes, *The History of the Institute of Bankers in Scotland* (n 11) and Edwin Green, *Debtors to Their Profession: A History of The Institute of Bankers 1879–1979* (n 9).

21 The Bills of Exchange Act 1882 and the Cheques Act 1957.

22 T Peter Lee, 'Significant Development in the United Kingdom in 1979' (1979) 2 Journal of Comparative Corporate Law and Securities Regulation 335.

for their SME customers (e.g. foreign exchange, international trade finance, export guarantees).

However, the number of people with bank accounts in the first half of the 20th century was quite low, with many workers receiving weekly wages paid in cash. The banking industry was also paper-intensive, with customers receiving their paid cheques back with their statements, and, of course, having a bank account had a cost. Free banking was first introduced by Midland Bank plc in 1984.[23] **6.13**

From the late 1960s onwards, things began to change with the advent of computerisation,[24] an increased focus on profitability,[25] market reform, new financial instruments, credit scoring, increased quantification, competition, consolidation and increased regulation. **6.14**

The 1980s was a period of major change. In the early 1980s, the new Conservative government commissioned a review of financial services regulation that was reported in 1984 (the Gower review[26]) and led to the enactment of the Financial Services Act 1986. This introduced a system of regulation that segmented the financial services market to be regulated by Self-Regulating Organisations (SROs), for example for life assurance and unit trusts the Life Assurance and Unit Trust Regulatory Organisation (LAUTRO), and for investment management services the Investment Management Regulatory Organisation (IMRO) – all co-ordinated by an overarching Securities and Investment Board (SIB). The provision of banking services continued to be regulated by the Bank of England (BoE), albeit mainly with a prudential focus. **6.15**

The government at this time also decided to de-regulate the UK's financial markets, in a process that came to be known as the 'Big Bang'.[27] The 'Big Bang' occurred on 27 October 1986, and its major change, for the purposes of this chapter, is that it allowed high street banks to buy investment banks (e.g. Barclays acquiring deZoete and Bevan and Wedd Durlacher and creating Barclays DeZoete Wedd (BZW) – now Barclays Capital) and investment **6.16**

23 'Seismic Changes over Seven Decades' (Winter 2023) *Chartered Banker Magazine* 24–27.

24 Bernardo Bátiz-Lazo and Trevor Boyns, 'The Business and Financial History of Mechanisation and Technological Change in Twentieth-Century Banking' (2004) 14(3) *Accounting, Business & Financial History* 225.

25 Milton Friedman, *Capitalism and Freedom* (University of Chicago Press 1962); 'The Social Responsibility of Business is to Increase Its Profits' *New York Times Magazine* (13 September 1970) 122.

26 Department of Trade and Industry, *Review of Investor Protection* (Cmd 9125, 1984).

27 Iain Martin, *Crash Bang Wallop: The Inside Story of London's Big Bang and a Financial Revolution that Changed the World* (Hodder & Stoughton 2016).

banks to buy high street banks (e.g. JP Morgan acquiring Chase Manhattan). This process unwound a separation of investment banking and commercial banking that – even though the period was not without its problems[28] – had provided a degree of stability for some 50 years.

6.17 After a series of regulatory failures in the 1990s,[29] notably the Bank of Credit and Commerce International (BCCI) [30] and Barings,[31] and a series of customer mis-selling events, such as pension mis-selling[32] and endowment mortgage mis-selling,[33] the new Labour government, in 1997, decided to shake up regulation. In this shake up they made the BoE independent (but took banking supervision away from it) and created a new super regulator,[34] the Financial Services Authority (FSA). The FSA was established in 1998, got full powers in 2001 and took on the responsibility for supervising both the prudential and conduct aspects of banking, insurance and securities businesses.

6.18 In the early 1980s there was a very clear distinction between the business models of commercial banking and investment banking, each with a very distinct culture. These cultures, discussed later, were encapsulated in the terms '*banker–customer relationship*' for commercial banks[35] and '*my word is my bond*' for investment banks'.[36]

6.19 The two key distinctions in these two business models were (1) the level of information asymmetry and (2) the nature of the bank-customer relationships. The commercial banks in their branches provided banking services to their

28 Margaret Reid, *The Secondary Banking Crisis 1973–75: Its Causes and Course* (2nd edn, Hindsight Books 2003).

29 Thomas Charles Baxter Jr, 'Breaking the Billion Dollar Barrier – Learning the Lessons of BNL, Daiwa, Barings, and BCCI' (1997) 1(1) *Journal of Money Laundering Control* 15.

30 Lord Justice Bingham, 'Inquiry into the supervision of the Bank of Credit Commerce and International' (22 October 1992) https://assets.publishing.service.gov.uk/media/5a7c6dbbe5274a5590059cd3/0198.pdf; Mohammed B Hemraj, 'The Regulatory Failure: The Saga of BCCI' (2005) 8(4) Journal of Money Laundering Control 346.

31 Board of Banking Supervision, 'Report into the circumstances of the collapse of Barings' (18 July 1995) https://www.gov.uk/government/publications/report-into-the-collapse-of-barings-bank.

32 Julia Black and Richard Nobles, 'Personal Pensions Misselling: The Causes and Lessons of Regulatory Failure' (1998) 61(6) *Modern Law Review* 789.

33 Paul Farrow, 'Endowment Mis-Selling Is a National Scandal' *The Telegraph* (2 October 2002) http://www.telegraph.co.uk/finance/personalfinance/borrowing/mortgages/2828940/Endowment-mis-selling-is-a-national-scandal.html.

34 Clive Briault, 'The Rationale for a Single Financial Services Regulator' (1999) FSA Occasional Paper 2; 'Revisiting the Rationale for a Single Financial Services Regulator' (2002) FSA Occasional Paper 16.

35 Eliahu Peter Ellinger, 'The Bank as a Fiduciary and as a Constructive Trustee' (1994) 9 *Banking and Finance Law Review* 111.

36 'Lord Mayor Charles Bowman Launches "Business of Trust" Programme' *Newsroom City of London* (London, 15 November 2017).

local community, personal customers and SME businesses – often customers with a low level of financial/business knowledge and who often relied on their bank for both advice and business support. Investment banks on the other hand had knowledgeable counterparties, or customers with the ability to pay professionals (e.g. accountants and lawyers) for advice.

Post-Big Bang and during the 1990s much of the commercial banking sector shifted to a profit-maximising transactional approach which caused problems with customer service and led to a number of consumer mis-selling scandals, such as endowment mortgage mis-selling,[37]pensions mis-selling[38] and, more recently, payment protection mis-selling.[39] The FSA attempted to correct the customer service problem with its Treating Customer Fairly (TCF) programme, of which more later. **6.20**

The Great Financial Crisis (GFC) of 2007/9 seriously damaged the reputation of the banking industry, and led to numerous initiatives to try and fix it, such as the introduction of ring-fenced banking,[40] a Parliamentary Commission on Banking Standards (PCBS) – Changing Banking for Good,[41] the creation of a Banking Standards Board in 2015[42] and a number of regulatory initiatives to improve the reputation of the sector, such as the Senior Manager and Certification Regime (SMCR).[43] **6.21**

Following the 2010 UK election and the creation of a new coalition government, a decision was taken to completely change the regulatory architecture **6.22**

37 See Paul Farrow, 'Endowment Mis-Selling Is a National Scandal' (n 33).

38 See Julia Black and Richard Nobles, 'Personal Pensions Misselling: The Causes and Lessons of Regulatory Failure' (n 32).

39 Eilís Ferran, 'Regulatory Lessons from the Payment Protection Insurance Mis-selling Scandal in the UK' (2012) 13(2) *European Business Organization Law Review* 247.

40 Independent Commission on Banking, 'Final Report' (2011) https://webarchive.nationalarchives.gov.uk/ukgwa/20131003105424/https:/hmt-sanctions.s3.amazonaws.com/ICB final report/ICB%2520Final%2520Report%5B1%5D.pdf; Peter McCormack, 'Ring-Fenced Banking: Regulation and Practice' (2015) Dissertation, University of London https://sas-space.sas.ac.uk/6345/.

41 Parliamentary Commission on Banking Standards, 'Changing Banking for Good, Volume I: Summary and Conclusions and Recommendations' (2013) https://www.parliament.uk/globalassets/documents/banking-commission/banking-final-report-volume-i.pdf; 'Volume II: Chapters 1 to 11 and Annexes, together with formal minutes' (2013) https://www.parliament.uk/globalassets/documents/banking-commission/banking-final-report-vol-ii.pdf.

42 Banking Standards Board, 'Banking Standards Review' (2014) https://financialservicescultureboard.org.uk/pdf/banking-standards-review.pdf.

43 Anat Keller and Andreas Kokkinis, 'The Senior Managers and Certification Regime in Financial Firms: An Organisational Culture Analysis' (2022) 22(1) *Journal of Corporate Law Studies* 299.

again[44] – a so-called twin peaks approach[45] – which has now been in place since 1 April 2013. It is not clear that this architecture change delivers regulation more effectively or efficiently.[46] The new approach created a new subsidiary of the BoE, the Prudential Regulation Authority (PRA),[47] which has since been integrated into the BoE, with the old Financial Services Authority re-named the Financial Conduct Authority (FCA) and responsible for protecting the consumer.[48]

6.23 It is the FCA that took over responsibility for the FSA's TCF programme, and that is taking the lead on purposeful culture and consumer duty.

C. STRUCTURE

6.24 As noted, the 1980s was a period of substantial regulatory change, leading to changes in the way that financial services firms are structured and as a consequence changes in the culture of the organisations. It is arguable that some of these changes have contributed to some of the problems that regulators are trying to address today.

6.25 The issue of combined investment bank and commercial bank cultures was first recognised in the aftermath of the 1929 Wall Street Crash[49] and led to the introduction of the Banking Act 1933[50] in the United States. This Act is better known as the Glass–Steagall Act (GSA) after the two sponsoring Senators.[51] The Act separated commercial banking (which supports the national economy – personal customers and SME businesses) and investment banking. The former is generally tended to be lower risk (sometimes referred to as boring

44 Amendments made to the Financial Services and Markets Act by the Financial Services Act 2012.

45 The twin-peaks approach had been recommended in the mid-1990s but not pursued. Michael Taylor, *Twin Peaks: A Regulatory Structure for the New Century* (Centre for the Study of Financial Innovation 1995); Michael Taylor, *Peak Practice: How to Reform the UK's Regulatory System* (Centre for the Study of Financial Innovation 1996).

46 FSA, 'The Turner Review' (2009) https://webarchive.nationalarchives.gov.uk/ukgwa/20130410182055/http:/www.fsa.gov.uk/pubs/other/turner_review.pdf; Eilís Ferran, 'The Break-up of the Financial Services Authority' (2011) 31(3) *Oxford Journal of Legal Studies* 455.

47 Andrew Bailey, Sarah Breeden and Gregory Stevens, 'The Prudential Regulation Authority' (2012) Bank of England Quarterly Bulletin Q4 https://www.bankofengland.co.uk/-/media/boe/files/quarterly-bulletin/2012/the-prudential-regulation-authority.pdf.

48 Financial Services and Markets Act 2000, Section 1B last amended 29.8.2023 by Financial Services and Markets Act 2023 (c. 29), ss. 25(2), 86(3); S.I. 2023/779, reg. 4(p).

49 John Kenneth Galbraith, *The Great Crash 1929* (Penguin Books 1954).

50 Howard H Preston, 'The Banking Act of 1933' (1933) 23(4) *The American Economic Review* 585.

51 Senators Henry Glass and Carter Steagall.

banking[52]), with the latter having a higher risk profile. The GSA also created the Federal Deposit Insurance Corporation. Most modern economies for most of the twentieth century had a similar form of structural separation (*de facto* in the UK) and also introduced deposit protection.

As memory of the Wall Street Crash and the Great Depression of the 1930s faded these separation principles were slowly chipped away. Friedman's 1970 *New York Times* article on profit maximisation,[53] and deregulation in the US in the 1970s and in the UK in the 1980s, completely changed the banking landscape, with the GSA principles finally repealed during the Clinton administration.[54] **6.26**

Commercial Banking vs Investment Banking

An important aspect in considering governance and culture is the nature of the bank's business, and more importantly the nature of its customers. **6.27**

Commercial banking historically served local communities (and is sometimes referred to as community banking, high street banking or branch banking) and supported personal customers and local businesses. This activity was characterised by the banker–customer relationship – a relationship of trust and confidence. **6.28**

Personal customers of the bank in a local community trusted their banker to act in their best interest and not allow them to over-borrow or mis-sell them products that benefited the bank but not the customer. SME businesses run by skilled mechanics, electricians, plumbers, and the like who generally did not have training in management, economics, law, accounting, banking, and finance relied on their banker to ask relevant questions. Branch bankers generally observed a duty of care to the customers in their community – which is what made them pillars of the community. **6.29**

Investment banking was and is largely transaction-driven and its customers are knowledgeable, sophisticated corporates. Many of the large investment banks were unlimited liability partnerships – a structure that creates a strong culture of managed risk-taking and high rewards. The big three, Goldman Sachs, Morgan Stanley and JP Morgan, are now all public companies and **6.30**

52 Elizabeth Warren, *This Fight Is Our Fight: The Battle to Save Working People* (William Collins 2017) 69.

53 See Milton Friedman, *Capitalism and Freedom*; 'The Social Responsibility of Business is to Increase Its Profits' (n 25).

54 Financial Services Modernization Act 1999 (known as the Gramm–Leach–Bliley Act after the Senators who sponsored it).

their employees do not put their capital at risk (unless they are shareholders). Some investment banks have clearly taken on more risk than the companies could manage (e.g. Bear Stearns, Lehman Brothers, and others). A suggestion to resolve this problem is the re-introduction of personal liability for investment bankers.[55]

6.31 Commercial banking was branch-based, focused on relationships and characterised by the '*banker-customer relationship*', with bankers acting in the best interests of their customers.[56] Investment banking on the other hand was transaction-based and adhered to the standard '*my word is my bond*'. The relationships were characterised by different information asymmetries – the general public in the high street banking context needing much more support than the knowledgeable counterparties in the investment banking markets. The combination of transaction-driven cultures with relationship-driven cultures has proved very problematic.[57]

6.32 Another issue that disconnects a bank from its customers is the growth of securitisation. In principle, one would think that granting a mortgage to a customer is an opportunity to build a long-term relationship with the customer (originate to hold) and reflective of a traditional banking transaction, that is, the bank covers its costs and makes a profit on the difference between what it pays its depositors and charges the borrower. However, many banks now securitise a large proportion of their mortgages (originate to distribute), and their income is the fee they charge for selling the mortgage before immediately selling it on to someone else.

6.33 To support the culture in the commercial banking industry, an obvious step would be to separate commercial and investment banking – as occurred in 1933 to deal with the Wall Street Crash. This was considered by the Independent Commission on Banking in the aftermath of the GFC (although the 'banker–customer relationship' was not their focus) and a halfway house of ring-fenced banking was agreed.[58]

---

55 Claire A Hill and Richard W Painter, *Better Bankers, Better Banks: Promoting Good Business through Contractual Commitment* (University of Chicago Press 2015).

56 See Eliahu Peter Ellinger, 'The Bank as a Fiduciary and as a Constructive Trustee' (n 35).

57 Philip Augar, *The Bank that Lived a Little: Barclays in the Age of the Very Free Market* (Penguin 2018).

58 See Independent Commission on Banking, 'Final Report' (2011) (n 40).

In the US there was considerable pressure for the reintroduction of Glass–Steagall, albeit in 2015.[59] It is easier to make major changes in the immediate aftermath of a crisis; as time passes this becomes much more difficult. Indeed, in the UK, banks have been pushing back on ring fencing for some time.[60] **6.34**

D. PURPOSEFUL CULTURE

The FCA issued a Discussion Paper in March 2020 titled 'Transforming culture in financial services: Driving purposeful cultures',[61] with contributions from a range of interested parties. **6.35**

Culture has been a subject of interest in the wider commercial world for many years, with leading author Edgar Schein defining it as: **6.36**

> [a] pattern of basic assumptions [...] invented, discovered, developed by a given group as it learns to cope with its problems of external adaptation and internal integration [...] that has worked well enough to be considered valid and, therefore, to be taught to new members as the correct way to perceive, think and feel in relation to those problems.[62]

In respect of purpose, the FCA noted that a firm's individual purpose is its own responsibility, and proposed that there are four common elements of a healthy culture: **6.37**

1. A meaningful purpose;
2. An inclusive environment where it is safe to speak up;
3. Effective leadership and governance; and
4. Employees that have the necessary capabilities and are motivated by appropriate incentives.[63]

It is the fourth element where professional institutes can make a significant and important contribution. A key component of adopting a healthy culture is 'putting a clear, meaningful purpose at the centre of a firm's business model, **6.38**

---

59 Kevin Cirilli, 'Warren, McCain Introduce Bill to Bring Back Glass–Steagall' *The Hill* (7 July 2015) https://thehill.com/policy/finance/247093-warren-mccain-introduce-bill-to-bring-back-glass-steagall/.

60 Stephen Morris, Nick Megaw, and Laura Noonan, 'Banks Set for Clash with UK Regulator over Ringfencing Rules: Industry Wants an Easing of the Post-Crisis Restrictions That Keep Retail and Investment Operations Apart' *Financial Times* (London/New York, 8 February 2021) https://www.ft.com/content/e19ef658-992a-497d-b73b-bf051aabf674.

61 See Financial Conduct Authority, 'DP 20/1: Transforming culture in financial services – driving purposeful cultures' (n 6).

62 Edgar H Schein, *Organisational Cultures and Leadership: A Dynamic View* (Jossey-Bass 1985).

63 Financial Conduct Authority, 'FCA Encourages Firms to Develop Purposeful Cultures' (5 March 2020) https://www.fca.org.uk/news/press-releases/fca-encourages-firms-develop-purposeful-cultures.

strategy and culture'.[64] If the bank's purpose is to support local communities (personal customers and SME businesses) then a business model, strategy and culture focused on the old-fashioned banker-customer relationship of trust and confidence is likely to serve the bank well and allow it to take the benefits of the customer lifecycle[65] and the service–profit value chain.[66]

6.39 As Peter Drucker once observed, profit for a company is like oxygen for a person, and a company cannot survive without it. A bank must generate a profit to survive and to be able to continue providing services to its customers. However, Drucker went on to note that although breathing is essential for life it is not life's purpose, and in the same way that profit is essential for a bank's survival it should not be its purpose. The bank must define its purpose and align its strategy, business model and culture around its purpose.[67]

6.40 'Purpose is the gravitational force that draws in and aligns teamwork, engagement, inspiration and creativity.'[68] Once the bank has decided what its purpose is it can consider the induction programme for new joiners (junior, middle, senior and board staff), the training that will support its chosen purpose – both values training[69] and technical training[70] – and the ongoing continuing professional development[71] required to establish and maintain a supportive culture.

6.41 Another very useful tool for establishing/re-establishing purposeful culture is the balanced scorecard.[72] Using a flexible scorecard for performance assessment, whereby the bank can flex the weight of the purposeful culture component, can help ensure the correct behaviours. This, combined with the appropriate training and continuing professional development, and supported

---

64 See Financial Conduct Authority, 'DP 20/1: Transforming culture in financial services – driving purposeful cultures' (n 6).

65 See Peter McCormack and Jonathan Deacon, 'Can Trust Be Restored to High-Street Banking: A 20-Year Challenge?' (n 8).

66 James L Heskett, Thomas O Jones, Gary W Loveman, W Earl Sasser Jr., and Leonard A Schlesinger, 'Putting the Service-Profit Chain to Work' (1994) 72(2) Harvard Business Review 164.

67 Peter Drucker, 'Quotes' *Goodreads* https://www.goodreads.com/quotes/10516297-profit-for-a-company-is-like-oxygen-for-a-person.

68 See Financial Conduct Authority, 'DP 20/1: Transforming culture in financial services – driving purposeful cultures' (n 6).

69 Simon Thompson, 'The Development and Implementation of Professional Standards for UK Bankers: A Practitioner Perspective' in Costanza A Russo, Rosa María Lastra and William Blair (eds), *Research Handbook on Law and Ethics in Banking and Finance* (Edward Elgar Publishing 2019) 149, 159.

70 Ibid.

71 Ibid 166.

72 Robert S Kaplan and David P Norton, *The Balanced Scorecard* (Harvard Business School Press 1996).

by a speak-up arrangement[73] in support of the firm's culture, will help ensure that the bank's purposeful culture is embedded and persists – helping the bank meet treating customers fairly and consumer duty expectations. If the bank does not take the initiative, it will most likely end up in the position noted in the Salz Review: 'if culture is left to its own devices it shapes itself, with the inherent risk that behaviours will not be those desired.'[74]

Although the above can make a difference in one bank, the trust issue in banking is a sectoral issue. In the context of restoring trust, one of the reasons why industry-wide professionalism underpinned by a professional institute is so important is that 'a few bad apples can create a negative reputational externality for the whole industry, even if most institutions are behaving ethically'.[75] This is a sectoral issue and requires a co-operative effort between commercial banks, regulators and professional institutes – an ecosystem.[76] **6.42**

Counter Culture

In the context of the distinction between relationship-driven and transaction-driven cultures, if one considers the rather colourful language of 'tone from the top', 'tune in the middle' and 'echo from the bottom', it is necessary to understand the risks posed to purposeful culture from top, middle and bottom. **6.43**

At the top, the board and executive, it is important to select directors with a cultural fit to the bank's purpose. It may be difficult to change from a director who has had a lifetime career in a transaction-based environment to one who is relationship-based, or from a lifetime career dealing with knowledgeable counterparties to one dealing with customers who need continuing support. **6.44**

It is also somewhat surprising that many firms do not invest more in developing executive talent internally as part of leadership succession, and instead go to the market for senior executives, often at hugely inflated salaries. This is particularly surprising in mutual organisations which one would expect to have strong purposeful cultures in support of their members, with the risk of a counterculture that takes the bank/building society in the wrong **6.45**

---

73 Amy C Edmondson, *The Fearless Organization: Creating Psychological Safety in the Workplace for Learning, Innovation, and Growth* (John Wiley & Sons Inc 2018).

74 Anthony Salz and Russell Collins, 'Salz Review – An independent review of Barclays' business practices' (2013) https://www.wsj.com/public/resources/documents/SalzReview04032013.pdf.

75 Anjan V Thakor, 'Ethics, Culture, and Higher Purpose in Banking: Post-Crisis Governance Developments' (2021) 17(5) *International Journal of Central Banking* 51.

76 See Sian Fisher, 'Insurance: A Purpose for the Profession', p 26 in Financial Conduct Authority, 'DP 20/1: Transforming culture in financial services – driving purposeful cultures' (n 6).

direction (a possible factor in the Britannia Building Society and Co-operative Bank merger).[77]

6.46 This counterculture risk also exists in middle management, particularly in large organisations.[78] It is a risk that has increased in the past 50 years, with more and more managers not being satisfied with their organisation, and more and more middle management being co-located in big urban centres, making moving easier. De-centralised regional offices might help here.

6.47 The bottom probably presents the least risk, as there is considerable opportunity to influence junior staff into the bank's culture; however, if the behaviours from middle management and senior management are not consistent with the bank's purposeful culture, the bank may have high turnover in its junior staff.

6.48 In all three layers, commercial banks, working with professional institutes and regulators, can help ensure the consistency and integrity of their purposeful culture. At the more junior level, the provision of basic banking training – both values training (e.g. professionalism and ethics[79]) and relevant technical training – will help underpin culture.

6.49 In the 1980s, when commercial banks were still very branch-based and focussed on servicing local communities, most English banks used to allow their junior staff day release – one day a week to attend local further education colleges to learn foundational economics, accounting, law and banking (stage 1 of the bank exams). This created a solid foundation of knowledge to serve customers – particularly local SME customers.

6.50 Another development in the past 40 years has been the huge increase in numbers of young people who go to university, with banks now recruiting predominantly university graduates with a myriad of different degrees. In a commercial banking environment, it remains important that all staff have a solid foundation in banking, including those working in technology, marketing, compliance, finance and human resources. Without this common training, it becomes

77 Christopher Kelly, 'Failings in management and governance: Report of the independent review into the events leading to the Co-operative Bank's capital shortfall' (30 April 2014) paras 6.9, 7.33, and 14.49 iv and v https://assets.ctfassets.net/5ywmq66472jr/3LpckmtCnuWiuuuEM2qAsw/9bc99b1cd941261bca5d674724873deb/kelly-review.pdf.

78 See Lesley Carline and Duncan Watson, 'A Fresh Purpose for the Pensions Sector', p 31 in Financial Conduct Authority, 'DP 20/1: Transforming culture in financial services – driving purposeful cultures' (n 6).

79 Chartered Banker Institute, 'Certificate in Professionalism and Ethics' https://www.charteredbanker.com/qualification/certificate-in-professionalism-and-ethics.html.

more difficult to create a culture where everyone is pulling in the direction of serving the customer. As Jan Carlzon noted, in a customer-focused organisation you should be focused on serving the customer and if you are not directly serving the customer you should be focused on serving someone who is.[80] In this context, it is necessary for everyone to understand and support the customer service culture of the bank. Indeed, this suggests that senior management should operate an inverted pyramid where they are empowering the organisation in the direction of customer service.

E. CORPORATE GOVERNANCE

In respect of tone from the top, the Basel Committee's Corporate Governance principles note that corporate governance, amongst other things, determines how a Board will: **6.51**

> align corporate culture, corporate activities and behaviour with the expectation that the bank will operate in a safe and sound manner, with integrity and in compliance with applicable laws and regulations.[81]

This of course requires a board that is compositionally competent (i.e. has the right mix of skills) and that is clear on the purpose of the bank, i.e., whether it is a relationship driven bank (commercial bank) or a transaction-driven bank (investment bank). If the Board is not clear on its purpose and the culture that is necessary to support that purpose (including the required values training and technical training) then its ability to set the 'tone from the top' is compromised. A board can establish consistency by agreeing a 'culture blueprint'. **6.52**

In ensuring that the bank is internally consistent and supports behaviours that are aligned with its purpose, and that are evidenced in its decisions, the bank needs to have a framework that facilitates measurement and monitoring. This consistency can be achieved through: **6.53**

> [a] culture blueprint or framework which demonstrates how culture, purpose, values and strategy are all aligned can act as a lens through which decisions are made and actions taken.[82]

80 Jan Carlzon, 'Quotes' https://www.azquotes.com/author/22935-Jan_Carlzon.

81 Basel Committee on Banking Supervision 'Corporate Governance Principles for Banks' (2015) para 3 https://www.bis.org/bcbs/publ/d328.pdf.

82 Financial Reporting Council, 'Corporate Governance Code Guidance' (2024) https://www.frc.org.uk/library/standards-codes-policy/corporate-governance/corporate-governance-code-guidance/.

6.54 The Basel Corporate Governance principles go on to say:

> The board should set the 'tone at the top' and oversee management's role in fostering and maintaining a sound corporate and risk culture. Management should develop a written code of ethics or a code of conduct. Either code is intended to foster a culture of honesty and accountability to protect the interest of its customers and shareholders.[83]

6.55 The 2024 Basel Core Principles for Effective Banking Supervision expects bank supervisors to 'determine that banks have robust corporate governance policies and processes covering, for example, corporate culture',[84] with an expectation that the Board 'establishes and communicates corporate culture and values (e.g. through a code of conduct)'.[85]

6.56 In its recent review, the UK's Financial Reporting Council (FRC) also noted that the Board plays a critical role in setting the tone from the top. The FRC in its guidance[86] on the new UK Corporate Governance Code[87] (effective January 2025) notes that:

> [a]n effective board defines the company's purpose and sets a strategy to deliver it, underpinned by the values and behaviours that shape its culture and the way it conducts its business. It understands the main trends and factors affecting the long-term sustainable success, resilience and future prospects of the company.[88]

6.57 Culture is not directly observable but is reflected in the behaviour of the employees of the bank – whereby it can be visible to bank management, supervisors and the general public.

6.58 The FRC goes on to highlight the importance of the board developing 'a common and consistent understanding and language around culture'[89] and noting influencing factors such as corporate history, sub-cultures and regulatory requirements. Having established a culture and developed language to aid understanding, the board must 'articulate the corporate culture'[90] and set the 'framework of values and attitudes, ethics and behaviours which support a

---

83 See Basel Committee on Banking Supervision, 'Corporate Governance Principles for Banks' (n 81) para 14.

84 Basel Committee on Banking Supervision, 'Core Principles for Effective Banking Supervision' (April 2024) Principle 14, Para 40.32 https://www.bis.org/bcbs/publ/d573.pdf.

85 Ibid para 40.33 (5).

86 See Financial Reporting Council, 'Corporate Governance Code Guidance' (n 82).

87 Financial Reporting Council, 'Corporate Governance Code' (2024) https://www.frc.org.uk/library/standards-codes-policy/corporate-governance/uk-corporate-governance-code/.

88 See Financial Reporting Council, 'Corporate Governance Code Guidance' (n 82) para 9.

89 Ibid para 21.

90 Ibid para 20.

positive culture'[91] – a positive culture being 'one based on transparency, trust, respect and inclusion'.[92]

In a commercial banking context, if the board has decided on a customer-focused, relationship-driven culture, it is important to have some way to measure this so that it can be reflected in a flexible balanced scorecard. **6.59**

Customer satisfaction is at the heart of the ability to up-sell and cross-sell relevant financial products that meet an individual customer's needs. If the board believes that in order to be successful, customer satisfaction must be at the heart of its culture, then, as Bouvin notes, decision making should be devolved to those in the bank 'who know and best understand' the 'customers' needs and circumstances'.[93] In this context, the board should recognise the role that professional education can play in supporting its chosen culture. **6.60**

F. PROFESSIONALISM

A common question in banking has been whether banking is a trade or a profession. While many products in investment banking are actively traded between market counterparties, in commercial banking, the information asymmetry and duty of care that is encapsulated in the banker–customer relationship arguably make it worthy of professional status and all that goes with establishing that status – in particular professional training. **6.61**

McGrath and Walker, with a focus on retail banking (commercial banking), assert that 'professionalisation will help to develop bankers with a professional, pro-social identity, in which there is a recognition of broader obligations to society, that exist independently of the profit-driven nature of banking and the hierarchy of their own firms'.[94] **6.62**

They are supported in this view by Mark Carney, who suggests that one of the three key components of restoring morality to markets is 'renewing a sense of vocation in finance'.[95] Indeed, this has been a theme for Carney for some time. **6.63**

---

91 Ibid para 20.

92 Ibid para 19.

93 Anders Bouvin, 'You Can't Digitise Empathy' (Summer 2021) *Chartered Banker Magazine* 48.

94 Joe McGrath and Ciaran Walker, *New Accountability in Financial Services: Changing Individual Behaviour and Culture* (Palgrave Macmillan 2022) 171.

95 Mark Carney, *Value(s): Building a Better World for All* (HarperCollins 2021).

6.64 In a speech Carney gave in Canada prior to becoming the Governor of the Bank of England, he noted that 'virtue cannot be regulated, and that even the strongest supervision cannot guarantee good conduct' and that what is needed is a re-discovery of core values and a return to old-fashioned banking. He went on to say that this responsibility begins with boards and senior management and that they need to define clearly the purpose of their organisations and 'promote a culture of ethical business throughout'. However, in asserting that the top-down approach is not enough, he noted that employees 'need a sense of broader purpose, grounded in strong connections to their clients and their communities (the banker–customer relationship) and that bankers need to see themselves as custodians of their institutions, improving them before passing them on to their successors'.[96] He continued the theme, after becoming Governor of the Bank of England, in another speech in 2014.[97]

6.65 The role of bankers as pillars of the community for much of the 20th century recognises the role that they played in supporting local communities as a 'quasi-public servant and fiduciary'[98] with a higher purpose to support SME businesses and the community's personal customers – a focus on the banker–customer relationship. The challenge in trying to achieve cultural change is to re-connect banks with their customers and re-discover a higher purpose.

6.66 Quinn and Thakor define higher purpose as 'a pro-social contribution goal that transcends the usual business goals like profit maximization but is intrinsically a part of the business of the organization'.[99]

6.67 McGrath and Walker identify four characteristics of professionalism:

1. Academic training in a body of specialised knowledge to exercise skilled judgements;
2. Members' commitment to serve a positive social purpose;
3. Mechanisms for members to be disciplined by their community for failing to honour those duties; and

---

96 Mark Carney, 'Rebuilding Trust in Global Banking' (2013) speech at the 7th Annual Thomas d'Aquino Lecture on Leadership, Lawrence National Centre for Policy and Management, Richard Ivey School of Business, Western University, Ontario https://www.bankofcanada.ca/wp-content/uploads/2013/02/remarks-250213.pdf.

97 Mark Carney, 'Inclusive Capitalism: Creating a Sense of the Systemic' (2014) speech at the Conference on Inclusive Capitalism, London https://www.bankofengland.co.uk/publications/Documents/speeches/2014/speech731.pdf.

98 Arthur M Lamport, 'Banking: Business or Profession' (1931) 122(3) *Bankers Magazine* 317.

99 Robert E Quinn and Anjan V Thakor, *The Economics of Higher Purpose: Eight Counterintuitive Steps for Creating a Purpose-Driven Organization* (Berrett-Koehler Publishers 2019) 3.

4. An underlying code of ethics.[100]

Training here needs to focus on individuals as it is the way that human interactions are managed and decisions made that banks need to influence. As Thompson notes, 'it is individuals working in the banking industry who make decisions';[101] this position is also supported by Edelson, who notes that 'banks are complex organisms driven by the sum of their human interactions and decisions'.[102] 6.68

The PCBS seemed to conflate investment banking and commercial banking, came to the conclusion that banking was not a profession, and suggested the establishment of an all-encompassing professional body.[103] This suggestion probably contributed to the demise of the Financial Services Culture Board (FSCB) (the re-named BSB) and the drift from banking to wider financial services. The FSCB did some very good work;[104] however, the standards required for dealing with knowledgeable counterparties in a transaction environment and those required for dealing with SME businesses and personal customers (where there can be a high degree of information asymmetry) are very different – consider, for instance, the difference between the Goldman Sachs business model/customers and the Lloyds Banking Group business model/customers. 6.69

It is arguable that banking had achieved professional status in the 20th century – the English Institute of Bankers had 110,000 members in 1979[105] providing professional service to customers in branches around the country. It is equally arguable that it lost its professional status in the 21st century – evidenced by the large number of bank branches that have become retail sales outlets. In this latter case the challenge is to restore professionalism (and the banker–customer relationship of trust and confidence) – a challenge that professional institutes are uniquely qualified to support as part of a wider ecosystem aimed at embedding purposeful culture and consumer duty. 6.70

---

100 Joe McGrath and Ciaran Walker, *New Accountability in Financial Services: Changing Individual Behaviour and Culture* (n 94) 175.

101 Simon Thompson, 'The Development and Implementation of Professional Standards for UK Bankers: A Practitioner Perspective' (n 69) 150.

102 Frank Elderson, 'Treading Softly Yet Boldly: How Culture Drives Risk in Banks and What Supervisors Can Do About It' (2023) speech at the 10th Conference on the Banking Union https://www.bankingsupervision.europa.eu/press/speeches/date/2023/html/ssm.sp230919~589c61455b.en.html.

103 Parliamentary Commission on Banking Standards, 'Changing Banking for Good, Volume I: Summary and Conclusions and Recommendations' (n 41) Vol I, para 94; Vol II, para 604.

104 Banking Standards Board, 'Statement of Principles for Strengthening Professionalism' (2018) https://financialservicescultureboard.org.uk/bsb-statement-of-principles-for-strengthening-professionalism/.

105 Edwin Green, *Debtors to Their Profession: A History of The Institute of Bankers 1879–1979* (n 9) xv.

CBI Efforts to Restore Banking Professionalism

6.71 In October 2011 (although conceived in 2008 in the aftermath of the GFC), the CBI and nine commercial banks founded the Chartered Banker Professional Standards Board (CB:PSB) and published *Our Commitment to Professionalism in Banking*.[106] They defined professionalism as:

6.72 the knowledge, skills, values, attitudes and behaviours expected of a professional.[107]

6.73 They also identified two key areas for the development of training to support professionals to meet expected professional attributes[108]:

1. Professional values and attitudes – the day-to-day conduct expected of all bankers; and
2. Professional knowledge and skills – the specialist body of knowledge and skills required to perform a professional role.

6.74 Training for the first is provided by a long-standing CBI course called 'Professionalism and Ethics' and the second is provided by the CBI's professional suite of technical exams, leading to Certified (CCBI), Associateship (ACBI) and Membership/Chartered Banker (MCBI) status.

6.75 The CB:PSB also published a Chartered Banker Code of Professional Conduct, with the 2016 version setting out expectations that professional bankers would demonstrate their personal commitment to professionalism in banking by:

1. Treating all customers, colleagues and counterparties with respect and acting with integrity;
2. Developing and maintaining their professional knowledge and acting with due skill, care and diligence; considering the risks and implications of their actions and advice, and holding themselves accountable for them and their impact;
3. Being open and cooperative with the regulators; complying with all current regulatory and legal requirements;
4. Paying due regard to the interests of customers and treating them fairly;
5. Observing and demonstrating proper standards of market conduct at all times;
6. Acting in an honest and trustworthy manner, being alert to and managing potential conflicts of interest; and

---

106 Chartered Banker Professional Standards Board, 'Our Commitment to Professionalism in Banking' (2011) https://www.charteredbanker.com/resource_listing/cpd-resources/our-commitment-to-professionalism-in-banking.html.

107 Simon Thompson, 'The Development and Implementation of Professional Standards for UK Bankers: A Practitioner Perspective' (n 69) 154.

108 Ibid.

7. Treating information with appropriate confidentiality and sensitivity.[109]

Seven years after the CB:PSB was established, the Independent Monitoring Panel's 2018 Annual Report noted: 6.76

> Our perception was that banks' main boards were not necessarily aware of CB:PSB professional standards and we considered this detrimental to the initiative – senior focus can unlock resource and give profile that ensures action.[110]

Following the publication of the 2018 CB:PSB Independent Monitoring Panel Report, the CB:PSB was transitioned into the CBI in June 2019.[111] Although banks do individually interact with the CBI, this unfortunately marked the end of the banks' active and collective involvement in this initiative, and from the comment in the final report (above) it seems that the main Boards were not engaged in this important initiative. 6.77

G. THE DEMISE OF THE BRANCH

As we have noted, historically, most workers in commercial banking served the community in branches and learnt their knowledge and skills on the job. Progression in the branch network was dependent on completing the bank exams. Where the branch manager and all of the senior staff had completed their bank exams, and junior staff were working towards completing them, there was a common knowledge base that supported a purposeful culture of customer service (supporting the local community). 6.78

Although the CBI did not specifically identify the demise of the branch in its submission to the PCBS as a reason for the decline in the professional standards that supported a strong culture in commercial banking, some of the issues that it did identify can be seen as a symptom of loss of branches: 6.79

109 Chartered Banker Professional Standards Board, 'The Chartered Banker Code of Professional Conduct' (2016) https://www.charteredbanker.com/resource_listing/cpd-resources/chartered-banker-code-of-professional-conduct.html.

110 Chartered Banker Professional Standards Board, 'Independent Monitoring Panel Annual Report' (2018) https://www.charteredbanker.com/resource_listing/cpd-resources/cb-psb-independent-monitoring-panel-report-2018.html.

111 Chartered Banker Professional Standards Board, 'Background and Transition' (2024) https://www.charteredbanker.com/the-institute/global-network-2021/employers/chartered-banker-professional-standards-board2.html.

- The increasing career specialism of individuals employed in the financial services and lack of demand for well-qualified, experienced, generalist bankers with all round experience;
- A shift away from banking as a structured lifelong career;
- Changes in recruitment and onboarding policies;
- Recruitment of non-bankers (e.g. sales and marketing specialists) directly into senior roles;
- Increased use of technology (e.g. credit scoring) reduced the need for highly skilled qualified professionals exercising professional judgement;
- A regulatory focus on firms rather than individuals;
- A 'tick box' approach to regulation and compliance which devalued professional judgement at all levels, from judging the appropriate amount of capital to set aside to 'Know Your Customer' rules;
- Lack of encouragement and support for professional banking qualifications and membership of professional banking institutes from employers, regulators, and policymakers; and
- A general change in banking culture from stewardship to sales.[112]

6.80 It's important to recognise that when talking about the demise of the branch we are talking about the demise of a bank that serves the local community as opposed to the continued existence of a bricks-and-mortar sales outlet – which is what the transaction-driven approach has turned many bank branches into.

6.81 The use of branches has been declining now for a number of years, a process that started in the 1960s with the introduction of the credit card (a revolving credit facility) and the introduction of Automated Telling Machines (ATMs).[113] In the 21st century, telephone banking, internet banking and more recently mobile banking have all chipped away at branch visitation. The decline in the use of cash in the post-Covid environment has been another nail in the coffin and it remains likely that many more branches will close.[114]

6.82 It is unreasonable to expect banks to maintain large costly estates to serve customers that no longer come into branches; however, banks still need to serve their customers, and must think of innovative approaches to reconnect with their customers. Abbey National (acquired by Santander in 2004) was innovative in this area and looked at a franchising model that would let local bank

---

112 Chartered Banker Institute, 'Response to the Parliamentary Commission on Banking Standards' (2012) para 27 https://www.charteredbanker.com/static/uploaded/73af0ae6-87da-4109-ba88cf4e5d79a256.pdf.

113 See Ian Peacock, *Bankers: From Pillars to Pariahs* (n 19).

114 House of Lords Library, 'Closure of High Street Banks: Impact on Local Communities' (19 January 2024) https://lordslibrary.parliament.uk/closure-of-high-street-banks-impact-on-local-communities/.

staff take the lead in serving their communities.[115] This model did not take off at the time but, with significant advances in technology, might be looked at again.

Another Abbey National innovation was putting Costa coffee shops in branches.[116] Given that branches are closing, this is unlikely to be a model going forward; however, the reverse could be a very workable model, that is, to have a bookable bank office in a retail outlet (that could be booked by one of several banks) for meeting customers. **6.83**

Take any large retail bank and decentralise: that is rather than having one very large office in London, have a reduced office in London and a matrix of regional offices. Each regional office, say the York Regional Office, would have a set of local sort codes and accounts covering the former surrounding local branches. Each town where there was a branch would have ATMs and a bookable office (possibly in a coffee shop, other retail outlet, or office space). A customer who wanted a face-to-face meeting could either visit the regional office or book a local meeting in the local 'banking office'. The local banking office could even be shared, that is, booked by different banks on different days. This type of approach is already being looked at for ATMs.[117] **6.84**

Handelsbanken operates a decentralised model in the UK, with its Head of External Affairs noting that 'when it comes to business development and customer banking decisions, our local branch teams are in the driving seat, closely supported by their head office colleagues[…] giving them the means and accountability to run their own show with a rock-solid framework of operating principles'.[118] The bank's long-term view allows it to build deep relationships with its customers. **6.85**

For many years commercial banks have been using innovation primarily as an opportunity to reduce costs and increase profits, and in doing so they have disconnected themselves from their customers. Branches are likely to continue to close and commercial banks must innovate (using all the technology available) to bring banking back to local communities and re-connect with their **6.86**

---

115 'Abbey National Announces Plans to Offer Franchises' (3 July 2000) Money Marketing https://www.moneymarketing.co.uk/news/abbey-national-announces-plans-to-offer-franchises/.

116 'Abbey Opens First Costa Coffee Branch' (1 August 2000) Finextra https://www.finextra.com/newsarticle/210/abbey-opens-first-costa-coffee-branch.

117 FCA, 'PS 24/8: Access to Cash Feedback to CP23/29 and final rules' (July 2024) https://www.fca.org.uk/publication/policy/ps24-8.pdf.

118 See Richard Winder, 'When What + How = Why', pp 16–18 in Financial Conduct Authority, 'DP 20/1: Transforming culture in financial services – driving purposeful cultures' (n 6).

customers. This does not mean sacrificing profit, as re-connecting with customers will help banks recognise the customer lifecycle and realise the lifetime value of their customer relationships.[119]

H. REGULATION

6.87 Llewellyn[120] notes that one of the core objectives underpinning the economic rationale for financial regulation is protecting the consumer. The role of the regulator is one of having 'the moral responsibility for seeing that other people act rightly and, when they do not, the responsibility for acting to correct the problem'.[121] This can be separated into two parts: the prospective setting of regulation to ensure the right behaviours, and a retrospective dimension of taking action against those, both firms and individuals, that have not acted rightly.[122]

6.88 Following the transition of the SROs and the SIB to the FSA, the FSA in 2001 responded to the poor treatment of customers with a programme called Treating Customers Fairly.[123] This was a major programme for most of the first decade of the 21st century and reported regularly on progress.[124] The programme did not produce the desired outcomes and firms continued to adopt transaction-based profit-maximising approaches, the most egregious of which led to the payment protection insurance mis-selling problem.[125]

6.89 The GFC of 2007/9 and a change of government led to the adoption of a twin peaks regulatory model and the creation of a new consumer-focused regulator, the Financial Conduct Authority (FCA). The FCA has identified a key problem in banking and the wider financial services industry to be culture,

---

119 See Peter McCormack and Jonathan Deacon, 'Can Trust Be Restored to High-Street Banking: A 20-Year Challenge?' (n 8).

120 David Llewellyn, 'The Economic Rationale of Financial Regulation' (1999) FSA Occasional Paper No 1.

121 Dennis Thompson, *Restoring Responsibility: Ethics in Government, Business and Healthcare* (Cambridge University Press 2005) 245.

122 Robert Schwartz, 'Regulatory Ethics in Theory and Practice: Comparing Two Cases' (2007–08) 10(1) *Public Integrity* 37, 38.

123 Financial Services Authority, 'Treating Customers Fairly After the Point of Sale', (June 2001).

124 Financial Services Authority, 'Treating Customers Fairly: Progress Report' (2002); 'Treating customers fairly – Towards fair outcomes for consumers' (2006) (https://www.fca.org.uk/publication/archive/fsa-tcf-towards.pdf; 'Treating customers fairly initiative: progress report', (2007).

125 See Eilís Ferran, 'Regulatory Lessons from the Payment Protection Insurance Mis-selling Scandal in the UK' (n 39).

and their response to this problem has been to introduce a consumer duty.[126] It remains to be seen if this approach will be successful.

For much of the 25-year period up to the emergence of the recent GFC, regulation was not particularly effective, especially in the consumer arena, with increased mis-selling scandals, and ever increasing fines that seemed to have little effect. 6.90

A commercial bank, acting in the best interests of its customer should identify its customer's needs, develop products that meet that need and provide them at a fair price. The number of mis-selling scandals demonstrates that this has proven a challenge for a sector that benefits from an information asymmetry and is motivated by profit-maximisation incentives. 6.91

The PCBS noted that a large number of senior bankers were operating with 'insufficient personal responsibility',[127] and a broad outcome in the aftermath of the GFC has either been the introduction of, or the enhancement of existing, personal accountability regimes. In the UK an Approved Person Regime was introduced when the FSA was established, enhanced in the immediate aftermath of the GFC, and ultimately replaced by the SMCR with a focus on Senior Management Functions (SMF) and a certification regime requiring annual certification. These are all good steps, and support clarity of accountability and responsibility at the bank – with the interactions of the various individual responsibilities captured in a Management Responsibilities Map. 6.92

In respect of protecting the customer, one rationale for the existence of financial regulation is the need for trust and confidence between the customer and the bank.[128] With the TCF programme, the regulator took a principles-based approach in the hope that the banks would take ownership and resolve this issue themselves. 6.93

A principles-based approach is intended to produce a situation where: 6.94

> [r]egulators and regulatees move from a directing relationship of telling and doing, to a relationship of responsibility, mutuality, and trust in which regulators communicate their goals and expectations clearly in principles and apply those principles predictably, regulatees adopt a self-reflective approach to the development of processes and practices

---

126 See Financial Conduct Authority, 'Policy Statement PS22/9: A new Consumer Duty, Feedback to CP21/36 and final rules' (n 7).

127 See Parliamentary Commission on Banking Standards, 'Changing Banking for Good, Volume I: Summary and Conclusions and Recommendations' (n 41) Vol 1, para 8.

128 See David Llewellyn, 'The Economic Rationale of Financial Regulation' (n 120).

> to ensure that those goals are substantively met, and, critically, both trust each other to fulfil their side of this new regulatory bargain.[129]

6.95 In a damning indictment after the GFC, Hector Sants, the chief executive of the FSA, observed that 'a principles based approach does not work with individuals who have no principles'.[130]

6.96 A key focus of professional bodies is ensuring that individuals have principles, a focus that would benefit from greater regulatory support (as part of an eco-system) to ensure that those entering the financial services professions, in particular commercial banking, are members of professional bodies that provide the training to ensure that they have the right principles.

6.97 Professional banking institutes have been aided in this activity by the publication of the United Nations Principles for Responsible Banking, which the CBI is taking a lead on in training provision.[131]

6.98 In dealing with regulation it is much better if a bank internalises regulation into its own purposeful culture so that behaviours are a requirement of the banks' culture rather than something externally imposed – an approach that requires 'a more active engagement with the values underlying the legislation'.[132]

6.99 There may be a regulatory pendulum at play here in that as trust and confidence increases, regulatory intensity will decrease. At the current time, with the poor TCF outcomes and the introduction of consumer duty, the commercial banking sector is experiencing increasing regulatory intensity. Re-establishing the banker–customer relationship, rebuilding trust with both customers and regulators may lead to a reduction in regulatory intensity.

6.100 The challenge for the banking sector is that this cannot be achieved by any one bank alone. It is a sectoral challenge and again one where professional bodies working with banks and regulators can make a significant contribution by agreeing cultural underpinnings of both values training (professionalism and ethics) and relevant technical training.

---

129 Julia Black, 'The Rise, Fall, and Fate of Principles-Based Regulation' (2010) LSE Law, Society and Economy Working Papers 17/2010 https://eprints.lse.ac.uk/32892/1/WPS2010-17_Black.pdf.

130 Hector Sants, 'Delivering Intensive Supervision and Credible Deterrence' (2009) speech at the Reuters Newsmakers event, 12th March 2009.

131 CBI, 'Principles for Responsible Banking Academy' https://www.charteredbanker.com/prbacademy.html.

132 David Jackman, 'Values-Led Regulation' in Chris Moon and Clive Bonny (eds), *Business Ethics* (Profile Books 2001) 186.

Indeed, when the FSA was first being set up an ethical approach to regulation was suggested[133] and considered[134] albeit that the regulator continued with the compliance approach which arguably in many cases has sadly led to box-ticking regulation. 6.101

Although the new Consumer Duty may encourage some box-ticking, there is also a danger that rules-based regulation can encourage firms to look for safe harbours with a de-risking outcome. This process of de-risking can reduce the variety of products that are available to meet the differing needs of customers. This would be a very poor outcome and would reflect firms managing regulatory risk and not engaging with the spirit of purposeful culture and consumer duty. 6.102

I. CONCLUSION

In the context of seeking to establish a purposeful culture, and recognising the higher purpose aspect of providing products and services to the sectors that support the national economy (SME businesses) and the financial wellbeing of the nation (personal customers), banks need to re-connect with their customers with a purposeful culture that re-establishes the banker–customer relationship and recognises the lifetime value of a customer. 6.103

A clear separation between transaction banking and relationship banking, a recognition of the continuing need to consider the pressures for short-term profit maximisation versus long-term profit optimisation and a return to working with professional institutes to establish a solid ethical and technical educational foundation that restores trust and returns bankers to their professional and esteemed position as pillars of the community would benefit bankers, customers and wider society. 6.104

Professional institutes' reason for existence is to raise the standards of professionalism and technical knowledge that support a purposeful culture that re-connects the financial services industry, and the banking sector in particular, with its customers. 6.105

133 Andrew Newton, *Compliance: Making Ethics Work in Financial Services* (Financial Times Management 1998).

134 Financial Services Authority, 'Discussion Paper 18: An ethical framework for financial services' (2002) https://www.handbook.fca.org.uk/archive/2003/08/DP18.pdf; David Jackman, 'Why Comply?' (2001) 9 *Journal of Financial Regulation and Compliance* 211.

6.106 With the folding of the CB:PSB into the CBI in 2019, the closure of the FSCB in 2023 and the pushback on ring-fencing, the commercial banking sector appears to be withdrawing its engagement from an ecosystem that was intended to support the restoration of trust to the commercial banking sector. In a governance context, it is essential that those setting the tone at the top engage with professional institutes so that bottom-up training matches, supports and reinforces that tone.

6.107 Although we now have the FCA's Consumer Duty, it may not prove an adequate substitute for an ecosystem where regulators, professional institutes and commercial banks (including building societies and credit unions) work together to agree on the professionalisation of the commercial banking sector – a sector that should ideally have a relationship-driven commitment to support SME businesses and personal customers. Given the recent closure of the FSCB, professional institutes may be able to make a significant contribution in continuing the purposeful culture/standards/consumer duty impetus.

6.108 The CBI, which will be celebrating its 150th anniversary in 2025, has 'a mission to enhance and sustain socially purposeful, responsible, professional banking in the public interest' and in addition to 'developing and supporting bankers' education and professional development throughout their careers' it hosts the PRB Academy, developing global education and training on the United Nations Principles for Responsible Banking.

7

ESG STRATEGIES AND THEIR IMPACT ON CORPORATE CULTURE

Isabel Kelly and Joanne Goddard

This chapter explores how ESG (environment, social, governance) strategic management has evolved and its effect on aspects of culture, including trust, values, purpose, people, innovation and leadership. The discussion provides an overview of these developments from early voluntary efforts known as Corporate Social Responsibility, through the need for companies to expand their responsibility following the financial crash of 2008, and up to today's ESG disclosure legislative requirements. The chapter concludes by canvassing a new type of financial services sector culture which is emerging among companies driven by 'purpose' and ESG. 7.1

Both authors of this chapter have worked in 'ESG' functions, or earlier iterations of what is now called ESG, as in-house practitioners at large companies and as consultants for companies of different sizes in a variety of industry sectors. As such, this chapter builds upon real-world experience of advising corporate clients and integrates recommendations for enhancing ESG management. 7.2

A. WHAT IS ESG?

7.3 Environmental, Social and Governance (ESG) has become a widely used term to refer to the actions companies take to address the interests of a set of stakeholders broader than investors or owners. These stakeholders include employees, customers, communities and the environment. While the concept of ESG is open-ended and as such not amenable to a universal definition, the following working definition can be useful for the purposes of our discussion:

7.4 ESG is a collective term for a business's impact on the environment and society as well as how robust and transparent its governance is.[1]

7.5 ESG compliance increasingly requires data capture for reporting, as well as integration into financial reporting and risk assessment. The UK Financial Conduct Authority (FCA) writes:

> ESG and sustainability are hugely important. But terms such as 'climate', 'environment', 'sustainable' and 'ESG' are often used loosely across the financial sector; and sometimes interchangeably.[2]

7.6 There is some controversy over the use of the term 'ESG'. Notably, BlackRock CEO Larry Fink, who gave prominence to the concepts of ESG in his 2021 and 2022 letters to CEOs and investors, announced in 2023 that he would stop using the term due to its politicisation, particularly in the USA.[3]

7.7 Some companies approach ESG from a risk perspective or for harm reduction, while others embrace ESG by making it part of their company purpose and embedding environmental and social change into their corporate identity.[4] Many larger institutions have been doing environmental and social work for many years; others are just starting, driven by new legislative requirements. While many aspects of a healthy corporate culture lie in robust governance which has existed in legislation and regulation for a very long time, we focus

---

1 British Business Bank https://www.british-business-bank.co.uk/business-guidance/guidance-articles/sustainability/what-is-esg-a-guide-for-smaller-businesses.

2 Financial Conduct Authority, A Strategy for Positive Change: Our ESG Priorities (November 2022) available at https://www.fca.org.uk/publications/corporate-documents/strategy-positive-change-our-esg-priorities.

3 I Binnie, BlackRock's Fink Says He's Stopped Using 'Weaponised' Term ESG, *Reuters* (New York, 26 June 2023) https://www.reuters.com/business/environment/blackrocks-fink-says-hes-stopped-using-weaponised-term-esg-2023-06-26/.

4 In this chapter, we focus on financial services institutions headquartered in the UK and non-UK entities (Europe & US) with a significant UK presence. These institutions include banks, accountancy firms, asset managers, investment managers, pension providers, building societies, credit rating agencies and insurance providers.

in this chapter on the cultural impact of adding environmental and social considerations within a business.

Regardless of the term used, the inclusion of environmental and social considerations is largely accepted in an increasing number of businesses in the UK as a legitimate area of activity, with some companies believing that it can add to value creation and a positive corporate culture. This development can be seen in the change of tone of business and management disciplinary discourse in the past decade, such as the Future of the Corporate Project led by Professor Colin Mayer.[5] This is also reflected in increased involvement of consultancy firms in assisting companies to develop credible and ambitious ESG policies and processes, including score cards. 7.8

B. THE KEY TENETS OF COMPANY CULTURE

Company culture can be hard to define or measure, but broadly it is understood to be the characteristic values, behaviours and mindsets that are expected and encouraged within an organisation. Culture is learned and transmitted to employees both consciously and unconsciously. A good culture instils a sense of accountability and responsibility within company employees and sets the groundwork for good governance, ethics and legality. In a speech to the Westminster Business Forum in June 2023, Emily Shepperd, the FCA's Chief Operating Officer, said: 7.9

> Culture remains central to our supervisory model. It is what underpins outcomes – firms with healthy cultures will be best equipped to adapt to a changing world and to consumers with changing expectations.
>
> Culture underpins conduct and therefore business performance and confidence. [...]
>
> Culture is not just the slogan on your website. It is the very essence of what your organisation stands for, embodied by how it conducts itself.[6]

The introduction of ESG principles into company culture reintroduces a new set of external stakeholders who must be considered in decision-making. These stakeholders may be positively or negatively impacted by a company's operations and may highlight competing interests. The needs and interests of one stakeholder may conflict with those of another, creating a need to balance priorities and manage any trade-offs. Done well, a good corporate culture creates 7.10

5 https://www.thebritishacademy.ac.uk/programmes/future-of-the-corporation/.

6 E Shepperd, Cultural Evolution: How Culture Must Change To Meet Expectations (Westminster Business Forum (Online), 26 June 2023).

a working environment that attracts and retains employees who feel pride in their work, leading to good brand reputation and customer loyalty.

7.11 In the early 2000s Silicon Valley tech companies were famed for their corporate culture: having meetings sitting on bean bags, endless free snacks available, driving Segways (a type of scooter) around the office, company yoga. This new corporate culture was aligned with the creation of new tech products which revolutionised how people work and live and presented a 'fail fast' approach to innovation. Employees' experience of going to an office changed radically and often included elements of corporate social responsibility such as being given time to volunteer with charities or to support nonprofit organisations to make better use of technology. People were encouraged to 'bring their whole self to work' rather than leave what they care about at the office door, as previous generations had done.

7.12 These practices led to companies making claims about how their products, particularly social media platforms, were supporting social change, including playing a role in the 'Arab Spring' in the early 2010s. These types of claims have more deeply embedded the sense within employees that they are working for an organisation that is aligned with their values and sensitive to social justice and environmental sustainability more broadly. This new ethos for employees can be also attested in situations where employee expectations are frustrated, leading to protests such as those against Amazon and McKinsey due to failures to reduce carbon emissions. Thus, Wright and Nyberg argue that:

> This employee critique from within corporations can also serve as a check upon overly optimistic 'green' pledges and 'greenwashing'.[7]

7.13 In parallel, technological innovations have sparked the idea of a sharing economy as 'an ecosystem where people rent, borrow, or trade instead of own'.[8] This concept appears to align to kindness and community to describe the commercial activities of companies creating tech platforms to enable people to monetise their underused assets, such as a spare bedroom, or a car which spent most of its time parked on a driveway. Even as these tech companies have matured, and the shine has worn off their claims to be disrupting social norms or capitalism, the strong desire of many people to work for a company which they feel has purpose beyond making profit remains as a recruitment

---

7 C Wright and D Nyberg, Corporations and Climate Change: An Overview (2024) *WIREs Climate Change* DOI: 10.1002/wcc.919, 10.

8 B Laker, Redefining Leadership: The Rise and Evolution of The Sharing Economy, *Forbes* (6 July 2023).

tool for many companies. In the financial services sector the sharing economy is apparent in the open data concept that entails moving from data ownership to data sharing.

C. CSR: AN INEFFECTIVE ADD-ON

Prior to the adoption of ESG as a term, early ventures into being a *responsible company* were widely termed Corporate Social Responsibility (CSR). CSR was defined in the 1980s as follows: 7.14

> The social responsibility of business encompasses the economic, legal, ethical, and discretionary expectations that society has of organizations at a given point in time.[9]

In this era, companies, including major investment banks, started developing codes of ethics. A prominent example was the Lehman Brothers code of ethics. Codes can potentially act as a powerful tool in promoting CSR but in practice, they often amount to little more than a window-dressing exercise: 7.15

> Codes have emerged as one of the major CSR (corporate social responsibility) instruments by which companies align their actions and values with those of their customers, enacting a concept known as ethical consumerism [...] They have the ability to transform organizational cultures and function best when communicated effectively and culturally embedded in the organization; otherwise, they remain as separate documents that are often seen as external to the company's mission and purpose.[10]

Not all but many of these types of programmes were siloed, understaffed and underfunded, and made little impact on the wider company culture. CSR in larger companies was often delivered through a separate philanthropic foundation with the same name as the company. The foundation's core activities were to support employee volunteering days and payroll giving and match funding and grants to nonprofits. However, this was very much an add-on to the core business. A typical annual CSR report would lay out its strategy covering community, environment and people, and sometimes include its supply chain. These focus areas were taken from frameworks or guidance from early proponents of CSR support – organisations such as Business in the Community. 7.16

---

9 EM Epstein, The Corporate Social Policy Process: Beyond Business Ethics, Corporate Social Responsibility, and Corporate Social Responsiveness (1987) 29(3) *California Management Review* 99, 104.

10 B Stevens and S Buechler, An Analysis of the Lehman Brothers Code of Ethics and the Role It Played (2013) 10(1) *Journal of Leadership, Accountability and Ethics* 43, 43 http://www.na-businesspress.com/jlae/stevensb_web10_1_.pdf.

7.17 Businesses shaped their programmes into these strategic stakeholder groups and reported on their associated actions for each group. This worked well to some extent, and people in the business sector could point towards the 'good' things they (or rather a small team within the organisation) were doing as a company. This shows that at this stage the majority of companies were not genuinely embracing CSR but instead cherry-picking aspects of their philanthropic and pro bono activities to improve their reputation. For instance, in 2006 and 2007, Lehman Brothers released Global Philanthropy reports sharing its philanthropic activities, including giving $millions of nonprofit donations, matching employee donations and championing employee volunteering programmes around the world. Lehman Brothers also had a Code of Ethics. However, a 2013 study of Lehman Brothers' code found that 'the culture at Lehman was not tied to the code and it did not play a significant role in the organization'.[11] Delivering CSR and having a Code of Ethics proved insufficient to drive behaviours to prevent what followed in 2008:

> The collapse of Lehman Brothers followed by the close of its London office and other international subsidiaries sent shock waves through the global financial markets with a widespread ripple effect. [...] Stock markets plunged, resulting in the worst economic downturn in global markets since the Great Depression of the 1930s.[12]

D. THE EMERGENCE OF 'ESG'

7.18 The seismic events of 2008 rocked the entire economy, with blame firmly placed on banks. Trust was very quickly eroded and broad sectors of society questioned the societal purpose of banks and the financial system and who it serves. Stories emerged about poor behaviour being financially rewarded, misselling, and people being driven to take risks by being incentivised by personal and company short-term gain. The finance sector urgently needed to increase its level of transparency and trust, reinstate its commitment to all its stakeholders including customers, employees and the community, and recognise its role in addressing climate change.

7.19 While banks were failing or struggling to survive, other financial services industry companies were trying to retain the trust stakeholders placed in them and differentiate themselves from banks. Insurers, mutuals and building

---

11 Ibid.

12 Lehman Brothers 1850–2008, Global Impact of the Collapse, Harvard Business School Baker Library Bloomberg Center, https://www.library.hbs.edu/hc/lehman/exhibition/global-impact-of-the-collapse.

societies had to try harder to demonstrate their *value to society*, and CSR messaging started to change. It was no longer sufficient to arrange a strategy or report into stakeholder groups; *materiality* was looming on the horizon.

Encouraged by early standard setters such as the Global Reporting Initiative (GRI) *materiality* was being used to refer to matters that were most important to the business. Building trust through transparency was up in the top right-hand corner of the materiality matrix. Reports were now being developed with new subject areas including: 7.20

- Trust and transparency
- Climate change and environment
- Responsible procurement
- Attracting and retaining employees
- Sustainable investment

Sustainability reporting consultants saw a clear need to increase the credibility of reporting and, in some cases, advocated for change in these areas to improve disclosure. 7.21

> Financial services started to move away from a philanthropic/foundation-based approach towards issues like financial literacy - where they can use their professional skills for targeted impact. This change of direction began to impact strategy, reporting and organisational culture. And, over time, we have seen other material issues move into sustainability strategy e.g. cybersecurity and business ethics. These remain hugely relevant as trust is so key for financial firms.[13]

Building (or rebuilding) trust through corporate responsibility became a focus for the sector. This started to affect the way programmes were delivered; more partnerships were developed to tackle issues that were applicable across all companies. ESG collaborations such as the United Nations Principles for Responsible Investment (UN PRI),[14] Equator Principles,[15] UN Environment Programme Finance Initiative (UNEP FI)[16] and Accounting 7.22

13 V Taylor, CEO, Flag Communication Ltd, quoted in private email conversation with the authors (included with full permission).

14 UNPRI was launched in 2006 but started to scale after the financial crash https://www.unpri.org/about-us/about-the-pri. Guiding Principles on Business and Human Rights, Implementing the United Nations "Protect, Respect and Remedy Framework" https://www.ohchr.org/sites/default/files/documents/publications/guidingprinciplesbusinesshr_en.pdf.

15 The Equator Principles were formulated in 2003 and the latest iteration of the Principles is from July 2020. https://equator-principles.com/about-us/.

16 https://www.unepfi.org/about/.

for Sustainability[17] gained prominence during this period, focusing on areas such as climate change, human rights and responsible investment.

7.23 Financial firms were able to collaborate in these forums without competitiveness getting in the way. The focus was on solving joint global issues, gaining traction for internal support within their firms to change cultural behaviours over time. All this new activity became labelled as ESG and this is now the term used by the majority of financial firms. ESG is also used to describe how the investment community assesses and issues material to understand the value or risk of a corporate entity.

7.24 Although ESG has been widely adopted as a term within the financial services industry, not all organisations use this term. In research carried out by the authors, they found that the term used often indicates the level of ESG integration maturity that the firm has. For example, if a firm uses the term 'philanthropy' as the only way to reference the way they interact with the external community and society, it is likely they will have a less well-integrated practice of managing environmental and social issues. Aligned to this is the value created within those practices, Philanthropy has a high cost to the business but a low value, whereas at the other end of the scale, ESG has a lower cost and brings higher value to the business.

7.25 Along with a change of name, increasing professionalisation of the ESG industry began. Leading academic institutions offer well-regarded courses in this area, including the Cambridge Institute of Sustainability Leadership and Cranfield School of Management. ESG or sustainability professionals have an industry body – the Institute of Corporate Responsibility and Sustainability[18] – which offers continuing professional development opportunities, as well as thought leadership and events.

E. THE 'G' OF ESG

7.26 While CSR was an exercise in *corporate compassion* and appeared to make little difference to the culture of the financial services sector, the introduction of ESG standards means that companies no longer have to simply *care*; they have to comply.

---

17 https://www.accountingforsustainability.org/en/about-us/overview.html.

18 https://icrs.info/.

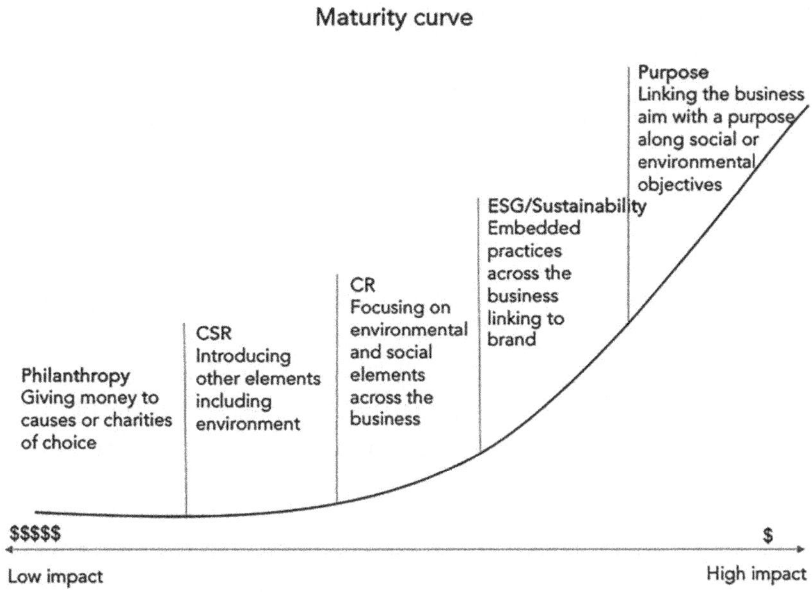

Figure 7.1 *Maturity curve*

Before the introduction of standards, some companies became signatories to voluntary, non-legally binding frameworks which incorporate ESG factors. For example, the UN Principles for Responsible Investment voluntary framework which was introduced in 2006 had, as of 2024, more than 345 signatory banks committed to taking 'action to align their core strategy, decision-making, lending and investment with the UN Sustainable Development Goals, and international agreements such as the Paris Climate Agreement'.[19] **7.27**

These voluntary frameworks are quickly being enhanced or replaced by legislation, regulation and reporting compliance to frameworks such as the Taskforce on Nature-related Financial Disclosures (TNFD)[20] and the IFRS (International Financial Reporting Standards) Sustainability Disclosures Standards.[21] In the UK there is legislation, regulation and guidance which embody different elements of ESG responsibilities and reporting obligations under UK law that require public companies, large private companies and certain financial institutions to disclose ESG-related risks and opportunities from a financial and governance risk perspective. **7.28**

19 https://www.unepfi.org/banking/bankingprinciples/.

20 Taskforce on Nature-related Financial Disclosures, https://tnfd.global/about/.

21 IFRS, https://www.ifrs.org/issued-standards/ifrs-sustainability-standards-navigator/.

7.29 Companies are expected to provide evidence and data to show outcomes and impact on a range of ESG issues, including environmental matters, employee issues, social issues and human rights, throughout their operations and supply chain. This evidence and data must be integrated into its traditional corporate governance reporting, as well as into investment decisions, supply chain management and financial reporting.

7.30 Some European Union (EU) directives and regulations which were in force prior to Brexit were transposed into UK law through the European Union (Withdrawal) Act 2018. Even regarding EU legislation that came into force after the UK's withdrawal from the EU, some legislation applies to UK firms managing EU Funds, for example the Sustainable Finance Disclosure Regulation which mandates disclosures on sustainability risks and impacts in financial services.[22]

7.31 The EU's Corporate Sustainability Reporting Directive (CSRD), effective as of January 2023, requires that all large companies and publicly listed entities (except listed micro-enterprises) disclose information on the risks and opportunities arising from social and environmental issues.[23] Companies must also report on the impact of their activities on people and the environment. The first reports under the CSRD are due in 2025. The CSRD will apply in certain cases to UK companies from 2028, for instance, if their securities are listed on an EU regulated market or if they exceed certain financial thresholds of turnover within the EU either through direct provision of services or through a branch.

7.32 The CSRD requires published data to be assured. The move to assured data may combat accusations of *greenwashing* and could lead to a level of trust in the sustainability reporting process and, by implication, in companies who report assured data. Pizzi et al. find that firms reporting against required ESG regulations has not led to the expected increase in companies adopting more sustainable practices:

> The introduction of strict requirements by regulators has favored the increasing adoption of accountability technologies by worldwide companies. Another relevant contribution has also been provided by financial operators, which have launched many initiatives to promote the adoption of more transparent behaviors by listed companies. [...] However,

---

22 Regulation (EU) 2019/2088 of the European Parliament and of the Council of 27 November 2019 on Sustainability-Related Disclosures in the Financial Services Sector OJ L 317, 1 https://eur-lex.europa.eu/legal-content/EN/TXT/?uri=CELEX:32019R2088.

23 Directive (EU) 2022/2464 of 14 December 2022 as regards Corporate Sustainability Reporting OJ L 322, 15.

> the quantitative increase associated with sustainability reporting regulation does not necessarily lead to a qualitative increase in the sustainable practices adopted by companies.[24]

Their evidence shows that external assurance improves the legitimacy of ESG information, as 'an effective way to collect independent information about sustainability information "robustness".' Sustainability practitioners have long advocated for assurance over sustainability data, and the introduction of the CSRD is very helpful in this regard. The Pizzi et al. research demonstrates that this is needed alongside mandated reporting to maintain trust in all organisations. It is yet to be seen, but arguably, regulation *levels the playing field*, with all companies required to report to the same standards, countering the argument that it can be uncompetitive and costly to 'do the right thing'. **7.33**

F. THE IMPACT OF ESG ON CULTURE

Many elements shape a company's culture, but here we will focus on those that intersect with and can be positively influenced by ESG. As mentioned above, there is an increasing amount of powerful ESG-specific legislation and regulation in addition to the traditional governance required by all companies, which is having a significant influence on behaviour in financial services companies. But there is also 'soft power' coming from customers, employees and investors to ensure that environmental and social impact are embedded as core parts of a company's strategy. This can have a positive impact on people and behaviours as well on how a business sets its priorities and objectives. **7.34**

1. Trust and Transparency

Transparency of reporting and disclosure became a core part of how firms started to win back the trust of their key stakeholder customers after 2008, including under the heading of Treating Customers Fairly. The following extract from Aviva's 2014 Corporate Responsibility Report demonstrates this: **7.35**

> Following the financial crisis in 2008, our industry continues to score poorly across various trust surveys. To increase trust, we need to keep our promises and act responsibly and ethically every day. [...] Our purpose is to free people from fear of uncertainty. We focus on helping people protect themselves and prepare for the future. Being clear about how

24 S Pizzi, A. Venturelli and F Caputa, Restoring Trust In Sustainability Reporting: The Enabling Role Of The External Assurance (2024) 68:101437 *Current Opinion in Environmental Sustainability* 1.

we can help and what we offer is a critical part of this commitment. So is keeping things as straightforward and user friendly for our customers as possible.[25]

7.36 In the past decade or so, a focus on customer needs has started to appear in CSR reporting, driven by the Global Reporting Initiative (GRI)[26] Standards GRI416 (Customer Health and Safety), GRI417 (Marketing and Labelling) and GRI418 Customer Privacy, which in turn reflected on strategy and culture. The GRI makes a clear link between transparent sustainability reporting and building and maintaining trust:

> Transparency on the sustainability impacts of a business is essential for continuous improvement as well as for stakeholder relationships. Without transparency, there is no trust – and without trust it is very complex to do business, markets do not function efficiently, and institutions lose their legitimacy.[27]

7.37 Trust in the sector started to improve. This improvement was much needed in light of the Edelman Trust Barometer that shows that trust in financial services was lower than in any other sector in 2011 and 2012.[28]

7.38 By 2017, it is interesting to note that the general public trusted financial services more than general business sectors.[29]

7.39 The barometer, however, reveals a much more nuanced picture. Not all financial services firms are perceived in the same way by the general public. Comparatively, insurance companies and asset managers do not fare as well as banks and payment services providers, as the diagram below shows:

7.40 Anecdotal evidence within the financial services industry points towards insurance companies ranking lower than banks due to the perception of low payouts on claims, although, according to the Association of British Insurers, in 2015, insurance companies paid out on average 97% of consumers' claims on vital protection policies.[30] It is, therefore, hard to counter the long-standing

---

25 'Building our Future' Aviva Corporate Responsibility Report 2014 available at https://static.aviva.io/content/dam/aviva-corporate/documents/investors/pdfs/reports/2014/CR-Report-2014.pdf, 13.

26 https://www.globalreporting.org/standards/.

27 The GRI Standards, A Policymakers Guide, 3 available at https://www.globalreporting.org/media/nmmnwfsm/gri-policymakers-guide.pdf.

28 Edelman Trust Barometer Global Report 2012 available at https://www.slideshare.net/slideshow/2012-edelman-trust-barometer-global-deck/11205162#10.

29 Edelman Trust Barometer, 2017 Financial Services Report (March 2017) available at https://www.slideshare.net/EdelmanInsights/2017-edelman-trust-barometer-financial-services-results?from_search=0 .

30 ABI, https://www.abi.org.uk/data/.

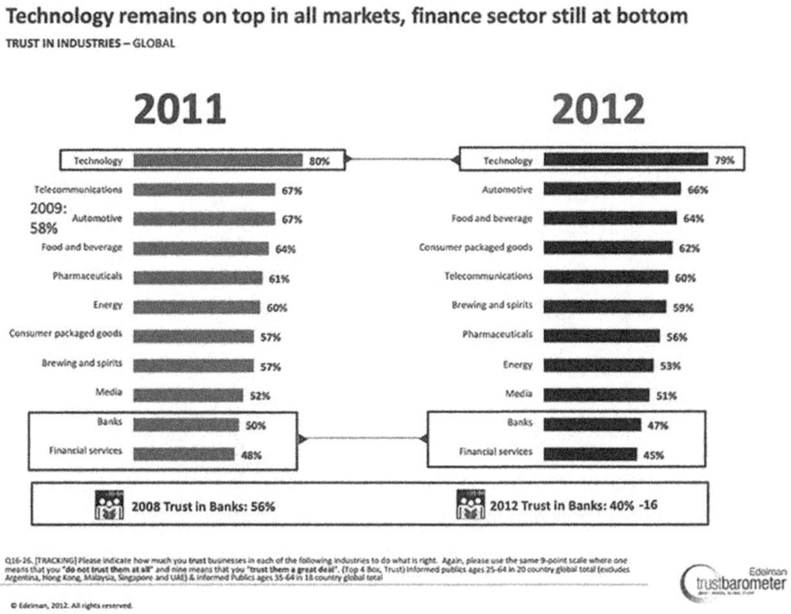

Source: Edelman Trust Barometer 2012

Figure 7.2 Technology remains on top in all markets, finance sector still at bottom

perception of the public but increased transparency could provide a good starting point.

2. Values

While there is a generational difference in expectations and perhaps a stronger moral compass for many younger people, it does not take long for a poor culture to crush their ideals and shape their decision-making to fit within a corporate culture designed solely to value maximum gain for the company or the people in charge. This problem can be overcome by building trust and focusing on increased transparency and disclosure that can, in turn, influence strategies within firms to think about the way they do business, and how to act internally as well as externally. 7.41

Indeed, corporate values increasingly include a link to the company's ESG strategy and company values have become more visible. Rather than just being meaningless words, they are linked to behaviours and used to support business decisions. Values are also closely aligned with business ethics, with the 7.42

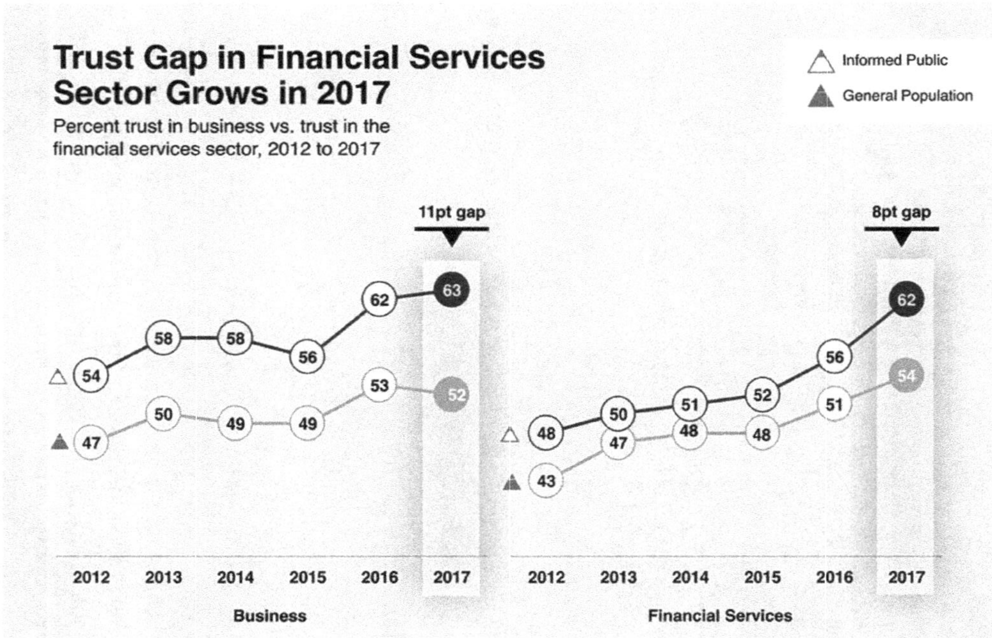

Source: Edelman Trust Barometer 2017

Figure 7.3 *Trust gap in financial services sector grows in 2017 (Percent trust in business vs. trust in the financial services sector, 2012 to 2017)*

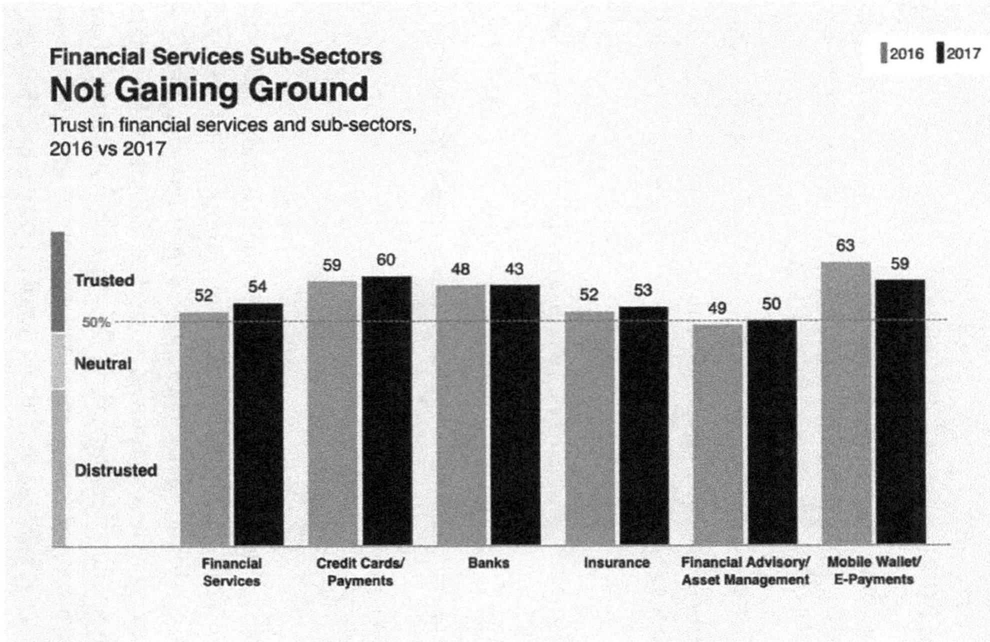

Source: Edelman Trust Barometer 2017

Figure 7.4 *Not gaining ground: financial services sub-sectors (Trust in financial services and sub-sectors, 2016 to 2017)*

behaviours expected of employees, suppliers and other business partners laid out within Business Ethics Codes. Core values often include principles like integrity, innovation, respect, and customer focus. These are intended to guide the company's actions and daily decision-making. They help the most junior to the most senior, the newest to the longest-serving, to make decisions based on principles rather than arbitrary in-the-moment factors that reflect personal or organisational gain.

7.43 The Institute of Business Ethics states:

> A code of business ethics reflects how the organisation operates its business model – how it relates to the communities in which it does business and how to express the corporate values it considers important.[31]

7.44 Values are often linked to corporate culture. A recent report from the Institute of Business Ethics found that a good corporate culture can enhance investment performance and boost productivity and employee wellbeing in the following ways:

> ***Strong investment case:*** *Incorporating cultural evaluation can significantly enhance investment performance and reduce risk*
> ***Improved business outcomes:*** *Good cultures boost productivity, employee wellbeing, innovation, and sustainability*
> ***Established discipline:*** *Cultural evaluation is a proven method with valuable insights for investors*
> ***Systematic assessment:*** *Culture can be evaluated systematically, using human judgement, and must be weighted not calculated*
> ***Technology's role:*** *New tools are emerging to support cultural assessment.*[32]

7.45 Having processes in place, aligned to a clear set of values, is more likely to result in transparent and accountable decisions. In an unpublished piece of research, a large global bank found that it takes just 18 months for employees' values to merge with those of their employer, within which time they start making decisions which are in the interests of the organisation rather than based on a set of values, ethics or governance. Values can also be aligned to a company's purpose. Values, purpose and ESG overlap but are not the same thing: values can drive purpose, purpose can include ESG, and all have an impact on culture.

---

31 The Institute of Business Ethics, Code of Ethics available at https://www.ibe.org.uk/knowledge-hub/ibe-business-ethics-framework/code-of-ethics.html accessed 10 September 2024.

32 A Gillar, Is Organisation Culture the Next Frontier in Investment, A Report for the Institute of Business Ethics (August 2024).

3. Purpose

A company's purpose has traditionally been expressed as the commercial reason it exists, but it can also be linked to or be the driving force behind its ESG strategy. Arguably, a company's primary purpose is to deliver its core service or product and to make profit: if a company is not financially viable, it cannot deliver anything for its wider stakeholders in society or the environment. A great company purpose should, however, align both commercial and ESG objectives, and a good strategy shows how they work together to deliver for all stakeholders. Profit and purpose can and should go hand in hand, with environmental and social stakeholders, as well as shareholders, clients and employees, being an integrated part of delivering both. **7.46**

In the Principles for Purposeful Business, Professor Colin Mayer writes: **7.47**

> We concluded that *the purpose of business is to solve the problems of people and planet profitably, and not profit from causing problems.*
>
> ... that a *corporate purpose* identifies how the company assists people, organisations, societies and nations to address the challenges they face, while at the same time avoiding or minimising problems companies might cause and making them more resilient in the process.[33] (emphasis added)

Having clarity of purpose can also help to direct employees of financial services companies to make good decisions on a daily basis. A commentator has opined that a clear corporate purpose is essential to enable financial firm staff to realise that customer loyalty and attracting talented workers are more important than short-term profit maximisation.[34] **7.48**

The articulation and communication of purpose within a company is critical to activating it. Having a purpose encompassing all stakeholders does not mean just adding the word 'sustainability' to an existing commercial purpose. To be an authentic driver of behaviours and decision-making, employees need to know how they can engage with supporting delivery of the purpose goals and objectives, alongside the work they do, which is focused on profit. Ideally, this is seamless within their daily life and not felt to be 'extra' or a burden. **7.49**

4. People

Being known as an employer with a genuine commitment to ESG, inclusivity and diversity offers an advantage in today's hiring market. Offering a flexible **7.50**

---

33 The British Academy, Principles for Purposeful Business (2019) available at https://www.thebritishacademy.ac.uk/publications/future-of-the-corporation-principles-for-purposeful-business/.

34 D Rouch, The Social Licence for Financial Markets: Reaching for the End and Why It Counts (2020).

and appealing work environment where employees feel a sense of belonging and alignment with the company's values, helps organisations to attract and retain top talent. Companies with outdated and unappealing cultures may find it costly to retain people, creating a risk to business continuity and success. Attracting and retaining talent is a constant battle for companies, leading them to offer a broad range of benefits and workplace enhancements. Attitudes are changing among younger employees, who have no expectation of staying in one job or even one industry sector for more than a few years.

7.51 While salary, bonus and benefits – including being able to work from home – are still very important to most employees, an increasing number of the younger workforce say they want to work for companies which have purpose, with which they share values, and which are taking responsibility for their environmental and social impact. Anecdotally, the pressure felt by companies to answer questions from potential employees about their ESG work – and its authenticity - during the interview process has encouraged them to improve and advance their ESG activity.

7.52 According to Deloitte's Global 2024 Gen Z and Millennial Survey: Living and Working with Purpose in a Transforming World:

> Environmental sustainability remains a top concern for Gen Zs and millennials, with 62% of Gen Zs and 59% of millennials reporting feeling anxious or worried about climate change in the past month. [...]
>
> The majority of Gen Zs (86%) and millennials (89%) say having a sense of purpose is important to their overall job satisfaction and well-being. And these generations are increasingly willing to reject assignments or employers who don't align with their values. When employers take that feedback and respond positively, employee loyalty tends to be much higher.[35]

7.53 It is not just the younger generation that seeks to work for responsible companies. Following the 2008 financial crisis, one UK building society – a mutual that had shifted towards a quasi-bank model before 2008 – found that reviving its credentials as a mutual focused on serving its members also reinvigorated its longest-serving employees. Many of these employees remembered the values that had originally inspired them to join the company.

7.54 As companies undergo periods of change due to having a new leader, changes in demand for their product, reputational downturn or rationalising a sprawling

35 Deloitte, Global 2024 Gen Z and Millennial Survey: Living and Working With Purpose in a Transforming World available at https://www.deloitte.com/content/dam/assets-shared/docs/campaigns/2024/deloitte-2024-genz-millennial-survey.pdf?dlva=1.

company, developing a clear purpose, and engaging employees and other stakeholders in a bigger vision of their company can prove to be a useful tool.

In November 2014, UK fintech company Sage hired a new CEO to take the 35-year-old FTSE100 company to its next stage of growth. While Sage had been giving volunteer time for many years through a UK CSR programme, there was no global strategy with a clear vision, mission, structure and funding model. Sage decided to commit to giving 2 per cent of employee time, 2 per cent of free cash flow and 2 donated licences of its three flagship products to support eligible registered nonprofits. As a company which is passionate about its SME customer base, it became clear that the focus for Sage's philanthropy should be on creating social equality and economic opportunity in the communities where they operate around the world. When the Sage Foundation was launched as the vehicle for delivering its social impact activities there was tangible excitement from employees: for many of them it was something they had longed for, with one employee even saying he'd thought he was going to have to leave the company to fulfil his philanthropic passion, but now he had five volunteering days, access to grants and the company's endorsement to bring his passion for social change into the workplace, he was more than happy to stay where he was.[36] 7.55

5. Innovation

Our knowledge of the industry indicates that ESG consultants and practitioners are often impatient for companies to develop and better fund their strategies to accelerate their mitigation of climate change, or make systemic social change or human rights impact in their supply chain. Examples of Social Innovation products funded around the world include an app to improve financial confidence for people without bank accounts in South Africa, identity verification for those without formal documentation in India and an online debt renegotiation platform in Brazil.[37] 7.56

At the same time, more traditional CSR-type activities are still in place, including offering volunteering days, payroll giving, match funding and giving grants to nonprofits. For these activities, however, budgets now tend to be smaller, and activities are more likely to be tied into a thematic focus aligned with the company's commercial objective. Employees are encouraged and 7.57

36 The case study on Sage is available on the Profit With Purpose website https://profitwithpurpose.co.uk/work/.

37 Profit with Purpose case study available at https://profitwithpurpose.co.uk/2020/10/14/experian-elevating-and-aligning-corporate-responsibility-with-global-company-vision/.

supported to volunteer around these themes, for example financial literacy for young people or people with vulnerabilities or supporting entrepreneurship programmes. Or volunteering might be tied into other company priorities such as developing diverse talent, offering training on jobs using new technologies, or even innovation and product development.

7.58 Experian provides a constrictive example of an innovative approach to integrate ESG into its business model. In 2019, Experian decided to elevate and align its corporate responsibility vision and strategy to the company's growth strategy, to make the best use of Experian's resources and to set goals and metrics to show progress towards its social impact objectives. As the world's largest credit bureau, Experian's corporate literature espouses financial inclusion as a high priority. Committed to '*creating a better tomorrow*', the core business is built around the power of data and its ability to transform lives around the world, helping people to realise their dreams – whether that means buying a house or a car, celebrating a wedding, funding their family's education or starting a new business. Since 2013, Experian has funded social innovation projects aimed at promoting financial well-being and helping people who have low credit scores or are credit 'invisible' due to having a limited financial track record. The programme has reached over 34 million people worldwide and provides around US$1.2 million in internal product development funding each year, resulting in innovations and products aimed at promoting financial inclusion under the Experian brand.

6. Boards and Executive Leadership

7.59 A company culture is heavily influenced by its leaders not only by the adoption of a certain rhetoric but most crucially by example. According to the dominant view of culture in the industry, culture is set from the top and received by people throughout the organisation. However, a top-down approach creates rules to be followed but does not create an engaged culture where less senior people are listened to.

7.60 There is still a reluctance among many boards and company leaders to accept that environmental and social issues are legitimate boardroom concerns. The introduction of standards and legislation is having a significant positive effect, but there are still too many boards and leaders who are focused solely on short-term financial results. Ignoring the wider picture of external social, environmental and geo-political factors creates a risk and governance blind spot, which does not help an organisation understand its clients' changing needs or identify new opportunities.

While not directly related to the financial services sector, analysis of recent UK corporate scandals, including at the Confederation of British Industry and the Post Office has included commentary on the failures of cultures, even 'toxic' cultures, created by boards and leadership. Poor leadership culture can lead to 'group think', or the dominance of one view or one person. **7.61**

> We know now that there is a big gap between what these organisations and their leaders say is important and what actually happens within them. Noticing and learning about that gap is what understanding culture is all about. It should be the number one priority for senior leaders. But ask them what's on their priority list, and they're likely to talk about quarterly results, growth or hitting targets.[38]

One of the approaches to improving board and leadership culture and decision-making is to add more diversity: diversity of background, experience, sex, race and ways of thinking: **7.62**

> Companies with more diverse Boards are also more likely to demonstrate higher business ethics and corporate citizenship scores, be better at attracting and retaining talent, and have more robust climate strategies.[39]

In 2022, the FCA published a policy decision on 'Diversity and inclusion on company boards and executive committees'[40] intended to improve 'transparency on the diversity of company boards and their executive management for investors and other market participants'. Leading up to this decision, the FCA published a discussion paper in 2021 titled 'Diversity and inclusion in the financial sector – working together to drive change' in which it stated: **7.63**

> We expect to see diversity and inclusion become part of how we regulate and part of how the UK financial sector does business. [..] Our goal is to see increased diversity and inclusion in financial services translate into safer and sounder firms with better internal governance and risk management, a more innovative industry, and financial products and services that meet the diverse needs of consumers.[41]

---

38 C Bishop, For All the Scandals, A Toxic Culture In Places Like The CBI and the Met Can Be Changed, *The Guardian* (London,18 April 2023) available at https://www.theguardian.com/commentisfree/2023/apr/18/toxic-culture-cbi-metropolitan-police.

39 World Economic Forum, Women Are Poised To Reshape Financial Markets – As Investors And Financial Decision-Makers (7 June 2024) available at https://www.weforum.org/agenda/2024/06/women-shape-influence-revolutionize-financial-markets/.

40 FCA, Diversity and Inclusion on Company Boards and Executive Management, Policy Statement PS22/3, (April 2022) available at https://www.fca.org.uk/publication/policy/ps22-3.pdf.

41 FCA, Diversity and Inclusion In The Financial Sector – Working Together To Drive Change, Discussion Paper DP21.2 (July 2021), 4 available at https://www.fca.org.uk/publication/discussion/dp21-2.pdf.

7.64 Another approach to focusing the minds of leadership on both profit and purpose is to integrate ESG factors into remuneration and reward, which ensures that an appropriate level of attention and priority is given to ESG factors. Integration into both short and long-term incentive plans is becoming more common, particularly in larger listed companies. PWC, in its 2021 publication The Leadership Agenda, writes:

> By now it's safe to say that to remain competitive, relevant, and respected – externally and internally – a public company, regardless of sector, must establish an ESG agenda too. As one example, remuneration may become a litmus test for financial regulators assessing whether banks, asset managers, and insurers are taking climate change seriously enough. Including ESG metrics in executive pay packages is a tangible way to close the say–do gap for a skeptical audience…[42]

7.65 The inclusion of ESG factors into incentives and remuneration across businesses would also be a useful approach for middle management, which can be a sticking point for activation of ESG strategies. They are often described as the 'squeezed middle'; their reward is determined by delivering their significant commercial targets and they are not similarly incentivised to deliver the non-financial targets, leading to inevitable prioritisation of the financial targets for themselves and their teams.

G. STRATEGY NOT TACTICS

7.66 As consultants, we often begin working with companies that already have some environmental and social impact initiatives in place – such as conducting a carbon footprint assessment or making charitable donations. However, many clients have not connected these efforts to the broader need for embedding ESG principles across their entire business. This integration is crucial not only for meeting reporting requirements but also for unlocking cultural benefits that enhance employee engagement and organisational identity.

7.67 When companies view ESG as a distraction or merely a compliance exercise, they overlook its deeper value. Stakeholders – including employees, clients and suppliers – perceive ESG as fundamental to an organisation's culture and long-term success. To bridge this gap, we collaborate with companies to develop a tailored framework that aligns all ESG elements with their core purpose as a business. Our approach helps them see how ESG activities both stem from

42 PwC, The Leadership Agenda (2021) available at https://www.pwc.com/gx/en/issues/esg/exec-pay-and-esg.html.

and contribute to their purpose, mission, and values, creating a cohesive and impactful strategy.

Our clients are often surprised to discover that an 'ESG consultant' — which they initially perceive as an add-on, an afterthought or a siloed function to be kept in a cupboard — actually provides a comprehensive view of their entire business. The strategies we develop not only align with their broader ambitions but also address critical business priorities such as risk management, cost efficiency, growth, profitability, talent acquisition and retention, employee engagement, reward systems and innovation. 7.68

In the following paragraphs we describe our process in more detail. When we start working with a client, we already have in mind the journey needed to create their ESG strategy framework. Many clients are already doing more than they realise. At an early stage we focus on their company vision: what is their purpose as a company? What are they aiming to achieve commercially? How can that purpose expand to include their ambitions for society and the environment? At this stage, we often find that the CEO is already considering broader goals beyond the bottom line but has not fully incorporated these into daily work objectives. For example, one client shared that they were using the Japanese concept of Ikigai (which roughly translates to 'a reason for being' or 'having a meaningful direction or purpose in life') to embed values and purpose beyond profit into their business.[43] 7.69

Next, we guide leadership through a brief exercise looking at the UN's Sustainable Development Goals (SDGs) to identify three or four of these on which their company could focus. Many leaders are unfamiliar with the full range of social and environmental issues relevant to their business, and the SDGs provide structured language and clear parameters to help identify areas for positive impact. Often, leadership teams quickly converge on the same SDGs, creating a shared sense of focus and direction. From this, we help companies articulate their 'north star': a big headline or tagline that sets out their ESG vision, inspires employees and engages stakeholders. 7.70

We then identify the resources the company can apply to its environmental or social initiatives. These resources might include employee time and expertise, a percentage of profits allocated to nonprofit partnerships or modifications to 7.71

43 Profit with Purpose Helps Aferian Create An ESG Strategy Aligned Culture to a Culture of Collaboration and Ikigai available at https://profitwithpurpose.co.uk/2021/08/12/profit-with-purpose-helps-aferian-create-an-esg-strategy-aligned-to-a-culture-of-collaboration-and-ikigai/.

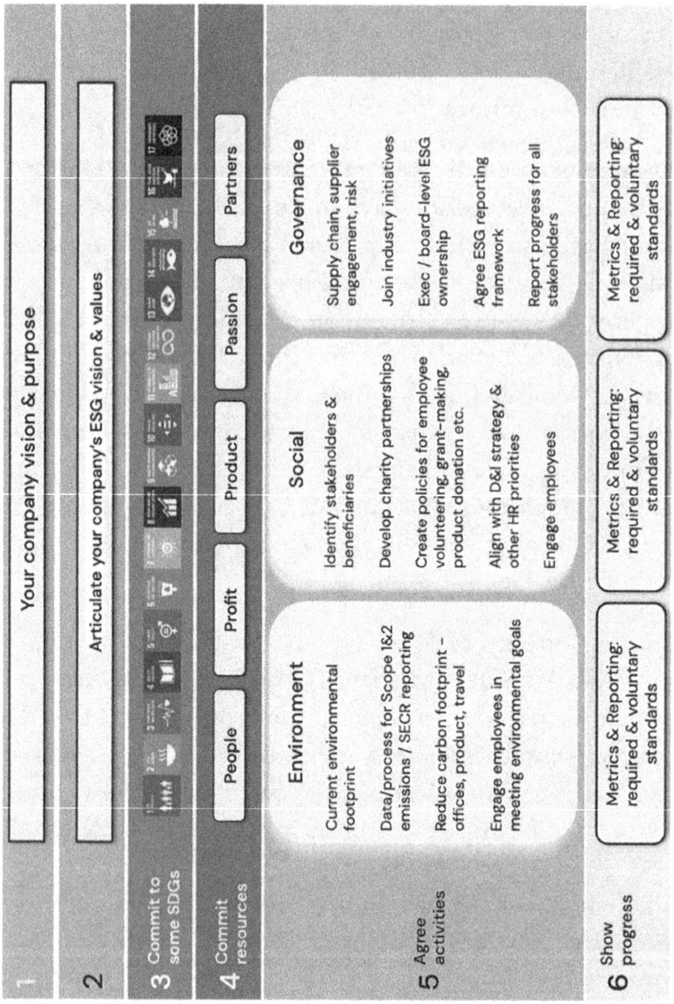

Source: ESG Experts Ltd

Figure 7.5 *ESG Consultants standard workflow*

commercial products or services to reduce carbon intensity or support impact outcomes. Increasingly, ESG legislation requires companies to extend their ESG efforts along their supply chains, making partners and suppliers valuable collaborators in achieving these goals.

Afterwards, we consolidate all the existing ESG-related efforts a company has done. They might already know their carbon footprint, or have started some reporting, making charitable donations, engaging employees in activities or addressing diversity at all levels, including the board. We assess everything being done, identify gaps and make recommendations to fill those gaps in a way which meets both the company's level of ambition and regulatory requirements. 7.72

Finally, we establish a set of short-, medium- and long-term metrics to activate their ESG strategy framework. These metrics align with regulatory reporting and relevant subsets of a number of existing standards and frameworks – for example, the EU Corporate Sustainability Reporting Directive (CSRD) includes 1,100 metrics – so we ensure a company's metrics align with those that are mandatory as well as those which support its chosen ESG goals. These metrics track progress toward the company's ESG ambitions and 'north star', supporting both regulatory compliance and storytelling. Additionally, most companies now require a tech platform to capture data and report on ESG metrics and progress effectively. 7.73

H. THE DAWNING OF A NEW FINANCIAL SERVICES CULTURE

Over the past ten years some of the oldest financial services companies, along with new challenger companies and others who sit in between, have completely changed how they work, how they are structured as a company and how they promote their company and services. They may not use the term 'ESG', but these companies fully embrace the concept of aligning profit with purpose and embedding social and environmental objectives into the core of their business. They have values which correspond to ESG, promote ethical behaviours and have a willingness to be transparent. This, in turn, attracts both customers and employees who choose these companies to align with their own values. 7.74

Some of these companies have certified as B Corporations (B Corp), which are 'companies verified by B Lab to meet high standards of social and 7.75

environmental performance, transparency, and accountability'.[44] To certify as a B Corp a company must also amend its Articles of Association 'to embed a commitment to consider the impact of decisions on all stakeholders'.[45] It must also implement a comprehensive framework of impact measures, against which they are assessed on initial certification and then every three years. The impact measures cover environmental and social factors as well as having a requirement for a company to have 'positive workplace cultures with meaningful workplace dialogue' and to measure workplace culture and take action to improve it.

> Workplace culture refers to the attitudes, beliefs, and values within a workplace that influence many aspects of workers' experiences, such as those related to workers' sense of satisfaction, belonging, shared purpose, psychological safety, engagement, and happiness. A positive workplace culture exists when workers have positive experiences and there is ongoing dialogue. Positive workplace culture helps create a sense of shared purpose, which is vital for the success of purpose-driven companies. Therefore, the concepts of workplace culture, workplace dialogue, and shared purpose are intertwined.[46]

7.76 In 2024, there are over 200 UK companies with B Corp certification covering all aspects of financial services: Octopus Group, Triodos Bank, Tribe Capital, BKL accountants, Simply Business Insurance, Dudley Building Society, GSB Capital, Crown Agents Bank, ECI Partners private equity, Lombard Odier wealth and asset managers, Beckett Investment Management Group, Centrus corporate finance, AKO Capital and the UK's oldest privately owned bank (since 1672), C.Hoare & Co. These companies are well positioned to support future generations who increasingly require their financial services providers both to be well governed and to actively provide solutions to environmental and social issues.

7.77 EQ Investors, a firm of financial planners and investment managers, was a founding B Corp in the UK. Its founder, John Spiers, had 'a growing sense that capitalism is not working', and had been on a journey for many years to 'create a company with a strong focus on developing great relationships with clients – and to make sure everyone received a fantastic service, with shared values, shared goals, and shared purpose'.

---

44 BLab United Kingdom, What is a B Corp? https://bcorporation.uk/b-corp-certification/what-is-a-b-corp/.

45 Ibid.

46 Overview of the standards for B Corp Certification, https://standards.bcorporation.net/en-us/draft/topic/workplace-culture.

> Some clients come to us purely because we are B Corp certified. Almost all clients recognise and appreciate it. [...] It's a unique selling point for us. The fact we can say we are also an equitable and ethically minded company means a lot to prospective clients. It also helps with attracting employees – they recognise and mention in our B Corp status in interviews. When we re-certify every three years, we create B Corp working groups to involve employees. As a staff-owned B Corp, we are part of a community of businesses worldwide building a more inclusive and sustainable economy.[47]

I. CONCLUSION

Significant progress has been made in the past ten years towards legitimising non-financial concerns and social and environmental considerations, as factors which are central to financial services businesses and their cultures. There is increasing respect for, understanding of and professionalisation of ESG factors, which has had some impact on the culture of companies: on boards, employees, leadership, investors, industry bodies and regulators. **7.78**

There is a higher degree of acceptance of the legitimacy of ESG, balanced with the need to remain commercially viable. However, there is still a long way to go before all financial services companies accept that they should seek profit with purpose. **7.79**

In a 2024 interview for ESG Summit Europe, Ioannis Ioannou, Associate Professor of Strategy and Entrepreneurship at the London Business School, observed: **7.80**

> More broadly, it is worth remembering that the path to integrating sustainability into business strategy is fraught with challenges, including the need for cultural change within organizations, the development of new capabilities, and the management of stakeholder expectations. Companies that have seen early success often share common traits, such as strong leadership commitment to sustainability, the ability to innovate in response to sustainability challenges, and the integration of sustainability into core business metrics and decision-making processes.[48]

---

47 J Spiers, 'View from the Chair: Capitalism Is Under Threat', 9 October 2023, available at https://eqinvestors.co.uk/individuals/hub/article/capitalism-is-under-threat.

48 I Ioannou, Innovation is Essential for the Strategic Integration of ESG Criteria (ESG Summit Europe, 10 April 2024) available at https://www.esgsummiteurope.com/blog/a-gathering-to-cement-esg-criteria/.

8

PURPOSE-LED COMPANIES IN FINANCIAL SERVICES – A CASE STUDY

Fliss Berridge

BE HELPFUL. AND KIND. THE END.

A cost-of-living crisis persists.[1] Yet in 2023 the four biggest banks in the UK amassed an eye-watering £44 billion in profit.[2] Regulators and academics continue to question the state of financial services in the UK. **8.1**

It is time for change in finance. The traditional bank template of maximising profit irrespective of consequence needs re-drawing. There is an alternative: the '*purpose*-driven' model, melding reasonable profits with a purpose that benefits the most in society, as well as the richest few. **8.2**

While the UK is reasonably well off on the global scale, annual wellness studies show money does not buy commensurate happiness. What's going wrong? Can the internal workings of businesses behaving better make a difference? If so, what does that look like? And what has *being helpful and kind* got to do with anything? **8.3**

To be successful you need to alleviate, or solve, a problem – to be helpful. So being helpful can be turned into a business case. Giving people knowledge, choice, capability and convenience is helpful. Making sure this is done in a way that does not otherwise cause harm is being true to this aim – kind. Being helpful, in a way that does not otherwise cause harm, can have a true impact on society, and can lead to a strong value-driven culture in financial firms. **8.4**

At fintech Ordo, we have built technology that helps people juggle their bills and flexibly manage their money. Mulling the point of our company, we briefly entertained being a lifestyle app and then narrowed this down to financial management. Given the emotional toll personal finances can take, we thought that our services could bring some peace to people's minds. We settled on the motto of '*Helping people improve their financial wellbeing*'. This was the artist's impression of what we wanted our newly built company to achieve. We had established our 'why?', our Purpose (for the time being). We inscribed it on flip-chart paper, blu-tacked it to a wall and measured our outcomes by it. **8.5**

Since then, to reflect our B2B focus, we have incorporated providing competition to the Goliaths that are the card schemes and banks. The end goal is to provide better services to businesses and consumers, that in turn enable them **8.6**

---

1 All weblinks were last accessed 26 December 2024.

2 According to research and analysis carried out by CityAM. Lars Mucklejohn, 'Lloyds, HSBC, Barclays and Natwest post record £44bn profits from global interest rate hikes' CityAM (22 February 2024) (22 February 2024) https://www.cityam.com/big-banks-see-record-44bn-profit-from-interest-rate-hikes/.

to manage their finances better. Curiously, we also find ourselves heading back towards *smart* financial and life management, completing the circle to re-visit the point where we once thought we could begin.

8.7 And as for *how* we work, we choose to commit to behaving in an open, considerate and positive way towards everyone we work with: our staff, customers, suppliers and fellow ecosystem participants. We try to work and behave in a way that works for, and respects, each of them whilst working for us. We could summarise our Purpose and way of working as 'doing helpful stuff while being kind': a positive version of Google's former motto, '*Don't be evil*'.

8.8 This is a case study of my fintech, Ordo. It's my experience of delivering financial services in a way that puts People and Purpose first, rather than supranormal profits. It's a description of how we came about and my view of what has been significant. It demonstrates the importance of Purpose in our past, present and future. It shows how Purpose has influenced how we behave in a sector that unfortunately finds it hard to hit the headlines for anything to be proud of.

A. SOCIETY TODAY

1. The Incumbent Finance Sector

8.9 As well as the continuing cost-of-living crisis, by the end of 2023 the UK was in recession,[3] and a record number of businesses went insolvent.[4] However, atop this sinking ground, bank profits soared.[5] This despite some institutions only still standing because they were propped up by the taxpayer,[6] and many having been embroiled in various scandals.[7]

---

3 Office for National Statistics (ONS), 'Quarterly economic commentary: October to December 2023' (28 March 2024) https://www.ons.gov.uk/economy/nationalaccounts/uksectoraccounts/articles/quarterlyeconomiccommentary/octobertodecember2023.

4 Sam Gruet, 'Number of companies going bust hits 30-year high' *BBC* (30 January 2024) https://www.bbc.co.uk/news/business-68140635#:~:text=The%20number%20of%20companies%20that,rising%20costs%20and%20interest%20rates.

5 As reported by CityAM. Lars Mucklejohn, 'Lloyds, HSBC, Barclays and Natwest post record £44bn profits from global interest rate hikes' (n 2).

6 National Audit Office, 'Taxpayer support for UK banks: FAQs' (last updated November 2020) https://www.nao.org.uk/taxpayer-support-for-uk-banks-faqs/.

7 See SFO, 'SFO concludes investigation into LIBOR manipulation' (18 October 2019) https://www.sfo.gov.uk/2019/10/18/sfo-concludes-investigation-into-libor-manipulation/; Financial Conduct Authority, 'FCA fines Metro Bank PLC £10 million and publishes Decision Notices for two of its former executive directors' (12 December 2022) https://www.fca.org.uk/news/press-releases/fca-fines-metro-bank-plc-decision-notices-two-former-executives and 'PPI complaints' (24 February 2023 and updated 2

Some would suggest it is supranormal profits, as opposed to reasonable profit or ordinary wealth, that needs addressing. A Joseph Rowntree Foundation report from 2024 indeed says this.[8] If you have a segment of society stretching the income scale so far in the wealth direction, the gap between rich and poor is going to cause problems. Where a nation has significant wealth and economic disparity, there will be poverty.[9] 8.10

2. Disparity between Rich and Poor

The disparity between rich and poor grew throughout the 1980s and has stayed stubbornly and consistently wide since the 1990s.[10] When the cost-of-living crisis triggered by COVID hit, it was those below the gap, with less disposable income, who felt, and still are feeling, the brunt.[11] The Office for Budget Responsibility predicts that disposable income will not get back to pre-COVID levels until the end of 2025/2026.[12] 8.11

When you factor overall wealth into the equation, not just income, the picture is even starker. When taking all a person's assets into consideration, in 2021, the richest 10 per cent owned over half[13] the UK's wealth; the bottom 50 per cent owned less than 5 per cent.[14] It is overall wealth – which includes how much you take home at the end of the day, week or month, as well as what you have to fall back on, both liquid and illiquid – that impacts health, wellbeing and poverty. As the May 2024 Joseph Rowntree Foundation report found, more than a quarter of adults at the start of 2020 said they would not be able to manage on their savings for a month if they lost their income.[15] 8.12

December 2024) https://www.fca.org.uk/consumers/ppi-complaints; Dominic Lindley, 'The top 10 retail banking scandals: 70 billion reasons why shareholders must play a greater role in changing bank culture' New City Agenda (11 April 2016) https://newcityagenda.co.uk/the-top-10-retail-banking-scandals-50-billion-reasons-why-shareholders-must-play-a-greater-role-in-changing-bank-culture/.

8 Sarah Kerr and Michael Vaughan, 'Changing the narrative on wealth inequality' (2 May 2024) Joseph Rowntree Foundation https://www.jrf.org.uk/wealth-funding-and-investment-practice/changing-the-narrative-on-wealth-inequality.

9 Ibid.

10 Brigid Francis-Devine, 'Income inequality in the UK' (17 April 2024) House of Commons Research Briefing https://commonslibrary.parliament.uk/research-briefings/cbp-7484/#:~:text=According%20to%20the%20Resolution%20Foundation,rise%20for%20the%20top%20half.

11 David Finch, 'The cost-of-living crisis is a health emergency too' (7 October 2022) Health https://www.health.org.uk/news-and-comment/blogs/the-cost-of-living-crisis-is-a-health-emergency-too; Jade Meadows and others, 'The Impact of the Cost-of-Living Crisis on Population Health in the UK: Rapid Evidence Review' (2024) 24 *BMC Public Health* 561 https://doi.org/10.1186/s12889-024-17940-0.

12 Office for Budget Responsibility, 'Economic and fiscal outlook – March 2024' (6 March 2024) https://obr.uk/efo/economic-and-fiscal-outlook-march-2024/#chapter-1.

13 57 per cent.

14 Sarah Kerr and Michael Vaughan, 'Changing the narrative on wealth inequality' (n 8).

15 Ibid.

8.13 There seems to be no end to the disparity in the short term. At the point of writing, the Resolution Foundation says that in 2024/25, the bottom half of households will see a 1 per cent *decrease* in their income, but the top half will yield a 1 per cent *increase*.[16]

8.14 Another way of putting it is: for 2024/25, the top 10 per cent of households by savings will receive around 65 per cent (£60bn) of interest. This works out at roughly £20,000 each before tax. At the bottom end of society, those households with the lowest amount in savings stand to reap just 2 per cent of the interest available: about £100 each.[17]

3. Just How Rich Is the UK?

8.15 Wealth is important – both nationally and individually. It is surplus funds that are needed for investment, both nationally and individually. Wealth can give you buying strength, reassurance and courage. Wealth gives you choices.

8.16 At a national level, wealth-fuelled investment pays for research, new infrastructure and services. In 2024, the International Monetary Fund ('IMF') ranked the UK as the 6th richest nation, out of 180+ countries, in terms of GDP, a key measure of output.[18] To be able to readily compare that to other countries and understand how expensive it is to live and buy the same basket of goods across multiple countries, the 'Purchasing Power Parity' ('PPP') measure is used in conjunction with GDP. For GDP-PPP, the UK ranks 23rd.[19] If you then factor in a country's share of the world for its GDP-PPP, the IMF puts the UK at number 9.[20]

8.17 While these measures hide the disparity of the spread of wealth, generally, being in the top 10 wealthiest countries globally out of more than 180 demonstrates some national success. So, are UK citizens content with being sixth richest and ninth strongest purchaser in the world?

---

16 Brigid Francis-Devine, 'Income inequality in the UK' (n 10).

17 Adam Corlett, 'The Living Standards Outlook – Summer 2023 Update' (September 2023) Resolution Foundation https://www.resolutionfoundation.org/publications/living-standards-outlook-summer-2023/.

18 Caleb Silver, 'The top 25 economies in the world: Ranking the richest countries in the world' (Updated 4 October 2024) https://www.investopedia.com/insights/worlds-top-economies/#:~:text=Nominal%20GDP%20Per%20Capita%20in%20Current%20U.S.%20Dollars%3A%20%2451%2C0706,%2C%20insurance%2C%20and%20business%20services.

19 International Monetary Fund, 'GDP per capita, current prices' (2024) https://www.imf.org/external/datamapper/NGDPDPC@WEO/OEMDC/ADVEC/WEOWORLD.

20 Ibid.

4. Is the UK Happy?

A collaboration between the United Nations Sustainable Development Solutions Network, the Oxford Wellbeing Research Centre and Gallup has produced a global happiness report since 2012.[21] Production began in response to a worldwide call for government policy to be more/also focused on improving wellbeing. It assists governments in considering and improving the happiness of their citizens. **8.18**

So, has UK wealth bought our happiness? **8.19**

We give ourselves 6.7 out of 10![22] **8.20**

In the March 2024 World Happiness Report, the UK scrapes into the top 20 happiest nations (number 20). Finland came in at number 1 for the seventh year in a row. Most of the Nordics are happier than the UK, as well as the Antipodeans, Kuwaitis, Canadians and Irish, among others. The US, France and Germany do even worse than the UK. **8.21**

The World Happiness Report uses the self-assessed Cantril Ladder methodology as its measure.[23] The Cantril Ladder is the most widely used test for assessing subjective topics[24] such as wellbeing and happiness. It is recommended by the Organisation for Economic Cooperation and Development ('OECD').[25] But use of a ladder with a bottom and top, representing worst and best possible lives, has been argued to give more credence to power and status and less weight to relationships and mental health, for example.[26] It is sobering that the sixth/ninth richest nation, the UK, even with a correlation between wealth and happiness, only makes it to number 20 for happiness and wellbeing. So, what is behind people's feelings about money and finances? **8.22**

---

21 John F Helliwell and others (eds), World Happiness Report 2024 (Wellbeing Research Centre, University of Oxford 2024) https://worldhappiness.report.

22 Ibid chapter 2.

23 Ibid.

24 Gallup, 'Understanding how Gallup uses the Cantril Scale: Development of the "Thriving, Struggling, Suffering" categories' https://news.gallup.com/poll/122453/understanding-gallup-uses-cantril-scale.aspx.

25 OECD, 'Illustrative examples of subjective well-being measures in OECD Guidelines on Measuring Subjective Well-Being' (Paris 2013) https://doi.org/10.1787/9789264191655-9-en.

26 Anders H Nilsson, Johannes C Eichstaedt, Tim Lomas, and others, 'The Cantril Ladder Elicits Thoughts about Power and Wealth' (2024) 14 Scientific Reports 2642 https://www.nature.com/articles/s41598-024-52939-y#:~:text=The%20Cantril%20Ladder%20is%20among,)%20to%20best%20(top).

5. How Does Money Make You Feel?

8.23 Subconscious beliefs and attitudes about finance can have deep psychological foundations.[27] Budgeting, spending, saving and borrowing are tools for carving out a better life for some. For others, financial planning is an enigma to be feared, filed and forgotten.

8.24 Try this:

8.25 *Money* knocks at your door. What does Money look like?[28]

8.26 Your instinctive vision could be a revelation.

8.27 For many, it is not only a bleak picture. It causes that stomach-plummeting-through-the floor-feeling; sad, baleful emotions that negatively affect your health. In 2023, the Office for National Statistics ('ONS') reported more people needing access to credit, and fewer people saving. This led to lower feelings of wellbeing and a lot of anxiety.[29] Recent data[30] from the mental health charity, Mind, showed nearly a third of people were worried about bills, and 37 per cent of anxious people felt ashamed.

8.28 It's not only consumers as individuals. Managing money is a chore for those running small and medium sized businesses ('SMEs') too. Ordo commissioned some research into how SMEs feel about money. In June 2020, our research found that business owners spend nearly 10 hours per week dealing with accounts-based tasks[31] and 45 per cent said they regularly had to work overtime to keep on top of business admin.[32] It is no surprise, then, that 40 per cent of respondents said that managing accounts and payments was the worst part of owning a business.

---

27 Emilia White, 'Behavioral finance: How our subconscious beliefs impact our real-world dollars' (2020) https://afmfa.com/behavioral-finance-how-our-subconscious-beliefs-impact-our-real-world-dollars/.

28 Sadly, I can't claim this wonderful visual. I read it in Psychologies magazine years go. I have asked many people since, revealing much.

29 Office for National Statistics, 'How are financial pressures affecting people in Great Britain?' (22 February 2023) https://www.ons.gov.uk/peoplepopulationandcommunity/wellbeing/articles/howarefinancialpressuresaffectingpeopleingreatbritain/2023-02-22 People who were behind on or struggling with bill payments, or using more credit than usual, had lower well-being and higher anxiety.

30 Mental Health Foundation, 'Financial strain is driving the UK's anxiety' (15 May 2023) https://www.mentalhealth.org.uk/about-us/news/financial-strain-driving-uks-anxiety.

31 Survey results reported in many publications, including Richard Jenkins, 'Small businesses unaware how much cash they lose every time they're paid for work' *Daily Star* (12 Jun 2020) https://www.dailystar.co.uk/life-style/money/small-businesses-unaware-how-much-22180678.

32 Ibid.

Clearly, there is room for helping consumers and businesses deal with their finances. 8.29

6. A Bit of Corporate Governance

An important element of Ordo's back story is to do with corporate governance. 8.30 It is not everyone's thriller read, but knowing the basic rules is essential for understanding their impact on corporate goings-on. It is corporate governance that is the backbone of financial regulation principles,[33] and its failure sent the planet's financial markets tumbling in the 2008 financial crisis.[34]

For the governing body of a company or organisation, usually a board, to be 8.31 effective, best practice is that it should comprise 8 to 12 diverse people including independent directors. Those directors should possess a range of skills, have varied experience, think differently, be different to each other and come from a variety of backgrounds.

The Corporate Governance Code, no matter the version, requires that a com- 8.32 pany appoint and maintain an effective board which is responsible for the long-term success of the company. A board and its committees should have a mix of skills, experience, knowledge and independence. There should also be a dialogue with shareholders (or guarantors in the case of a company limited by guarantee, which is a common form for not-for-profit companies) – distinct from directors. A board sets and oversees the strategy of an organisation, holding executives to account for delivery of the strategy. Shareholders or guarantors hold the board to account.

Once an effective board is in place, how it runs a company is partly set by 8.33 its so-called Articles of Association, a set of rules of what a company can and cannot do, at a mechanical and process level. Articles will, for example, describe how shares may or may not be transferred and set out the process for effecting any transfers, and how directors must be appointed and for what

33 Financial Reporting Council, 'Corporate Governance (overview)' (4 October 2023) https://www.frc.org.uk/library/standards-codes-policy/corporate-governance/corporate-governance-overview/.

34 Grant Kirkpatrick, 'The Corporate Governance Lessons from the Financial Crisis' (2009) 2009(1) OECD Journal: Financial Market Trends https://doi.org/10.1787/fmt-v2009-1-en; Simon Deakin, 'Corporate Governance and Financial Crisis In The Long Run' (2010) Centre for Business Research, University of Cambridge Working Paper No. 417 https://www.jbs.cam.ac.uk/wp-content/uploads/2023/05/cbrwp417.pdf.

length of term. Changing an organisation's Articles requires 75 per cent[35] shareholder backing.[36]

7. The UK's Online and Mobile Bank Transfer System – The Faster Payments Scheme

8.34 Prior to founding Ordo, the co-founders ran the UK's online and mobile bank transfer system, the Faster Payments Scheme Limited (the 'Faster Payments Scheme'). The Faster Payments Scheme is the central monopoly system that facilitates all the online and mobile bank transfers in the UK 24x7, 365 days a year. It is a company limited by guarantee, with the guarantors being the financial institutions that participate in the system.

8.35 Being a popular market player with strong market power means the Faster Payments Scheme could be a concentrated risk channel. Arguably, it is intrinsic to UK society. There are no exact alternatives. It could cause great harm to the UK and its people if it went wrong. It must be robust. Consequently, HM Treasury designated the Faster Payments system as systemically important,[37] and it is overseen by the Bank of England. It must abide by the Principles for Financial Market Infrastructures, governed jointly by the Committee on Payments and Market Infrastructures and the International Organisation of Securities Commissions ('CPMI-IOSCO').[38]

8.36 In addition, and in contrast, the Payment Systems Regulator (the 'PSR') regulates the payment systems. The PSR, being an economic regulator, has a competition, end-user and innovation perspective. The Faster Payments Scheme must abide by directions given by the PSR, which include having open and non-discriminatory access requirements, considering user needs and directors avoiding conflicts of interest with infrastructure suppliers.[39]

8.37 The Faster Payments Scheme is paid for by the financial institution participants in the payment system and is run on a cost recovery basis. In a bid to

---

35 Companies Act 2006, section 21.

36 If a company is limited by guarantee rather than shares (as the UK's internet and mobile bank transfer system, the Faster Payments Scheme Limited, is), the company will have guarantors rather than shareholders. Changing such an organisation's Articles requires the backing of 75 per cent or more of its guarantors.

37 HM Treasury, 'Designation of Payment Systems: Response to the Consultation' (March 2015) https://assets.publishing.service.gov.uk/media/5a7f67cfe5274a2e87db5a85/Designated_Payment_Systems_FINAL_17.03_21_05.pdf.

38 BIS, 'Principles for Financial Market Infrastructures (PFMI)' (16 April 2012) https://www.bis.org/cpmi/info_pfmi.htm.

39 Payment Systems Regulators, 'General directions' https://www.psr.org.uk/how-we-regulate/regulatory-framework/general-directions/.

grab market share in the mid-1980s, banks stopped charging consumers for some bank account services if the customer was in credit. Sending and receiving faster payments for consumers was made free as part of the *free-if-in-credit* banking model as a result of competition; a result that has largely been good for consumers. Consequently, as with all business cost, it is in the Faster Payments Scheme participants' interests to keep the costs of operating the payment system low.

B. THE NEXT LAYER OF PAYMENTS INNOVATION

The payments innovation of 2008 was real-time payments in the form of the Faster Payments Scheme. Fast forward ten years, and European payments laws and a UK bank competition crackdown were to collide in an attempt to catalyse the next payments frontier. **8.38**

In 2017, the UK's national competition regulator, the Competition and Markets Authority ('CMA'), concluded there was a lack of competition in the retail banking market.[40] As a result of years of a stagnant market dominated by players not innovating or providing value for money, consumers and small businesses were suffering and paying over the odds. The CMA's competition remedy was to mandate that the nine largest banks in the UK and Northern Ireland[41] build and expose standard Application Programme Interfaces ('APIs'). In the UK, this competition remedy, comprising mandated technology build and participation in a market, is known as Open Banking and operates under the CMA's Retail Banking Market Investigation Order 2017 (the 'CMA Order').[42] Effectively, the CMA mandated the standardised implementation of the Payment Services Directive 2 ('PSD2') as a competition remedy on the banks, in lieu of potential further legal action against retail banks for anti-competitive behaviour. **8.39**

The Open Banking regulatory remedy permitted FCA-authorised fintechs to securely connect to these exposed and (supposed) standardised APIs. Once connected, fintechs could provide what banks had not: innovative services to businesses and consumers that drove down costs. **8.40**

40 Competition and Markets Authority, Retail Banking Market Investigation Order 2017 (2 February 2017 last updated 15 May 2020) https://www.gov.uk/government/publications/retail-banking-market-investigation-order-2017#:~:text=Details,enterprise%20(SME)%20banking%20markets.

41 Allied Irish Bank – AIB Group UK, Bank of Ireland, Barclays, Danske Bank (Northern Bank Limited), HSBC, Lloyds Banking Group, Nationwide Building Society, NatWest Group and Santander.

42 Competition and Markets Authority, Retail Banking Market Investigation Order 2017 (n 40).

8.41 Innovative Open Banking services operate at a competitive layer above the systemically important Faster Payments system. The digital journey, and the business and consumer proposition, would be provided by the fintech. The actual money transfer would still be completed via the systemically important Faster Payments system, in accordance with the CPMI-IOSCO principles and subject to Bank of England and PSR oversight and regulation respectively. As Open Banking operates *competitively* at a digital layer abstracted from the Faster Payments system, Open Banking services could never be provided by the central not-for-profit monopoly payment system itself.

1. The Impact of Open Banking

8.42 Open Banking allows the collection of payments (mostly by businesses) securely and instantly at low cost, with payment landing in their account automatically correctly referenced. Open Banking does this without the need for a payer to input references, account details or card numbers. The burden of securely collecting and storing account details is removed for businesses, and payers are spared the responsibility and hazard of typing in numbers, which can easily go wrong.

8.43 With Open Banking, because payment is instant, both in and out (unlike cards and direct debit) payers (mostly consumers) can be far more agile with managing their finances. A consumer can wait seconds before a bill becomes overdue before making payment and still pay on time. This gives people more time to pay a bill, or to arrange for money to be available for them to clear a debt. It means transfers between accounts can be made seconds before an invoice needs to be paid. This not only gives people the ability to manage their finances more dynamically, but it can save people money too. Open Banking can save penalty fees that would have otherwise been levied had someone gone overdrawn or had a direct debit payment bounce due to inherent rigidity. It also means people can make instant loan repayments, whereby lowering the capital-attracting interest. On the flip side, it can make money. Savers can instantly increase capital-earning interest or move money to a higher yielding account earning a higher rate, immediately.

8.44 Money moving in real time also means whenever someone checks their bank balance, they can be confident it is accurate. Any payments sent via Open Banking will have debited when sent and cleared when received. This means the balance showing is, to the penny, an accurate statement of how much money someone has in their account. This is as opposed to card payments, which may show confusingly as pending for days or just be deducted from an account working days later; or direct debits, which take multiple working days to clear, tying up funds for longer.

The benefits of Open Banking for consumers and businesses can be summarised as follows: **8.45**

Consumers: **8.46**

(i) Instant money transfer – allowing for more time to cancel, pay, and/or gather required funds, enabling dynamic, flexible and controllable finances;
(ii) Instant balance recognition – enabling accurate financial management;
(iii) Enhanced security – reducing fraud and mistaken payments;
(iv) Digitised payment journey – smooth joined up payment requests available across multiple channels (text message, data message such as WhatsApp, paper bills, email, eCommerce 'Pay now' buttons, QR codes and in-person) making paying easy, convenient and efficient;
(v) Indirect cost saving – saving money.

Businesses: **8.47**

(i) Instant money transfer – boosting liquidity;
(ii) Lower fees – saving costs;
(iii) Broader availability for businesses than Direct Debit – better choice and access;
(iv) Automatic reconciliation – better services and indirect cost savings;
(v) Enhanced security – reducing fraud and mistaken payments;
(vi) Reduced regulatory burden – as less data is collected, less data must be securely stored, whereby easing compliance with GDPR and making card scheme regulatory requirements irrelevant, freeing up business capacity;[43]
(vii) Certainty of payment – in common with Faster Payments, cheques and cash, purchase protection insurance is not automatically bundled in with payment method as with card chargebacks; and
(viii) Easy to integrate – API and cloud native services are quicker and easier to implement, resulting in convenient, efficient and low-cost accessibility.

2. The Limitation of the CMA Order and the Need to Expand Open Banking

Traditionally, repeated payments are either made via card details being held on file, or by direct debit. These mechanisms were invented in the 1960s and took off in the 1980s. The UK was a very different society 65 years ago. Most people had working structures that meant they were paid, predictably and reliably, the same amount every month. Nowadays, job security and regularity is **8.48**

43 Minimal data is stored by the fintech as less data is required to initiate a payment. Data is stored securely in compliance with FCA requirements.

absent for many people. Millions in the gig economy, some by choice, others not, have incomes that are changeable in terms of both amount and frequency. Together with the self-employed, for those with portfolio careers, and those whose income is contingent and therefore sporadic, traditional payment methods are at odds with their life and financial situation.

8.49 For businesses too, there are disadvantages to taking repeated payments such as gym subscriptions, ongoing charity donations, and the like by card. Card payments are messy once a card expires or is lost or stolen. And the concentrated market with Visa and MasterCard makes it difficult for some businesses to broker a good deal. But with the UK being such a card-dominant society, even more so since COVID, most businesses view card payment acceptance as essential.

8.50 The UK is unique in being so heavily reliant on cards without an available alternative. Consequently, successive UK governments[44] and regulators want Open Banking to be a real competitor to card payments. This is such an important goal that it is part of the PSR's strategy,[45] and comes under the competition objective of the Financial Conduct Authority.[46]

8.51 However, despite the UK's mandated approach to implementing PSD2 seeing some success – in July 2024 there were more than 10 million users of Open Banking[47] – it was envisaged by many that Open Banking would be more mainstream by now.

8.52 This lack of mainstream adoption is, in part, due to the artificial restriction on what was mandated in the CMA Order. At the time of writing, mid-2024, pursuant to the CMA competition remedy, Open Banking can be used for single payments, and a slither of repeated payments meeting certain criteria.

8.53 In Open Banking, the authorisation of a mandate to collect repeated payments (such as direct debits) is called Variable Recurring Payments ('VRP'). The CMA Order-mandated banks allow regulated fintechs access to facilitate

---

44 Niamh Curran, 'UK election 2024: What each party's manifesto outlines for fintech' *Finextra* (2 July 2024) https://www.finextra.com/the-long-read/1060/uk-election-2024-what-each-partys-manifesto-outlines-for-fintech; see also Labour under Strategic partnership through industrial strategy https://labour.org.uk/change/kickstart-economic-growth/.

45 Payment Systems Regulator, 'Strategy' (January 2022) https://www.psr.org.uk/media/m2kfxfkg/psr-strategy-jan-2022.pdf.

46 FCA, 'Our strategy 2022–2025' https://www.fca.org.uk/publication/corporate/our-strategy-2022-25.pdf.

47 'Open banking marks major milestone of 10 million users' *Open Banking* (23 July 2024) https://www.openbanking.org.uk/news/open-banking-marks-major-milestone-of-10-million-users/.

single payments and VRPs. However, following lobbying from the banks, fintech access for facilitating VRPs was restricted. The final restricted VRPs included relate to the provision of credit, lending, credit cards, savings and alternatives to high-cost bank overdrafts – an attempt to engineer the outcome of making people's money work harder for them.[48] It means that repeated bill payments such as utility bills and council tax, and gym and streaming subscriptions, for example, are excluded from mandated access for fintechs.

The restricted VRPs that are mandated have been nicknamed '*sweeping*' or '*me-to-me*' payments. To qualify, the payments are required to move between accounts in the same name: for example, from a person's current account to their credit card, loan account or savings account. **8.54**

Financial institutions are not granting fintechs access to facilitate payments if they are not within the CMA Order. For as long as financial institutions deny (even upon being paid) fintechs access to provide unrestricted VRP, businesses, their customers and UK plc are being denied the benefits of Open Banking outlined above. **8.55**

However, there are structural reasons why this market will not come to fruition via market forces alone. Regulatory intervention is needed to break open the market, allowing Open Banking providers to properly compete with incumbent players Visa and MasterCard, and the card-issuing banks. **8.56**

In response to the lack of voluntary competitive market progress on unrestricted VRPs, regulators and government have collectively set up a specific body to oversee and ensure development. The PSR, FCA, CMA and HM Treasury have formed the Joint Regulatory Oversight Committee[49] ('JROC'), which is requiring the ecosystem to collaborate, and is determining when to intervene at the point that cooperation is impossible. **8.57**

3. Competing with Cards

Both single and recurring payments can be made by card. Recurring card payments are where the payer (knowingly or otherwise) consents to their card details being held on file for future payments to be taken without needing to **8.58**

48 Competition and Markets Authority, 'Letter to Charlotte Crosswell, Implementation Trustee of the Open Banking Implementation Entity' (14 March 2022) https://assets.publishing.service.gov.uk/media/622ef71fd3bf7f5a86be8fa4/Sweeping_clarification_letter_to_be_sent_14_March_2022__.pdf.

49 HM Treasury, 'Recommendations for the Next Phase of Open Banking in the UK' (17 April 2023) https://www.gov.uk/government/publications/recommendations-for-the-next-phase-of-open-banking-in-the-uk.

authorise each payment. This arrangement is also known as card-on-file and as a continuous payment authority ('CPA').

8.59 The card schemes and card issuers (banks and Payment Services Providers) receive revenue for card and business usage, the card-issuing banks every time a card payment is made. This is the case for single and recurring card payments.

8.60 For Open Banking to be a success, and to enable it to compete with Visa, MasterCard and banks, a final step needs to be unlocked: we need to be able to pay *all* our bills, those subscriptions we have signed up to, using Open Banking.

8.61 However, the economic reality is that there can be no *market* resolution to:

(i) the conflict of interest which financial institutions and card schemes have with Open Banking being successful – card payments generating income for banks and card schemes, and competing Open Banking VRP set to cannibalise this revenue; and
(ii) each bank being a gatekeeper to fintech access, allowing fintechs to provide Open Banking services to businesses and consumers.

8.62 If a bank is going to lose revenue, it is not going to allow a fintech access enabling the fintech to provide alternative improved services.

8.63 I can prove card revenue is working for banks and card schemes. The plethora of offers and inducements for people to use one card over another, be it cashback, loyalty points or free flights, is evidence that cards work for banks and card schemes. Despite the cost of the rewards and incentives offered, card schemes and card issuers still obviously find it profitable; it would not make business sense for them to offer and run the reward schemes otherwise.

8.64 These reward schemes are not funded by bank and card schemes. We are in a bizarre societal position where the more affluent of us are reaping rewards that are paid for, at least in part, by the less well-off. While some of us are building up a good credit score from sipping our free coffee, others are denied an overdraft or full current account facilities and affordable credit because they have got less to live on. Having less to live on may have resulted in missed payments and penalty fees, or maybe not. Either way, such a level of income and payment history marks them out as higher risk, which means they attract higher fees, putting them in an endless negative high-cost spiral.

8.65 This is the uncomfortable economic reality. It is how the market is structured. To this extent, it is not players behaving badly. But the conflict is irreconcilable, the market power of incumbents unbreakable.

This market structure is holding up expansion, and the regulator needs to intervene. 8.66

4. The PSR's 2023 Christmas Present

Following years of cross-industry work, in December 2023 the PSR published its proposal for unlocking the next phase of low-cost, secure Open Banking technology. 8.67

The PSR's proposal may seem radical to some – for a limited initial phase, it is proposing a centrally set price between fintech and payment service provider/bank. That central price, for phase 1, is proposed to be zero due to cross-industry agreement that there is no additional functional build to do, and the fintech Open Banking market still needs support to be able to compete with Visa, MasterCard and financial institutions. Contrast this with these bill payments being made by card, where the bank would earn revenue each time ... some parties do not like this proposal. But that does not mean it is wrong. Competition necessarily has winners and losers, and the losers often do not like it. The regulator's goal is to enable competition which, in turn, will mean a better deal and improved services for businesses and consumers. To this end, their centrally set price model is the *only* model that will work efficiently and lead to an expedited take-off of an initial phase. 8.68

At the time of writing, the final announcement of the PSR, as part of JROC, is eagerly awaited. 8.69

5. What's the Case for Purpose?

Open Banking has already taken years of time and effort to try to break open the payments market beyond regulatory mandate. Further work yet is required. Regulators and government do not move at the pace investment backed fintechs ideally need them to, and of course, not every decision or edict goes your way. For any industry or initiative that is complex or contentious, persistence, tenacity, stamina and commitment are essential. 8.70

Research shows that people who have a Purpose are more resilient and bounce back from setbacks quicker.[50] In a survey conducted by the Economist's Intelligence Unit, more than 60 per cent of executives said a sense of Purpose 8.71

---

50 Stacey M Schaefer, Jennifer Morozink Boylan, Carien M van Reekum, Regina C Lapate, Catherine J Norris, Carol D Ryff and Richard J Davidson, 'Purpose in Life Predicts Better Emotional Recovery from Negative Stimuli' (8 May 2013) NIH National Library of Medicine https://www.ncbi.nlm.nih.gov/pmc/articles/PMC3827458/.

means they can be nimbler in innovating and responding to market disruption. Separately, studies have also shown that employees who work for a company that has a clear Purpose are more engaged and motivated,[51] and likely to contribute to greater productivity and innovation.[52] In this sense, every employee is an integral part of the innovation and creative side of the business and has their part to play in coming up with ideas, whereby problem solving and value providing.[53]

8.72 Working for a company with a Purpose could give people what they need to go the distance in a complex and contentious environment with protracted progress. One thing above all else gives people the endurance to last for the long haul: taking breaks and leave when needed. This includes taking leave of checking work devices, be it LinkedIn, Slack, email or anything else.

8.73 Not checking your emails takes bravery and self-discipline. The Economist recently quoted research by Melissa Mazmanian from the University of California, Irvine and Wanda Orlikowski and JoAnne Yates of MIT Sloan School of Management. In 2013, they devised the label 'autonomy paradox'. This contradiction refers to the modern world where, armed with post-COVID flexible working and the prevalence of smartphones and Wi-Fi, our increased flexibility actually means it's harder for people to draw boundaries and have the courage to fully switch off.[54]

8.74 With the multitude of communication channels now utilised, being able to trust you are truly allowed to switch off, ready to return rested, is key.

C. ORDO'S STORY

8.75 Ordo's tale is one of three parts: the past, the present and the future. While it is not Christmas, there is a hint of the ghost of payments past.

---

51 Naina Dhingra, Andrew Samo, Bill Schaninger and Matt Schrimper, 'Help your employees find purpose – or watch them leave' (5 April 2021) *McKinsey* https://www.mckinsey.com/capabilities/people-and-organizational-performance/our-insights/help-your-employees-find-purpose-or-watch-them-leave.

52 CIPD, 'Employee engagement and motivation' (8 July 2024) https://www.cipd.org/uk/knowledge/factsheets/engagement-factsheet/.

53 EY Global, 'Why business must harness the power of purpose' (15 August 2018) https://www.ey.com/es_pe/purpose/why-business-must-harness-the-power-of-purpose.

54 Bartleby, 'How to Take Proper Breaks from Work – The Matinée Test' *The Economist* (15 August 2024) https://www.economist.com/business/2024/08/15/how-to-take-proper-breaks-from-work.

1. The Past

(a) The Faster Payments Access project

In 2013, those that would become my Ordo co-founders and I ran the online and mobile payment transfer system for the UK, the Faster Payments Scheme. **8.76**

During our tenure, we initiated an 'Access project' to open up the payment system to more participants. TransferWise (now just Wise) was one of the first to join, through Raphaels Bank. This was one of the first new Faster Payments Scheme participants in a long time, and Transferwise was keen to mark itself out as innovative and cutting edge. Its premise: to fix the overseas transfer market. It would provide multiple currency accounts, and not charge through the nose for it. It is all just the same electronic money and holding of funds; why should it cost *so* much more? **8.77**

There was a launch event. It included the daring spectacle of making the virgin Faster Payments bank transfer – live, in real time, projected super-sized onto a wall. The moment our private conversations paused arrived. TransferWise CEO Kristo Kaarmann said a few words: the speech was short, each sentence staccato, some would say apprehensive. Nervous laughter propping up bravado; an attempt to signal to self-doubt that it had no place in the room where innovation was being done. **8.78**

With online banking payment set up, there was nothing else to do but press 'Pay'! Holding our breath for what felt like a commercial break, but which was actually a fraction of a second, we saw one bank account decrement and another increment on the wall projection. There was a brief cheer and applause, a collective relieving exhale, and the confident chatter returned. Mission accomplished. Or more accurately: mission commenced. **8.79**

We began opening the Faster Payments system in 2013 – we thought that near-instant money transfer shouldn't be the last innovation in financial services, and it shouldn't be the preserve of the usual ten incumbent banks. The more institutions that are part of the Faster Payments clearing and settlement system, the more of society can go about their everyday lives managing their money on the move. Every customer of every participant in the Faster Payments Scheme knew exactly where they were with their finances, able to juggle who to pay what and when, within an instant of a bill becoming due. **8.80**

Getting money in and being able to pay bills immediately, perhaps just before they become overdue, is crucial for some; being able to pay instantly a mere convenience for others, and an essential driver for economic growth. Why **8.81** should this flexibility and control, financial agility and dynamism not be available to everyone with a bank account? And why should this capability not be available to challenger banks giving the incumbents some competition? There's no reason why.

8.82 And so the award-winning Access project[55] was off. We recruited can-do onboarding managers to ensure swift progress and designed processes to make it as easy as appropriate to join the systemically important domestic real-time payment system. We worked with the Bank of England and the FCA to change their requirements, introduced the concept of gateway aggregators to make payment system access secure but efficient, developed a new risk assurance framework, and created a new model for FCA regulated non-bank Payment Services Providers, such as Ebury and others, to join.

8.83 By April 2018 we had gone from the Faster Payments Scheme being the exclusive playground of the same 10 incumbent banks who had not provided much innovation, to around 18 participating without a single glitch. Today, that number is 45 and counting.

8.84 And here began the rumblings of our first transformative challenge. The first vibrations heralding a shift in focus and culture. The beat would steer us to be guided by fulfilling a Purpose, rather than simply operate and function as back-office plumbing for financial institutions. It was a shift that would lead to all the payment systems in the UK being restructured and amalgamated, and the beginning of our mission-driven fintech, Ordo.

(b) Turkeys voting for Christmas

8.85 The Faster Payments Scheme's Articles of Association contained a payment scheme participant right that betrayed how the organisation had historically been viewed and operated. This right would be the impetus for change.

8.86 Change comes when you're running from pain or to reward. We were beginning to feel a pain that would only get worse, and we saw the potential for reward. The reward was one for society, resulting from greater competition in payment services and between financial institutions. But as is the way with competition, what is good for some means others are losing. Not everyone was in favour. We needed turkeys to vote for Christmas.

---

55 For the Faster Payments Scheme Limited winning the Industry Achievement award with Raphaels Bank: 'The Card and Payments Awards 2017: The winners' https://ffnews.com/newsarticle/faster-payments-and-raphaels-bank-recognised-for-industry-achievement-of-the-year/.

No financial institution ever waived its right to have a director on the board. When there are ten participants together with a chair plus a couple of independent directors, this is manageable. But by 2018 there were up to 18 institutions participating. The board of this critical national infrastructure would soon become unwieldy. The board also risked being wildly motivated by participating financial institution interests, rather than what was best for the country's online and mobile payment system. **8.87**

In addition, some participant-appointed directors wanted to sit on the boards of both the Faster Payments Scheme and the technology infrastructure provider to the Scheme – a single person sitting on the board of both customer and supplier. Whilst a customer and supplier need to work together, the customer does need to hold the supplier to account, and the interests of both can never be fully protected by the same person. **8.88**

To stall the progress of our Access project in order to stop adding directors to the board would mean the number of businesses and consumers benefiting from real time bank transfers would be curtailed. It would not be good for project momentum, the UK economy, competition or society. But to continue adding directors to the board would detrimentally affect the effectiveness of the board, and not just from the perspective of the number of chairs and sandwiches required. **8.89**

To establish a more effective board, we needed to change this financial institution director appointment right in our Articles. We also needed to add a prohibition on infrastructure supplier directors also sitting on our board. To change our Articles, we needed the current board (comprising a majority of appointees from participating financial institutions) to recommend these changes to guarantors. Then we needed a vote of 75 per cent of our guarantors, the participating financial institutions, to make these Article changes. **8.90**

We needed to get buy-in for change. We needed to make change undeniable. To achieve that, we needed to collectively establish the *point* of the Faster Payments Scheme – its Purpose. Up to that stage, it had been thought of as back-office plumbing, under bank control and operated for their benefit. That was looking at it from the payment system participant point of view. It was a description of functionality, and not the whole picture. It certainly was not a Purpose from an end-user or economic societal perspective. **8.91**

The Purpose of an organisation is its vision, not its functionality. We took a first principles approach to discovering the true Purpose of the Faster **8.92**

Payments Scheme. We broke the problem down into constituent elements and analysed them individually. What did the Faster Payments Scheme do, what did it achieve, how, for whom? And crucially, why?

(c) The governance project

8.93 Our encroaching pain allowed us to force addressing the issue. If ignored, it would intensify to eventually become an ineffective and cumbersome board, risking the safe and secure operation of the systemically important payment system. We would have to justify to the Bank of England and the PSR how and why we had let matters get to this point.

8.94 Any earlier approach to change the payment system's Purpose from being bank back-office plumbing would have been rejected. But by allowing innovation, having more participants join, and enduring the mild but intensifying pain of an ever-expanding board, change became necessary, rather than a choice.

8.95 To determine the Purpose of the Faster Payments Scheme, we held a series of workshops with all the directors, their alternates, and staff. I began an opening presentation with '*Imagine you're a tree*', which was certainly a different way of thinking for career bankers on the board! The point was, the Faster Payments Scheme originally began running out of the already established CHAPS, the high-value wholesale bank settlement system. Same personnel, two systems. What began as a seedling in a supportive pot grew to become so useful and popular that it required re-potting into its own pot, to stand on its own two roots, with its own gardeners.

8.96 In 2014, the Faster Payments Scheme processed 1.1 billion payment transactions with a value of £904 billion.[56] It was something different to what was originally envisaged when it was part of CHAPS. It had outgrown its first pot and was successfully standing tall and strong in its own ground, doing its own thing. It was therefore a fitting time to review what the Purpose of the organisation was after such growth and consider whether adjustments were appropriate.

8.97 The successes of the Faster Payments Scheme were evident: challenger banks such as Monzo and Starling had joined; non-banks such as Ebury were participating; consumers and businesses across the country were exploiting the

56 Faster Payments have since greatly increased even further in popularity. In 2023, the system processed 4.5 billion transactions with a value of £3.7 trillion. Pay UK, 'Faster Payment System' https://www.wearepay.uk/what-we-do/payment-systems/faster-payment-system/.

advantages of an open Faster Payments system and wide availability of real-time payments.

Given this, it was untenable to continue as if the payment system was merely back-office plumbing for the good of participating payment service providers alone. In analysing the situation and how Faster Payments was being used, we came to agree that the Faster Payments Scheme Purpose was to: 8.98

- enable a vibrant and globally competitive UK economy;
- allow Payment Service Providers to deliver services that are safe and secure, real-time, simple to use and economically efficient; and
- stimulate and grow the UK payments market.

From an economic perspective, the point of the payment system was enabling greater financial speed for users of the system, enabling people to send and collect money in a more agile and dynamic manner, all benefiting UK plc; its Purpose was to serve its end users, not only the participating institutions. The fact that the financial institutions used the payment system to effect the transfers people wanted to make was just the functionality. The benefit was for UK citizens and businesses, not the participating payment service providers. When looked at from this perspective, from the point of view of users of the payment system making and collecting payments, the Purpose becomes clear. 8.99

With Purpose set, we then tackled what that organisation needed to look like to flourish. Having an unwieldy board was not on the list! We applied the principles of the Corporate Governance Code to each element of the Faster Payments Scheme and its activities. This allowed us to ask our directors to reflect and consider whether the set-up of the Faster Payments Scheme, its board composition, its overlap of guarantor members with the board, its overlap of participant board directors also sitting on the board of the material infrastructure supplier to the payment system, Vocalink, was appropriate. 8.100

Applying the Principles of the Corporate Governance Code to our new Purpose-driven organisation allowed us to successfully challenge the status quo. Having an overly large board, consisting mostly of people who worked in financial institutions who were also the guarantors of the company, and some of whom were also directors of our material supplier, was not setting the company up for success to fulfil its Purpose in the long term. Discovering and committing to our Purpose was critical. 8.101

Following further rounds of small group meetings, staff briefings and question-and-answer sessions, we set criteria for the Faster Payments Scheme board 8.102

appointments. We retained all our independent directors, who were crucial for impartial judgement. We lessened the participant directors, who were crucial for expert participant knowledge and experience, to a few. Participant directors were to be interviewed and appointed based on a mix of skills and experience that would enhance the Faster Payments Scheme board holistically.

8.103 From being dominated by bank directors, we managed to initiate the Access project to open up the payment system to more and new types of competing payment service providers, win an award, and set up the organisation to have a corporate structure and board fit for such a strategically important UK utility: all made possible by setting our newly defined public Purpose as our north star.[57]

2. The Present

8.104 Using our knowledge of Faster Payments, the underlying payment method for Open Banking, and our market disruption experience, we embarked upon our next challenge. It would be one that would see us taking on the Goliaths of Visa, MasterCard and the banks. And we would hear a whisper from the ghost of our recent past reminding us of the importance of a company Purpose, both for us and the ecosystem.

(a) The origins of Ordo

8.105 In May 2018 we co-founded our fintech, Ordo.[58] Ordo would provide innovative Open Banking services for invoicing, call centres, online and in-person payments. Our services would be fully hosted and managed solutions for businesses, using the Faster Payments system for the underlying payment, moving money in real-time.

8.106 Ordo was our own company, to build from the ground up, exactly as we wanted it. And what did we want our company to be, to stand for? Our experience at the Faster Payments Scheme showed us that business should always begin with what its Purpose is. As we discovered, a Purpose is how a business helps, not a functional tech description, or a purpose of 'making money'; it is what is enabled when your business does what it does, what it gives people.

---

57 At the time of leaving the Faster Payments Scheme, the regulators were re-organising the UK payment systems to be amalgamated into one company. The Payment Systems Operator of all the UK's systemically important monopoly payment systems today is Pay.UK https://www.wearepay.uk.

58 Ordo is the trading name of The Smart Request Company Ltd (company number 11338545) and regulated by the Financial Conduct Authority (FRN 836070).

Our efforts at the Faster Payments Scheme not only meant that more financial institutions than ever were able to offer real-time payments, but they were also reachable by Open Banking providers like Ordo. We knew Open Banking was going to be about enabling people and businesses to manage their finances better, while passing costs savings to businesses, allowing greater flexibility, control and payment certainty. We had the green shoots of some ideas for Ordo's Purpose. **8.107**

(b) Our Purpose and financial wellbeing

Learning from the Governance project at the Faster Payments Scheme, we went back to first principles to establish the Purpose of Ordo. Given the flexible management capability enabled by Open Banking, and the psychological effects of money, building services that give financial control, dynamism and insight could help people make more of their money. The result of this, we hoped, would be less anxiety, and more financial freedom and choice. **8.108**

And so, our Purpose was crafted: **8.109**

To improve the financial wellbeing of individuals, businesses, social enterprises, charities, community groups and the public sector by helping them to be more in control of their finances. We do this by: **8.110**

- *enabling payers to securely and simply see what they've been asked to pay, trust who's asking, and then choose how and when they make or don't make payments;*
- *enabling billers to securely, simply and cost effectively provide information to, and request payments from, their customers without having to gather, store and protect payers' private financial information; and*
- *enabling billers to understand the status of their payment requests and receive settlement irrevocably and without delay from their customers, directly into their bank accounts.*

Peace of mind, especially over something as taxing (pun intended) as money, is a fundamental human need. Feeling in control of, and having choices over, your finances contributes to financial and personal security. While we could not do anything about how much money people took home, giving people ability to juggle and be creative and savvy with their money was something we could contribute to. Our services could help people deal with life's financial admin, enhance their financial resilience and maybe result in more positive mental health. **8.111**

(c) As academics and regulators would say: 'Operationalising Purpose'

We had established our '*why?*' Next was to truly make our company driven by it. *How* were we going to achieve this? **8.112**

8.113 There are two subjects that people can often feel nervous about: money and technology. Trying to help people improve their financial wellbeing using technology was going to be tricky.

8.114 Having a brand that was approachable and dependable, a tone of voice that sounded like a trusted critical financial friend, was essential. We briefed a digital agency for our logo design. When we explained our Purpose, they suggested we were a lifestyle service/app. That seemed quite broad and vague at the time, and nothing to do with our beloved payments! But five or six years later, we would find ourselves revisiting this concept.

8.115 We also engaged a customer experience agency to help us design our app and online journeys. We conducted independent user testing that informed the functionality and design of our service, in line with our Purpose. For example, to enable people to use Ordo to both pay and receive money, they would have something like email boxes for the various payments: a sent box for payment requests sent, and an inbox for payment requests received which the user needed to pay.

8.116 We initially coloured the inbox of requests-for-payment *received*, that is, bills that needed paying, red, because finances are important and bills needing paying require attention. The sent box, containing payment requests for money *sent* were in calming teal, because you should be thinking straight when you're requesting money from people. Our user testing strongly indicated we should switch these colours. The feedback was that if someone saw a list of their bills colour coded red, they would never look at them! Avoiding tackling finances was the exact opposite of what we were trying to achieve – improved financial wellbeing is not gained by being in denial and avoiding demands. Listening to the feedback, we swapped the colour coding. We made payment requests received, the bills that needed paying, calming Ordo teal.

8.117 Our user testing also demonstrated different approaches to financial management. During our research, we asked our testers how and when they settle bills with reference to their due date. Some people said as soon as they arrived, so they know the task is done. Strikingly, however, another person said that for big companies, they deliberately waited until they started receiving red demand letters. There was a feeling that they were big, so they deserved to wait. A payment to a big corporate was treated differently to paying a small company; these were paid promptly, with recognition that smaller businesses needed cash flow more keenly. This led us to incorporating filtering, sorting and searching functionality via due date, as well as by amount, payment status and invoice date.

This evidential attunement to user needs is a direct response to being Purpose-driven; every decision and every product feature must be made in the context of people being able to use it to improve their financial wellbeing. Four years later, with the introduction of the FCA's Consumer Duty, we had plenty of examples to demonstrate that we had designed our services to result in good customer outcomes. **8.118**

(d) The inside story on Purpose-driven companies

In the past, at the Faster Payments Scheme, we used a newly defined Purpose as both a catalyst to trigger change and a benchmark against which all changes were calibrated. It allowed us to carve a new path in terms of organisational outlook, culture, governance and board composition. In the present, as five co-founders, we were guided by our Purpose in designing and building our services from the outset. In the wake of the financial crisis and the LIBOR and other scandals,[59] regulators and academics are trying to engender companies behaving well internally, to influence and result in good outcomes. So how does being Purpose-driven affect the way we run Ordo internally? **8.119**

I'm an advocate of complementing methodologies: Brene Brown's vulnerability and daring ethos, and servant leadership style. Vulnerability and leading by example are crucial for nurturing open, ethical, brave and encouraging environments – the sort of environments that are fertile ground for innovation and for finding new solutions to old problems. Emphasising these qualities leaves space for people to feel confident and accepted enough to throw out ideas and challenge, and autonomous enough to create and experiment. **8.120**

In a post-COVID era of working from home and communicating via video calls, this style must be very intentional, obvious and deliberate. It has to be worked hard at to work. Making time to share wins, needs, concerns and **8.121**

59 Serious Fraud Office, 'SFO concludes investigation into LIBOR manipulation' (n 7); Financial Conduct Authority, 'FCA fines Metro Bank PLC £10 million and publishes decision notices for two of its former executive directors' (n 7); 'PPI Complaints' (n 7); 'FCA fines five banks £1.1 billion for FX failings and announces industry-wide remediation programme' (12 November 2014, updated 4 November 2019) https://www.fca.org.uk/news/press-releases/fca-fines-five-banks-£11-billion-fx-failings-and-announces-industry-wide-remediation-programme; Dominic Lindley, 'The top 10 retail banking scandals: 70 billion reasons why shareholders must play a greater role in changing bank culture' (n 7); Joanna Partridge, 'Major banks shared sensitive bonds information in online chats, CMA finds' *The Guardian* (24 May 2023) https://www.theguardian.com/business/2023/may/24/major-banks-shared-sensitive-bonds-information-in-online-chats-cma-finds.

updates on Teams calls ensures the team remains cohesive. Multiple teams need to be clear on a direction to collaborate on all aspects of a solution, rather than feeling demotivated and directionless, resulting in unnecessary unsellable tech.

8.122 Despite now being a largely remote working company, we strive to ensure our employees know the big-picture vision for the company and the strategy to achieve it. Ideas are shared early, and comments, views and feedback always listened to.

8.123 Being guided by the company Purpose, including when it may evolve, means everyone in the team is clear on what we are trying to achieve. Our commercial models, products and services can flex to better suit our customers, with staff being at the forefront of ensuring our propositions are fit for any given situation.

8.124 Working to adopt this open, inclusive and challenging culture, trying to make the right decisions for our business and our customers for the long term, while making a difference in society is not always comfortable. It means dwelling for a time on the harder decisions, not just skipping to the easiest and quickest solution to move through feeling uncomfortable as soon as possible.

8.125 A while ago I had a regulatory question. I feared I had interpreted an issue wrongly, or at least, that a different interpretation could be reached and therefore our position was at risk. What I wanted to be a quick call with my boss to confirm my initial view allowing me to move on from this uncomfortable thought was not to be. An hour and half later, we had walked through the relevant materials, analysed the situation from different viewpoints, looked at what competitors were doing and surmised what their view could be and argued with it, and only then come to affirm my initial view. That was an hour and half of feeling sick! But as Brene would say, we 'rumbled with vulnerability',[60] dwelled on the problem to dig around for a while and think through arguments and challenges. Once we had stopped digging around, we felt even more confident in the original view, and so more comfortable – the work variation of that sporting phrase, *No pain, no gain.*[61]

---

60 Brene Brown, 'Let's rumble' *Brene Brown* (1 May 2019) https://brenebrown.com/articles/2019/05/01/lets-rumble/.

61 Michael Kent, *The Oxford Dictionary of Sports Science & Medicine*, 'The "no pain, no gain" concept' (2006, published online 2007) https://www.oxfordreference.com/display/10.1093/oi/authority.20110803100238248#:~:text=The%20concept%20that%20an%20athlete,see%20principle%20of%20progressive%20overload).

This situation arose again later, except this time I was the person being consulted, along with others from the team. There was a vibe of wanting to agree a particular course of action immediately; the sharing was just so everybody knew what was going on. The team wanted to implement the change they had resigned themselves to, move on, and stop thinking about and feeling it. Armed with this recent experience proving that *rumbling with vulnerability* gives greater comfort in the long run, and it being more likely we would reach a better solution, I stuck with the sick feeling … and I kept the team in there with me – lucky people! As before, after discussion and comprehensive consideration of alternatives however unlikely or seemingly inappropriate, we concluded the initial suggestion was the best way forward. Now we could implement the original solution, knowing why we chose that option, that it was in line with our Purpose, and that it was good for our customers. **8.126**

Doing something thoughtfully and purposefully, after due consideration and spending time with the difficult stuff (feeling sick is optional!), is very different to doing the same thing, unexamined, because you're afraid. **8.127**

A balance needs to be struck between problem-dwelling to ensure you arrive at the appropriate solution, and too much, or disproportionate, analysis and consideration. It will often be those driven by tasks, the ones who like getting things off their desk and ticking off a to-do list, who will be quick to come to a solution. This personality type will need encouragement to dwell and support in experiencing being uncomfortable; those with more cautious hyper-vigilant or perfectionist tendencies may need to be supported in moving through options more quickly, making the degree of analysis appropriate for the task and situation. The important thing is not that one way is best, it is recognising what the people involved and the situation at hand need. **8.128**

(e) When the going gets tough, the Purpose-driven stick with it

Ordo creates new solutions that reflect society today, not in the 1960s when cards and direct debit were invented. Today's society is dynamic and instant – if people's financial lives cannot keep up with this, the finance industry is failing them. Successfully pursuing our Purpose of enabling people to improve their financial wellbeing means being able to offer people the benefits of agile, dynamic, controllable and flexible Open Banking for all their payments. **8.129**

To achieve this and provide services that reflect all that modern life and work has evolved to be in the UK, we must be able to compete on a level playing field with Visa and MasterCard. We must be able to provide unrestricted Variable Recurring Payments, VRP, which is like a smart direct debit. **8.130**

8.131 Our functionality for full VRP is available and live now. However, to set up and manage Open Banking VRP mandates, we need banks to grant us access to set up the mandate on the consumer's account when the consumer is agreeing to a repeated bill or subscription. As the bank will lose card issuer revenue if the consumer were to switch to using Open Banking VRP, only one bank is currently allowing fintech access for a premium – and one bank does not allow a business to collect payments from all its customers. A network effect is needed; that is, at least 90 per cent of the current account market needs to participate in facilitating VRP for it to be fit for purpose for businesses to use for payment collection.

8.132 Challenging the status quo and delivering new technology that will make a difference in society is a Purpose staff can get behind and support. Having a Purpose that staff can get behind and that enables them to feel they're a part of making a difference in society will engender resilience. And this resilience helps when you hit the obstacles you can't control, like restricted bank access preventing you from deploying your services, enabling creative minds to devise innovative solutions that get you a step forward.

8.133 We are in the midst of contributing to multiple cross-industry working groups aimed at splitting open the dominance of incumbent card schemes and payment service providers/banks. They comprise many parties whose interests are polar opposite. On many occasions I'm giving a view that I know will rankle with the reams of people that are on calls representing the banks and card schemes. When you're challenging incumbents with much more resources and deeper pockets, you need resilience by the bucketload.

8.134 For long, tough paths, a Purpose gives you a reason to keep turning up to meeting after meeting feeling like you're going round in circles. It gives you the endurance and perseverance needed to stick with it. As a fintech raising risk investment rather than an incumbent relying on established revenue lines, grit and determination are high on the list of must-have characteristics.

3. THE FUTURE

Open Finance and beyond: the Open (and connected) Economy

8.135 Comprehensive Open Banking services covering all payment and bill types by fintechs are just the beginning. The next stage is so-called Open Finance, which will see more types of accounts securely exposed to Open Banking capability: secured savings and investments, pensions, mortgages, life assurance – a single holistic view of a person's financial situation, from which informed decisions can be made. These informed and accurate decisions can then be acted upon, securely and instantly, facilitated by businesses at low cost.

While Open Finance is a useful next step, it is just a fuller (and therefore more accurate) view of a person's financial position. This is important, but all it needs is broader plumbing, the digitising of more connections that make managing finances and paying for things more convenient and efficient than it is today. The business collecting side of the journey has been digitised. There is still work to be done to make it efficient and valuable for the consumer. The real benefits will come when there are not only more Open Finance connections, but also smart data linking all those accounts, and the use of AI to lighten the burden of analysing all the data and financial insights. It is the timesaving decisioning and automatic analysis and value-add service that will really transform people's lives – nudges and suggestions that respond in a tailored way to a consumer's financial profile, spending habits and dynamic money situation. **8.136**

Today, even with Open Banking and with Open Finance to come, manual assessment and initiation of a digital process is necessary to take an action, albeit a lower cost and more efficient and convenient digital process. In the future, 'smart payments' will fully exploit technology, allowing people to reap benefits – freeing up time and mental energy, encouraging healthy long-term habits. **8.137**

All those things we used to carry around in wallets – contact details, diary appointments, business cards, the scraps of paper covered in scribbles to remember, a couple of precious photos of loved ones, shopping lists – they have expanded and moved on to the computers that rarely leave our hands. That is convenient. But benefit and transformation will come once time, management and manual monitoring are removed from the admin of our lives, freeing up time and headspace for things that matter most. Creating a service to help people manage all their life admin and personal finance management – a lifestyle app or service … where have I heard that before?! **8.138**

What will be needed to build a solution for tackling life's financial to-do list? It will require a comprehensive, useful and ethical platform to garner wholesale trust and adoption. It will need engaged, inspired and creative staff, just like people driven by a Purpose. Businesses focus on money alone at their peril. **8.139**

D. REFLECTIONS

1. Beyond the Web Page

8.140 Corporate missions aren't new. Amazon strives 'to be Earth's most customer-centric company … Earth's best employer and Earth's safest place to work'.[62] Yet it stars in multiple TV exposes[63] and court battles evidencing that staff are treated badly and are not safe at work, and setting out its extensive data use. Financial technology company Revolut wants '[t]o simplify all things money'.[64] Yet in taking three years to get a banking licence it has allegedly created a toxic long working hours culture.[65]

8.141 Being Purpose-driven involves more than a webpage. If your mission is to improve people's financial wellbeing (and with it, people's daily lives), it is disingenuous to allow your own workplace to be noxious. To go beyond the webpage, academics and regulators have turned to 'operationalising purpose'. At its heart is being kind while doing helpful things, and still making money.

8.142 The outcome regulators want is for financial services to truly *earn* their profits, in a decent way. To acknowledge and remedy things when they go wrong, in a decent way. Regulators are trying to deal with companies cutting corners, faking documents, fixing interest rates, exploiting customers, walking over workers, buying silence, all in the hunt for ever more revenue. It is hoped that a company fulfilling a societal mission would behave better. Behave better, whilst still making a bob or two million satisfying shareholders and keeping the economy churning.

---

62 Amazon, 'Mission' https://www.aboutamazon.co.uk/who-we-are.

63 Channel 4, 'The Great Amazon Heist' https://www.channel4.com/programmes/the-great-amazon-heist; BBC, 'Amazon: What They Know About Us, Panorama Investigates' https://www.bbc.co.uk/programmes/m000fjdz; Maria Ward-Brennan, 'Amazon hit with "biggest ever" UK class action in £1bn legal case' *CityAM* (6 June 2024, updated 7 June 2024) https://www.cityam.com/amazon-hit-with-biggest-ever-uk-class-action-in-1bn-legal-case/; Reuters, '$1.3 bln UK lawsuit accuses Amazon of misusing small sellers' data' (6 June 2024) https://www.reuters.com/sustainability/13-bln-uk-lawsuit-accuses-amazon-misusing-small-sellers-data-2024-06-06/; Mike Scarcella, 'FTC lawsuit over Amazon's Prime program set for June 2025 trial' *Reuters* (12 June 2024) https://www.reuters.com/legal/litigation/ftc-lawsuit-over-amazons-prime-program-set-june-2025-trial-2024-06-12/.

64 Revolut, 'About' https://www.revolut.com/about/#.

65 Kalyeena Makortoff and Anna Isaac, 'Revolut: Can the Chancellor's fintech favourite fix its image problem?' *The Guardian* (20 February 2023) https://www.theguardian.com/business/2023/feb/20/revolut-can-the-chancellors-fintech-favourite-fix-its-image-problem; Andrew Liptak, 'A report describes high turnover and toxic workplace culture at finance startup Revolut: Another alleged that the company turned off anti-money laundering software for three months last year' *The Verge* (3 March 2019) https://www.theverge.com/2019/3/3/18248826/revolut-workplace-culture-burnout-finance-app-reports; John Reynolds, 'Fintech can be a "brutal" workplace but are "toxic" claims over-egged?' *The Fintech Times* (21 January 2023) https://thefintechtimes.com/fintech-can-be-a-brutal-workplace-but-are-toxic-claims-over-egged/.

2. How to Do Things Differently and Be Believed

In a capitalist culture, and financial services in particular, where competition, long hours and success at all costs can make cutting corners seem inevitable, how can you be believed when you say you want to do things differently? How do you get your employees to believe you do not expect them to check emails while on leave, for example, or work when they are ill, while still having growth ambitions? **8.143**

For people to feel brave enough to do things differently, they must trust you mean what you say. Leaders must be first to skitter across the brave new glass floor revealing the chasm beneath, to prove it is safe, and demonstrate that there are not unpleasant repercussions. **8.144**

This is where the characteristics of daring and servant leadership resonate. Daring leadership is the concept of showing vulnerability: sharing when things go wrong, or when mistakes have been made, and demonstrating that blame is not apportioned. Instead, effort is put into finding solutions. *Living* your values, rather than just a virtual display of them. Proving that checking emails while on leave is not expected, for example, can only be achieved by leaders being brave enough to abandon their inboxes while on leave too. **8.145**

While having responsibility in an organisation requires you to be there when needed for important and urgent matters – even when on leave, if possible – it also requires you to demonstrate what the organisation stands for. If your organisation stands for respecting people and fostering resilience by improving wellbeing, then you must respect yourself, your choices and time, and use the tools available to keep yourself mentally and physically healthy, like taking leave, too. This behaviour models buy-in to what would otherwise be just words, and builds trusting and open cultures. Psychology calls it vicarious reinforcement: modelling the behaviour you want to see so that people believe it for themselves and then follow. **8.146**

Demonstrating bravery to switch off, and showing openness and vulnerability, is crucial for creating an environment where people feel psychologically safe. When people feel psychologically safe and job secure, they'll take breaks when they need to, allowing them to actively participate in and contribute to the company in day-to-day operations when they're in the (virtual) office. In a culture where all employees are rested and working at full steam, they'll come up with the innovative and creative ideas needed, and you'll be getting the best out of a team. When a company is innovative and creative, it can be nimble **8.147** and deftly navigate obstacles along the way. When its work force is tired, it will be demotivated and unable to devise solutions.

8.148 Proving and displaying humility, bravery and transparency is a choice; it shows you can be trusted. Brene Brown defines one component of trust as 'choosing courage over comfort, choosing what's right over what's fun, fast or easy, and *practising* your values not just *professing* your values'.[66]

8.149 Our Purpose was to enable people to improve their financial wellbeing. We try to work in a way that is in keeping with this Purpose: treating ourselves, staff, suppliers and customers well, giving people want they need, being compassionate. In summary, '*being helpful and kind*'. Many years later it would occur to me that this is the positive version of Google's old motto '*Don't be Evil*'.

8.150 Looking back at how we have worked with our company over the past six years, here are some basic things we do to *practise* our values and not just profess them:

- *Value people* – paying people appropriately in recognition of their skills, experience and talent, not just the minimum we think we can get away with. This includes suppliers, especially small suppliers, creating wholesome partnerships rather than a race to the bottom. This does not mean paying over the odds, but not scraping to rock bottom where making a margin necessitates cutting corners;
- *Value people's contribution* – investing in employee skills helps staff feel valued and motivated, as well as benefiting the company. It will broaden what employees are able to offer a company and bring new opportunities;
- *Value people's health* – equipment: as we largely work remotely, making sure staff have the equipment they need for their health is essential. Purchasing equipment that staff want, enabling them to do their job well, again helps staff feel valued and motivated, as well as making employees comfortable and able to work efficiently;
- *Respect people's preferences* – travel: giving employees choice about when they travel, whether it is an early start because they prefer to be at home overnight, or travelling the night before and requiring accommodation because they prefer to avoid last-minute potential travel disruption;
- *Acknowledge people aren't robots* – taking leave: senior team members not checking emails while on leave, ensuring people see that it is expected they switch off when not at work. Having 30 days' annual leave and encouraging this to be taken. We think this is more effective than unlimited leave, which can seem unbelievable;
- *Recognise people have other things in their lives* – flexible working hours: responding to when people work best while balancing with people being available to work with team members;

---

66 Brene Brown, 'Dare to lead: The BRAVING Inventory' https://brenebrown.com/resources/the-braving-inventory/.

- *Respect people's time* – working late infrequently and only on urgent and important matters: working outside of working hours (whatever they are) should be the exception, not the norm, and expressly stating that work can wait unless it is urgent and important ensures issues are given the attention they deserve. Working late is not a virtue; working till burnout is not glamorous – it is bad for your brain, we should not do it, and managers and companies should not expect it;
- *Fostering a positive, growth mindset culture* – cultivated by never asking "how did this happen?" when a mistake comes to light, instead focusing on what is needed for a solution. And taking time to absorb a disappointing event, then seeing what can be made of it to keep progressing;
- *Seek difference* – making a conscious effort to be openminded when hiring, meaning we consider those that might not ordinarily get an interview, as well as the commonly known diversity criteria;
- *Live our values* – holding suppliers to high standards: for example contractually requiring suppliers to pay at least the Living Wage to all staff, including overseas; and
- *Be empathetic* – remote working: with new staff joining just before March 2020, and now being nearly fully remote, it is important to keep evaluating what kind of team collaboration is needed. Too many calls can be unproductive, too few can be isolating, and when and how to meet in-person is regularly reviewed. We do not rely on seeing people on camera to know whether they are ok. It is often hard for people to ask for support and requiring them to show up on camera when they are not feeling good is not going to work. Berating someone for not putting their camera on (as I heard one bank do) is tantamount to victim-blaming and does no good apart from allowing the blaming manager to feel temporarily powerful. You must work harder at working out how people are faring when you are remote, but that does not excuse you from working at it. When we do meet in-person, we hire rooms from a social enterprise helping homeless women in central London. Getting our work done while enabling people to improve their skills and living situation – it's our vision to a tee.

3. Customer Attraction

Our Purpose has influenced the types of customers we attract, too. We have multiple not-for-profit credit and lending customers, so-called CDFIs (Community Development Financial Institutions). Not only are they an ethical lifeline for people who have limited access to mainstream financial services, but they also have complementary financial goals. Some aim to improve financial literacy, others focus on making credit affordable preventing resorting to unregulated loan sharks, and another prioritises public sector key workers. **8.151**

We have also attracted public sector serving customers who are not driven solely by profit but are instead focused on ensuring funding goes towards services for citizens, with minimal amounts going on costly service provision. **8.152**

8.153 In the energy sector, we have partners that have developed solutions with us that tackle not only money management, control and flexibility, but also use Open Banking data and AI to help those in hardship. The solution directs people to the most appropriate department, be that for top-up payments or tariff changes, and includes direction to hardship teams and debt management charities when needed.

8.154 In a post-pandemic society, with inflation just about under control in a cost-of-living crisis, we find ourselves serving customers that are trying to help the less well-off – those that often find themselves paying more for the same, the so-called poverty premium, despite being the least able to afford it. Our Purpose supports their Purpose. We have strong partnerships and have adapted our commercial models to suit them and their mission.

8.155 Being Purpose-focused on financial wellbeing has shaped our company. It means we attract more mission-motivated people, staff and customers. We have also had success in engaging with regulators on what is next for Open

8.156 When you are in the business of innovation, it can feel like you are pulling a dead weight behind you. While we continue to argue for expanding Open Banking to VRP for various use cases, we are lobbying for the building blocks to be put in place for the stage beyond that. Again, this is not for the faint-hearted. A Purpose-driven workforce that is inspired for what the future could be, where things work better, will be stronger. Resilience, perseverance and desire to make a difference are essential qualities, and having a Purpose will attract the right people for the job. Your Purpose-driven staff who are more engaged and motivated are also loyal, which is good for them and good for business … and you need that sort when you are at the front, forging the road ahead, with doubters and detractors all around.

4. Is Being Purpose-driven a Winner?

8.157 Putting people's financial wellbeing at the heart of what we build and how we operate, and stepping up to challenge the dominant incumbents, has allowed us to attract talented employees, secure investment, win awards, gain customers and greatly influence regulators. We have fulfilled our FCA Consumer Duty obligations by default. It means there is a point to continuing to collaborate and argue to bring about the expansion of Open Banking Variable Recurring Payments, Open Finance, and beyond to smart data and Personal Financial Management, however hard that may be with inherent conflicting economic market structures.

Living out a Purpose may seem a harder option at first. But the benefits are a subtle design that adds credibility and authenticity, and a touch of competitor-distinguishing flair. Our experience bulldozes excuses for running a business any other way. We are proving every day that people, be they employees, investors, customers, suppliers or regulators, are intrigued with the strong Purpose-driven dynamic. And to be true to your Purpose, it must be reflected in your underlying values and everyday actions showing what you stand for. Be helpful and kind; make a difference in society; it doesn't have to compromise success. **8.158**

What type of business are you running: is it *for* all humans, or *against* them? **8.159**

***** **8.160**

The End (again) **8.161**

9

INTERNAL COMPLIANCE, RISK MANAGEMENT, AND THEIR IMPACT ON CULTURE IN FINANCIAL FIRMS

Kosmas Kaprinis

A. INTRODUCTION

9.1 Modern societies are witnessing a shift towards a more holistic and integrated approach in the evolution of risk management regulations.[1][2] This development is propelled by several factors, including the necessity to bolster organisational resilience, maintain compliance with regulatory standards and tackle new challenges such as cyber threats and risks associated with climate change. In the aftermath of the 2007–09 crisis, there has been a similar emphasis on the need for a transformed regulatory culture within financial services.[3] Notably,

1 All weblinks were last accessed on 26 December 2024.

2 OECD, 'Regulatory Policy and Governance: Supporting Economic Growth and Serving the Public Interest' (2011) https://doi.org/10.1787/9789264116573-en; Ulrich Beck, *Risk Society: Towards a New Modernity* (Sage Publications 1992).

3 See generally, Financial Stability Board, 'Guidance on Supervisory Interaction with Financial Institutions on Risk Culture: A Framework for Assessing Risk Culture' (7 April 2014) https://www.fsb.org/2014/04/140407/; Group of Thirty, 'Banking Conduct and Culture: A Call for Sustained and Comprehensive Reform' (2015) https://group30.org/publications/detail/166 arguing that the financial system was

the sufficiency of risk management processes was seen not only as a matter of formal risk management framework deficiencies, but also as an issue of organisational culture.[4] Weaknesses in cultural norms and behavioural practices around risk are frequently cited as early indicators of significant compliance problems in banks, such as anti-money laundering, fraud and cybersecurity breaches.[5] Given this hypothesis, it seems logical to examine culture, which is widely recognised as a key influence of individual employee behaviour.

The current discourse on risk culture tends to equate 'good' risk culture with conservative risk-taking behaviours, where an organisation's risk appetite is tightly controlled to avoid regulatory breaches.[6] However, this cultural shift towards heightened risk aversion can also raise concerns about its potential effects on growth and profitability, as institutions may become overly cautious and miss out on profitable opportunities.[7] Research has indicated that while a risk-averse culture may protect against downside risks, it could simultaneously hinder a bank's competitive positioning and long-term innovation strategies.[8] As an intangible social phenomenon, risk culture presents challenges in its definition, yet it remains a concept that should be evaluated and 9.2

---

weakened before the 2007–09 financial crisis by 'poor cultural underpinnings'; Frank Elderson, 'Treading Softly Yet Boldly: How Culture Drives Risk in Banks and What Supervisors Can Do About It' (Speech at the 10th Conference on the Banking Union, Frankfurt am Main, 19 September 2023) https://www.bankingsupervision.europa.eu/press/speeches/date/2023/html/ssm.sp230919~589c61455b.en.htm linking culture to the Significant financial scandals over the past two decades, such as the collapses of Lehman Brothers and Silicon Valley Bank); William C Dudley, 'Enhancing Financial Stability by Improving Culture in the Financial Services Industry' (Speech at the Workshop on Reforming Culture and Behavior in the Financial Services Industry, Federal Reserve Bank of New York, 20 October 2014) https://www.newyorkfed.org/newsevents/speeches/2014/dud141020a.html.

4 For an overview of these arguments, see Alessandro Carretta, Vincenzo Farina and Paola Schwizer, 'Risk Culture and Banking Supervision' (2017) 25(2) *Journal of Financial Regulation and Compliance* 209.

5 Elizabeth Sheedy and Bree Griffin, 'Risk Governance, Culture, and Behaviors in Banks' (2015) FIRN Research Paper No. 2529803 ssrn.com/abstract=2529803; Karl Bengtsson, *Risk Culture in Financial Institutions: Understanding Risks and Addressing Failures* (PhD thesis, University of Gothenburg 2020) https://www.e-helvetica.nb.admin.ch/api/download/urn%3Anbn%3Ach%3Abel-1496988%3ADis4935.pdf/Dis4935.pdf.

6 Daniela Coluccia and others, 'Does Risk Culture Affect Banks' Volatility? The Case of the G-SIBs' (2017) 15(1) *Corporate Ownership and Control* 33.

7 Explaining the downside risk aversion in the context of banking see Donald C Keenan and Arthur Snow, 'Greater Prudence and Greater Downside Risk Aversion' (2010) 145(6) *Journal of Economic Theory* 2018.

8 Fenghua Song and Anjan V Thakor, 'Bank Culture' [2017] Journal of Financial Intermediation ssrn.com/abstract=3069252; Fenghua Song and Anjan V Thakor, 'Bank Culture' (2019) 40 *Journal of Financial Intermediation* 100813 https://doi.org/10.1016/j.jfi.2017.11.001; Andrew G Haldane, 'Why Banks Failed the Stress Test' (Speech at the Marcus-Evans Conference on Stress-Testing, London, 9–10 February 2009) https://www.bankofengland.co.uk/speech/2009/why-banks-failed-the-stress-test; Sebastian Fritz-Morgenthal, Julia Hellmuth and Natalie Packham, 'Does Risk Culture Matter? The Relationship between Risk Culture Indicators and Stress Test Results' (2016) 9(1) *Journal of Risk Management in Financial Institutions* 71.

controlled.[9] Various recommendations from regulatory bodies vary in their emphasis of the elements that constitute an organisation's risk culture. The main objective for regulators is to encourage the establishment of monitoring systems and dependable risk culture interventions that can be validated for regulatory assessment.[10]

9.3 Financial firms operate in highly regulated environments, making effective compliance management crucial. Compliance and risk management frameworks are vital for ensuring that banks function within legal parameters while minimising potential risks. Practices around risk management and compliance not only affect internal governance but also have external consequences, such as influencing systemic stability and public trust in the financial system.[11] Along with regulators, compliance departments also strive to quantify risk culture using metrics and expand their influence with financial institutions. Furthermore, compliance divisions, which traditionally relied on manual processes and human decision-making, are increasingly incorporating AI and automated systems to improve efficiency and precision. This technological shift not only transforms operational workflows but also reshapes the cultural dynamics within these departments.[12]

9.4 The chapter is structured as follows. Section B provides an overview of the organisational framework of compliance and risk management functions within financial institutions; Section C elaborates on the definition of risk culture in the context of the financial sector; Section D examines the European Central Bank's (ECB) initiatives regarding risk culture, as the ECB is a leading regulatory authority in this domain, along with the fact that the EU and UK financial markets exhibit significant interconnectedness; Section E provides recommendations for enhancing compliance and risk management processes in relation to risk culture; and Section F concludes. We argue that the primary challenge in addressing risk culture within compliance departments

---

9 Aparna Gupta and Abena Owusu, 'Identifying the Risk Culture of Banks Using Machine Learning' (2024) 20(2) *International Journal of Managerial Finance* 377.

10 De Nederlandsche Bank, 'Supervision of Behaviour and Culture: Foundations, Practice & Future Developments' (2015) https://www.dnb.nl/media/1gmkp1vk/supervision-of-behaviour-and-culture_tcm46-380398-1.pdf.

11 For example, Vilma Deltuvaitė, 'The Importance of Systemic Risk Management in the Banking Sector' (2012) 17(3) *Economics and Management* 869; Bahriye Basaran-Brooks, 'Money Laundering and Financial Stability: Does Adverse Publicity Matter?' (2021) 30(2) *Journal of Financial Regulation and Compliance* 196; Ibrahim Adeniran and others, 'Strategic Risk Management in Financial Institutions: Ensuring Robust Regulatory Compliance' (2024) 6(8) *Finance & Accounting Research Journal* 1582.

12 Basel Committee on Banking Supervision, 'Compliance and the Compliance Function in Banks' (2005) www.bis.org/publ/bcbs113.pdf.

is not the necessity for organisational restructuring, but rather a lack of clear conceptual understanding of risk culture. Our recommendations emphasise the significance of experimenting with compliance practices, empowering mid-level management, increasing the involvement of compliance and risk managers in business operations and recognising the value of informal networks among compliance professionals.

B. AN ORGANISATION FRAMEWORK OF INTERNAL COMPLIANCE IN FINANCIAL INSTITUTIONS

The debate surrounding risk culture is often examined in relation to the organisational structure of the compliance and risk management processes. The Three Lines of Defence (TLD) model plays a crucial role in defining risk oversight within a bank's internal control framework.[13] It categorises responsibilities into three distinct tiers, assisting banks in effectively identifying, managing and escalating risk-related issues throughout the organisation.[14] The TLD model suggests that the primary responsibility for risk management lies with the business units, often referred to as the 'first line of defence'. Within this first line of defence, business units assume risks and are held directly responsible for managing their operations, with all employees recognising their role in risk mitigation by adhering to internal policies and complying with external regulations. The first line of defence encompasses both 'front office' and 'back office' departments.[15] 9.5

13 For an explanation of the TLD model in the banking sector see EBA, 'Final Report on Guidelines on Internal Governance under Directive 2013/36/EU (EBA/GL/2021/05)' (July 2021) https://www.eba.europa.eu/sites/default/files/document_library/Publications/Guidelines/2021/1016721/Final%20report%20on%20Guidelines%20on%20internal%20governance%20under%20CRD.pdf; Tomasz Braun, *Compliance Norms in Financial Institutions: Measures, Case Studies and Best Practices* (Springer 2019).

14 Basel Committee on Banking Supervision, 'Principles for the Sound Management of Operational Risk' (2011) www.bis.org/publ/bcbs195.htm (underscoring the significance of the TLD model in managing risks); Michael Power (ed), *Riskwork: Essays on the Organizational Life of Risk Management* (Oxford University Press 2016) (discussing the implementation of the TLD model as the analytical framework of risk governance in financial institutions); Howard Davies and Maria Zhivitskaya, 'Three Lines of Defence: A Robust Organising Framework, or Just Lines in the Sand?' (2018) 9(1) *Global Policy* 34; Kinil Doshi, 'Breaking Down Barriers: Adapting Three Lines of Defense for Ever Changing Banking Regulations' (2024) 9(2) *International Journal of Finance* 75; Yusarina Mat Isa and others, 'Money Laundering Risk: From the Bankers' and Regulators Perspectives' (2015) 28 *Procedia Economics and Finance* 7.

15 For instance, functions such as Legal, HR, and IT comprise the first line of defence and are responsible for managing their risks withing their division and implementing the relevant control processes. For an analysis, Alexander Dill, *Anti-Money Laundering Regulation and Compliance: Key Problems and Practice Areas* (Edward Elgar Publishing 2021) 175 et seq.

9.6 The second line of defence is composed of specialised risk management and compliance functions, which operate independently from the first line. From an operational standpoint, this function encompasses core compliance activities that ensure that the bank adheres to applicable laws and regulations. Key aspects of compliance work include: (i) Regulatory Compliance: guaranteeing conformity with laws and regulations established by domestic and international regulatory bodies; (ii) Internal Policies: creating and implementing internal codes of conduct and operational procedures; (iii) Training: conducting regular instructional programmes to inform employees about compliance requirements and ethical conduct. It has been argued that the compliance/second line of defence has transformed over time, transitioning from a reactive function to a proactive approach that anticipates regulatory shifts and emerging risks.[16]

9.7 Internal audit serves as the third line of defence, conducting independent evaluations of the first and second lines of defence. Specifically, internal auditors evaluate how well the other two lines operate, identifying gaps and advocating potential improvements. Their findings inform senior management about compliance issues requiring attention or remediation. By offering an independent perspective, the third line of defence reinforces the overall governance framework and supports continuous improvement.[17]

9.8 While the TLD model establishes a structured approach to risk management, its practical implementation can present challenges, particularly in striking a balance between control oversight and business operations.[18] Issues may arise when the lines of defence become blurred, for instance, when risk managers become too involved in operational decision-making or when auditors

16 Vivian Ofure Eghaghe and others, 'Advancing AML Tactical Approaches with Data Analytics: Transformative Strategies for Improving Regulatory Compliance in Banks' (2024) 6(10) *Finance & Accounting Research Journal* 1893; Mohammed Ahmad Naheem, 'Anti-Money Laundering/Trade-Based Money Laundering Risk Assessment Strategies – Action or Re-Action Focused?' (2019) 22(4) *Journal of Money Laundering Control* 721 discussing this proactive approach in the area of AML.

17 Institute of Internal Auditors, 'The Three Lines of Defence in Effective Risk Management and Control' (2013) IIA Position Paper www.iia.nl/actualiteit/nieuws/the-three-lines-of-defense-in-effective-risk-management-and-control--iia-position-paper; Melanie Roussy and Michelle Rodrigue, 'Internal Audit: Is the "Third Line of Defense" Effective as a Form of Governance? An Exploratory Study of the Impression Management Techniques Chief Audit Executives Use in Their Annual Accountability to the Audit Committee' (2016) 151 *Journal of Business Ethics* 853; Samar Pratt and Erika Peters, 'Internal Audit: Raising the Bar in Auditing Financial Crime Risk' (2017) 1(3) *Journal of Financial Compliance* 237.

18 Ulrich Bantleon and others, 'Coordination Challenges in Implementing the Three Lines of Defense Model' (2020) 25 *International Journal of Auditing* 59; Jonas Schuett, 'Three Lines of Defense against Risks from AI' (2023) 15 *Law, Innovation and Technology* 45; Ruchi Agarwal and Sanjay Kallapur, 'Cognitive Risk Culture and Advanced Roles of Actors in Risk Governance: A Case Study' (2018) 19 *The Journal of Risk Finance* 327 proposing an operational layer between the first and second lines of defence.

participate in setting internal policies. In contrast, regulatory expectations call for a clear distinction between the roles of each line to avoid conflicts of interest and ensure the robustness of the control framework.[19] We argue that while the TLD model serves as a useful benchmark, it does not fully capture the complexities of real-world organisational dynamics. For example, banks have opted for hybrid approaches or have implemented more than three lines of defence to address complex risk profiles or integrate emerging risk areas, such as data governance and cyber risk management.[20] For the purposes of our analysis, we shall concentrate on the second line of defence, which incorporates the units responsible for executing the core of risk management and compliance activities.

Risk Management Frameworks in Financial Institutions

From the mid-1990s onwards, the field of risk management has witnessed the development of various frameworks describing the organisational structure of compliance and risk management functions. As per risk management theory, a comprehensive risk management framework of a financial institution typically consists of four key elements: identifying risks, evaluating their impact, implementing mitigation strategies, and conducting ongoing monitoring and reporting.[21] **9.9**

First of all, a crucial component is the identification of risks, focusing on credit, market, operational, and reputational risks. This risk identification process extends beyond assessing risks associated with the company's existing business model, including further assessments of potential emerging risks. The latter evaluations should be conducted at least once a year to ensure the **9.10**

---

19 For a critique of the TLD model, also Kumbirai Mabwe, Robert Webb and Patrick John Ring, 'Operational Risk and the Three Lines of Defence in UK Financial Institutions: Is Three Really the Magic Number?' (2017) 12 *The Journal of Operational Risk* 53; Donna Turner, 'Three Lines of Defence – Is It the Right Model?' (2022) 5 *Journal of Financial Compliance* 237; Shruti Kashyap and Einar Iveroth, 'Transparency and Accountability Influences of Regulation on Risk Control: The Case of a Swedish Bank' (2020) 25 *Journal of Management and Governance* 475.

20 For example, research proposing a 'four lines of defence' model: Volodymyr Chaplyha, 'The Improved "Four- Line Model" of the Organization of the Risk Management System in Banks and Banking Groups of Ukraine' (2023) *Herald of Economics* 161; Alette Tammenga, 'The Application of Artificial Intelligence in Banks in the Context of the Three Lines of Defence Model' (2020) 94 *Maandblad Voor Accountancy en Bedrijfseconomie* 219 discussing the integration of AI and machine learning in risk management.

21 For an analysis, McKinsey & Company, 'The future of operational'-risk management in financial services' (2020) www.mckinsey.com/capabilities/risk-and-resilience/our-insights/the-future-of-operational-risk-management-in-financial-services; Elisabetta Gualandri, 'Basel 3, Pillar 2: The Role of Banks' Internal Governance and Control Function' (2011) CEFIN Research Paper No 0027 https://ssrn.com/abstract=1908641; Anthony Saunders and Marcia Millon Cornett, *Financial Institutions Management: A Risk Management Approach* (McGraw-Hill 2014).

organisation remains responsive to shifts in both market conditions and regulatory requirements. By taking a proactive stance on risk identification, companies can anticipate potential issues before they become problematic, thereby establishing a robust compliance framework.[22]

9.11 Second, the process of risk assessment encompasses the formulation of approaches to address key compliance concerns. Typically, the evaluation procedure seeks to establish the intrinsic risk level for an organisation in relation to risk areas identified by the compliance department. In particular, risk professionals evaluate two key factors: the probability of a risk materialising and the potential impact of such an event on the company and its clients. By prioritising risks according to this analysis, financial institutions can strategically allocate resources to address areas with the highest risk exposure.[23]

9.12 The third aspect involves risk mitigation techniques, such as diversification, hedging and insurance.[24] The risk management protocols and compliance guidelines of each bank should be customised to address the unique characteristics of its offerings and its customer base, formalised and documented. It is subsequently the responsibility of compliance staff to regularly assess whether the organisation is adhering to its own policies and procedures.

9.13 The fourth aspect of risk management involves the ongoing monitoring risk exposures and reporting this information to top-level executives and regulatory authorities. A financial institution's compliance framework should be designed to produce reports and data that cover operational, financial and compliance-related matters, addressing both internal and external elements that affect the institution's regulatory and compliance risks. Once a risk officer has identified and collected this information, it must be efficiently distributed to the appropriate staff members throughout the organisation for examination and evaluation.

9.14 In the following sections, we contend that the organisational structure of compliance and risk management departments has little impact on the development of a strong risk culture.[25] Instead, the core of the cultural debate revolves

22 Ortwin Renn, *Risk Governance: Coping with Uncertainty in a Complex World* (Routledge 2008).

23 Georges Dionne, 'Risk Management: History, Definition, and Critique' (2013) 16(2) *Risk Management and Insurance Review* 147.

24 Geoffrey Poitras, 'Chapter 6 – Risk Management: Hedging and Diversification' in *Risk Management, Speculation, and Derivative Securities* (Elsevier 2002).

25 Harold Weston, Thomas A Conklin and Kristen Drobnis, 'Assessing and Re-Setting Culture in Enterprise Risk Management' (2018) 85 *Assurances et gestion des risques* 131.

around factors such as the autonomy of compliance staff and an environment of constructive criticism within compliance teams. These elements, rather than organisational structure, are central to shaping the compliance culture of a financial institution.

C. TOWARDS A DEFINITION OF REGULATORY CULTURE IN FINANCIAL SERVICES

The concept of culture itself is subject to debate.[26] The difficulty in defining culture is not unique to the financial services sector, as evidenced by the broader discussions on organisational culture across various industries.[27] Various theoretical perspectives and research methodologies emphasise different aspects of organisational culture.[28] Culture is intrinsically linked to the risk framework of a financial institution, encompassing the 'collective mindset and the shared set of norms, attitudes and behaviours related to the awareness, management and control of risks at all levels in a bank'.[29] In terms of other definitions of risk culture, the Institute of International Finance (IIF) defines risk culture as 'the norms and traditions of behaviour of individuals and of groups within an organisation that determine the way in which they identify, understand, discuss and act on the risks the organisation confronts and the risks it takes'.[30] The Basel Committee for Banking Supervision (BCBS) offers 9.15

26 The term 'culture' has a wider meaning than 'risk culture'. For an analysis, Marvin Bower, *The Will to Manage: Corporate Success Through Programmed Management* (McGraw-Hill 1966); Edgar H Schein, 'Organizational Culture' (1990) 45(2) *American Psychologist* 109; Terrence Deal and Allan Kennedy, *Corporate Cultures: The Rites and Rituals of Corporate Life* (Perseus Books 2000), referring to organisational culture as 'the way we do things around here'; Benjamin Schneider, Mark Ehrhart and William Macey, *Organizational Climate and Culture* (Routledge 2017), defining culture as 'the shared basic assumptions, values, and beliefs that characterize a setting and are taught to newcomers as the proper way to think and feel, communicated by the myths and stories people tell about how the organization'.

27 Lisa Interligi, 'Compliance Culture: A Conceptual Framework' (2010) 16 *Journal of Management & Organization* 23; Alison Dempsey, *Principles, Process, Responsibility: Exploring Ethics as a Meta-Regulatory Framework for Evolving Governance Discourse* (PhD thesis, University of British Columbia 2012).

28 Michael Power, Simon Ashby and Tommaso Palermo, 'Risk Culture in Financial Organisations: A Research Report' (2013) Centre for Analysis of Risk and Regulation, London School of Economics Report (http://eprints.lse.ac.uk/67978/1/Palermo_Rsik%20culture%20research%20report_2016.pdf?_gl=1*1azbqkw*_ga*MTk5OTI1MjMzMS4xNzUxMzYxODg0*_ga_LWTEVFESYX*czE3NTEzNjE4ODQkbzEkZzAkdDE3NTEzNjE4ODkkajYwJGwwJGgw*_gcl_au*MTQ1NTE1MTQ2NC4xNzUxMzYxODkw) noting that 'while culture can be associated with leadership, learning, and performance, it can also be related to control, ideology, and oppression.'

29 Frank Elderson, 'Treading Softly Yet Boldly: How Culture Drives Risk in Banks and What Supervisors Can Do About It' (Speech, 19 September 2023) https://www.bankingsupervision.europa.eu/press/speeches/date/2023/html/ssm.sp230919~589c61455b.en.htm.

30 Institute of International Finance, 'Reform in the Financial Services Industry: Strengthening Practices for a More Stable System: The Report of the IIF Steering Committee on Implementation' (2009); Financial Stability Board, 'Guidance on Supervisory Interaction with Financial Institutions on Risk Culture: A

a similar definition, referring to it as the 'bank's norms, attitudes and behaviours related to risk awareness, risk-taking and risk management and controls that shape decisions on risk'.[31] The FSB and ECB propose four building blocks that comprise a sound risk culture of a financial institution: 'tone from the top, accountability of employees, adequate incentives and effective communication and challenge'.[32] Frank Elderson, Vice Chair of the Supervisory Board of the ECB, recently observed that 'Culture is often the invisible hand that nudges banks towards either prudent risk management or reckless behaviour'.[33] Elderson further characterises risk culture as the 'software' of governance, encompassing the attitudes and norms influencing individual behaviour within the formal structure of management policies (contrasting governance as 'hardware'). He posits that a robust encourages innovation and customer service while ensuring compliance with regulatory requirements and internal controls. In contrast, a weak culture will lead bank employees to overlook risk controls in favour of short-term gains. Overall, these definitions underscore the importance of personal attitudes and social interactions with departments in shaping a bank's risk culture. They further highlight the importance of risk culture in establishing a proactive and consistent approach to managing risk within banking institutions.[34]

Framework for Assessing Risk Culture' (2014) www.fsb.org/2014/04/140407/ For a review of definitions, Jurgen Bott and Udo Milkau, 'Risk Culture and the Role Model of the Honourable Merchant' (2018) 11(40) *Journal of Risk and Financial Management* 1.

31 Basel Committee on Banking Supervision, 'Corporate Governance Principles for Banks' (2015) www.bis.org/bcbs/publ/d328.htm; in general, see Nicola Bianchi and Franco Fiordelisi, *Measuring and Assessing Risk Culture* (Springer 2017).

32 For a definition of risk culture by the EBA, see paragraph 13 EBA, Guidelines on Internal Governance under Directive 2013/36/EU (EBA/GL/2021/05) (https://www.eba.europa.eu/sites/default/files/document_library/Publications/Guidelines/2021/1016721/Final%20report%20on%20Guidelines%20on%20internal%20governance%20under%20CRD.pdf): 'Risk culture means an institution's norms, attitudes and behaviours related to risk awareness, risk-taking and risk management, and the controls that shape decisions on risks. Risk culture influences the decisions of management and employees during the day-to-day activities and has an impact on the risks they assume'; Berta F Muniz, Jose M Montes Peon and Camilo J Vazquez Ordas, 'Misconduct and Risk Climate in Banking: Development of a Multidimensional Measurement Scale' (2020) 11 *Global Policy* 73 introducing a framework to evaluate risk culture in banks, based on the four foundational elements outlined by the FSB; also Elizabeth A Sheedy and Denise Jepsen, 'How to Measure Risk Culture in Australian Superannuation Funds' Macquarie University Faculty of Business & Economics Research Paper ssrn.com/abstract =3128693.

33 Elizabeth A Sheedy and Denise Jepsen, 'How to Measure Risk Culture in Australian Superannuation Funds' (2018) Macquarie University Faculty of Business & Economics Research Paper https://ssrn.com/abstract=3128693; Frank Elderson, 'Treading Softly Yet Boldly: How Culture Drives Risk in Banks and What Supervisors Can Do About It' (n 30).

34 Yuliani Yuliani, 'Risk Management Strategies in Financial Institutions' (2024) 1 *Management Studies and Business Journal (PRODUCTIVITY)* 154; Paolo Agnese and Paolo Capuano, 'The Culture of Risk Governance in Financial Institutions' (2021) 14 *Journal of Risk Management in Financial Institutions* 301.

How Does 'Good' Culture Look for Compliance Departments of Banks?

The foundation of effective risk culture in financial institutions lies in the autonomy of the internal control functions. Studies have highlighted that these governance frameworks foster a stronger risk culture by establishing distinct lines of responsibility and accountability, thus improving the efficacy of compliance and risk management systems. According to this view, governance structures should forbid 'dual-hatting', where individuals simultaneously hold positions in control functions and business roles, as this could undermine the objectivity and independence necessary for effective internal control.[35] For example, a risk manager with financial or managerial responsibilities in an operational unit may struggle to objectively assess that unit's risks.[36] Likewise, merging the internal audit function with other roles, such as compliance, could reduce its effectiveness and jeopardise the integrity of the third line of defence. **9.16**

Second, a robust risk culture is linked to a 'challenge culture' within compliance departments, emphasising the need to empower compliance staff to actively question practices without fear of negative consequences. This challenge culture involves creating an environment where compliance and risk management personnel are encouraged to voice concerns, offer alternative perspectives and hold all levels of the organisation, including top management, accountable for their risk management decisions. To ensure the effectiveness of this approach, certain practices should be established: (i) Direct board access: compliance officers should have unimpeded communication channels with senior management and relevant committees to report compliance matters; (ii) Cultivation of an inquisitive mindset: promoting an inquisitive approach in compliance means nurturing an atmosphere where questioning and critical thinking are not only allowed but actively promoted. This approach includes understanding the underlying reasons for compliance regulations and how they align with the organisation's overall risk management strategies; (iii) Effective record-keeping: consistent documentation of compliance interactions with leadership ensures that concerns and recommendations can be traced and referenced.[37] **9.17**

---

35 Andrew Ellul, 'The Role of Risk Management in Corporate Governance' (2015) 7 *Annual Review of Financial Economics* 279.

36 Nikki Cornwell and others, 'The Role of Data Analytics within Operational Risk Management: A Systematic Review from the Financial Services and Energy Sectors' (2022) *Journal of the Operational Research Society* 374 discussing how managers may be prone to underestimating risks in their own units; Erastus Karanja and Mark A Rosso, 'The Chief Risk Officer: A Study of Roles and Responsibilities' (2017) 19 *Risk Management* 103.

37 Doriana Cucinelli and Arturo Patarnello, 'Bank Credit Risk Management and Risk Culture' in Francesca Arnaboldi and others (eds), *Risk Culture in Banking* (Palgrave Macmillan 2017) 321. For a review of these

While there is considerable discussion about fostering a 'challenge culture' within compliance departments, its practical implementation often falls short due to organisational power dynamics and a lack of psychological safety. We believe that the substantial influence held by leaders in financial institutions can suppress the open voicing of concerns or disagreements by compliance professionals, especially when the latter challenge established business strategies or decisions.

9.18 Third, a strong risk culture is fundamentally shaped by accountability. Scholarly research indicates that an effective accountability framework within a bank necessitates a clearly defined structure of roles and responsibilities.[38] This concept extends beyond simply assigning responsibilities; it involves ensuring that all personnel and departments comprehend the potential impacts of their choices and actions. A robust accountability culture promotes proactive risk management practices, encouraging employees across all levels to take charge of risk-related duties and compliance obligations. This emphasis on accountability is particularly crucial for top executives and board members, who must actively supervise risk-taking activities and uphold the integrity of risk management protocols throughout the organisation. As explained above, the 'Three Lines of Defence' model is frequently referenced as a valuable framework in promoting accountability in risk management. For example, the UK SMCR marks an important advancement in strengthening accountability and governance within the financial sector. By emphasising individual responsibility, it aims to ensure that senior executives cannot evade accountability for their actions or omissions.[39]

D. INSIGHTS FROM THE ECB ON RISK CULTURE

9.19 The ECB's regulatory approach remains highly relevant for the UK even after Brexit, for several key reasons. First, the ECB establishes rigorous regulatory standards that often shape global practices and influence international norms. Furthermore, the UK and EU financial markets remain deeply interconnected. Despite the UK's departure from the EU, numerous financial institutions

---

points see Lucas Gonçalves De Lima, 'Essentials of Risk Management in the Banking Sector' (2024) 14 *Revista Sistemática* 1344.

38 Oliver Wyman and G30, 'Banking Conduct and Culture – A Permanent Mindset Change' (2018) www.oliverwyman.com/our-expertise/insights/2018/dec/banking-conduct-and-culture-the-g30-report.html; Elizabeth Sheedy and Dominic SB Canestrari-Soh, 'Does Executive Accountability Enhance Risk Management and Risk Culture?' (2023) 63 *Accounting & Finance* 4093.

39 See Chapter 1 for a relevant analysis.

continue to manage cross-border operations between the two regions. In this context, the UK's financial services sector is pursuing equivalence agreements to maintain access to the EU market post-Brexit.[40]

The ECB has made risk culture a top priority, especially since the global financial crisis highlighted the importance of robust risk management frameworks within banking institutions. According to the ECB, deficiencies in risk culture can signal deeper governance issues that may precede broader financial difficulties. This supervisory focus encompasses not just the technical aspects of banking governance, but also cultural dimensions, aiming to promote an organisational mindset conducive to prudent risk management. The aim is to encourage a risk culture where employees at all levels are aware of their responsibilities and act in a manner that supports the institution's long-term stability and regulatory compliance. **9.20**

The supervisory approach of the ECB incorporates the 'three lines of defence' model. The central bank mandates that these divisions (risk management, compliance, and audit) possess adequate authority, status, reporting lines and resources to carry out their responsibilities efficiently. As regulatory standards evolve, financial institutions are compelled to continuously update their governance frameworks to address emerging risks. These challenges encompass not only financial risks but also non-financial ones, such as geopolitical risks, technological innovations (e.g., artificial intelligence) and environmental, social and governance (ESG) risks. The ECB further emphasises that banks must demonstrate their internal governance practices through tangible actions, rather than relying solely on formal policies. **9.21**

As previously mentioned, risk culture in the EU regulation context is broadly categorised into four dimensions: leadership tone, effective communication and diversity, accountability, and incentives and remuneration. Financial institutions are required to examine all these aspects to provide a comprehensive assessment of their risk culture standing. The ECB conducts internal governance evaluations, resulting in specific qualitative requirements and recommendations that banks must implement within a given timeframe. It is important to note that risk culture is equally significant for all banks, regardless of their size. In line with the principle of proportionality, the governance arrangements of banks should be aligned with the nature, scale, and complexity of the **9.22**

40 For a discussion on the topic, John Armour, 'Brexit and Financial Services' (2017) 33 *Oxford Review of Economic Policy* 54; Eilis Ferran, 'The UK as a Third Country Actor in EU Financial Services Regulation' (2017) 3 *Journal of Financial Regulation* 40.

risks embedded in their business model. However, it is worth mentioning that in its supervisory approach, the ECB recognises national differences in the various governance structures presented across the euro area.[41]

9.23 At the European Union level, the Capital Requirements Directive (CRD), transposed into national legislation, outlines the regulatory requirements for banks' internal governance. The CRD mandates robust governance frameworks, effective risk identification processes and sufficient internal controls. Complementing the CRD, the European Banking Authority (EBA) provides guidelines that further elaborate on internal governance standards. The EBA's Guidelines on Internal Governance (EBA/GL/2021/05) outline the practices banks should follow to cultivate a risk culture that emphasises compliance and sound risk management. This includes measures to ensure the accountability of senior management and to integrate risk considerations into business decision-making.[42]

9.24 Risk culture is a central component of the Single Supervisory Mechanism's (SSM) Supervisory Review and Evaluation Process (SREP), which aims to assess the governance and risk management frameworks of financial institutions within the Euro area. The SSM has developed an approach to assess governance and risk culture that integrates key European regulations, including the Capital Requirements Directive IV (CRD IV) and guidelines from the European Banking Authority (EBA). This approach also incorporates international best practices, such as principles from the Financial Stability Board (FSB) and recommendations from Group of Thirty (G30) reports. By integrating these regulatory frameworks and industry standards, the SSM strives to establish a consistent basis for conducting supervisory assessments throughout the eurozone.

41 Article 74(2) Directive 2013/36/EU of the European Parliament and of the Council of 26 June 2013 on access to the activity of credit institutions and the prudential supervision of credit institutions and investment firms, amending Directive 2002/87/EC and repealing Directives 2006/48/EC and 2006/49/EC, OJ L 176, 27.6.2013, p. 338–436 (CRD); also European Central Bank, 'Draft Guide on Governance and Risk Culture Consultation Document' (July 2024) www.bankingsupervision.europa.eu/legalframework/publiccons/pdf/ssm.pubcon202407_draftguide.en.pdf noting that 'good governance and risk culture are equally important for all banks, whatever their size', indicating that the Guide will be applicable smaller institutions as well.

42 CRD, recital 54 (stating that 'Member States should introduce principles and standards to ensure effective oversight by the management body, promote a sound risk culture at all levels of credit institutions and investment firms'); also Title V of the EBA Guidelines on internal governance under Directive 2013/36/EU (EBA/GL/2021/05); for an analysis, B Snijder-Kuipers and others, 'New EBA Guidelines – Management Body and AML/CFT Compliance Officer' (2023) 24 *Finance and Capital Markets* (formerly *Derivatives & Financial Instruments*) research.ibfd.org/#/doc?url=/document/dfi_2023_04_e2_3.

The ECB Draft Guide on Governance and Risk Culture (the 'Guide') is the latest regulatory statement addressing key supervisory areas in banking risk culture.[43] The forthcoming Guide aims to provide banks with practical insights and expectations to strengthen governance and foster a robust risk culture within the EU banking sector. This document outlines the ECB's recommendations for banks' risk culture, significantly expanding upon the 2016 Single Supervisory Mechanism (SSM) Statement on Governance and Risk Appetite.[44] The guide is a result of the ECB's in-depth risk culture assessments of selected banks and an examination of global practices in this field. Although the Guide does not impose legally binding obligations, it outlines various recommended practices, serving as benchmarks for effective risk management and governance structures. These practices, recognised as 'good practices', include frameworks and approaches that promote thorough checks and balances, alongside fostering a risk-aware mindset in decision-making processes.[45] Additionally, the Guide identifies several 'red flags', which are indicators of potential shortcomings in risk culture, such as the absence of independent risk functions, inadequate board oversight, or insufficiently articulated risk appetites. Banks are encouraged to undertake a comprehensive gap analysis to compare their existing governance frameworks against the standards and expectations articulated in the Guide. A crucial aspect emphasised by the ECB in this new guidance is the incorporation of risk considerations into strategic decision-making processes. Furthermore, the Guide underscores the importance of establishing clear accountability within organisations as a fundamental principle. This emphasis on accountability aims to foster an environment where individuals comprehend their specific roles and, more importantly, recognise how their actions impact the organisation's risk profile. Moreover, national regulatory bodies will be urged to align their evaluations of domestic banks with the standards and recommendations outlined in the guide. 9.25

The ECB notes that the primary determinant of cultural effectiveness in banks is the tone set from the top by the bank's management bodies. In order to improve this cultural trait, certain banks have established dedicated committees within their supervisory boards to oversee risk culture, conduct and 9.26

43 European Central Bank, 'Draft Guide on Governance and Risk Culture Consultation Document' (n 42).

44 European Central Bank, 'SSM Supervisory Statement on Governance and Risk Appetite', www.bankingsupervision.europa.eu/ecb/pub/pdf/ssm_supervisory_statement_on_governance_and_risk_appetite_201606.en.pdf.

45 See examples of good practices provided by the ECB for other regulatory areas, such as environmental regulation, European Central Bank, 'Thematic Review on Climate-Related and Environmental Risk: Compendium of Good Practices' (November 2022) www.bankingsupervision.europa.eu/ecb/pub/pdf/ssm.thematicreviewcercompendiumgoodpractices112022~b474fb8ed0.en.pdf.

ethics. Some institutions utilise a risk culture dashboard, which is regularly presented to the board and used to scrutinise senior management decisions. This dashboard also includes metrics to assess the implementation of the organisation's code of conduct. Additionally, many banks promote leadership examples through senior management communications to employees about culture and conduct during company-wide meetings. Moreover, banks have been instructed to enhance their management body's expertise by conducting frequent training sessions.[46]

9.27 In terms of supervisory tools, regulators primarily concentrate on written records. This focus on documentation allows leadership to actively track risk culture and ensure compliance with risk policies and controls across all divisions of the bank. The ECB is expected to seek extensive written proof that management fosters a positive approach to prudent risk management throughout the bank. In this respect, supervisors may review various documents: organisation-wide messages such as employee memos and town-hall meetings; meeting minutes demonstrating management's openness to constructive criticism and diverse viewpoints; training materials that incorporate prudent risk management principles; reporting channels to confirm employees' comfort in raising concerns without fear of negative consequences. The ECB further utilises boardroom observation as a key method to assess whether constructive challenge of culture takes place at the board level. Regulators attend board meetings selectively, aiming to evaluate board dynamics and their ability to effectively challenge management, reporting that they rarely observe indications of constructive challenge.[47]

9.28 Risk culture is frequently associated with an institution's risk appetite framework (RAF), with the ECB considering a comprehensive RAF as essential to robust governance. It is a dynamic, evolving company policy that is regularly updated and reviewed by senior management to reflect the bank's current risk profile and any emerging threats or opportunities. The RAF serves as a formal representation of the boundaries that decision-makers commit to adhere to within their risk management activities. Financial institutions are expected to integrate internal monitoring mechanisms to evaluate compliance with the

46 For similar arguments Alan Morrison and Joel Shapiro, 'Governance and Culture in the Banking Sector' (11 February 2016) ssrn.com/abstract=2731357 identifying 'tone from the top' as a crucial tool for formulating an appropriate regulatory culture.

47 Martin Arnold, 'ECB sparks staff revolt over board's "disrespectful" approach to climate change' *Financial Times* (5 March 2024) www.ft.com/content/65fcb775-43ae-472b-89bb-c75941146f46, arguing that the ECB is exceeding its authority by monitoring culture and participating in board sessions.

RAF, employing tools such as a risk appetite dashboard. This dashboard allows for a benchmark between the current risk exposure, established limits and the defined risk appetite, covering both financial and non-financial risks.[48]

The ECB has also initiated targeted 'risk culture deep dives' for a select group of banks to gain deeper insights into their risk culture. These deep dives are thorough examinations providing the ECB with a detailed understanding of a bank's risk management and cultural practices. The assessments focus on key elements such as governance frameworks, the involvement and roles of the board of directors, the alignment and operationalisation of risk appetite frameworks and the effectiveness of risk communication throughout the organisation.[49] This analysis is carried out using a combination of techniques, including direct observation of day-to-day practices, structured surveys and in-depth interviews with employees across different levels of the organisation. The results of the deep dives, combined with an examination of global efforts in this field, will shape the upcoming ECB Guidelines on Governance and Risk Culture.[50] 9.29

It should be noted that the UK and EU have generally taken distinct approaches to managing risk culture in financial institutions.[51] The comparison underscores the UK's emphasis on personal accountability versus the EU's comprehensive governance approach. The UK SMCR is focused on individual accountability, implementing strict regulations and enforcement measures to hold senior managers individually responsible for failings. Conversely, the EU framework emphasises collective responsibility and extensive guidelines for organisational risk management, placing less emphasis on individuals. Similarly, the EBA guidelines stress a holistic governance model with rigorous oversight but without the individual focus of the SMCR. They are more principles-based compared to the prescriptive nature of SMCR, and the mechanisms for enforcing cultural change are less defined compared to the SMCR. 9.30

---

48 Also, Walter Gontarek, 'Risk Governance of Financial Institutions: The Growing Importance of Risk Appetite and Culture' (2016) 9 *Journal of Risk Management in Financial Institutions* 120.

49 The deep dives employ organisational psychologists and other experts to analyse the underlying behavioural factors that shape the bank's risk culture. Also, KPMG, 'Diving Deep on Risk Culture' (2023), kpmg.com/bh/en/home/insights/2023/12/diving-deep-on-risk-culture.html this exercise building upon the ECB's recent evaluation of management bodies and the Dutch central bank's assessment of bank culture carried out in 2015.

50 Frank Elderson, 'Treading Softly Yet Boldly: How Culture Drives Risk in Banks and What Supervisors Can Do About It' (n 30).

51 For an analysis of SMCR, Anat Keller and Andreas Kokkinis, 'The Senior Managers and Certification Regime in Financial Firms: An Organisational Culture Analysis' (2022) *Journal of Corporate Law Studies* 299.

9.31 Despite increased regulatory scrutiny, the ECB has determined that banks have not made adequate progress in improving their risk culture.[52] The ECB has stated its intention to strengthen its supervisory efforts for banks under its jurisdiction, ensuring that appropriate measures are taken to improve governance standards. We anticipate that comprehensive risk culture assessments will serve as a template for on-site inspections across a broader range of financial institutions in the EU.[53] We believe that conducting risk culture deep dives could similarly benefit UK banks by helping to identify and address potential weaknesses in risk management practices. However, the implementation of such deep dives should be approached with caution. Given that the ECB's deep dives remain relatively untested, any adoption in the UK should align with existing regulatory frameworks and consider the unique needs and challenges of the UK banking sector.

E. RECOMMENDATIONS FOR A SOUND RISK CULTURE IN COMPLIANCE DEPARTMENTS

9.32 The below proposals are largely underdeveloped and based on anecdotal evidence. They provide, though, some directions on the study of risk culture within compliance departments.

9.33 First, we contend that experimentation plays a crucial role in transforming culture within compliance departments.[54] The conventional, rule-based approach that follows predetermined guidelines can often result in a risk-averse environment that stifles learning from errors. By adopting a more experimental mindset, compliance departments can cultivate a culture that welcomes innovation and ongoing learning. In this respect, insights can be gained from other regulated sectors, including medicine, aviation and pharmaceuticals, which have long incorporated trial and error into their processes, even in highly controlled environments.[55] We have noticed that compliance departments in banks are

---

52 European Central Bank, 'Draft Guide on Governance and Risk Culture Consultation Document' (n 42); Andrea Enria, 'Just a Few Bad Apples? The Importance of Culture and Governance for Good Banking' (Speech at the Conference of the Federation of International Banks in Ireland, Dublin, 20 June 2019) https://www.bankingsupervision.europa.eu/press/speeches/date/2019/html/ssm.sp190620~f9149fe258.en.html.

53 See also KPMG, 'Diving Deep on Risk Culture' (n 50).

54 For a similar analysis, see James Hennessy, 'Emerging Trends in Culture Reform: The New York Fed's Perspective' (Speech 93862, Federal Reserve Bank of New York, 2022) https://21211564.fs1.hubspotusercontentna1.net/hubfs/21211564/Compendium%20Files/Compendium%202023%20v16.pdf.

55 For example, Michael C Christensen and others, 'On the Role of Randomized Clinical Trials in Medicine' (2007) 16 Economics of Innovation and New Technology 357 analysing the benefits of randomised

transitioning from rule-based to risk-based approaches, opening up possibilities for experimentation. This shift allows for testing behavioural interventions to boost compliance rates and evaluating the efficacy of compliance programs. For instance, a financial institution could conduct a trial to determine if customised email notifications about compliance duties lead to higher completion rates than standard reminders. Moreover, these departments can explore various training techniques, such as gamified modules or scenario-based learning, to identify which methods are most effective in helping staff retain regulatory information. Compliance teams can also employ simulations to evaluate how well the bank's systems and personnel manage hypothetical regulatory crises or adapt to new regulatory requirements. Moreover, the implementation of practices such as 'regulatory sandboxes' has proven effective in nurturing innovation within financial institutions. These sandboxes enable companies to evaluate new products and services in a controlled setting under regulatory supervision, striking a balance between innovation and risk management.[56] All these methods allow financial institutions to learn from failures in a secure environment, promoting a dynamic and responsive compliance culture that addresses emerging risks.

Second, in contrast with the majority of policy guidelines, we argue that middle management, rather than leadership of compliance departments, can function as critical agents for cultural change.[57] Their dual role as implementers of strategy and influencers of daily practices provides them with the necessary leverage to drive meaningful cultural shifts. Research indicates that middle managers play a crucial role in connecting top-level leadership with junior staff.[58] Studies also suggest that middle managers can cultivate an environment of transparency and responsibility by actively promoting communication 9.34

controlled trials in medicine.

56 Dirk Zetzsche, Ross Buckley, Douglas Arner and Janos Barberis, 'Regulating a Revolution: From Regulatory Sandboxes to Smart Regulation' (2017) 23 *Fordham Journal of Corporate & Financial Law* 31; Ahmad Alaassar, Anne-Laure Mention and Tor Helge Aas, 'Exploring How Social Interactions Influence Regulators and Innovators: The Case of Regulatory Sandboxes' (2020) 160 Technological Forecasting and Social Change 120257 www.sciencedirect.com/science/article/pii/S0040162520310830.

57 Paul Cox and Diandra Soobiah, 'An Empirical Investigation into the Corporate Culture of UK Listed Banks' (2018) 26 *Journal of Financial Regulation and Compliance* 120.

58 Anneloes Raes, Marielle Heijltjes, Ursula Glunk and Robert Roe, 'The Interface of the Top Management Team and Middle Managers: A Process Model' (2011) 36 *Academy of Management Review* 102 discussing how middle managers influence employees' motivation and commitment; Edmar Saturnino César, Sandrielem Da Silva Rodrigues and Poliano Bastos Da Cruz, 'Compliance Mediation between the Demographic Characteristics of Intermediate Management and the Financial Performance of Banking Branches' (2021) 5 *New Challenges in Accounting and Finance* 17; James B Abugre and Kester Adebola, 'An Examination of Training and Development of Middle Level Managers in Emerging Economies' (2015) 23 *International Journal of Organizational Analysis* 545.

and reinforcing a culture where employees feel safe to voice concerns without fear of repercussions.[59] They can convert high-level compliance goals into concrete actions, thus acting as catalysts for organisational change. When middle managers demonstrate ethical behaviour and prioritise risk management, they establish a tone that resonates throughout the organisation. Additionally, middle managers can play a vital role in creating psychological safety, a crucial component in fostering a speak-up culture. In this regard, middle managers often face a dual pressure: the need to deliver on performance targets while upholding cultural standards. To drive meaningful cultural change, they require strong support from senior leadership. Without visible backing or adequate resources, their efforts risk losing credibility and effectiveness.

9.35 Our third recommendation is to encourage the deeper involvement of compliance and risk managers in business operations. In contrast with many policy prescriptions analysed above, we advocate the inclusion of compliance personnel on key organisational decision-making committees. In this role, they function not only as technical specialists but also as catalysts for change and strategic collaborators. Research highlights the dual role of risk management positions, emphasising a shift toward a 'risk management of everything' approach.[60] This perspective views risk as a broad organisational concern rather than a purely technical discipline. This facilitates the incorporation of risk considerations into core business activities and ensures that risk is factored into strategic planning, rather than being treated as an afterthought. This integration also allows risk professionals to build relationships with various business units, which is crucial for aligning risk management with business goals. Furthermore, it underscores the need for risk managers to become fluent in different business 'languages', adapting their communication styles to suit diverse organisational audiences.[61] The appointment of Chief Risk Officers (CROs) reflects this shift, as they are increasingly engaged in firm-level strategic decision-making. Additionally, Enterprise Risk Management (ERM) has risen in importance, allowing organisations to take an integrated approach

59 Neal M Ashkanasy, Celeste PM Wilderom and Mark F Peterson (eds), *The Handbook of Organizational Culture and Climate* (2nd edn, SAGE Publications 2011).

60 Anette Mikes, 'Risk Management and Calculative Cultures' (2009) 20 *Management Accounting Research* 18 identifies two archetypes: the 'quantitative enthusiast', who emphasises technical risk metrics, and the 'holistic facilitator', a business partner who integrates risk awareness to drive organisational change; Michael Power, *Organized Uncertainty: Designing a World of Risk Management* (Oxford University Press 2007); also Alan Brener, 'The Role of Compliance as a "Gate-Keeper" Function in Financial Services: Reality vs Regulatory Conception' (2019) 30 *European Business Law Review* 965.

61 Ekaterina Vasilyeva, Maria Bultseva and Nadezhda Lebedeva, 'Face Concerns in Intra- and Intercultural Business Communication' [2022] *Journal of Intercultural Communication Research* 237.

to risk management that is both defensive and strategic, moving away from traditional siloed practices.[62]

Additionally, we emphasise the significance of informal networks among compliance experts in cultivating a strong regulatory culture within financial organisations. These unofficial networks enable compliance professionals to engage in candid conversations about regulatory expectations, exchange insights on best practices and discuss emerging risks more flexibly and dynamically than traditional hierarchical structures allow.[63] Such interactions facilitate the exchange of diverse viewpoints and foster a sense of unity among compliance professionals. The trust established through informal communication also contributes to a culture of transparency, where staff members feel at ease discussing potential compliance challenges without fear of repercussions. Additionally, these interactions can further enhance formal structures by providing an additional channel for communication and knowledge sharing. For instance, while the 'Three Lines of Defence' model provides a clear distinction of roles in risk management, informal networks can help bridge the gaps between these lines by promoting cross-functional dialogue and ensuring that insights from the first line (business operations) reach those in the second and third lines.[64] 9.36

Finally, research should concentrate on the impact of integrating technologies such as artificial intelligence, regulatory technology and supervisory technology into compliance and risk management processes.[65] These technological advancements not only optimise regulatory procedures but also trigger significant changes in risk culture.[66] This cultural impact extends beyond operational efficiency; employees must adjust to new working methods where 9.37

62 Andre P Liebenberg and Robert E Hoyt, 'The Determinants of Enterprise Risk Management: Evidence From the Appointment of Chief Risk Officers' (2003) 6 *Risk Management and Insurance Review* 37; Jeffrey Brown, Michael Duane and Til Schuermann, 'What Is Enterprise Risk Management?' (2019) 12 *Journal of Risk Management in Financial Institutions* 311.

63 Michael Roemer and Mark Buckle, 'A Culture of Learning: Reinforcing a Firm's Values, Ethics and Culture through Building a Learning Environment in Compliance' (2017) 1 *Journal of Financial Compliance* 7; Michele M Fleming, 'The Imperative of Building and Fostering a Strong Compliance Culture in the Evolving Cross-Border Payments Space' (2024) 18 *Journal of Payments Strategy & Systems* 73; Jeffrey C Morton, 'The Development of a Compliance Culture' (2005) 6 *Journal of Investment Compliance* 59.

64 Michael Power, *Riskwork: Essays on the Organizational Life of Risk Management* (Oxford University Press 2016) suggesting that informal networks can significantly enhance the effectiveness of risk management by encouraging the flow of information that may not surface through formal reporting channels.

65 Douglas Arner, 'Janos Barberis and Ross Buckley, FinTech, RegTech, and the Reconceptualization of Financial Regulation' (2017) 37(3) *Northwestern Journal of International Law & Business* 371.

66 Rafael Becerra-Vicario and others, 'The Impact of Artificial Intelligence in The Financial Sector: Opportunities and Challenges' (2024) 5 *International Journal of Business & Management Studies* 33; Nitin Rane, Saurabh P Choudhary and Jayesh Rane, 'Acceptance of Artificial Intelligence Technologies in

decision-making increasingly relies on data-driven insights rather than conventional judgment. The integration of AI and other technologies should be, therefore, complemented by a risk-aware culture that encourages ethical AI usage and continuous adaptation to emerging risks.

F. CONCLUSIONS

9.38 Over the past years, regulatory bodies and supervisors worldwide have placed increased emphasis on risk culture as part of the risk management framework of financial institutions. The focus on culture and conduct indicates a recognition that financial stability is as much about sound governance and ethical behaviour as it is about technical compliance. We view these developments as an indication that culture has been firmly established as a supervisory priority, and banks should anticipate heightened scrutiny in this area in the near future. Various academic fields explore risk culture-related topics from different methodological perspectives.[67] This multidisciplinary approach provides a wealth of theoretical and empirical evidence to inform business practices and enhance legal frameworks of banks. While these studies have yielded valuable insights, further research is needed to understand how risk culture transformation initiatives can be effectively implemented within the organisational practices of compliance departments. As analysed above, risk culture is an ambiguous concept, comprising both formal and informal processes, with the latter being more difficult to observe.[68] In our view, this qualitative nature of risk culture poses a significant challenge for compliance functions and risk management.[69]

Business Management, Finance, and e-Commerce: Factors, Challenges, and Strategies' (2024) 5 *Studies in Economics and Business Relations* 23.

67 For a review, Joachim Kunz and Marc Heitz, 'Banks' Risk Culture and Management Control Systems: A Systematic Literature Review' (2021) 32 *Journal of Management Control* 439 reviewing 103 articles that examine risk culture in banks, categorising them into three main areas: assessment of risk culture, its relationship with management controls, and its development over time; Bernhard Streicher, Eric Eller and Moritz Bielefeld, 'The Risk Culture Framework: Introducing an Integrative Framework for Holistic Risk Analysis' (2023) 13 SAGE Open https://journals.sagepub.com/doi/10.1177/21582440231191789 introducing a Risk Culture matrix that differentiates between three influence domains: person, social context, and risk situation; Phil Kelly, 'Conceptualising Business Risk Culture: A Study of Risk Thinking and Practice in Contemporary Dynamic Organisations' (2009) 1 *International Journal of Business Continuity and Risk Management* 19.

68 Financial Stability Board, 'Guidance on Supervisory Interaction with Financial Institutions on Risk Culture. A Framework for Assessing Risk Culture' (2014) www.fsb.org/2014/04/140407, explaining that risk culture changes and adapts over time in response to various factors, such as mergers and acquisitions, as well as fluctuations in market conditions.

69 Altaaf Osman and Charlene C Lew, 'Developing a Framework of Institutional Risk Culture for Strategic Decision-Making' (2020) 24 *Journal of Risk Research* 1072.

Specifically, regulatory bodies expect that financial institutions cultivate a prudent approach to risk management, which does not necessarily entail adopting an overly cautious stance over risk decisions.[70] Instead, it aims to foster risk behaviour that allows banks to take acceptable risks, enabling sustainable growth without financial instability.[71] In this context, many financial professionals have mistakenly equated the implementation of culture with over-regulation, viewing it as a regulatory approach that adds new layers of compliance policies. Moreover, evaluating the suitability of a specific risk culture should be aligned with each bank's business strategy. This consideration is particularly crucial in the financial services industry, which encompasses a diverse range of organisations (from local/regional institutions to global conglomerates) operating across various sectors (including retail, commercial, investment, insurance and fintech).[72] A key policy question that emerges is whether regulators should promote a standardised risk culture for all financial institutions or consider embracing 'pluralism and diversity in the cultural aspects of risk'.[73] Furthermore, it could be argued that the discourse on risk culture has diverted to an ethical debate, reflecting a regulatory desire to reintroduce ethical considerations into organisations through their risk management processes.[74] In conclusion, while there are numerous valid perspectives on risk culture in banking institutions, they need to be synthesised to develop a more unified understanding. This integration would enable financial institutions to cultivate the risk culture of compliance departments in a suitable direction. **9.39**

In terms of recommendations, we believe that experimentation can help banks create compliance practices that are more effective, efficient and adaptable, while fostering a culture of learning and continuous improvement. Empowering middle managers with the right resources and support is equally critical in promoting a strong compliance culture. As key influencers within organisations, middle managers can model compliant behaviour, provide constructive feedback and build engagement and trust among teams. Furthermore, the **9.40**

---

70 Alessandro Carretta, Vincenzo Farina and Paola Schwizer, 'Banking Regulation Towards Advisory: The "Culture Compliance" of Banks and Supervisory Authorities' (July 2005) ssrn.com/abstract=764244.

71 Frank Elderson, 'Banks' Governance and Risk Culture a Decade On: Progress and Shortcomings' (ECB The Supervision Blog, 24 July 2024) https://www.bankingsupervision.europa.eu/press/blog/2024/html/ssm.blog240724~a4e2c38688.en.html.

72 Michael Power, Simon Ashby and Tommaso Palermo, 'Risk Culture in Financial Organisations: A Research Report' (n 29) explaining that within organisations risk cultures can vary significantly and may not be uniformly distributed.

73 Ibid; Alessandro Carretta, Vincenzo Farina and Paola Schwizer, 'Banking Regulation Towards Advisory: The "Culture Compliance" of Banks and Supervisory Authorities' (n 71).

74 Rutger Claassen, 'Financial Crisis and the Ethics of Moral Hazard' (2015) 41 *Social Theory and Practice* 527.

growing adoption of a 'risk management of everything' approach highlights the recognition of the interconnected nature of risks and the need for holistic management strategies. This shift calls for risk managers to not only meet compliance requirements but also play a strategic role in business decision-making. Additionally, informal networks among compliance professionals further strengthen compliance culture by encouraging curiosity, sharing best practices and exchanging knowledge and experiences. Lastly, while AI offers significant potential for innovation and efficiency in compliance and risk management, it also demands a cultural transformation within banks. Successfully leveraging AI requires a balanced approach that embraces its benefits while addressing ethical and regulatory challenges to ensure responsible and effective implementation.

10

BANKS' ANTI-MONEY LAUNDERING EFFORTS – THE ROLE OF REGTECH AND AI AND CULTURE

Babajide Oniwinde

A. OVERVIEW

The principal aim of this chapter is to examine how banks engage with anti- **10.1**
money laundering regulations. The chapter delves into the interplay between banks' internal culture and the anti-money laundering framework and how banks' significant investment in advanced technology is transforming financial crime prevention.

The banking industry is vital to maintaining the stability of every financial **10.2**
system and mitigating systemic risk to an economy.[1][2] However, that stability

1 All weblinks were last accessed on 20 December 2024.

2 Liang Dai, Dan Luo and Ming Yang, 'Disclosure of Bank-Specific Information and the Stability of Financial Systems' (2024) 37(4) *The Review of Financial Studies* 1315.

is increasingly threatened by the negative consequences of money laundering.[3] Money laundering is a form of financial crime.[4] It involves concealing and hiding the true source and origin of proceeds of crime such as drug dealing, terrorist acts and corruption.[5] Money launderers take advantage of every opportunity to convert illicit funds into legal money, using various financial institutions and professionals.[6] Hence, it is critical to build a strong and formidable anti-money laundering system to keep banks from being negatively impacted and exploited by illegitimate operations.[7]

10.3 The perceived risk of banks being used as a channel for financial crime has inevitably prompted global and regional policymakers to subject banks to stringent regulations aimed at preventing money laundering; these laws establish standards and criteria that banks must follow.[8] Furthermore, national regulatory bodies have been established to ensure adherence to these anti-money laundering regulations.[9] Indeed, banks frequently incur large financial fines, forfeitures and other consequences for non-compliance with AML legislation and standards.[10] Additionally, protecting consumer interests, upholding financial system stability and combating financial crime are primary objectives of banking regulation.[11]

10.4 AML standards are a deterrent to illicit activities and, unsurprisingly, banks have responded in their adherence, their internal culture and their growth trajectory, particularly with technological advancement, to significantly improve

3 Marek Kot, 'Money Laundering as a Major Risk to the Stability of the Banking Industry' (2021) 65(4) *Prace Naukowe Uniwersytetu Ekonomicznego we Wrocławiu* 77.

4 Muhammad Saleem Korejo, Ramalinggam A/L A. Rajamanickam and Muhamad Helmi Md. Said, 'The Concept of Money Laundering: A Quest for Legal Definition' (2021) 24(4) Journal of Money Laundering Control 725.

5 Michael Levi and Melvin Soudijn, 'Understanding the Laundering of Organized Crime Money' (2020) 49 *Crime and Justice* 579.

6 Reeda Al Sabri Halawi, 'Dirty Money in the Banking Sector' (2019) 22(3) *Journal of Money Laundering Control* 527.

7 Esat Durguti, Erëza Arifi, Emine Gashi and Muhamet Spahiu, 'Anti-Money Laundering Regulations' Effectiveness in Ensuring Banking Sector Stability: Evidence of Western Balkan' (2023) 11(1) *Cogent Economics & Finance* 2167356.

8 Ilaria Zavoli and Colin King, 'The Challenges of Implementing Anti-Money Laundering Regulation: An Empirical Analysis' (2021) 84(4) *Modern Law Review* 740.

9 Isaac Ofoeda, Elikplimi Komla Agbloyor and Joshua Yindenaba Abor, 'Financial Sector Development, Anti-Money Laundering Regulations and Economic Growth' (2024) 19(1) *International Journal of Emerging Markets* 191.

10 *Financial Conduct Authority v NatWest Bank Plc* [2021] Sentencing Remarks (Southwark Crown Court, 13 December 2021).

11 Darshan Kumar and Mark Eshwar Lokanan, 'Money Laundering Influence on Financial Institutions and Ways to Retaliate' (2023) 26(1) *Journal of Money Laundering Control* 133.

their compliance.[12] However, to effectively combat money laundering, it is vital to have the correct culture. This chapter, therefore, creates an opportunity to examine and offer valuable insight into how banks are engaging with AML regulations having regard to their internal culture. In terms of method for gathering data for this chapter, data has been obtained from regulatory texts, and from writings in journals that have gone through peer-review, that explored the interplay between banks and AML frameworks. This chapter also has an empirical element by drawing upon previously conducted interviews with 20 compliance professionals within the banking industry on the point of culture of compliance.[13]

B. CATALYST FOR AML COMPLIANCE IN BANKS

This section will explore the key factors that drive AML compliance in banks, highlighting the regulatory pressures that act as a catalyst for robust AML frameworks. Insofar as banks are concerned, the legal framework against money laundering and counter-terrorist financing consists of two components: first, a list of criminal offences that broadly target money laundering and terrorist financing activities; and second, a comprehensive set of regulations requiring banks to implement suitable internal controls and procedures to prevent ML and TF.[14] For example, UK banks must abide by the Proceeds of Crime Act of 2002, the Terrorism Act of 2000's money laundering rules and the Money Laundering Regulations 2017, which are enforced by the regulator, the Financial Conduct Authority (FCA). Penalties for contravention of these regulations may result in heavy administrative fines, the cancellation of a necessary licence, the criminal prosecution of specific executives and officers, and serious harm to a bank's reputation. **10.5**

Hence, financial institutions ought to serve as gatekeepers, since failure to ensure proper compliance procedures when facilitating banking transactions can aid the perpetration of financial crime. In addition, banks are required by the relevant regulatory framework to carry out due diligence on customers, report suspicious activity regarding specific transactions,[15] designate a **10.6**

12 Moh Zali and Ach Maulidi, 'Fighting Against Money Laundering' (2018) 5(3) *BRICS Law Journal* 40.

13 Babajide Oniwinde, 'To What Extent Does a Focus on Accountability Promote Regulatory Compliance in the UK Financial Services Sector?' (2024) Doctorate thesis, Anglia Ruskin Research Online (ARRO) https://hdl.handle.net/10779/aru.25133663.v1.

14 Andreas Kokkinis and Andrea Miglionico, 'Money Laundering and Terrorist Financing' in Andreas Kokkinis and Andrea Miglionico, *Banking Law* (Routledge 2021) 179.

15 *Shah & Anor v HSBC Private Bank (UK) Ltd* [2012] EWHC 1283 (QB).

dedicated nominated officer, guarantee that senior management bears overall accountability for preventing money laundering and terrorist financing and proliferation financing and carry out regular risk assessments.[16] Furthermore, institutions must ensure that dedicated professionals responsible for compliance are equipped with the necessary resources. Especially important are resources relating to customer due diligence investigations, suspicious activity reporting, beneficial ownership procedures, and Politically Exposed Persons (PEP)/sanctions screening.[17] However, in-house nominated AML compliance professionals, usually referred to as Money Laundering Reporting Officers, tend to have an ambiguous role within the banks, with competing objectives of law enforcement and profit-making.[18] Nonetheless, these compliance professionals and relevant personnel get ongoing training, professionalisation, skill development and support to guarantee adequate adherence to the anti-money laundering regulations.[19]

10.7 In addition, compliance programmes are essential to the efficient execution of money laundering regulations and compliance requirements. These programmes must be updated often to stay current with the most recent changes in the financial crime landscape. Indeed, the field of compliance and regulations designed to combat international financial crime is intricate and dynamic, and meeting compliance requirements may be costly and time-consuming.[20] As such, banks have been investing significantly in technology to strengthen their controls against money laundering.[21] But even with the variety of rules and regulations, global exchange of best practices and the significantly rising number of compliance employees and technologies, banks continue to lag well below expectations on a national and international scale.

---

16 Philip Ruce, 'Anti-Money Laundering: The Challenges of Know Your Customer Legislation for Private Bankers and the Hidden Benefits for Relationship Management ("The Bright Side of Knowing Your Customer")' (2011) 128(6) *The Banking Law Journal* 548.

17 Financial Action Task Force, 'Guidance to Risk-Based Approach Banking Sector' (FATF Statement, 23 October 2014).

18 Colleen P Eren, 'Cops, Firefighters, and Scapegoats: Anti-Money Laundering (AML) Professionals in an Era of Regulatory Bulimia' (2020) 2(1) *Journal of White Collar and Criminal Crime* 47.

19 Eleni Tsingou, 'New Governors on the Block: The Rise of Anti-Money Laundering Professionals' (2018) 69(2) *Crime, Law and Social Change* 191.

20 Nurul Liyana Bahrin, Sharifah Norzehan Syed Yusuf, Kamaruzzaman Muhammad and Erlane K Ghani, 'Determinants of Anti-Money Laundering Program Effectiveness among Banks' (2022) 11(1) *International Journal of Management and Sustainability* 21.

21 UK banks and FinTechs face an annual compliance cost of 38.4 billion pounds. Janine Hirt, 'LexixNexis Risk Solution Report' (2024) https://risk.lexisnexis.co.uk/insights-resources/white-paper/true-costs-of-compliance 2024.

The challenges faced by banks in their engagement with anti-money laundering regulations are evident from the magnitude of enforcement actions that have been taken against banks by regulators over the past decade. For instance, HSBC was fined USD 1.9 billion in 2012 for laundering USD 15 billion from Russia and USD 7 billion from Mexico.[22] Similarly, Standard Chartered Bank was fined USD 340 million in 2012 for laundering USD 250 billion for Iran and Libya. ING Bank was fined €775 million in 2018 for weak internal controls that allowed customers to launder funds without explaining their source of funds. In 2019 UBS was fined USD 4.2 billion for facilitating tax evasion and for inadequate controls to prevent money laundering. In 2021, NatWest was fined GBP 264.8 million for AML failure in monitoring approximately GBP 365 million of suspicious transactions by one commercial customer.[23] **10.8**

In 2022, Danske Bank was fined USD 2 billion for processing through its Estonian branch USD 160 billion of suspicious transactions and facilitating access to the US financial system for customers who resided in high-risk jurisdictions such as Russia; exposure to this case has also led to the criminal charge and conviction of the former CEO of Swedbank.[24] In 2023 the US Fed fined Deutsche Bank USD 186 million for failing to address anti-money laundering issues within the bank.[25] The demise of Credit Suisse bank and its takeover by UBS in 2023 was caused by US tax evasion fines, Swiss court criminal charges for money laundering and UK fines for bribery scandal.[26] In 2024 the CEO of TD Bank announced that he was stepping down on the back of AML failures that took place under his watch after the bank revealed it had set aside USD 3 billion to cover fines from US regulators who alleged that drug traffickers had used the bank to launder at least USD 650 million over a five-year period.[27] **10.9**

Faced with such a predicament of impending enforcement action, many banks apply extreme measures and exit product lines, countries and clients that they **10.10**

22 Carrick Mollenkamp and Brett Wolf, 'HSBC to Pay $1.9 Billion US Fine in Money-Laundering Case' (Reuters, 11 December 2012).

23 *Regina (The Financial Conduct Authority) v National Westminster Bank Plc* [2021] (Southwark Crown Court, 13 December 2021).

24 Stefania Palma and Richard Milne, 'Danske Bank to Pay $2bn Penalty for Defrauding US Banks' *Financial Times* (13 December 2022) https://www.ft.com/content/6a17f771-7c13-43f1-9d11-2e401db8e48f.

25 Pete Schroeder and others, 'US Fed Fines Deutsche Bank $186 Million for Slow Progress against Money Laundering' *Reuters* (19 July 2023) https://www.reuters.com/business/finance/fed-fines-deutsche-bank-186-mln-insufficient-progress-addressing-anti-money-2023-07-19/.

26 Sam Jones and Owen Walker, 'Credit Suisse Found Guilty over Bulgarian Drug Money Failings' *Financial Times* (27 June 2022) https://www.ft.com/content/58b59fde-0f4a-4da2-b68e-e824eee9380e.

27 Robb M Stewart and Vipal Monga, 'TD Bank Taps Veteran to Succeed Bharat Masrani as CEO' *WSJ* (19 September 2024) https://www.wsj.com/business/td-bank-ceo-bharat-masrani-to-retire-be-succeeded-by-raymond-chun-5bd94406.

struggle to service due to regulatory obligations. Frequently, operational compliance difficulties paired with ever-rising fines directly conflict with banks' abilities to maximise their resources for the financial benefit of their customers and shareholders. Thus, when the costs and risks (driven by compliance concerns, among others) do not match the expected financial returns and benefits, banks may ultimately 'de-risk' by reducing or terminating their financial transactions and banking relationships.[28] The question arises as to whether banks are failing in their fight against anti-money laundering. Is technology the answer? Is the 'right culture' the answer?

C. IS REGTECH/AI THE ANSWER TO COMBATING FINANCIAL CRIME?

10.11 This section of this chapter delves into the ways in which Regulatory Technology (RegTech) and Artificial Intelligence (AI) have been innovatively impacting AML compliance frameworks, focusing on preventing financial crimes. With the increasing complexity of financial transactions, banks have begun to comprehend that their legacy systems are insufficient to keep pace in the fight against financial crime and that they would have to embrace advanced technology to have any chance of success.[29]

10.12 AML compliance processes have evolved from the manual procedures used in the 1980s for spotting large deposits to a bank account. In the 1990s rules-based systems automated various operations while enhanced transaction monitoring became necessary in the 2000s following various regulations that preceded the events of 9/11. The 2010s saw a technological revolution as AI and machine learning were introduced to analyse customer behaviour, detect complex patterns and learn from historic data. Financial technology (FinTech) refers to the application of innovative and developing technology in the financial services sector.[30] FinTech accelerates the delivery of financial products and services, but since it interacts with customers online through platforms such as websites and mobile apps rather than face-to-face, it poses the risk of identity theft and impersonation, which in turn enhances the risk of money laundering. This risk is mitigated through RegTech tools which have become prominent in streamlining and automating routine AML processes and regulatory

28 Noémi També Bearpark and Dionysios S Demetis, 'Re-thinking De-risking: A Systems Theoretical Approach' (2022) 25(1) *Journal of Money Laundering Control* 27.

29 Dionysios S Demetis, 'Fighting Money Laundering with Technology: A Case Study of Bank X in the UK' (2018) 105 *Decision Support Systems* 96.

30 Indrani Bhattacharjee et al. (2024), The Rise of Fintech: Disrupting Traditional Financial Services' (2024) 30(4) *Educational Administration: Theory and Practice* 89–97.

reporting. A report shows that UK banks were spending billions of pounds yearly on RegTech/AI for customer profiling and transaction monitoring.[31] AI uses a range of algorithms and methods to monitor markets, clients and financial transactions in order to detect different banking patterns.[32] Similarly, machine learning algorithms are increasingly used to predict different forms of criminal behaviour.[33]

Undoubtedly, these latest technologies involve simplifying or automating customer due diligence verifications. Indeed, this involves the use of technology such as facial recognition and ID authentication using machine learning, voice biometrics for remote customers, optical character recognition, and comparing a self-taken photo with a passport, resulting in enhanced customer experience, document authentication, digital identity verification, verification of liveliness and detecting anomalies and fraud in transactions based on historic data.[34] Furthermore, biometrics using devices, such as fingerprint scanning, provide increased security and a seamless user experience. Meanwhile, device-related measures, such as SMS, PIN code and two-factor authentication, are employed for the verification of email addresses and phone numbers. Indeed, these additional steps are intended to enhance verification processes to prevent impersonation and identity theft.[35] Also, AI systems are monitoring credit card transactions and other online payments using pattern recognition and device fingerprint information to detect anomalies and potential fraud.[36] **10.13**

Moreover, the utilisation of data obtained from devices, such as phone geolocation data, IP addresses and URLs, is beneficial for improving consumer behavioural analysis and personal profiling to tailor individual risk profiles.[37] This involves grasping customers' typical location, and typical movement behaviours **10.14**

31 Barbara Pianese, 'UK Banks' Compliance Spending Surges amid Regulator's AML Concerns' (*Banking Risk and Regulation*, 5 August 2024) https://www.bankingriskandregulation.com/uk-banks-compliance-spending-surges-amid-regulators-aml-concerns/.

32 Rashid Alhajeri and Abdulrahman Alhashem, 'Using Artificial Intelligence to Combat Money Laundering' (2023) 15 *Intelligent Information Management* 284.

33 Georgios Pavlidis, 'Deploying Artificial Intelligence for Anti-Money Laundering and Asset Recovery: The Dawn of a New Era' (2023) 26(7) *Journal of Money Laundering Control* 155.

34 Douglas W Arner and others, 'The Identity Challenge in Finance: From Analogue Identity to Digitized Identification to Digital KYC Utilities' (2019) 20 *European Business Organization Law Review* 55.

35 Eray Arda Akartuna, Shane D Johnson, and Amy E Thornton, 'The Money Laundering and Terrorist Financing Risks of New and Disruptive Technologies: A Futures-Oriented Scoping Review' (2023) 36(4) *Security Journal* 615.

36 Aaron Joseph Tsapa, 'Artificial Intelligence Use Cases for Banking Anti-Money Laundering' (2023) 1(2) *Journal of Artificial Intelligence, Machine Learning & Data Science* 259.

37 Georgios Pavlidis, 'Deploying Artificial Intelligence for Anti-Money Laundering and Asset Recovery: The Dawn of a New Era' (2023) 26(7) *Journal of Money Laundering Control* 155.

analysing account login patterns and flagging multiple accounts accessed from the same IP address. Efforts are being made to implement measures that facilitate the sharing of CDD data among institutions and utilise AI/machine learning analytics to monitor transactions for suspicious activities and speedily analyse large datasets, spot patterns and use predictive analysis to anticipate money laundering risks.[38] Additionally, enhancing probabilistic matching and analytics technologies is intended to enhance the effectiveness of PEP/sanctions screening processes and more accurately detect possible individuals and entities with increased confidence.[39]

10.15 Furthermore, sophisticated matching technologies, such as analytics-driven 'fuzzy matching', can detect records with approximate rather than exact matches, allowing data that appears similar but not identical to be reviewed. This approach is believed to lessen dependence on external vendor information.[40] It is thought that incorporating machine learning into data analytics capabilities will allow for the creation of personalised transaction profiles for customers, improving the ability to detect suspicious transactions.[41] By incorporating biometrics and other technologies, banks could potentially implement genuine behaviour-based monitoring.

10.16 Nevertheless, the expense of utilising these technologies may be too high for smaller firms. On the one hand, FinTech companies, such as challenger banks, typically have restricted budgets for enhancing AML technology and are constantly looking for adaptable pricing models from their vendors.[42] On the other hand, FinTech banks can benefit from their technology-driven platforms without facing significant legacy issues that major banks encounter. With large banks, numerous departments work in various locations around the world and need a certain level of standardisation among those locations, making the combination of RegTech and AI with current legacy systems challenging and

---

38 Devraj Basu and Godsway Korku Tetteh, 'Using Automation and AI to Combat Money Laundering' (Financial Regulation Innovation Lab White Paper Series, University of Strathclyde, March 2024) https://www.strath.ac.uk/media/departments/accountingfinance/fril/whitepapers/Using_Automation_and_AI_to_Combat_Money_Laundering.pdf.

39 Ana Isabel Canhoto, 'Leveraging Machine Learning in the Global Fight Against Money Laundering and Terrorism Financing: An Affordances Perspective' (2021) 131 *Journal of Business Research* 441.

40 Martin Jullum and others, 'Detecting Money Laundering Transactions with Machine Learning' (2020) 23(1) *Journal of Money Laundering Control* 173.

41 Emmanuel Hayble-Gomes, 'The Use of Predictive Modeling to Identify Relevant Features for Suspicious Activity Reporting' (2023) 26(4) *Journal of Money Laundering Control* 806.

42 Douglas W Arner, Jànos Barberis and Ross P Buckley, 'FinTech, RegTech, and the Reconceptualization of Financial Regulation' (2017) 37 *Northwestern Journal of International Law and Business* 371.

requiring a significant amount of time.[43] For example, CitiBank uses AI to help with risk assessment by analysing customers' transactional and behavioural patterns on a global scale. The system uses recognition patterns to assign a score to high-risk activities for money laundering, identifying alerts that require immediate attention.[44] Similarly, Standard Chartered Bank uses AI technology to monitor and analyse transactions in real-time for risk-free banking operations. This technology watches every transaction in real-time, providing immediate alerts for any fraudulent activities and reducing the window for potential money laundering attempts.[45]

Blockchain analysis tools are crucial for AML monitoring of cryptocurrency **10.17** and digital assets, enabling the tracking and identification of suspicious transactions.[46] This empowers institutions to effectively observe cryptocurrency transactions.[47] These systems are specifically designed to monitor, detect patterns and flag potentially suspicious activities in the digital space. They also provide a comprehensive overview of financial transactions, allowing institutions to manage the flow of money. AI systems are crucial in automating the process of aligning reporting requirements with global AML laws.[48]

Banks use AI systems to detect and predict potentially suspicious actions, **10.18** speed up decision-making and provide quick reports to regulatory entities in some cases automated with reduced human intervention.[49] However, relying too much on AI and RegTech may lead to decreased human oversight, causing a lack of alertness. This situation may arise when there are technology malfunctions or when AI learns incorrect patterns or cannot recognise particular subtleties, resulting in wrong or biased decision making.[50] Furthermore, using

43 Jane Walshe and Tom Cropper, 'Should You Be Banking on RegTech?' (2018) 10(2) *Journal of Securities Operations & Custody* 167.

44 Georgios Pavlidis, 'Deploying Artificial Intelligence for Anti-Money Laundering and Asset Recovery: The Dawn of a New Era' (2023) 26(7) *Journal of Money Laundering Control* 155.

45 Lucinity, 'Anti-Money Laundering Compliance: AI's Impact – Transform FinCrime Operations & Investigations with AI' (8 April 2024) https://lucinity.com/blog/reshaping-anti-money-laundering-compliance-the-impact-of-ai-on-financial-integrity.

46 Joana Lorenz and others, 'Machine Learning Methods to Detect Money Laundering in the Bitcoin Blockchain in the Presence of Label Scarcity' (2020) Proceedings of the First ACM International Conference on AI in Finance 1.

47 Fabian Maximilian Teichmann and Marie-Christin Falker, 'Money Laundering via Underground Currency Exchange Networks' (2021) 29(1) *Journal of Financial Regulation and Compliance* 1.

48 Peter Yeoh, 'Artificial Intelligence: Accelerator or Panacea for Financial Crime?' (2019) 26(2) *Journal of Financial Crime* 634.

49 Martin Jullum and others, 'Detecting Money Laundering Transactions with Machine Learning' (2020) 23(1) *Journal of Money Laundering Control* 173.

50 Jane Walshe and Tom Cropper, 'Should You Be Banking on RegTech?' (2018) 10(2) *Journal of Securities Operations & Custody* 167.

AI and RegTech involves managing large amounts of sensitive financial data, raising concerns about basic human rights and the security of data privacy.[51] The use of compliance technologies is more common for automating tedious tasks and reducing operational costs.[52] Nevertheless, banks may incorrectly assume they are following anti-money laundering rules by only concentrating on meeting the criteria, resulting in a false sense of security while neglecting efficient methods to identify and stop money laundering.[53]

10.19 Technologies can serve as a strategic tool for meeting regulatory requirements and expectations in relation to preventing money laundering. While regulators tend to claim they are technology-neutral, their response to RegTech/AI have been encouraging, acknowledging the practical benefits of these technologies.[54] However, it appears that the rapid pace of technological innovation outstrips regulators' ability to adapt. 'Markets and technology are moving quicker than regulators could accommodate', commented one interview participant (Participant 20 – Compliance Officer, Banking). Additionally, malicious actors can use AI to evade detection, mimic legitimate transactions and generate voice, images and videos impersonating individuals.[55] As stated by another interview participant, 'regulation has been trying to catch up with technology while bad actors can easily use technology to evade regulatory radar' (Participant 10 – Compliance Officer, Payment Services FinTech).

10.20 Compliance technologies used by high-volume banks can sometimes burden compliance teams with excessive false alerts.[56] These alerts stem from regulatory red flags that rarely signal actual suspicious behaviour yet must still be investigated, which can be resource-intensive and costly.[57] Consequently, banks are cautious in adopting new technologies, wanting to see concrete

---

51 Astrid Bertrand, Winston Maxwell, and Xavier Vamparys, 'Do AI-Based Anti-Money Laundering (AML) Systems Violate European Fundamental Rights?' (2021) 11(3) *International Data Privacy Law* 276.

52 Aaron Joseph Tsapa, 'Artificial Intelligence Use Cases for Banking Anti-Money Laundering' (2023) 1(2) *Journal of Artificial Intelligence, Machine Learning & Data Science* 259.

53 Zhiyuan Chen and others, 'Machine Learning Techniques for Anti-Money Laundering (AML) Solutions in Suspicious Transaction Detection: A Review' (2018) 57 *Knowledge and Information Systems* 245.

54 Johnathan McCarthy, 'The Regulation of RegTech and SupTech in Finance: Ensuring Consistency in Principle and in Practice' (2023) 31(2) *Journal of Financial Regulation and Compliance* 186.

55 P. Faisal Islam, 'Using Malicious AI to Immunize AML Programs: Redefining the AML Paradigm' (Global Compliance Institute) https://www.gci-ccm.org/.

56 Utku Görkem Ketenci and others, 'A Time-Frequency Based Suspicious Activity Detection for Anti-Money Laundering' (2021) 9 *IEEE Access* 59957.

57 Ilaria Zavoli and Colin King, 'The Challenges of Implementing Anti-Money Laundering Regulation: An Empirical Analysis' (2021) 84(4) *Modern Law Review* 740.

evidence that it will lead to increased efficiency.[58] Participants interviewed highlighted the resource challenges involved. 'There is pressure of asking and getting resources and tools and technology needed to carry out compliance; the board might be too slow to deliver on this' (Participant 4 – Compliance Officer, Banking). Furthermore, staying abreast of technological developments is another hurdle, as one participant noted: 'Another challenge is being on top of the technology one uses' (Participant 7 – Compliance Officer, Investment Management).

10.21 All in all, modern banking environments, such as digital banking, amplify the role of technology. 'Nowadays IT is not just a thing to help business in digital banking; IT is the whole business' (Participant 9 – Compliance Officer, Banking). These sentiments also reflect broader shifts in workplace dynamics, where technology facilitates agile and remote working: 'The culture of agile way of work, and remote working technology means no more hierarchy in the office building' (Participant 20 – Compliance Officer, Banking). The use of Regtech/AI in AML is enhancing risk management by enabling the detection and identification of patterns and anomalies that may suggest potentially fraudulent activities. This thereby allows for prompt prevention and reporting of money laundering activities, ensuring compliance with strict international and regional regulations embedded in the system to uphold the integrity of the financial system.[59]

D. IS POOR CULTURE HINDERING THE FIGHT AGAINST FINANCIAL CRIME?

10.22 This section will explore the internal cultural dynamics within banks, examining how they impact AML compliance strategies. We identify forces of internal culture that influence the way in which banks engage with the AML framework.

1. Culture of Tick-box

10.23 A tick box mentality when engaging with the AML framework affects the integrity of organisations, and therefore necessitates a comprehensive and proactive compliance approach. Tick-box compliance involves systematically

58 Ahmed N Bakry and others, 'Automatic Suppression of False Positive Alerts in Anti-Money Laundering Systems Using Machine Learning' (2024) 80(5) *The Journal of Supercomputing* 6264.

59 Alhanouf Abdulrahman Saleh Alsuwailem and Abdul Khader Jilani Saudagar, 'Anti-Money Laundering Systems: A Systematic Literature Review' (2020) 23(4) *Journal of Money Laundering Control* 833.

using checklists to meet regulatory obligations.[60] A common pattern on the rise in banks and financial institutions, defined by superficial compliance with regulatory rules, is called a 'tick-box exercise'.[61] This pattern may have come about due to the shift towards risk-based regulation allowing banks more flexibility in meeting requirements.[62] Companies can abuse rule flexibility by creating procedures that seem to follow the rules but are only superficial and aimed at the bare minimum.[63]

10.24 In a culture of tick box, banks tend to prioritise fulfilling regulatory obligations without completely embracing a stronger dedication to anti-money laundering principles. As one compliance officer interviewed explained, 'people often perceive compliance as a cost centre and tick box process. Sometimes there is need to convince executives of the risk as things are not clear cut and it can become difficult to explain to them why they cannot do certain things if it is not prescribed' (Participant 14 – Compliance Officer, Investment Management). Even though employees are expected to follow certain rules, they often end up only meeting the basic expectations without showing any diversity in their actions.[64] Hence, financial institutions tend to adhere to a pre-established set of risks instead of evaluating the risk of money laundering/terrorist financing based on individual customers, products, services and case-specific circumstances.[65] In contrast, a principles-based regulatory approach can result in a higher level of actual adherence to the rule's intent compared to a checklist method.[66] This is because it necessitates firms to carefully consider how to adhere to the rule, thus aligning with management-based regulation.[67]

10.25 Indeed, the tick-box method can stem from self-protection and fear of prosecution; this is worrying as it impedes the assessment of ML/TF risks at the basic level, making it challenging to implement the required measures

60 Ronald F Pol, 'Anti-Money Laundering Effectiveness: Assessing Outcomes or Ticking Boxes?' (2018) 21(2) *Journal of Money Laundering Control* 215.

61 Ibid.

62 Gauri Sinha, 'Risk-Based Approach: Is It the Answer to Effective Anti-Money Laundering Compliance?' in Katie Benson, Colin King, and Clive Walker (eds), *Asset, Crime and the State* (Routledge 2020) 14.

63 Iris H-Y Chiu and Anna Donovan, 'A New Milestone in Corporate Regulation: Procedural Legalisation, Standards of Transnational Corporate Behaviour and Lessons from Financial Regulation and Anti-Bribery Regulation' (2017) 17(2) *Journal of Corporate Law Studies* 427.

64 Nurul Liyana Bahrin, Sharifah Norzehan Syed Yusuf, Kamaruzzaman Muhammad and Erlane K Ghani, 'Determinants of Anti-Money Laundering Program Effectiveness among Banks' (2022) 11(1) *International Journal of Management and Sustainability* 21.

65 Ibid.

66 Julia Black, 'Principles-Based Regulation: Risks, Challenges and Opportunities' (Principles-Based Regulation Conference, Sydney, 28 March 2007).

67 Ibid.

to reduce these identified risks.[68] Banks might focus on mere compliance with AML regulations instead of truly incorporating a strong and forward-thinking risk management system, leading to a lack of effectiveness in fighting money laundering and possibly diverting attention and resources away from regulatory goals.[69] To address this, effective leadership must model compliance behaviours to shape organisational culture positively. Interview participants emphasised that 'culture is what you do when nobody is looking', and leadership modelling the right behaviour can significantly influence employee attitudes and actions (Participant 19 – Compliance Officer, Banking). This requires not only clear communication about compliance expectations but also demonstrating consequences for breaches. As one participant noted, 'people can get complacent if there is no precedent [...] that breaches of rules result in regulatory action' (Participant 12 – Compliance Officer, Asset Management).

The FCA highlighted its dissatisfaction with tick-box compliance in its final **10.26**
notices, as seen in the case of Canara Bank. In that case, the FCA suggested that the checklists used for compliance monitoring were likely insufficient and not taken seriously enough by Canara's staff during the relevant period. Moreover, the FCA highlighted that the audits carried out monthly during the specified timeframe had limited scope that Head Office instructed internal auditors to perform a 'tick-box' review and that this was not enough for Canara to trust it as its third defence line.[70] In another case, the FCA discovered that the Group Financial Crime Risk Committee of Standard Chartered Bank was informed of a report stating that there had been a 'lack of proper evaluation of AML procedures for correspondent banking clients'. The report contained descriptions of the correspondent's controls that appeared to be copied and pasted, suggesting a superficial approach. The FCA stated that the review highlighted insufficient evaluations of the AML controls in the eight overseas branches and subsidiaries, with signs of a superficial approach rather than a thorough comprehension of the risks.[71]

68 Ilaria Zavoli and Colin King, 'The Challenges of Implementing Anti-Money Laundering Regulation: An Empirical Analysis' (2021) 84(4) *Modern Law Review* 740.

69 Muhammad Usman Kemal, 'Anti-Money Laundering Regulations and Its Effectiveness' (2014) 17(4) *Journal of Money Laundering Control* 416.

70 FCA, 'Final Notice – Canara Bank' (6 June 2018) https://www.fca.org.uk/publication/final-notices/canara-bank-2018.pdf.

71 FCA, 'Final Notice – Standard Chartered Bank' (5 February 2019) https://www.fca.org.uk/news/press-releases/fca-fines-standard-chartered-bank-102-2-million-poor-aml-controls#:~:text=The%20Financial%20Conduct%20Authority%20.

10.27 It is, therefore, crucial to implement AML/CFT measures that focus on mitigating risks rather than just going through the motions.[72] Constant demands for paperwork, regardless of the customer's risk level, can serve as a distraction.[73] For instance, during a time of guarding against identity theft, basic 'know your customer' verifications and other ineffective methods that do not pinpoint the main risk factors are ultimately useless and could potentially lead to harm.[74] Due to the dominance of a tick-box compliance culture, it is important for financial institutions to recognise the limitations of depending on a tickbox-focused approach for AML efforts and strive to cultivate a culture that goes beyond simple regulatory requirements.

2. Culture of Resistance to Change

10.28 This section will examine the impacts of a culture of resistance to change. It points out the need for promoting a responsive and flexible culture of compliance. The culture of resistance to change in AML compliance can be described as a mindset that hinders financial institutions from adopting new procedures, technologies or methods. Consequently, this opposition frequently presents itself as a hesitation to adopt new technologies that could improve the efficiency of anti-money laundering measures. Resistance in an organisation is a gradual reaction to or a refusal to cooperate with change, which can be deliberate or unintentional, hidden or open.[75] In addition, departments and employees might resist compliance efforts due to viewing them as a hindrance or obstacle to their regular tasks.[76]

10.29 There are two types of resistance to change in employees' attitudes within organisations: active and passive resistance.[77] Employees' active resistance is associated with manipulation, ridicule, criticism and the fear of losing their jobs. Passive resistance, conversely, consists of withholding information from others, being oblivious to problems and ignoring verbal instructions.[78] As a result, employees use resistance as a tactic to maintain the current method of

---

72 Marcus Killick and David Parody, 'Implementing AML/CFT Measures that Address the Risks and Not Tick Boxes' (2007) 15(2) *Journal of Financial Regulation and Compliance* 210.

73 Ibid.

74 Fabian Maximilian Teichmann and Marie-Christin Falker, 'Money Laundering through Consulting Companies' (2020) 28(3) *Journal of Financial Regulation and Compliance* 485.

75 Brandon Mathews and Christopher M Linski, 'Shifting the Paradigm: Reevaluating Resistance to Organizational Change' (2016) 29(6) *Journal of Organizational Change Management* 963.

76 Ibid.

77 Bernard Burnes, 'Understanding Resistance to Change – Building on Coch and French' (2015) 15(2) *Journal of Change Management* 92.

78 Ibid.

doing things when they are afraid of losing their job to others or to technology. Moreover, this approach includes challenging, resisting, disputing and interrogating levels of power and engaging in critical discussions in response to change management methods.[79] Resistance can have positive and negative impacts on a company as a whole. Resisting organisational change can result in negative consequences by encouraging counterproductive employee attitudes that impacts corporate performance.[80]

A resistance culture within financial institutions can impede progress in adopting modern AML strategies, relying instead on outdated techniques that expose vulnerabilities. This resistance often leads to inefficiencies and hinders innovation, such as leveraging emerging technologies and advanced analytics to combat money laundering effectively. As one participant noted, 'commercial pressure and a fast-paced environment can be found in FinTech where they are used to doing things very quickly. The key risk is change; ensuring one can keep up and accommodate the pace of change with rigorous compliance checks' (Participant 17 – Compliance Officer, Banking, FinTech). However, resistance can also be beneficial as it forces those initiating change to re-evaluate important decisions in order to achieve their objectives.[81] Furthermore, resistance can clarify unexamined thoughts that are not carefully considered or are simply a reaction to external events.[82] **10.30**

Addressing this resistance requires implementing change management strategies that foster a mindset which views change as an opportunity for growth. Moreover, evidence of cultural transformation includes allocating additional resources to compliance. 'Meaningful change in the culture of compliance can be evident by an increase in resources sent to compliance, increase in compliance headcount, increase compliance staff to sales staff ratio, increase in compliance budget, [and] increase in tools available in the market for compliance monitoring' (Participant 10 – Compliance Officer, Payment Services FinTech). By fostering a positive compliance culture and embracing operational changes, such as recognising the significance of IT and operational teams in regulatory **10.31**

---

79 David Rosenbaum, Elizabeth More, and Peter Steane, 'Planned Organisational Change Management: Forward to the Past? An Exploratory Literature Review' (2018) 31(2) *Journal of Organizational Change Management* 286.

80 Hary Febriansyah, Dematria Pringgabayu, Nurfaisa Hidayanti and Feny Citra Febrianti, 'Enhancing the Employee Engagement through the Organizational Climate (A Study of School of Business and Management)' (2018) 12(3) *Journal of Business and Retail Management Research* 104–12.

81 Gentisa Furxhi, 'Employees' Resistance and Organizational Change Factors' (2021) 6(2) *European Journal of Business and Management Research* 30.

82 Ibid.

processes, banks can better manage AML risks. Furthermore, embracing technological developments is another hurdle, as one participant noted: 'Another challenge is being on top of the technology one uses' (Participant 7 – Compliance Officer, Investment Management). 'Change in culture has shifted that and made others in the technology department realize that they conduct a significant function and they are responsible to the regulators for the work they do' (Participant 11 – Compliance Officer, Banking). These measures create a robust AML framework that evolves with emerging threats and ensures financial institutions remain resilient against money laundering activities.

10.32 A resistance culture in financial institutions can lead to outdated risk management techniques, inefficiencies and operational obstacles. This could cause organisations to ignore potential risks and money laundering techniques, leaving them exposed to vulnerabilities. The culture of resistance hampers innovation in the AML field, potentially causing financial institutions to overlook opportunities to use new technology and data analytics to identify and prevent money laundering.[83] Moreover, organisations should tackle the resistance to change in AML compliance by implementing change management strategies, offering extensive training and fostering a mindset that views change as a chance for growth.[84] No doubt, this approach can help banks adapt to the ever-changing money laundering risks, enhancing a robust and efficient AML framework. Hence, by acknowledging and taking proactive steps to address this cultural barrier, financial institutions can enhance their readiness to manage risks associated with money laundering.

3. Culture that Does Not Instil a Sense of Responsibility for AML

10.33 Having a strong sense of responsibility positively impacts the ability to detect cases of fraud and financial crime.[85] However, there is a prevalent culture in AML compliance characterised by a corporate mindset in which employees at various levels fail to fully acknowledge their individual and collective responsibility in upholding the AML protocols. As a result, this lack of accountability can be seen in inadequate reporting, lack of thoroughness in investigations and limited engagement in fulfilling AML obligations. At the same time,

---

83 Claudia Paula Fuioagă and Costache Rusu, 'Resistance of Changes Implementation' (2018) 6(2) *FAIMA Business & Management Journal* 66.

84 Esther Cameron and Mike Green, *Making Sense of Change Management: A Complete Guide to the Models, Tools and Techniques of Organizational Change* (Kogan Page Publishers 2019) 544.

85 Yulianti Yulianti and others, 'Effects of Professional Commitment, Commitment to Ethics, Internal Locus of Control and Emotional Intelligence on the Ability to Detect Fraud through Reduced Audit Quality Behaviors' (2024) 15(3) *Journal of Islamic Accounting and Business Research* 385.

a culture that lacks accountability leads to disjointed anti-money laundering efforts, with employees possibly not aiding in the overall compliance goals.[86] Consequently, the institution's divided structure hinders its capacity to efficiently identify and prevent money laundering.

Interview participants stressed that fostering an open culture where employees feel secure discussing mistakes and taking responsibility for escalating issues is vital to reducing, the institution's susceptibility to money laundering risks. One participant noted: 'Not many people appreciate accepting mistakes are made; they don't want to talk about their weaknesses so that better AML controls can be put in place. Instead of seen as an opportunity, self-reporting is seen as a threat' (Participant 7 – Compliance Officer, Investment Management). This lack of openness can prevent staff from fully engaging in compliance goals, increasing the institution's susceptibility to money laundering risks. Another participant highlighted the need for a 'clear and safe environment' where employees feel empowered to escalate concerns and make mistakes without fear, as failing to do so could undermine regulatory compliance and potentially lead to institutional failure (Participant 20 – Compliance Officer, Banking). **10.34**

Participants in the interview stressed that accountability needs to go beyond just committee frameworks. An instance of this is when Participant 1 emphasised the importance of people taking ownership of their actions instead of deflecting blame on to a group. In the same vein, Participant 8 highlighted the importance of individual responsibility, but also emphasised the need to promote collective accountability within the organisation to avoid singling out individuals. Implementing accountability involves establishing transparent audit trails and fostering employee allegiance to strengthen compliance initiatives (Participant 10). Nevertheless, certain employees may find it challenging to take on responsibility, particularly in intense scenarios with regulators or law enforcement (Participant 14). In the end, integrating accountability into organisational culture is essential. Staff members need to recognise their important influence on coworkers, clients and the organisation (Participant 12). By providing thorough training and strong structures, organisations can enable workers to take on accountability, establishing an AML compliance framework that is more cohesive, forward-thinking and able to withstand challenges. **10.35**

86 Angela Samantha Maitland Irwin, Kim-Kwang Raymond Choo and Lin Liu, 'An Analysis of Money Laundering and Terrorism Financing Typologies' (2012) 15(1) *Journal of Money Laundering Control* 85.

10.36 A final notice communication from FCA highlighted a lack of clear understanding about roles and duties at CB&S (Corporate Banking &Securities) division[87] FCA maintained that the front office team did not feel responsible for recognising and managing non-financial risks due to the existing corporate culture. As a result, the CB&S front office, known as the 'London Front Office', did not realise it had to fulfil its clients' KYC requirements. This was especially evident in the London Front Office, which did not acknowledge its duty to oversee Deutsche Bank's KYC requirements as the first line of defence. The complicated organisational structure of the company generated uncertainty regarding the distinct functions and duties of the London Front Office, operations team, and AML team. Therefore, the regulators concluded that Deutsche Bank's anti-money laundering control framework lacked sufficient monitoring and supervision.[88]

10.37 Similarly, the FCA raised concerns regarding SCB's failure to ensure a culture supportive of AML compliance in its operations in the United Arab Emirates as cited in the FCA final notice to another bank.[89] The primary reasons for this concern included insufficient resources at Financial Crime Risk, collaboration among staff in UAE branches to bypass controls, understanding of accounts used to avoid financial sanctions by other UAE workers, lack of action from the UAE government in addressing S2B access issues, and not taking a comprehensive approach to financial crime controls.[90] Also, in a NatWest matter, some bank employees responsible for handling cash deposits escalated suspicious issues to those investigating potential money laundering, but no appropriate measures were taken. Large amounts of Scottish banknotes spread across England, banknotes with a distinct musty smell and questionable actions while depositing money at NatWest branches were identified as warning signs.[91]

10.38 Having a whistleblowing policy can provide a sense of responsibility to employees. Whistleblowing is often driven by a sense of obligation to the company, noticing changes in colleagues, governance failures, and obvious criminal

---

87 FCA, 'Final Notice – Deutsche Bank' (30 January 2017) https://www.fca.org.uk/publication/final-notices/deutsche-bank-2017.pdf.

88 Ibid.

89 FCA, 'Final Notice – Standard Chartered Bank' (5 February 2019) https://www.fca.org.uk/news/press-releases/fca-fines-standard-chartered-bank-102-2-million-poor-aml-controls#:~:text=The%20Financial%20Conduct%20Authority%20(FCA,ever%20imposed%20by%20the%20FCA.

90 Ibid.

91 FCA, 'Agreed Statement – National Westminster Bank' (December 2021) https://www.fca.org.uk/publication/corporate/agreed-statement-facts-fca-national-westminster-bank.pdf.

behaviour.[92] Whistleblowers often view their responsibilities as assisting their organisations in preventing serious harm by reporting misconduct, using different methods to address issues like criminal activities or corruption, informing top management, and disclosing bad behaviour.[93] External whistleblowing might be required with whistleblower protection if money laundering concerns are not dealt with by internal management.[94]

Furthermore, improved governance and oversight is crucial for financial institutions to implement strong monitoring and management structures to guarantee responsibility and compliance with AML procedures. The concept of accountability within the business setting has evolved from the traditional notion of 'duty of care' to newer ideas such as 'duty of oversight', resulting in a shift from corporate to individual responsibility.[95] Therefore, it is important to have a culture of responsibility in order to ensure successful AML compliance and promote both individual and collective efforts to safeguard financial institutions. This culture can be fostered by ongoing education, effective communication and accountability. **10.39**

4. Culture of Optimism

Excessive managerial optimism within an internal culture often blinds financial institutions to underlying risks.[96] A culture of optimism in AML compliance involves a company mindset that tends to downplay or ignore possible risks linked to money laundering. The optimism could stem from mistaken overconfidence in current strategies, a lack of knowledge of new threats, or relying too much on old data without considering the dynamic nature of risks.[97] Bank executives frequently make decisions relying on 'delusional optimism' instead of rational assessment of gains, losses, and probabilities and **10.40**

92 Theo Nyreröd, Stelios Andreadakis, and Giancarlo Spagnolo, 'Money Laundering and Sanctions Enforcement: Large Rewards, Leniency and Witness Protection for Whistleblowers' (2023) 26(5) *Journal of Money Laundering Control* 912.

93 Zeinab Amini Yekta, 'Corporate Code of Ethics and Reporting Wrongdoing In Private Sector Organizations in Malaysia' (2010) 5 *International Journal of Business and Management* 84.

94 Folashade Adeyemo, 'Rebutting the Presumption: Are Whistleblowers Really Protected under PIDA and in the Case of the UK Banking Industry' (2020) *Journal of Business Law* 607.

95 Muhammad Saleem Korejo, Ramalinggam Rajamanickam, and Muhamad Helmi Md. Said, 'Financial Institutions and Anti-Money Laundering Violations: Who Is to Bear the Burden of Liability?' (2022) 25(3) *Journal of Money Laundering Control* 671.

96 Damiano B Silipo, Giovanni Verga, and Sviatlana Hlebik, 'Managerial Beliefs and Banking Behavior' (2023) 64(3) *Journal of Financial Services Research* 401.

97 House of Commons Treasury Committee, Banking Crisis: Dealing with the Failure of the UK Banks, Seventh Report of Session 2008–09 (House of Commons 2009) https://publications.parliament.uk/pa/cm200809/cmselect/cmtreasy/416/416.pdf.

understanding of the potential dangers.[98] Additionally, the culture of over-optimism transitions from focusing on market integrity to prioritising sales, leading to widespread greed, recklessness, and dishonesty.[99]

10.41 Behavioural economics shows that people have less influence on decision-making than they think. People often succumb to biases, causing them to rely on shortcuts in decision-making, show reluctance to let go of losses, demonstrate excessive confidence and optimism, be swayed by outside influences and social pressures, and opt for satisfactory solutions instead of aiming for the best possible outcomes according to their preferences.[100] Therefore, behavioural analysis indicates that as a result of these biases and shortcuts, people often make inadequate decisions and assessments. In terms of how a company views and deals with risks, there is a risk of misunderstanding the amount of control they have, which can result in excessive optimism and assurance in their abilities to manage risks.[101] This can be explained by unrealistic optimism and self-serving bias. Simply put, being overly optimistic may cause one to underestimate the chances of a negative event happening. Therefore, a culture of optimism may result in decreased vigilance towards new money laundering risks, as financial institutions might not fully recognise the importance of conducting a comprehensive due diligence.[102]

10.42 Bank executives' willingness to believe in positive forecasts despite industry conditions shows an optimistic bias, and overconfidence is a trait that impacts corporate CEOs.[103] Moreover, individuals in these powerful roles typically have an exaggerated belief in their own abilities and frequently believe they are unique cases.[104] This self-assurance motivates individuals to seek evidence that supports their beliefs and ignore opposing viewpoints. Optimism among executives can make even the most severe punishment ineffective in deterring them from committing such corporate violations.[105] Indeed, an overempha-

98 Dan Lovallo and Daniel Kahneman, 'Delusions of Success: How Optimism Undermines Executives' (2003) *Harvard Business Review* https://hbr.org/2003/07/delusions-of-success-how-optimism-undermines-executives-decisions.

99 Alison Lui, 'Greed, Recklessness and/or Dishonesty? An Investigation into the Culture of Five UK Banks Between 2004 and 2009' (2015) 16(2) *Journal of Banking Regulation* 106.

100 Manju Puri and David T Robinson, 'Optimism and Economic Choice' (2007) 86(1) *Journal of Financial Economics* 71.

101 Ibid.

102 Darshan Kumar and Mark Eshwar Lokanan, 'Money Laundering Influence on Financial Institutions and Ways to Retaliate' (2023) 26(1) *Journal of Money Laundering Control* 133.

103 Yueran Ma, 'Bank CEO Optimism and the Financial Crisis' https://papers.ssrn.com/abstract=2392683.

104 Ibid.

105 Ibid.

sis on optimism could result in inadequate allocation of resources for AML efforts; or for example, participants highlighted a disconnect between senior management's declarations and their actions: 'There are lots of speeches and declarations of intent from the top, but there is little change as leaders spend 70% of their time courting investors... if they don't make money, they will close shop' (Participant 5 – Compliance Officer, Payment Services FinTech). Another participant pointed out that while senior managers might vocalise the importance of compliance, their decisions are often driven by competitive and investor pressures: 'You don't start a bank to have the privilege of meeting AML rules... regulation is just a price that you pay' (Participant 9 – Compliance Officer, Banking).

Therefore, companies must promote a balanced and practical risk management approach to counter the prevailing optimism in AML compliance culture. This requires continuous training, staying current with industry developments, using cutting-edge technologies, and fostering a culture that encourages open discussions on potential risks.[106] Therefore, acknowledging the importance of a comprehensive risk-aware culture can help financial institutions enhance their defences against money laundering risks and enhance their AML framework. **10.43**

5. Culture of Gaming the Rules

Another concerning trend in AML compliance is where some companies prioritise taking advantage of loopholes in regulations rather than truly implementing effective AML measures. Likewise, it is observed that companies can create systems and processes that seem to follow regulations while exploiting the regulatory system by gaming or circumventing regulations.[107] **10.44**

Moreover, within the domain of AML, regulatory arbitrage includes taking advantage of regulatory gaps, manipulating rules for personal benefit, or using deceptive tactics to seem in compliance with AML laws while evading their true essence.[108] Financial institutions may participate in this practice in order to obtain a competitive edge or reduce the impact of regulatory obligations. Variances in regulations within different areas can give a competitive **10.45**

106 Nurul Liyana Bahrin, Sharifah Norzehan Syed Yusuf, Kamaruzzaman Muhammad and Erlane K Ghani, 'Determinants of Anti-Money Laundering Program Effectiveness among Banks' (2022) 11(1) *International Journal of Management and Sustainability* 21.

107 PCBS, 'Changing Banking for Good' (June 2013) HL Paper 27-II, HC 175-II https://www.parliament.uk/globalassets/documents/banking-commission/Banking-final-report-volume-i.pdf.

108 Karen Harrison and Nicholas Ryder, *The Law Relating to Financial Crime in the United Kingdom* (2nd edn, Routledge 2017).

edge. Businesses can choose to set up their activities in countries that have looser regulations to avoid being restricted by the compliance requirements of stricter regions. Institutions can engage in illicit financial activities without concern by operating in areas with lenient AML regulations or limited regulatory oversight. This practice, referred to as regulatory arbitrage, may reduce the impact of regulations. Moreover, regulatory arbitrage can lead to financial industry imbalances.

10.46 Ambiguous language in regulations can create opportunities for individuals or entities to exploit loopholes due to unclear wording. Jurisdictional gaps arise when various regulatory authorities have restricted supervision because specific industries or activities fall within their individual jurisdictions. This can lead to inconsistencies in enforcement or loopholes in regulations, which could be taken advantage of. Moreover, the complexities of AML regulations and responsibilities for compliance could create opportunities for exploitative tactics. Financial institutions might exploit uncertainties or inconsistencies in regulations to control reporting thresholds, conceal illicit transactions, or disguise information about beneficial ownership.[109] This form of 'innovative compliance' offers a new outlook on utilising the law in a disobedient and unconventional manner to circumvent legal requirements without violating them.

10.47 Overall, institutions that exploit the system may focus on meeting minimum requirements rather than addressing the real risks of money laundering, resulting in inadequate risk mitigation strategies. Financial institutions that exploit loopholes or do not comply with rules can weaken the regulatory system as a whole, reducing its effectiveness in combating money laundering. Businesses employing deceitful methods might surpass those adhering to AML regulations, jeopardising the sector's trustworthiness. In order to uphold a favourable reputation, companies need to focus on following regulations and implementing transparent policies that are in line with the intent of the law, rather than taking advantage of legal loopholes. Therefore, regulatory agencies and financial organisations can work together to enhance the AML structure to effectively combat money laundering threats.

6. Culture of Minimal or Non-compliance

10.48 A culture of minimal compliance or inadequate adherence to AML compliance standards refers to a failure to commit to strict regulatory procedures

---

109 André Spicer and others, 'A Report on the Culture of British Retail Banking' (2016) https://newcityagenda.co.uk/wp-content/uploads/2014/11/Online-version.pdf.

aimed at preventing money laundering. A culture that does not prioritise strict compliance with regulations can lead to financial institutions lacking proper diligence, ineffective reporting methods, and insufficient monitoring of suspicious activities.[110] The prevalent tendency to underestimate the significance of Know Your Customer protocols in anti-money laundering compliance poses substantial challenges for global financial institutions and regulatory bodies.[111] In a fiercely competitive market, financial institutions may prioritise cutting costs over enhancing KYC procedures. Consequently, this minimal compliance mentality could lead to inadequate resource allocation for KYC compliance, resulting in undertrained personnel, outdated technology, and limited due diligence procedures.[112]

Interview participants emphasised the role of organisational culture in shaping AML compliance practices, highlighting how a culture that truly values compliance manifests in tangible changes, such as increased resources, staff and technology dedicated to compliance functions. One participant explained that 'meaningful change' in compliance culture could be observed through greater budget allocation, increased compliance staff-to-sales ratios and expanded monitoring tools (Participant 10 – Compliance Officer, Payment Services FinTech). Another participant stressed that individuals more motivated by personal rewards rather than client benefit tend to 'exit themselves from the firm' as they misalign with the firm's cultural shift towards stringent compliance (Participant 6 – Compliance Officer, Private Banking). 10.49

In two FCA final notice cases, senior management at Sonali Bank UK Limited did not make sure that SBUK promoted a culture that prioritised strict adherence to regulatory duties, resulting in a culture of minimal or non-compliance within the company.[113] Likewise, Canara Bank's senior management did not create a thorough system of controls for dealing with AML and financial crime risks. Therefore, FCA concluded that Canara did not successfully establish a culture of compliance with its legal and regulatory obligations. Due to these 10.50

110 Howard Chitimira and Sharon Munedzi, 'An Evaluation of Customer Due Diligence and Related Anti-Money Laundering Measures in the United Kingdom' (2023) 26(7) *Journal of Money Laundering Control* 127.

111 Sue Turner and Jonathan Bainbridge, 'An Anti-Money Laundering Timeline and the Relentless Regulatory Response' (2018) 82(3) *The Journal of Criminal Law* 215.

112 Howard Chitimira and Sharon Munedzi, 'An Evaluation of Customer Due Diligence and Related Anti-Money Laundering Measures in the United Kingdom' (2023) 26(7) *Journal of Money Laundering Control* 127.

113 FCA, 'Final Notice – Sonali Bank (UK) Limited' (12 October 2016) https://www.fca.org.uk/publication/final-notices/sonali-bank-uk-limited-2016.pdf.

shortcomings, a culture of following the bare minimum rules, or not following them at all, continued to exist during that time frame at Canara Bank. [114]

10.51 Financial institutions may focus on quickness and effectiveness instead of following the proper AML process to meet business goals and revenue targets.[115] This pressure can lead to cutting corners in diligence procedures, lack of proper documentation, and delayed reporting of suspicious activities.[116] In turn, it may also create an environment where employees are motivated to bypass established protocols or ignore potentially dubious behaviours in order to expedite processes and avoid conflicts with colleagues or customers.

10.52 Additionally, financial institutions must invest in advanced tools to streamline AML processes and adhere to due process requirements through improved technology and automation. Automated systems can improve efficiency, accuracy, and consistency in due diligence processes and documentation.[117] However, institutions might not fully understand the importance of investing in advanced technologies or knowledgeable personnel to address intricate money laundering schemes. On these challenges, some compliance officers report struggles in securing resources from top management. As Participant 1, a compliance officer in asset management, observed, 'Senior management thinks compliance is just a "nice to have and not a necessity"'. Similarly, Participant 2 noted the difficulty in securing board-level approval for capital expenditure on compliance tools, which they linked to a cultural undervaluing of compliance's role in protecting the firm from regulatory and reputational risks. Participant 4, a banking compliance officer, further remarked on the frustration stemming from compliance often being perceived as a mere cost centre that is not directly adding to the revenue of the institution.

10.53 In the end, financial institutions and regulatory agencies face significant challenges when the culture overlooks AML procedural rights. However, financial institutions can enhance their AML procedures, diminish compliance risks and safeguard the integrity of the financial system by recognising the root causes of this culture and implementing pre-emptive actions. Financial

114 FCA, 'Final Notice – Canara Bank' (6 June 2018) https://www.fca.org.uk/publication/final-notices/canara-bank-2018.pdf.

115 Fabian Maximilian Johannes Teichmann and Chiara Wittmann, 'Compliance Cultures and the Role of Financial Incentives' (2024) 31(1) *Journal of Financial Crime* 226.

116 Ibid.

117 Eray Arda Akartuna, Shane D Johnson and Amy E Thornton, 'The Money Laundering and Terrorist Financing Risks of New and Disruptive Technologies: A Futures-Oriented Scoping Review' (2023) 36(4) *Security Journal* 615.

institutions can establish a culture of compliance focusing on AML due process, transparency, integrity, and trust in the global market through comprehensive training, enhanced oversight, and advanced technology.

7. Culture that Prioritises Revenue Generation over Market Integrity

The AML compliance culture of prioritising revenue over market integrity means that organisations focus too much on profit-making, even if it means not focussing enough on keeping the financial market safe and honest. Certainly, this unbalanced emphasis could result in AML procedures being compromised and insufficient actions taken against money laundering.[118] According to FCA final notice, in the case of State Street UK, the company did not recognise that a culture had developed in its UK TM business that subordinated the interests of clients to the generation of revenue for the firm and did not identify the very serious misconduct within the UK TM business. Consequently, State Street UK's breaches caused a significant risk that financial crime would be facilitated.[119] **10.54**

This underscores the importance of building a culture that aligns individual incentives with organisational goals. Competitive pressures, the need for shareholder returns, and misaligned management incentives have all played a role in the lack of effective regulatory compliance within banks.[120] 'Where people don't engage with the AML rules because they are more motivated purely by individual reward, rather than client and firm benefit, they would ultimately exit themselves from the firm as their personal characteristics would no longer fit a good culture' (Participant 6 – Compliance Officer, Private Banking). As noted by Participant 3 – Compliance Officer in Banking, 'the business side is rewarded with measures that are not in tune with what AML regulation is trying to achieve', with a focus on commercial profitability rather than customer outcomes. One compliance officer interviewed observed that the 'business side sees regulation as a hindrance to trying to get a business in a time-sensitive fashion', whereas compliance functions focus on creating a safer, long-term framework for business (Participant 8 – Compliance Officer, Payment Services FinTech). This prioritisation of revenue over market integrity can lead to operational challenges especially where pressure to acquire **10.55**

118 Fabian Maximilian Johannes Teichmann and Chiara Wittmann, 'Compliance Cultures and the Role of Financial Incentives' (2024) 31(1) *Journal of Financial Crime* 226.

119 FCA, 'Final Notice – State Street Bank Europe Limited' (30 January 2014) https://www.fca.org.uk/publication/final-notices/canara-bank-2018.pdf.

120 Peter Yeoh, 'Banks' Vulnerabilities to Money Laundering Activities' (2020) 23(1) *Journal of Money Laundering Control* 122.

customers in the competitive market, brings about tension between remuneration, profit maximisation and maintaining customer and market integrity.[121]

10.56 The majority of ethical issues are caused by avarice, which is made possible by pressure, opportunity, and incentives.[122] In some banks, a profit-driven mindset can overshadow ethical considerations, especially when client revenue targets come into play. For instance, one compliance officer explained that 'if the bank has zero tolerance for certain businesses, the starting point is to reject the business', but onboarding clients who bring significant revenue sometimes creates tension between supporting profitability and maintaining compliance standards (Participant 16 – Compliance Officer, Asset Management). Such a system can drive people towards certain behaviours by 'constantly pushing people with targets to hit, promotions to seek and recessions to try and survive, and so on' and so is 'likely to engender corporate crime'.[123] The 'enterprise culture' stresses the values of individualism and financial success and can lead to business practices that 'bend the rules' in the pursuit of profit or personal gain.[124] While banks certainly need profit to drive success and growth, purpose is also required to ground a company in its values and create a sustainable, healthy culture.[125]

10.57 Individuals and their decision-making are heavily influenced by the culture of their environment and financial incentives have a major impact on the compliance culture.[126] When employees are under pressure to fulfil inflated targets in order to generate profit for the business, they will do whatever it takes to hit those targets, whether they are met incorrectly or not.[127] The stronger the corporate culture, the more coherence there is between a manager's words and actions. Employees in such an environment understand that upholding moral principles is required and will be encouraged by higher-ups, even if it negatively impacts the bottom line.[128] In contrast, weak environments typically

---

121 Shenaaz Gani and Tafirei Mashamba, 'The Effect of Culture on Risk-Taking Activities of Banks' (2022) 6(3) *Corporate Governance and Organizational Behavior Review* 8.

122 Alison Lui, 'Greed, Recklessness and/or Dishonesty? An Investigation into the Culture of Five UK Banks Between 2004 and 2009' (2015) 16 *Journal of Banking Regulation* 106.

123 Gary Slapper and Steve Tombs, *Corporate Crime* (Longman 1999).

124 Barth and Sasan Mansouri, 'Corporate Culture and Banking' (2021) 186 *Journal of Economic Behavior & Organization* 46.

125 Ibid.

126 Fabian Maximilian Johannes Teichmann and Chiara Wittmann, 'Compliance Cultures and the Role of Financial Incentives' (2024) 31(1) *Journal of Financial Crime* 226.

127 Duc Duy Nguyen, Linh Hoai Nguyen and Vathunyoo Sila, 'Does Corporate Culture Affect Bank Risk-Taking? Evidence from Loan-Level Data' (2019) 30(1) *British Journal of Management* 106.

128 Ibid.

allow control mechanisms to be circumvented or disregarded, which opens the door to fraud.[129] This requires thorough training, strong internal controls and a dedication to maintaining the highest AML compliance standards.

E. CONCLUSION

This chapter has explored how banks engage with anti-money laundering regulations with a focus on the role of technology and organisational culture. Huge and increasing fines and sanctions imposed on banks for breaches in anti-money laundering indicate a deficiency in their efforts to combat financial crime. This chapter has highlighted how banks are deploying advanced technologies, such as artificial intelligence and machine learning, to enhance their AML compliance efforts. These technologies enable banks to improve their monitoring systems, detect suspicious activities more efficiently and adhere to the stringent requirements of AML regulations. However, while technology plays a critical role, the success of anti-money laundering efforts heavily relies on a strong internal culture that prioritises compliance and a deep commitment to the spirit of AML regulations. **10.58**

The chapter identified several problematic cultural dynamics within banks that may hinder their AML efforts. A 'tick-box' culture, where compliance is reduced to meeting minimal regulatory requirements. Similarly, a 'culture of resistance to change' slows the adoption of new AML technologies and processes. Other harmful dynamics include a culture that fails to instil personal responsibility for AML, and one that prioritises revenue generation over market integrity. While directives based on deterrence are effective in detecting and punishing inappropriate behaviour, the integration of good corporate values and self-regulation by companies is necessary to encourage long-term compliance, accountability and public trust. **10.59**

The chapter referred to insights from 20 compliance officers from the banking sector. Their comments indicated that while AI and other advanced technology facilitates business operations, it may also pose challenges, such as enabling bad actors to invent ways to bypass AML controls. In addition, rapid advancements in technology and market dynamics often outpace regulatory frameworks, creating significant challenges for compliance efforts. Nevertheless, technology is increasingly integral to ensuring regulatory compliance and **10.60**

129 Afroza Begum, 'Rebuilding Public Trust Through the Lens of Corporate Culture: An Inevitable Necessity to Sustain Business Success in Australia' (2022) 25(2) *Journal of Money Laundering Control* 280.

fostering an agile work culture. Institutions should therefore continue to allocate sufficient resources to compliance functions, integrate technological solutions and instil a culture of accountability across all organisational levels. Furthermore, achieving a robust culture of compliance requires active engagement from senior management and the board to prioritise AML adherence as a strategic objective. This chapter encourages banks to balance technological investment with a focus on cultivating the right cultural environment to effectively comply with money laundering regulations and combat financial crime.

11

NEW TECHNOLOGIES, CORPORATE GOVERNANCE AND CULTURE

Michael Anderson Schillig

A. INTRODUCTION

It is generally accepted that 'weak' corporate governance regimes in the financial sector, combined with a high-risk culture focusing on short-term profits, were key contributing factors to the Global Financial Crisis of 2007–8.[1] Unsurprisingly, therefore, the post-crisis reform efforts tried to also address, at least to some extent, any real or perceived corporate governance shortcomings, in addition to the introduction of macroprudential oversight and the strengthening of micro-prudential requirements.[2] With several scandals involving the mis-selling of financial products and benchmark rigging coming to light, the much more vague and intangible concept of corporate culture subsequently emerged as a regulatory focal point in its own right.[3] **11.1**

Still, according to the Swiss regulator Finma, the main reasons for the failure in 2023 of the banking giant Credit Suisse include 'recurrent scandals' that undermined the bank's reputation and the bank's 'poor risk management **11.2**

1 J Armour et al, *Principles of Financial Regulation* (OUP, 2016) 370.
2 I Chiu and J Wilson, *Banking Law and Regulation* (OUP, 2019) 563.
3 Ibid 506–7.

culture'.[4] Similarly, according to the Federal Reserve, Silicon Valley Bank's failure, also in 2023, can be directly attributed to its board of directors and senior management not doing their job:

> The board and management failed to effectively oversee the risks inherent in SVBFG's business model and balance sheet strategies. SVBFG did not take sufficient steps in a timely fashion to build a governance and risk-management framework that kept up with its rapid growth and business model risks.[5]

11.3 And the same has been said about Signature Bank's demise. According to the FDIC, Signature Bank's 'board of directors and management pursued rapid, unrestrained growth without developing and maintaining adequate risk management practices and controls appropriate for the size, complexity and risk profile of the institution'.[6]

11.4 Perhaps these are outliers, with problems attributable to the special circumstances in each individual case – prolonged mismanagement in the case of Credit Suisse; macro-factors such as rapid growth of the tech sector's deposit base and sudden high inflation for SVB and Signature. However, these failures could be a symptom of a wider malaise: a renewed deterioration of standards as the memory of the GFC fades, in accordance with what Coffee has termed the 'regulatory sine curve',[7] despite the post-crisis regulatory frameworks remaining in place largely unchanged. In that case, there likely will be more failures to come, which, if experience is anything to go by, will trigger calls for yet more and tighter regulation. However, it is worth pausing here to ask whether and to what extent new technologies can be used as a tool to address and mitigate (some of) the remaining governance and corporate culture shortcomings. Where technology can effectively and efficiently be deployed to this end, new regulation is still likely to be necessary but may have an entirely different focus and could potentially be less intrusive. This is the topic of the current chapter.

11.5 In the next section, corporate governance and corporate culture will be defined, their interaction in the financial sector explored and the regulatory framework discussed. The key insight here is that for the financial sector, the theoretical framework that underpins much of the corporate governance debate requires significant modifications. This will then be followed by an analysis of the

---

4 FINMA, *Report: lesson learned from CS Crisis* (Bern, 19 December 2023) 7.

5 Board of Governors of the Federal Reserve System, *Review of the Federal Reserve's Supervision and Regulation of Silicon Valley Bank* (April 2023) 2.

6 FDIC, *FDIC's Supervision of Signature Bank* (28 April 2023) 2.

7 J Coffee, 'The Political Economy of Dodd–Frank: Why Financial Reform Tends to be Frustrated and Systemic Risk Perpetuated' (2012) 97 *Cornell Law Review* 1019, 1029–1037.

potential impact of new technologies on corporate governance and culture. There are numerous technologies that have been transformative for the financial sector over the past decade or so.[8] Out of the ABCD technologies – Artificial Intelligence, Blockchain, Cloud Computing and (Big) Data – the focus will be on AI, and in particular on natural language processing and machine learning. Possible interactions are also varied: first and foremost, AI constitutes an investment project – financial institutions may spend huge amounts of money on AI investment opportunities which may never pay off; in fact, irrational AI exuberance may result in a bubble, to burst sooner or later.[9] However, of interest here is AI as a governance tool that may help to both measure corporate culture more reliably and to shape it directly by potentially enhancing governance decision making. Although some of the advances in this space are promising, they are by no means a panacea. Moreover, the deployment of any AI tools in this context will raise its own governance issues which will have to be addressed through law and regulation. There is an opportunity here, however, in the sense that refocused and targeted regulation may be better able to accommodate the corporate governance idiosyncrasies in the financial sector. The final section concludes.

B. CORPORATE GOVERNANCE AND CORPORATE CULTURE IN THE FINANCIAL SECTOR

Writing in 1776, Adam Smith famously proclaimed that the: **11.6**

> directors of [joint stock] companies being the managers rather of other people's money than of their own, it cannot well be expected, that they should watch over it with the same anxious vigilance with which the partners in a private copartnery frequently watch over their own [...] Negligence and profusion, therefore, must always prevail.[10]

Here, Smith neatly anticipates what much later became known as the principal–agent problem.[11] Ever since the 'separation of ownership and control',[12] their respective interests have been perceived as being radically different and **11.7**

8 L Lu, Global Fintech Revolution (OUP, 2024); R Buckley, D Arner and D Zetzsche, *FinTech: Finance, Technology and Regulation* (Cambridge University Press, 2024).

9 Goldman Sachs, GenAI: Too Much Spend, Too Little Benefit? (2024) 129 *Global Macro Research* 1.

10 A Smith, *An Inquiry into the Nature and Causes of the Wealth of Nations Volume II* 264–265 (RH Campbell and AS Skinner eds, Liberty Press 1976; first published in 1776).

11 MC Jensen and WH Meckling, 'Theory of the Firm: Managerial Behavior, Agency Costs, and Ownership Structure' in MC Jensen *A Theory of the Firm: Governance, Residual Claims, and Organizational Forms* (Harvard University Press 2003) 83, 86.

12 A Berle and G Means, *The Modern Corporation and Private Property* (Transaction Publishers, 2009), first published in 1932.

often in conflict: whereas the shareholders – as 'owners' of the means of production – are interested in the company earning the maximum profit, the management in control 'can serve their own pockets better by profiting at the expense of the company'.[13] This raises important normative questions: should the law strengthen the powers of those in control or the rights of shareholders? Should it ensure that corporations are operated primarily in the interests of the 'owners' or also in the interests of some other group or the community or society as a whole?[14]

11.8 The answer is straightforward when the firm is conceptualised as a 'nexus' for a set of contracting relationships among market actors.[15] Whereas any form of debt, in principle, is payable when due, equity is entitled (only) to what is left after debt has been discharged.[16] As a consequence, equity holders as the residual risk bearers have optimal incentives to monitor the management with a view to ensuring that they pursue optimal investment strategies.[17] The maximisation of shareholder value as directly observable in share prices becomes the overriding objective of corporate activity. Locked into this principal–agent relationship, the divergence of the interests of shareholders and management result in agency costs: efforts to commit the agent to act in the best interest of the principal (bonding cost), efforts to monitor the agent (monitoring costs) and a 'residual loss' caused by remaining divergences.[18] With the emphasis on shareholder wealth maximisation and a strong capital markets orientation, 'nexus of contract' theories have come to dominate policy debates in corporate law. Despite strong and persuasive criticisms at both descriptive and normative levels, the approach has been extremely influential and has informed scholarship as well as legislative and policy initiatives in the US, the UK and much of continental Europe over the last 50 years.[19] In the face of ever increasing inequality and impending environmental catastrophe, the tide seems to be slowly turning. However, at least for now, 'nexus of contract' and agency cost approaches remain prevalent in corporate law discourse.

---

13 Ibid 114.

14 Ibid 293.

15 Jensen and Meckling (n 11). The classical legal treatise is F Easterbrook and D Fischel, *The Economic Structure of Corporate Law* (Harvard University Press, 1991).

16 Easterbrook and Fischel (n 15) 67.

17 Ibid 68.

18 Jensen and Meckling (n 11) 86. However, provided that capital markets function properly, these costs will be internalised through the share price correctly reflecting the divergence of interests, ibid 90.

19 C Gerner-Beuerle and M Schillig, *Comparative Company Law* (OUP, 2019).

Accordingly, 'corporate governance' emerges as all those institutional structures that seek to constrain the principal–agent problem inherent in the public corporation.[20] These include the rules and principles that determine the delineation of the principals (shareholders), the selection, incentivisation and accountability of the agents (directors and managers), the allocation of decision-making powers between the corporate constituencies and various processes of decision-making and oversight. The underlying rules and principles derive from a multitude of sources: corporate law statutes and case law, listing rules of stock exchanges, soft-law measures such as corporate governance codes that rely on a comply-or-explain approach, but also social norms that may be enforced privately through reputational sanctions and market forces.[21] Corporate culture belongs to this latter category. **11.9**

Thus, what emerges is a distinction between corporate governance in a narrow sense, consisting of the institutional framework that can be defined by law and regulation and legally enforced,[22] and corporate governance in a broad sense that includes social norms, of which corporate culture is perhaps the most important manifestation. **11.10**

1. Corporate Governance (in the Narrow Sense)

With significant differences in detail, all major corporate law systems rely on a well-rehearsed panoply of measures that seek to reduce bonding and monitoring costs as well as the residual loss.[23] **11.11**

Historically, corporate law emerged from partnership law. In the archetypical partnership there is no separation of ownership and control; indeed, the partners are also the decision makers. Thus, an obvious way of ensuring that a company is run in the best interest of the shareholders is to give them the power to determine business strategy, select the relevant investment projects, hire the relevant personnel, and so on. This may indeed be the case for small partnership-like companies where ownership and control are not separated. However, for most sizeable corporations, in particular if they are publicly traded, such a set-up would be hopelessly inefficient.[24] Thus, centralised management where the day-to-day running of the business is assigned to a small group of experts, **11.12**

20 S Bainbridge, *Corporate Governance after the Financial Crisis* (OUP, 2012) 2.

21 Ibid.

22 Ibid.

23 Gerner-Beuerle and Schillig (n 19) Part II.

24 Investors with small stakes will usually lack the necessary expertise for running the business; they also would not have the time and money to acquire the necessary knowledge and vote their shares accordingly.

a board of directors, who in turn may delegate this decision-making power further to the managers – the separation of ownership and control – accounts for much of the modern business corporation's efficiency as compared to other types of business organisations.[25] It is a feature, not a bug. What remains for shareholders is control over certain 'structural' decisions: amendments of the articles of association, disposition of major revenue-generating assets and lines of business, or structural changes in the context of mergers and takeovers. Perhaps the most significant remaining shareholder power, however, is the decision on who will be appointed to the board of directors and who will be removed.[26] This is an important accountability channel as the board of directors selects the managers who are supposed to run the business in the best interest of the company. This makes perfect sense on paper. However, in practice shareholders in publicly traded corporations with widely dispersed ownership structures face a formidable collective action problem. Compared to exercising their voice by voting on structural or personnel decisions, it is often much cheaper for shareholders to exit the corporation if they are unhappy by cashing out their shares.[27] Moreover, individual shareholdings tend to be too small to make a difference, and with thousands or more of highly liquid shares in circulation, coordination is impossible. This is just as well, given that most investors follow a passive investment strategy – they have neither the time nor the expertise to monitor individual companies – and care primarily about the structure of their portfolio. Only institutional investors – activist hedge funds and pension funds with significant shareholdings – may be able to exert control over the board of directors and corporate management. But their interests are not necessarily aligned with those of the typical outside investor.[28]

11.13 Thus, in practice it will usually be the CEO who nominates the members of the board of directors, who will then in turn be confirmed with an overwhelming majority by the shareholders; the directors will then confirm/re-appoint the CEO and his team. Only on rare occasions may activist institutional investors vote down a management proposal or even remove an unwanted director. Therefore, bonding mechanisms are far from perfect. This is also true for a further shareholder remedy: holding directors and managers liable for a breach of the duty to avoid conflicts of interest or to take due care in the running of the business. To mount a derivate or class action, shareholders, individually or as a group, are not only subject to an asymmetry of information – with defendants

25 Gerner-Beuerle and Schillig (n 19) 42.

26 Ibid 8-26.

27 A Hirschman, *Exit, Voice and Loyalty* (Harvard University Press, 1972).

28 Armour et al (n 1) 372.

having access to much better information than any suing shareholder – but also face a free-rider problem: they would carry all the downside risk and costs of a failed action, whereas any benefits of success would accrue to all the shareholders collectively – a very weak incentive to go down that route.[29]

If bonding by using a stick – possible downvotes of directors and liability for breach of duty – doesn't work, perhaps a carrot is more promising. One way to align the interests of shareholders and managers is by tying managerial compensation to stock performance. Clearly, here managers should have a natural interest in maximising shareholder value, that is, share prices. To insulate managers from any underperformance beyond their control, which could result in an unduly risk-averse approach, managers may be given stock options instead. By duly calibrating the strike price, managers can benefit from rising share prices without facing any downside risk. But setting the strike price is crucial for appropriately incentivising managers, and the strike price is normally negotiated by the compensation committee of the board of directors, which means that much depends on the quality of the directors on the board.[30] **11.14**

How can the board of directors effectively monitor the managers if they rely on the latter's nomination and must be in their good books, and with shareholders being largely ineffective in taking control of the appointment process? The answer: a requirement for director 'independence', in the sense that there are no family, financial or employment ties between the director, on the one hand, and the firm and its managers, on the other. Importantly, a director will be independent if they are free from any conflict of interest; it says nothing about the director's competence or expertise, which, for example, may be vital for an adequate calibration of the strike price of managerial stock options.[31] **11.15**

Prior to the Global Financial Crisis, it was widely accepted that the corporate governance mechanisms for publicly traded large corporates were also adequate for banks, and that no specific corporate governance rules were required in addition to the regulatory oversight and supervision.[32] However, empirical evidence has shown that banks with the most 'pro-shareholder' boards and the closest alignment between executive compensation and share price were those **11.16**

29 Ibid 373.
30 Ibid 372–373.
31 Ibid 372.
32 Ibid 371.

that took the greatest risks prior to, and suffered the greatest losses during, the crisis.[33]

11.17 From a theoretical perspective, this can be easily explained. Banks are highly leveraged institutions: assets in the form of long-term loans are 'funded' by highly liquid deposits and other short-term debt instruments, with a tiny sliver of long-term debt and equity as mandated by minimum capital requirements. The leverage effect means that as long as the expected return on an investment project is higher than the interest rate payable on debt, increasing the total investment will increase the rate of return on equity.[34] Under normal circumstances, adding additional layers of debt and/or investing in ever higher variance projects would eventually result in increasing interest rates on debt and negate the leverage effect when the interest rate is equal to the expected return on the project. However, banks are unique in that they operate under an explicit or implicit public safety net. Retail depositors are weak monitors to start with and are protected by deposit insurance schemes that usually cover 100 per cent of the claims of most depositors.[35] As a consequence, most depositors will be insensitive to increased risk taking on the part of their bank. Moreover, the public guarantee that supports the deposit taking business may *de facto* be extended to other lines of business – notably securities business – carried out within the same group, increasing moral hazard and setting an incentive to engage in even riskier speculation.[36] Risky business may be shifted to the bank, with the consequence that any losses will be covered by the deposit guarantee scheme.[37] In addition, the holders of other short-term or long-term debt may benefit from the central bank's discount window and/or generous public bailouts. With a view to restoring market discipline and tackling moral hazard, all mature financial jurisdictions have introduced extensive resolution tools and powers. These enable a transfer of the viable parts of a failing institution's business – assets and liabilities – to a private sector purchaser or to a newly incorporated bridge bank, combined with the liquidation of the residual entity.[38] The transfer powers may further be used to separate

33 A Beltratti and RM Stultz, 'The Credit Crisis Around the Globe: Why Did Some Banks Perform Better?' (2012) 105 *Journal of Financial Economics* 1; DH Erkens, M Hung and P Matos, 'Corporate Governance in the 2007–2008 Financial Crisis: Evidence form Financial Institutions Worldwide' (2012) 18 *Journal of Corporate Finance* 389.

34 W Klein, J Coffee and F Partnoy, *Business Organization and Finance* (Foundation Press, 11th edn, 2010) 346.

35 M Schillig, R*esolution and Insolvency of Banks and Financial Institutions* (OUP, 2016) para 12.08.

36 R Herring and A Santomero, 'The Corporate Structure of Financial Conglomerates' (1990) *Journal of Financial Services Research* 471, 480.

37 P McCoy, *Banking Law Manual* (LexisNexis, 2014) §4.02.

38 Schillig (n 35) para 10.04–10.08, 10.35–10.40.

performing from non-performing assets and insulate the latter in an asset management company for eventual wind-down.[39] Formal bail-in tools may be available for a write-down or conversion of an institution's equity and debt instruments with a view to its recapitalisation as a going concern or for a reduction of its debt load in a gone concern scenario.[40] However, covered deposits will never be subject to bail-in and will always be part of a transfer package to a private sector purchaser or bridge bank.[41] Other debt may benefit from lender of last resort liquidity assistance pre-resolution, may be exempt from bail-in or may be transferred and thus also protected in full with generous government support.[42] Experience over the past decade has shown that despite these elaborate bank resolution frameworks, public bailouts are still the preferred mode of operation by regulators and policy makers.[43] Granted, shareholders may suffer a loss (albeit not necessarily)[44] when a bank fails, but downside exposure is limited due to the principle of limited liability. Moreover, a public intervention will likely prevent a failure from reaching systemic proportions. As a consequence, equity investors with a diversified portfolio have no incentive to monitor the risk associated with any particular investment, as their portfolio overall will remain protected.

In fact, the implicit or explicit government guarantee under which banks operate constitutes a put option that allows creditors to assign any losses in excess of shareholders' net worth to the taxpayer and a stop-loss call option on the firm's assets that allows the government as guarantor to take over the firm's assets when the shareholders' net worth approaches or becomes zero. This is the economic equivalent of holding an equity position.[45] Where the govern- **11.18**

39 Ibid para 10.12–10.13.
40 Ibid para 11.10–11.31.
41 Ibid para 11.13; 10.36.
42 Ibid 11.13–11.17, 11.50.
43 European Commission, Commission Staff Working Document: Impact Assessment Report accompanying the Proposals for a Directive of the European Parliament and Council amending Directive 2014/59/EU as regards early intervention measures, conditions for resolution and financing of resolution action; Regulation of the European Parliament and Council amending Regulation (EU) 806/2014 as regards early intervention measures, conditions for resolution and financing of resolution action; Directive of the European Parliament and Council amending Directive 2014/49/EU as regards the scope of deposit protection, use of deposit guarantee schemes funds, cross—border cooperation and transparency. SWD(2023) 225 final 30–31: between 2015 and 2022, European banks benefited from EUR58.2 bn of public financial support in the form of precautionary measures, liquidation aid and public aid in resolution (prior to the 8 per cent bail-in requirement taking effect), as compared to only EUR 6.9 bn of contributions from resolution funds and deposit guarantee schemes.
44 On the treatment of shareholders in Credit Suisse see Finma (n 4).
45 Edward J. Kane, A Theory of How and Why Central-Bank Culture Supports Predatory Risk-Taking at Megabanks 22 (Inst. For New Econ. Thinking, Working Paper No. 34, 2015), https://ssrn.com/abstract=2718733.

ment refuses to exercise the call option — because an institution is deemed to be 'too big to fail' — and continues to support the firm through liquidity assistance and explicit guarantees, it assumes a subordinated equity position with the taxpayer as residual risk bearer. The moral hazard-induced risk taking with a view to increasing the return on equity then directly transfers value from taxpayers through the put to shareholders, and through stock options to the managers of these firms.[46]

11.19 With the taxpayer emerging as the potential residual risk bearer in large banking institutions, it becomes obvious that by aligning management incentives with the interests of the shareholders, excessive risk taking was encouraged. Independent directors failed to exercise oversight, perhaps in the belief that regulators were applying proper risk controls,[47] or more likely with a view to not rock the boat and thereby increasing their chances for being reappointment. Thus, the more a bank operates in line with traditional shareholder-focused 'good' corporate governance, the riskier its business model may turn out to be, the higher the likelihood of failure and the bigger the losses eventually to be picked up by the taxpayer if the institution goes to the wall. Applying our corporate governance logic to the banking sector, therefore, would seem to require to align, at least to some extent, the interests of directors and managers (and shareholders) with those of the taxpayers, so as to mitigate the agency costs that emanate from these multi-level principal–agent relationships.

11.20 It could be argued that this is already the case and is achieved through the extensive regulation and supervision in the financial sector. The core of the banking system is a public–private partnership: to generate and distribute credit money as a public resource, the sovereign enrols privately owned banks with a view to exploiting their (real or perceived) informational advantage in spotting profitable investments.[48] The privilege of creating and distributing money comes at the cost of restricted and conditional access to banking activity and stringent regulatory oversight with a view to ensuring the safety and soundness of banks' public interest function, thereby also protecting the taxpayer. However, this may be insufficient. In general, corporate governance matters because it is impossible to write complete contracts that cater for all eventualities. In a world of incomplete contracts – our world – corporate governance informs and enables *ex post* decision making in unspecified contingent circumstances. In the same way that contracts are by necessity incomplete, regulation will always

46 Ibid 21.

47 Armour et al (n 1) 377.

48 R Hockett and S Omarova, 'The Finance Franchise' (2017) 102 *Cornell Law Review* 1143, 1163–1164.

remain incomplete as well. In fact, financial firms have an incentive to push the boundaries, seek to exploit loopholes and find ways to circumvent regulation that they perceive as limiting their earnings potential. Where regulation is incomplete and subject to circumvention, there would seem to be a need for further or additional alignment with the interest of taxpayers.

This doesn't seem to have been achieved by the post-Crisis reform package, addressing certain corporate governance issues. Pursuant to the EU's CRR/CRD IV package, the management body should always commit sufficient time and possess adequate knowledge, skills and experience to fully understand the business of the firm and its risk exposure. To avoid groupthink and to facilitate critical exchange, management boards should be sufficiently diverse as regards age, gender, geographical provenance and educational and professional background so as to present a variety of views and experiences.[49] The management body should be accountable for the overall risk strategy and for the adequacy of the risk management system.[50] A separate risk committee should be set up and there should be an independent risk management function to form an effective and holistic view of the whole range of risk.[51] Further, institutions are required to establish and maintain remuneration policies and practices that are consistent with effective risk management for staff whose professional services have a material impact on a firm's risk profile (senior managers, risk-takers)—in particular, a remuneration structure that does not encourage excessive risk-taking or moral hazard and that is aligned with the long-term interests of the firm.[52] **11.21**

The US Dodd–Frank Act focused almost exclusively on executive pay with most provisions applying to all public companies, not just financials. Under the Dodd–Frank Act, the compensation of executives is subject to a non-binding shareholder vote ('say-on-pay'). On a 'comply or explain' basis, the Act requires compensation committees to be composed of independent directors subject to strict requirements of independence. It further requires the disclosure of information that shows the relationship between executive compensation actually paid and the financial performance of the company, based on any changes in the share price, dividends and distributions. Incentive-based compensation is subject to a three-year clawback period if it turns out that it has been erroneously awarded based on an accounting restatement. Each public company is required to disclose in the annual proxy statement whether its employees are **11.22**

49 Art. 91 of Directive 2013/36/EU.
50 Art. 88 of Directive 2013/36/EU.
51 Art. 76 of Directive 2013/36/EU.
52 Art. 92 of Directive 2013/36/EU.

permitted to purchase financial instruments that are designed to hedge or offset any decrease in the market value of equity securities granted to the employee by the issuer as part of a compensation package.[53] Specifically for financial institutions, the Dodd–Frank Act mandates the promulgation of rules by the appropriate federal regulator to ensure the disclosure of the structure of all incentive-based compensation arrangements in order to assess whether they provide excessive compensation or could lead to material financial loss to be covered by the institution, and to prohibit compensation arrangements that encourage inappropriate risk-taking.[54]

11.23 These reforms are based on the traditional paradigm of corporate governance; they fail to recognise the taxpayer as the (potential) residual risk bearer. To that extent, they are likely to be ineffective and insufficient to prevent any shortcomings in the future.

2. Corporate Culture

11.24 The concept of 'corporate culture' supplements corporate governance in the narrow sense; it is much more vague and therefore not easy to pin down. The UK Houses of Parliament Commission demanded regulatory reform to promote sounder cultures at banks,[55] with bank culture widely perceived as being of crucial importance for the prudential soundness of banks and their conduct in the marketplace.[56] Even though not in breach of prudential regulation, a bank may operate in a regulatory 'grey area' with hazardous practices at play that could drive the bank to ultimate failure.[57] Moreover, a particularly malicious culture may manifest itself in clear breaches of the law – consumer mis-selling, manipulation of trading benchmarks or money laundering – all with a view to boost quarterly earnings.[58] On that basis, it seems that culture may be viewed as the institutional concept that can act as the lever for addressing the incompleteness of contracts and regulation with a view to ensuring greater alignment of banking practices with the interests of taxpayers as residual risk bearers, and the public interest more generally.

53 Dodd–Frank Act, §§951–955, amending various provisions of the Securities Exchange Act 1934.
54 Dodd–Frank Act, §956.
55 House of Lords and House of Commons, Changing Banking for Good (Report of the Parliamentary Commission on Banking Standards) (12 June 2013).
56 Chiu and Wilson (n 2) 505.
57 Ibid 506.
58 Ibid 506–507.

As a mental construct, culture is hard to define and measure.[59] However, the literature on organisational culture has made significant advances in recent years. Schein's definition has been particularly influential.[60] He provides a 'dynamic definition of culture' as: 11.25

> the 'accumulated shared learning' of a group 'as it solves its problems of external adaptation and internal integration, which has worked well enough to be considered valid and, therefore, to be taught to new members as the correct way to perceive, think, feel, and behave in relation to those problems'.

'Accumulated learning' consists of a 'pattern or system of beliefs, values and behavioural norms that come to be taken for granted as basic assumptions'.[61] These patterns of beliefs and values give meaning to the daily activities of the group and provide a sense of identity and stability.[62] Importantly, according to Schein, culture operates at multiple levels. The first level consists of artifacts as visible and feelable phenomena: the architecture of a group's physical environment, its language, its technology and products, its style, its published lists of values and its observable rituals and ceremonies. The second level consists of the group's espoused beliefs and values of 'what is right or wrong, what will work or will not work'. At a third level, 'taken-for-granted underlying assumptions' tell group members how to perceive, think about and feel about things. These basic assumptions are generally non-confrontable and non-debatable and therefore extremely hard to change.[63] 11.26

Building on Schein's work, Grennan and Li define corporate culture as 'an informal institution typified by patterns of behaviour and reinforced by people, systems and events'.[64] Being an 'informal institution' sets culture apart from 'formal institutions' such as 'governance and compensation' – our corporate governance in a narrow sense. People, systems and events can have an impact on culture and can be the channel for cultural change. People – leaders, new employees and investors – may influence culture directly by promoting certain cultural values, say, integrity, or indirectly by sharing stories and anecdotes.[65] As Schein writes, 'leadership is key to learning. Learning occurs when 11.27

59 G Gorton, J Grennan and A Zentefis, 'Corporate Culture' (October 20, 2021) 3; available at https://ssrn.com/abstract=3928972.

60 E Schein, *Organizational Culture and Leadership* (Wiley, 5th edn, 2017).

61 Ibid 6.

62 Ibid 6–11.

63 Ibid 17–30.

64 J Grennan and K Li, 'Corporate Culture: A Review and Directions for Future Research' (April 2022) 5; available at https://ssrn.com/abstract=4095565.

65 Ibid 7.

something expected is not happening and the individual or the group feels hungry, hurt, disappointed, or in some other way "disconfirmed".' Leadership must then propose something new to try to get out of the difficulty and, if successful, this new approach may crystallise into shared beliefs and values and eventually become part of the shared assumptions.[66]

11.28 Given the importance of leadership for shaping and changing corporate culture, it is not surprising that individual behaviour and responsibility at senior management level and below are perceived as the key levers for regulatory intervention with a view to improving corporate culture in the financial sector.[67] Notably, the Parliamentary Commission took the view that individual responsibility would be key to enhancing banking culture and that individuals must be regulated more stringently in order to 'change banking for good'.[68] Implemented by the Financial Services (Banking Reform) Act 2013 (and subsidiary legislation), different regulatory regimes apply for 'senior managers' – including CEO, CFO, CRO, Head of Compliance, Chairman of the Board and of the Risk, Audit, and Compensation Committees – and for 'certified persons' – as the 'material risk takers' whose professional activities may have a material impact on the firm's risk profile. Senior managers are subject to regulatory approval for prescribed responsibilities within financial institutions. 'Certified persons' are to be certified by their banks themselves subject to regulatory criteria. For both categories, individuals must be 'fit and proper' in terms of reputation, integrity, level of competence, knowledge and experience. Certified persons must act with integrity, due skill, care and diligence, and must be open and cooperative with regulators. In addition, senior managers must take reasonable steps to ensure that the business is controlled effectively and complies with the relevant regulatory framework, that any responsibilities are delegated appropriately and that appropriate disclosures are made to the regulators. Senior managers are subject to enhanced responsibilities and may incur personal liability for failures within their areas of responsibility.[69]

11.29 As sensible as these regulatory changes are, there is a risk that good 'corporate culture' may be equated with compliance with the Senior Managers and Certified Persons Regime, without really impacting the deeper levels at which

66 Schein (n 60) 14.

67 A Keller and A Kokkinis, 'The Senior Managers and Certification Regime in Financial Firms: An Organizational Culture Analysis' (2022) 22 *Journal for Corporate Law Studies* 299, 306–9.

68 House of Lords and House of Commons (n 55) Volume I para 116.

69 Keller and Kokkinis (n 67) 303–305; Chiu and Wilson (n 2) 513–35.

corporate culture operates.[70] Again, the problem is the inescapable incompleteness of contracts and regulation, with any attempt at regulating corporate culture in a traditional way also remaining incomplete.

C. THE IMPACT OF NEW TECHNOLOGIES

The use of the newest technologies in finance ('FinTech') is nothing new or revolutionary.[71] In ancient times, writing;[72] in 1838, the telegraph; or in the 1960s, the ATM are perhaps the most prominent examples of technological innovations that were harnessed early on to provide financial products and services more efficiently, without necessarily changing the product or service itself.[73] Today the conversation is dominated by the ABCD technologies: Artificial Intelligence in its different manifestations; blockchain and distributed ledger technology, cloud computing and Big Data.[74] Some of these technologies may have a significant impact on corporate governance and corporate culture. **11.30**

For example, it has been said that blockchain technology could effectively address some of the issues that have bedevilled corporate governance ever since the separation of ownership and control. Decentralized Autonomous Organizations (DAOs) are a case in point. Established by computer code, DAOs are not based on incorporation statutes. Instead of being delegated to self-interested agents, certain management functions may be carried out by 'objective' and uncompromised algorithms that reliably codify and execute the objectives of the organization. Through decentralised governance mechanisms, token holders can effectively control key parameters of the smart contact protocol and democratically vote on any amendments and upgrades. At least theoretically, it is more easily possible for each token holder to take an active stance in the governance of their DAO and they have an incentive to do so because acting in the best interest of the platform increases the value of their share in the supply of the token.[75] More broadly, and moving beyond the DAO space into general corporate law, for about half a century, most investment securities – publicly traded shares and bonds – have been held and **11.31**

70 Keller and Kokkinis (n 67) 319–321.

71 Buckley, Arner and Zetzsche (n 8) 11–3.

72 W Goetzmann, *Money Changes Everything: How Finance Made Civilization Possible* (Princeton University Press, 2016) 19–30.

73 Lu (n 8) 14.

74 Ibid 16–31.

75 C Harvey, A Ramachandran and J Santoro, 'DeFi and the Future of Finance' (December 2020) 13 (available at: https://ssrn.com/abstract=3711777) 39.

transferred through an immobilised and/or dematerialised system of intermediated securities.[76] Within this system, (interests in) securities are transferred by book entry only. Following the clearing process, settlement requires the adjustment (crediting and debiting) of securities accounts across the various intermediaries – securities depositories, custodians, clearing members, and so on. Records have to be reconciled across multiple ledgers.[77] The system has a tendency to severely weaken the legal position of the end investor[78] and may even threaten the integrity of the established corporate governance system.[79] Blockchain enthusiasts have suggested that holding securities and settling trades through a blockchain-based system could address many of the ills of the current intermediated set-up.[80] Blockchain technology would 'allow votes to be quickly and securely recorded, streamlining a proxy voting process that has historically been labour-intensive and fragmented'.[81] As a result of greater speed, transparency and accuracy of blockchain voting, shareholders and governance token holders may be more inclined to cast their votes and participate in corporate governance more frequently.[82] Accordingly, for Yermack, blockchain technology has the potential of changing 'corporate governance as much as any event since the 1933 and 1934 securities acts in the United States'.[83] Although financial institutions are increasingly interested in exposure to crypto-assets, the widespread tokenisation of debt and equity instruments that would be necessary for this vision to become reality has not materialised (yet, and perhaps never will). As for DAOs, they seem to work reasonably well for

---

76 G Morton, 'Historical Introduction: The Growth of Intermediation and Development of Legal Analysis of Intermediated Securities' in L Gullifer and J Payne (eds) *Intermediation and Beyond* (Hart, 2019) 23.

77 P Paech, 'The Governance of Blockchain Financial Networks' (2017) 80 *Modern Law Review* 1073, 1079.

78 Most approaches for the classification and legal treatment of the end investor's entitlement provide some measure of proprietary protection, which remains vulnerable to inadequate segregation and shortfalls in the relevant securities accounts; UNIDROIT, *UNIDROIT Legislative Guide on Intermediated Securities: Implementing the Principles and Rules of the Geneva Securities Convention* (2017) 16–27. Crucially, the end investor can never have more rights than those granted by the most restrictive contract terms and applicable law within the chain of intermediation; E Micheler, 'Custody Chains and the Asset Values: Why Crypto-Securities are Worth Contemplating' (2015) 74 *Cambridge Law Journal* 505, 509–521; *Secure Capital SA v Credit Suisse AG* [2017] EWCA Civ 1486; *Eckerle v Wickeder Westfahlenstahl GmbH* [2013] EWHC (Ch) 68.

79 Vice Chancellor J Travis Laster, 'The Block Chain Plunger: Using technology to Clean Up Proxy Plumbing and Take Back the Vote' Keynote Speech Council of Institutional Investors (Chicago, 29 September 2016) 14. In a seminal article, Kahan and Rock have analysed the various pathologies of corporate voting in the US, arising predominantly as a result of securities intermediation; M Kahan and E Rock, 'The Hanging Chads of Corporate Voting' (2008) 96 *Georgetown Law Journal* 1127.

80 Laster (n 79) 16; L Lee, 'New Kids on the Blockchain: How Bitcoin's Technology Could Reinvent the Stock Market' (2016) 12 *Hastings Business Law Journal* 81, 82.

81 D Yermack, 'Corporate Governance and Blockchains' (2015) National Bureau of Economic Research Working Paper No. 21802, 24.

82 Ibid 25–26.

83 Ibid 1.

limited purpose projects in the DeFi ecosystem, for example, as automated investment funds, automated market makers or lending protocols. However, even here human decision making and governance remain crucial: the rules embedded in a protocol will have been coded by a handful of 'core developers' with enormous power; thus a new principal–agent relationship emerges, or perhaps just the old one in a different guise. At least for now, the technology seems unsuitable and wholly inadequate for addressing the incredibly complex and manifold governance issues at play in large financial institutions.

By contrast, AI and machine learning applications are widely used by financial **11.32**
institutions today, most prominently in AI trading, risk management, fraud detection, credit scoring and customer services.[84] It is important to distinguish between AI applications properly so called and more traditional automated decision-making and transaction execution. For example, traditional algorithmic trading is based on a set of predetermined rules or conditions, relating to time, price and quantity, determined by human traders and their analysis of market conditions. Although a certain predetermined trading strategy can be automated in this way, the rules themselves remain static and do not adjust automatically in accordance with changing market environments. By contrast, machine learning-based algorithms process and analyse vast amounts of data with a view to recognising patterns and trends, often invisible to the naked eye. By applying patterns identified in the historic training data to real-time market information, inferences can be made to determine the best trading strategy. By continuously learning and evolving, these systems can thus automatically adapt to changing market conditions and improve their predictions over time.[85] With its access to huge amounts of customer and transaction data which can be used as training data and input, the financial services industry is a particularly fertile ground for the deployment of such machine learning algorithms.[86] AI-powered risk models can be used to identify potential risks and anomalies in real-time, thereby improving risk assessment accuracy, financial

84 M El Hajj and J Hammoud, 'Unveiling the Influence of Artificial Intelligence and Machine Learning on Financia Markets: A Comprehensive Analysis of AI Applications in Trading, Risk Management, and Financial Operation' (2023) 16 *Journal of Risk and Financial Management* 434; X Bai et al, 'Leveraging Generative Artificial Intelligence for Financial Market Trading Data Management and Prediction' (2024) 1 *Journal of Artificial Intelligence and Information* 32; T Adeyeri, 'Economic Impacts of AI-Driven Automation in Financial Services' (2024) 12 *International Journal of Scientific Research and Management* 6779.

85 A Unger, 'AI Trading vs Algo Trading: Understanding the Key Differences and Benefits,' Medium (7 June 2023), available at https://medium.com/@AlexUnger/ai-trading-vs-algo-trading-understanding-the-key-differences-and-benefits-3b76c6e7bea3.

86 Bai et al (n 84) 33.

loss mitigation and compliance with prudential requirements.[87] By analysing transactional patterns, user behaviours and historical data, fraudulent activities can be identified much earlier, and money laundering and the financing of terrorism can be detected in real-time. As a result, customer assets can be protected, building trust and confidence in the financial sector.[88] As useful as they may be, these applications do not impact corporate governance and culture directly: an institution with a strong culture of compliance-consciousness will immediately address any issues in terms of fraud or money laundering or excessive risk taking flagged by its AI systems; however, if the culture is malicious, the mere availability of the AI's predictions is unlikely to trigger a change in behaviour as long as the firm's earnings are not negatively affected. Moreover, firms may even rely on embedded biases in AI models to harm their customers.[89] For example, it is not inconceivable that an algorithm may be trained and used with a view to pushing the firm's own financial products, rather than recommending more suitable offerings by third parties.

11.33 It is possible, however, to envisage a more direct impact on governance and culture. More reliably measuring corporate culture is the first important step.

1. Measuring Corporate Culture using Machine Learning

11.34 To be able to penetrate the deeper levels of corporate culture, it is essential as an initial step to get a reasonably good idea of what the culture of a particular firm is. This raises the issue of consistently and reliably measuring the corporate culture of a firm. Perhaps the most straightforward and traditional approach is surveying and interviewing executives and employees about the underlying values and norms within their organisations.[90] The disadvantages of this method are well rehearsed: potential selection bias and behavioural biases that make any observations less objective and reliable.[91] Other approaches rely on various proxies for firm culture, such as the executive's cultural heritage or personal traits, past performance or CSR-consciousness.[92] Although providing interesting insights, as far as culture is concerned, there seems to be a lack of granularity. It is here that new technologies, in the form of machine

87 Adeyeri (n 84) 6784.

88 Ibid.

89 CFTC Technology Advisory Committee Advances Report and Recommendations to the CFTC on Responsible Artificial Intelligence in Financial Markets, Release Number 8905-24, May 02, 2024, available at https://www.cftc.gov/PressRoom/PressReleases/8905-24.

90 e.g. J Graham, J Grennan, C Harvey and S Rajgopal, 'Corporate Culture: Evidence from the Field' (2022) 146 *Journal of Financial Economics* 552.

91 Grennan and Li (n 64) 11.

92 Ibid 12–15.

learning and natural language processing, may be able to provide more satisfying answers. According to Grennan and Li, applying advanced linguistic models to big data has become one of the fastest growing methods for measuring corporate culture.[93]

To quantify corporate culture, Grennan[94] uses employee reviews collected by career intelligence firms, who are dedicated to revealing what life is like for employees at the respective firms. The review process consists of employees answering questions about the corporate culture, firm values, work–life balance and work environment at the firm they are working at. The reviews collect data on the employee's work history, job title, employment status and job location, as well as the review date. Grennan uses data from multiple career intelligence firms with a view to representing employees at all levels within a firm's hierarchy. Reviewers remain anonymous, but their identity is authenticated by the collecting career intelligence firm. This ensures that there are no repeat reviews and reduces incentives for employees to post fake reviews out of fear of reprisals. Importantly, the reviews are provided by employees on a voluntary and unsolicited basis, which greatly enhances their reliability and mitigates potentially perverse incentives.[95] **11.35**

Using computational linguistic techniques, Grennan then transforms the more than 400 million words of text contained in 1.8 million employee reviews into seven quantitative measures of corporate culture: *adaptability*, *collaboration*, *customer-orientation*, *detail-orientation*, *integrity*, *results-orientation* and *transparency*. The measure is 'textual similarity' – a standard measure in computational linguistics – between a 'master text' and a given firm-year's aggregated reviews. The master texts describe the fundamental concepts related to the seven attributes of corporate culture and are determined by using an external lexical database of semantic relations (WordNet).[96] WordNet is a large English language lexical database, grouping together nouns, verbs, adjectives and adverbs to create sets of 'cognitive synonyms (synsets)', each expressing a distinct concept. These synsets are interlinked by means of conceptual-semantic and lexical relations, interlinking specific senses of words so that words that are found in close proximity to one another in the network are semantically disambiguated. **11.36**

93 Ibid 15.

94 J Grennan, 'A Corporate Culture Channel: How Increased Shareholder Governance Reduces Firm Value', available at https://ssrn.com/abstract=2345384.

95 Ibid 8.

96 https://wordnet.princeton.edu/.

11.37 All the reviews for a given firm-year are aggregated and the similarity between this aggregate text and the master texts are then calculated. The measures of corporate culture constructed in this way are akin to correlation coefficients: high, positive values mean that the firm displays more of that attribute of corporate culture whereas low or negative values indicate less of that attribute.[97] Grennan uses this quantification of culture to show that stronger governance can significantly change culture, which may benefit shareholders in the short term, but may not be in the shareholder's long-term interest.[98] For our purposes, it would seem feasible to create cultural attributes such as *compliance-consciousness* or *risk-awareness* and measure textual similarity between the respective master texts and aggregated employee reviews at individual firms. With unsolicited reviews coming from various levels within an institution, Grennan's method may be suitable to penetrate Schein's deeper levels of culture, going beyond what is advertised on corporate websites and marketing material.

11.38 In a similar vein, Li and co-authors propose a 'semisupervised machine learning approach for measuring corporate culture'.[99] As a starting point, they use the corporate values mentioned by S&P500 firms on their corporate website: *innovation, integrity, quality, respect* and *teamwork*. These serve as 'value words' expressing a core corporate value. They then use the 'word embedding model' as a new machine learning model to quantify text.[100] The 'word embedding model' is based on the well-established linguistic concept that words that co-occur with the same neighbouring words have similar meanings, and can thus identify synonyms from common neighbouring words.[101] This model is then used to train a neural network model to learn the meanings of all words and phrases in earnings call[102] transcripts based on their respect contexts. On that basis the authors build a 'culture dictionary' of words and phrases that appear in close association with a cultural value: for example, *alliance*, *ecosystem* or *win–win* and the like may be associated with *teamwork*. The *teamwork* score of a firm is based on the weighted-frequency count of those words and phrases in its earnings call transcripts.[103]

97 Ibid 9–10.

98 Ibid 50–51.

99 K Li et al, 'Measuring Corporate Culture Using Machine Learning' (2021) 34 Review of Financial Studies 3265, 3266.

100 Ibid.

101 Ibid 3273.

102 Earnings calls are conference calls between the management of a public company, analysts, investors and the media to discuss the company's financial results during a given reporting period, such as a quarter or a fiscal year, with the transcript being filed with the SEC.

103 Ibid 3266.

The authors' use of earnings calls as the basis for scoring corporate culture is based on the belief that culture is most significantly influenced by top management – in line with Schein's emphasis on the importance of leadership. To effectively implement a particular value, management themselves must live by that value and lead by example. Where this is the case, it is likely that their words in earnings calls will reflect the prevailing values that management seeks to instil in their respective organisations. The advantage of earnings calls is that they are not advertising material, but a forum to discuss the firm's business operations and performance. The authors use the question-and-answer section of a call instead of the scripted management presentation to mitigate against excessive self-promotion, since during QA there is little room for management to pick discussion topics.[104] The authors use this method to show that corporate culture correlates with business outcomes such as operational efficiency and risk-taking, and that the culture–performance link is more pronounced in bad times. **11.39**

These new methods seem more promising than traditional approaches and could potentially be utilised by both financial institutions and regulators, uniquely tailored to the financial services sector. It is not inconceivable that in institutions such as Silicon Valley Bank and Signature an excessive growth culture and/or general disregard for adequate risk management could have been identified very early on, either by current or former employees reviewing their experience at the firm, or through earnings calls with management boasting about their growth strategies. Based on these methods, a lack of, say, compliance-consciousness seems potentially detectable even before any issues may be flagged by the algorithms that analyse transaction data with a view to detecting fraud and money laundering. Importantly, any bank failure has potentially systemic implications, with taxpayers, as residual risk bearers, on the hook. If we accept that corporate culture in the financial sector is the lever for aligning management incentives with the interests of the taxpayers as principal, being able to detect, and therefore address, any misalignment early on seems essential. **11.40**

However, there are downsides. Earlier and better information on a firm's culture is useful only to the extent that regulators are willing and capable to act upon it. Notably, prior to SVB's and Signature's demise, regulators were well aware of liquidity and risk management issues but failed to escalate their **11.41**

104 Ibid 3266–3267.

concerns.[105] And a recent report on the UK's Financial Conduct Authority (FCA) found that the regulator is widely perceived as incompetent – slow in identifying and addressing wrongdoing with a view to protecting consumers – and lacking in integrity – being 'captured' by large authorised firms and being generally not transparent and unaccountable.[106] Moreover, from a technical perspective, reliable algorithms must be developed, trained and tested, which may be very costly. Fair competition requires some form of standardisation across the entire financial sector, and, in accordance with rule of law demands, there needs to be sufficient transparency on how these models work. This latter aspect may reduce the usefulness of these models, at least to some extent, in the medium and long-term: for example, where management is aware that their earnings calls are assessed for culture measurement purposes, they may become much more guarded over time and learn to use the right vocabulary to placate regulators. Grennan's model is not immune from this issue either. Firms could encourage and incentivise their employees to submit reviews that use the 'right' vocabulary. Such behaviour would have to be addressed through a regulatory scheme that imposes stiff penalties on firms that seek to influence their current and former employees in this way. This is the other side of the regulatory coin: regulation may be necessary to encourage and appropriately incentivise employees to submit 'honest' reviews in the first place. Thus, ensuring the integrity of the process through proper calibration of incentives will not be an easy feat. At least for now, both models seem to work reasonably well as a one-off snapshot, but as a long-term regulatory strategy they seem problematic and open to manipulation.

11.42 In short, technological advances in measuring corporate culture, although promising, do have some downside and need a lot more refinement to be useful as a long-term regulatory strategy. Crucially, their usefulness will depend on regulators acting upon any insights the new models may provide, as they stop short of impacting corporate culture directly.

2. Changing Corporate Culture: ML-Informed Appointments to the Board

11.43 Perhaps the 'healthy purposeful culture' envisaged by the FCA[107] can be achieved by technological means, if not today then maybe in the future.

105 United States Government Accountability Office, 'Preliminary Review of Agency Actions Related to the March 2023 Bank Failures' (April 2023) 17.

106 All-Party Parliamentary Group on Investment Fraud and Fairer Financial Services, 'Report on the Call for Evidence about the Financial Conduct Authority' (November 2024), available at https://www.appgifffs.org/.

107 FCA, 'Transforming Culture in Financial Services – Driving Purposeful Cultures' (2020) DP20/1.

Automated corporate management in 'self-driving corporations' could be based on algorithms that pursue set goals, precisely and thoroughly, by simply optimising a given goal function without acting in good or bad faith.[108] Leaving aside companies with limited functions such as SPVs in a securitisation chain, it is hard to imagine how the algorithmic goal function could be practically calibrated: shareholder value maximisation may be easy enough, but at what externalised cost and within which time horizon? There are myriads of potential goal conflicts that need to be resolved and external constraints that need to be observed.[109] 'Acting in the best interest of the company' seems to be one of those parts of the legal system that are not easily susceptible to computation.[110] This is even more true for the much more intangible concept of corporate culture. Indeed, going back to Schein's definition, corporate culture seems to be a uniquely human concept, based on the lived experience of individuals and their interaction with each other and the environment surrounding them. A machine learning algorithm will not be able to meaningfully engage with that, not now and perhaps never.[111]

Through a widely reported and commented-on stunt, a Hong Kong-based venture capital firm made headlines a decade ago by announcing that it had appointed an algorithm – VITAL (Validating Investment Tool for Advancing Life Sciences) – to its board of directors. According to media reports at the time, VITAL could vote like any other director on whether to invest in a specific company or not. It was appointed because of its ability to automate due diligence and use historical datasets to uncover trends that are not immediately obvious to humans. Although widely heralded as the 'world's first artificial intelligence director', VITAL wasn't actually a company director or allowed to vote; rather, the algorithm would make suggestions based on its data processing capacity that the board would then vote on.[112] Despite significant advances in AI since the launch, and subsequent retirement, of VITAL, the idea of 11.44

108 H Eidenmueller and G Wagner, Law by Algorithm (Mohr Siebeck, 2021) 176–177.

109 Ibid 178.

110 C Markou and S Deakin, 'Ex Machina Lex: Exploring the Limits of Legal Computability' in S Deakin and C Markou (eds) *Is Law Computable?* (Hart, 2020) 31.

111 We could envisage a world in which all human employees have been replaced by one or more interacting algorithms or robots. Perhaps, in this world there can be such a thing as machine culture that determines how the various algorithms interact. But this is likely to be very different from corporate culture as we understand it today, so much so that humans won't be able to understand it (in the same way that algorithms today do not and cannot understand human culture).

112 F Moeslein, 'Robots in the Boardroom: Artificial Intelligence and Corporate Law' in W Barfield and U Pagallo (eds) *Research Handbook on the Law of Artificial Intelligence* (Edward Elgar Publishing, 2018) 649, 649–650.

appointing algorithms to the boards of major companies doesn't seem to have caught on (just yet).

11.45 A less ambitious but perhaps more promising approach would be enrolling the help of machine learning techniques when it comes to selecting corporate directors. Given that the selection of directors is essentially a 'prediction problem',[113] Erel and co-authors have developed a machine learning algorithm that uses data on firms, their current board members and the attributes of potential directors to assess the quality of directors being considered for a given firm's board. The authors construct a large dataset of publicly traded US firms and independent directors appointed between 2000 and 2014. They then use several machine learning algorithms designed to predict director performance, using director, board and firm-level data available to the nominating committee at the time of the nomination.[114] Director performance is measured primarily by the level of shareholder support a director receives in annual director re-elections as a market-based measure of individual directors' performance. In particular, the authors use the algorithm to predict the average excess voting support relative to the slate of directors up for re-election over the first three years of director tenure.[115] Each algorithm was trained on data comprising the directors appointed between 2000 and 2011. The authors then compared the predictions to the observed out-of-sample data on the test set of directors appointed between 2012 and 2014.[116] They found that the algorithms made accurate out-of-sample predictions: directors identified by the algorithms as likely to have low (high) future shareholder support were in fact more likely to have low (high) support in subsequent elections.[117] By contrast, traditional econometric modelling was not capable to capture these effects.

11.46 By relying on advances in 'explainable AI', the authors were further able to unearth some of the features that are overvalued and undervalued by firms in the selection process.[118] Relative to algorithm-selected directors, management-selected directors with predictably low shareholder approval were more likely to be male, have larger networks and sit on more boards, which describes the stereotypical director in most large corporations. The algorithms would,

---

113 I Erel et al, 'Selecting Directors Using Machine Learning' (2021) ECGI Finance Working Paper No 605/2019, 1.

114 Ibid 2.

115 Ibid 5–9.

116 Ibid 9–11.

117 Ibid 12. The result was confirmed by using alternative measures of director performance (abnormal returns at the time of appointment, high dissent, turnover shortly after appointment).

118 Ibid 4.

therefore, seem to inject a healthy dose of diversity: directors who are not old friends of management and come from different backgrounds are more likely to monitor management more effectively, and less well-connected directors may be able to provide different and more useful opinions on policy.[119] The authors further found that firms that choose predictably bad directors tend to have weak governance structures. The authors emphasise that in their view, algorithms hold promise to complement human judgement rather than replace it, potentially expanding the set of possible candidates with the necessary skillset who would otherwise have been overlooked.[120]

Given the board diversity requirement under CRR/CRD IV, it seems that Erel et al.'s approach could be very usefully deployed in the financial services industry. Moreover, it does not seem to be inconceivable that machine learning approaches for measuring corporate culture could be combined with algorithms that can predict whether and to what extent a particular director will be likely to have a positive or negative impact on certain key attributes of culture. For example, using Li et al.'s word embedding approach it might be feasible to link changes in a financial firm's culture scores on, say, *compliance-consciousness* or *risk-awareness* to the appointment (and re-election) of individual directors in the past, to then predict how an appointment may impact the culture score on a test set going forward. If successful, the model could then be used for making recommendations to the nominations committee with a view to improving firm culture so that management's running of the business remains aligned with the interest of the residual risk bearers, the taxpayers. Moreover, under the UK's Senior Managers and Certification Regime, the regulators tasked with approving senior managers of financial firms could also draw on such a model, for example, with a view to vetoing a senior manager that the model flags as having a likely adverse cultural impact, as could firms when certifying their 'certified persons', with the relevant regulatory criteria being adjusted to that effect (i.e. 'no red flags' thrown up by the model as a prerequisite for certification). 11.47

A key problem is of course the availability of sufficient high-quality data to train and test the algorithms. Moreover, while natural language processing has become very robust and reliable over the past decade, this is not necessarily the case for predictive AI. As Narayanan and Kapoor write,[121] AI applications 11.48

119 Ibid 20–21.

120 Ibid 22–25.

121 A Narayanan and S Kapoor, *AI Snake Oil: What Artificial Intelligence Can Do, What it Can't, and How to Tell the Difference* (Princeton University Press, 2024) 9–10.

that claim to be able to predict social outcomes, including how well applicants are likely to do at a job, have proliferated over the last few years and are widely used by companies. The providers of these applications often fail to release any evidence that their products actually do what they promise to do and there is plenty of evidence to the contrary, showing that it is extremely difficult to predict individuals' future performance.[122] Inbuilt discriminations and biases as well as incentives for gaming the system may account for the low accuracy of these tools, in addition to the lack of availability of certain important factors within the training data. Narayanan and Kapoor do not think that things will improve over time, as these flaws are inherent.[123] Like everywhere else, relying on AI-based technological solutions in the corporate governance and culture context may seem attractive precisely because the governance structures themselves are weak, as is regulatory oversight. It would be more effective to improve the underlying governance framework with a view to enhancing accountability rather than by 'automating' decision making.[124]

11.49 Still, machine learning algorithms may provide useful insights when it comes to measuring and influencing corporate culture. This can be of great importance if we accept that corporate culture is the lever within the corporate governance armoury that can serve to align management incentives with the interests of taxpayers as the residual risk bearers in banking institutions. To be effective, this will require a regulatory underpinning with a focus that must be different from traditional regulatory frameworks. Regardless of whether the relevant algorithms are developed in-house or bought in by external providers, a new regulatory framework must ensure that these algorithms are well designed, appropriately trained and tested with sufficiently high-quality training data and test sets, and test outcomes have to be verified and interpreted prior to application, which then needs to be adequately supervised. Every stage within this process requires human value judgements, which cannot be automated and may be severely flawed.[125] The great advantage of this form of regulation, however, would be that it might be less intrusive than traditional regulation, respecting banking business as a form of private enterprise (albeit in a public–private partnership) while also ensuring that the interest of the taxpayer as residual risk bearer is adequately protected.

122 Ibid 10.
123 Ibid 11–12.
124 Ibid 263.
125 Eidenmueller and Wagner (n 108) 169–175.

D. CONCLUSION

Traditional corporate governance theory, based on a principal–agent and nexus of contract analysis, requires a modification for the financial sector. For financial institutions that operate under an explicit or implicit state guarantee, the shareholders are replaced as residual risk bearers by the taxpayer. Corporate culture can serve as an important lever for aligning management incentives with the interest of taxpayers, without interfering too much in the day-to-day business of banking institutions. In terms of measuring corporate culture and helping to influence it, natural language processing and machine learning hold some promise. The deployment of these new tools and methods will require a new regulatory framework with a different focus: designing, training and testing the relevant algorithms and effectively supervising their application. **11.50**

However, despite technological advances that can assist human decision making, installing and maintaining robust governance arrangements will remain key, as will having good and competent people at the level of the board of directors, senior management and below, and importantly also at the relevant regulators. AI may help in processing and analysing huge amounts of data and may also assist in automating some processes. But human individual accountability will remain essential and needs to be supported with the necessary human and material resources. **11.51**

12

FUTURE DEVELOPMENTS

Anat Keller and Andreas Kokkinis

12.1 The in-depth discussions in this book have raised pertinent questions about culture, accountability, transparency, social purpose and the formation of expertise in the financial services sector. In lieu of conclusions, the final chapter of the volume attempts to look at the future, but – inevitably – in doing so, it also takes the reader back to the fundamentals of governance and culture and the often-forgotten concept of professionalism. Broadly speaking, we foresee a transformation in the narrow understanding of governance as risk management towards a broader umbrella concept of purposeful culture, which, over time, is likely to gain more concrete content as a result of regulatory expectations and societal pressures. We are intrigued by the conceptualisation of culture as the core infrastructure of organisational decision-making that eventually determines the ultimate outcomes of external factors such as regulatory rules, while being gradually influenced by external rules and societal expectations too.[1] Indeed, UK financial regulators are paving the way to this future vision, which, however, remains within the framing of sustainable and inclusive growth. After setting out our broad vision for the rise of culture in finance, we will contextualise these changes by reference to two major developments that

1 This view of culture as infrastructure is shared by the management consultancy industry. See e.g., https://krausebellgroup.com/organizations-are-built-on-a-cultural-infrastructure/.

will undoubtedly impact all aspects of society, including the financial industry: the climate emergency and the impact of disruptive technologies.

A. THE RISE OF CULTURE

As explained in the first substantive chapter of this volume, the FCA encourages financial firms to develop a healthy, purposeful culture with a view to leading to better outcomes for consumers and markets. For the time being, the FCA has mostly refrained from dictating the essence of purposeful culture, thereby allowing each firm to frame and determine its manifestation and implementation. However, we already observe signs of concretisation of the concept of purposeful culture in the areas of diversity and inclusion, as a vehicle 'to deliver better internal governance, decision making and risk management'.[2] Contrary to the conventional corporate governance framing of diversity as a priority primarily for boards and senior management, the scope of the FCA expectations is broader and applies at all levels of firms with an emphasis on setting appropriate targets and preventing non-financial misconduct. The diversity and inclusion agenda remains, however, hostage to an instrumental view of the value of diversity as a means to an end. This reflects the FCA's lack of confidence in entering a field that is not traditionally associated with its ambit, and its attempt to justify the expansion of its remit by invoking the (tenuous) positive impact of diversity on the more traditional regulatory goal of customer outcomes.[3] **12.2**

In the future, we expect to witness a further shift away from technocratic risk management to an umbrella concept of culture that complements and encompasses risk management. After the 2008–9 global financial crisis, risk management has become the quintessential element of financial firm governance and formal processes, but without necessarily altering their underlying profit-oriented culture. This is precisely the potential contribution of a broad and bold understanding of purposeful culture, which is inextricably connected to **12.3**

2 FCA, 'The FCA and PRA propose measures to boost diversity and inclusion in financial services:' (September 2023) available at https://www.fca.org.uk/news/press-releases/fca-and-pra-propose-measures-boost-diversity-and-inclusion-financial-services.

3 There is generally an evidence gap on the impact of diversity on business outcomes. See Diversity Project, Diversity and inclusion in the financial sector – working together to drive change. FCA CP 23/20 Response, available at https://diversityproject.com/wp-content/uploads/2023/12/FCA-CP-2320-DP-Dec-23-Final.pdf, Review of research literature that provides evidence of the impact of diversity and inclusion in the workplace (July 2021), 21 available at https://www.fca.org.uk/publication/research/review-research-literature-evidence-impact-diversity-inclusion-workplace.pdf.

greater stakeholder orientation.[4] In this context, it is likely that firms will face increasing market pressure to adopt a more stakeholder-oriented approach to strategic management, primarily from the labour market. While the language used by the FCA does not yet tread onto the contentious topic of stakeholder governance, in the future, firms' social licence to operate may well encompass a shift away from narrow shareholder value maximisation, particularly in view of developments that will be analysed in the next two sections. If this shift materialises, it is likely to change the balance of power within firms. While power currently lies mostly in the hands of senior leaders with numerical skills who can deliver 'hard' financial outcomes, in the future, the rise of purposeful culture may necessitate a more holistic skillset that also encompasses 'soft' people skills. Such a shift may eventually undermine the stereotypical use of terms such as 'hard' and 'soft' that tend to perpetuate a hierarchical view that privileges 'hard' skills and feminises 'soft' skills in a male-dominated environment, thus coinciding with traditional and restrictive gender roles.[5]

12.4 In a sense, the FCA and PRA are ahead of the game in global terms, as they are pioneering a regulatory focus on culture – something that is not yet happening in other major jurisdictions such as the EU. Potentially, this can be explained in terms of the absence of a powerful stakeholder tradition in the UK, where the purposeful culture agenda is functioning as an oblique way towards a more inclusive approach to corporate governance. At the same time, UK regulators face the unavoidable challenge of reconciling purposeful culture with the new statutory secondary objective of supporting the competitiveness and growth of the UK financial services sector.[6] Given the inherent tensions between growth, sustainability and distributive outcomes, merely adopting the rhetoric of inclusive and sustainable growth will not be sufficient for regulators to navigate these tensions.

---

4 There is already an established practice of large global banks utilising stakeholder mapping. S Nestor and others, *Governance of Sustainability in the Largest Global Banks: A Study of the Top 30 European and North American Banks* (January 2023) available at https://sodali.com/uploads/insights/attachments/Banking%20Study%202023%20-%20Final%20web.pdf.

5 L Constantino and J Rodzinka, 'The Role of Soft Skills In Employability in the Financial Industry' (2022) 18(1) *Financial Internet Quarterly*, ISSN 2719-3454, Sciendo, Warsaw, 44–55 available at https://sciendo.com/article/10.2478/fiqf-2022-0004.

6 FSMA 2000, Section 1B(4A) and section 1EB. On the reasons for introducing this objective see HM Treasury, 'Financial Services Future Regulatory Framework Review: Proposals for Reform' (November 2021) CP 548, 30. For criticism of this addition see E Ferran, 'International Competitiveness and Financial Regulators' Mandates: Coming Around Again in the UK' (2023) 9 *Journal of Financial Regulation* 30. See also EV Lim, FSMA 2023 'Secondary Competitiveness and Growth Objective: A Step Back or a Step Forward?' (2024) 13(1) *Journal of Law and Jurisprudence* 109.

B. THE CLIMATE EMERGENCY AND CULTURE AND GOVERNANCE IN THE FINANCIAL INDUSTRY

The first exogenous pressure that we expect to impact governance and culture in financial services is related to climate change. The urgency of climate change is likely to become internalised by broader sections of the population in the foreseeable future as its tangible effects will become increasingly felt around the world in the form of extreme weather events and other types of natural disasters.[7] In such a world, stable inflation rates, financial stability and fair and functioning markets would take a back seat in the face of pressing imminent threats to human flourishing. It is thus likely to result in calls for financial services to play a major role in tackling the climate emergency. **12.5**

Faced with such powerful public expectations, financial firm leaders will have to rethink their strategy and discourse. To some extent, firms have already incorporated climate risk into their risk management models, although only a few have fully integrated sustainability into their internal credit ratings and operational risk models.[8] This trend is likely to be further supported by emerging prudential regulatory expectations that require consideration of climate risk when calculating capital adequacy.[9] Financial firms and especially large banks are thus likely to have to reposition themselves as paragons of sustainability and this will require them to have relevant expertise in leadership positions, so directors will need to demonstrate 'sustainability literacy' alongside typical financial expertise.[10] **12.6**

From the perspective of regulation, the FCA and PRA's statutory objectives already encompass environmental sustainability, as 'the nature regulatory principle' requires them to consider the UK's net zero greenhouse gas emissions target by 2050 and other environmental targets.[11] This new regulatory principle will further contribute to the shift of bank governance and culture away from narrow shareholder value maximisation. Thus, the move towards **12.7**

---

7 The final report of the Intergovernmental Panel on Climate Change in March 2022 left no doubt that climate change poses a clear and present danger for markets and the global economy.

8 Nestor and others (2023) (n 4), 8.

9 Basel Committee, Frequently asked questions on climate-related financial risks (December 2022) available at https://www.bis.org/bcbs/publ/d543.htm.

10 'While banks are now actively looking for board members with certain E&S experience, candidates must also still have relevant financial or senior leadership experience – they cannot be "one-trick ponies"'. Nestor and Sodali (2023) (n 4), 9.

11 Section 27 of FSMA 2023 inserting section 3B into FSMA 2000. FCA, Environmental Sustainability (available at https://www.fca.org.uk/about/how-we-operate/environmental-sustainability): "Our regulatory principles were updated in 2023, so we need to contribute towards environmental targets and the UK commitment to achieving net zero greenhouse gas emissions by 2050."

sustainability and the move towards stakeholder orientation are two mutually amplifying phenomena which will shape financial firm governance in the years to come.

12.8 In parallel, it is reasonable to expect that the financial sector will be characterised by an increasing role of insurance as a means to manage the risk of natural disasters. This is already reflected in the heightened focus of the FCA on insurance markets. As insurance firms are expected to take on the bulk of climate change risk, they will rationally invest resources to develop methods to quantify and mitigate the risk. This expertise will have broader values and can be utilised to encourage or require companies across all sectors to adopt climate-friendly policies.

C. TECHNOLOGICAL DISRUPTIONS AND THEIR IMPACT ON BANK GOVERNANCE AND CULTURE

12.9 The second exogenous factor to impact bank governance and culture is, in our view, the increasing effect of new technologies and associated technological risks. Cyber risks pose a threat not only to financial firms and their clients but also to financial stability. Already in 2020, the FSB warned that 'A major cyber incident, if not properly contained, could seriously disrupt financial systems, including critical financial infrastructure, leading to broader financial stability implications'. These risks are likely to intensify, particularly the risk of cyber-attacks as a form of cyber warfare. Payment systems and other financial market infrastructures may become a significant target for such attacks, potentially severely affecting economic activity.

12.10 Recent regulatory initiatives to bolster the financial industry's operational resilience are a turning point. They aim to ensure that financial firms and the financial sector as a whole can absorb and adapt to shocks and disruptions. Operational resilience is to be differentiated from existing risk management system expectations, which are already integrated into firms' organisational structures and decision-making processes. It requires a shift in framing risk and a proactive approach that assumes disruptions will occur, considering the firm's overall risk appetite and tolerance for disruption. Financial firms must utilise their existing governance structure to establish, oversee and implement an effective operational resilience approach. However, operational resilience will require a cultural change in light of its evolving and adaptive nature. This is reflected in the PRA's supervisory statement, which acknowledges the link between operational resilience and culture: 'The ability of firms to deliver their important business services within their impact tolerances depends upon appropriate reporting and accountability to be in place throughout the firm. Where limitations are identified, leadership from the firms' board and senior management is essential to prioritise the investment and cultural change required to improve operational resilience.'[12]

Furthermore, with the emergence of additional players, including fintech and big tech companies, providing services to the financial industry, the scope of risk management and governance is expected to become broader. For instance, financial firms and financial market infrastructure increasingly rely upon third parties to support their operation. Therefore, they will need to manage effectively the risk of disruption and harm to their customers and demonstrate to regulators their own resilience and good governance and that of their third-party service providers, taking into account the criticality of these services to their operation. **12.11**

Another area that will require particular attention in the financial industry and may result in substantive changes to governance and culture is fraud prevention. Enhanced consumer protection requirements, such as the new Consumer Duty and tackling specific challenges, including Authorised Push Payments, may not be sufficient to stem the tide. To improve customers' awareness and understanding of risks, we may witness an emerging role of financial institutions as financial education champions. The collaborative efforts of financial institutions and consumers to identify and prevent fraud risks may lead to the mitigation of APP fraud and fraud attacks more broadly. **12.12**

AI can play a key role in fraud prevention, improving efficiency and inclusion in loan and credit decisions and tailored financial advice. It also opens the door to many risks, including biases or errors in decision-making and even a destabilising effect on markets. In contrast to the EU's tailored AI regulatory regime, the FCA believes that the existing regulatory framework is sufficient to embrace the use of AI in finance. As a technology-agnostic regulator, the FCA suggests that 'there are already regulations and frameworks in place to facilitate the safe and responsible implementation of AI in financial services'.[13] It concludes that these frameworks provide the FCA with the tools to address **12.13**

12 *PRA Rulebook, Guidance SoP – Operational Resilience*, section 2, available at https://www.prarulebook.co.uk/guidance/statements-of-policy/sop---operational-resilience/2-the-relationship-between-operational-resilience-and-governance/15-12-2024?p=1.

13 J Rusu, 'AI: Flipping the Coin in Financial Services', The City and Financial Global AI Regulation Summit, 5 October 2023, available at https://www.fca.org.uk/news/speeches/ai-flipping-coin-financial-services.

material risks associated with AI and create incentives for the right outcomes. Most notably, these tools encompass the SMCR and the FCA's Principles for Businesses, including Consumer Duty, good governance and a healthy organisational culture. The latter 'helps cultivate an ethical and responsible environment at all stages of the AI lifecycle: from idea, to design, to testing and deployment, and to continuous evaluation of the model.'[14] However, it is doubtful whether AI's complexity challenges a technology-neutral approach. For instance, could a lack of explainability be incompatible with existing legal frameworks, considering that transparency is a pillar of governance? Where are ownership and responsibility for decision-making located?

12.14 The latter is of real concern and goes to the core of corporate governance. The FCA contends that legal responsibility for compliance with its high-level principles 'should be allocated to the actors in the AI life cycle best able to identify, assess and mitigate AI risks effectively'. Yet, AI supply chains can be complex and opaque and, thus, subject to the 'problem of many hands'.[15] In such an environment, attributing responsibility and allocating individual accountability for harm is far from straightforward.[16] Therefore, the siloed thinking that has applied since the GFC of allocating individual accountability under the SMCR may not apply in the AI era. Instead and to reflect the 'many hands' involved in AI use, collective accountability will become paramount.

12.15 Since the inappropriate allocation of AI liability and responsibility for AI governance could negatively impact innovation, the FCA prefers adopting a 'wait and see' approach. In particular, it suggests, 'It is too soon to make decisions about liability as it is a complex, rapidly evolving issue which must be handled properly to ensure the success of our wider AI ecosystem'. These issues will become even more pertinent with the anticipated rise in the use of AI by corporate boards in a wide range of strategic and personnel decisions.

---

14 J Rusu, 'Building better foundations in AI', The Alan Turing Institute's Framework for Responsible Adoption of Artificial Intelligence in the Financial Services Industry (FAIR) event (24 January 2023), available at https://www.fca.org.uk/news/speeches/building-better-foundations-ai. See also FCA, Artificial Intelligence (AI) update – further to the Government's response to the AI White Paper (April 2024), available at https://www.fca.org.uk/publications/corporate-documents/artificial-intelligence-ai-update-further-governments-response-ai-white-paper.

15 On the problem of many hands see DF Thompson, Chapter 1, 'The Problem of Many Hands' in *Restoring Responsibility Ethics in Government, Business, and Healthcare* (CUP, 2004), 11. In the context of AI see T M Lechterman, 'The Concept of Accountability in AI Ethics and Governance' in J Bullock and others (eds), *The Oxford Handbook of AI Governance* (Oxford University Press, 2024).

16 Information Commissioner's Office, 'How Do We Ensure Fairness in AI?' Available at https://ico.org.uk/for-organisations/uk-gdpr-guidance-and-resources/artificial-intelligence/guidance-on-ai-and-data-protection/how-do-we-ensure-fairness-in-ai/.

At the same time, the next decade is likely to witness the introduction of central bank digital currency (CBDC) as a means of payment. It seems that the UK will follow the option of a non-interest-bearing CBDC that will be exclusively utilised for payments and that retail customers will need to enter into an agreement with a bank or payment services provider to obtain a CBDC wallet. Thus, the implementation of the CBDC will not challenge the role of banks as financial intermediaries under these proposals.[17] The possible applications of this technology, however, are already fuelling a wave of radical thinking in the literature[18] arguing that CBDCs ought to be interest-bearing and made available by central banks directly to retail customers, thus bypassing the intermediating role of banks and payments services providers. To the extent that the inherent potential of the CBDC to render aspects of financial intermediation obsolete becomes widespread knowledge, the social licence of banks to operate will be impacted by stronger public demands for banks to deliver positive outcomes for customers. Bank boards and senior management will be obliged to grapple with these issues, as otherwise, a lack of public trust will eventually lead to political pressure to rethink the approach to the CBDC towards a model that would encourage disintermediation in the medium term. In other words, in the future landscape, large banks will need to justify the social value of their existence rather than be taken for granted, and banks' leadership and culture will have to adjust in the way their role is framed and communicated, as can already be seen in the tone adopted by some large retail banks in the UK. **12.16**

D. PROFESSIONALISM AND REGULATION

Having examined the two major exogenous parameters that we believe will greatly affect bank governance and culture in the next decade, the final section of the chapter canvasses what we would like to see happening in order for banks to rise to the challenges ahead to the benefit of society. While there are many possible reforms that may improve the current situation, we identify two main avenues for change that are both politically feasible (as they do not require legislative change or taking a confrontational approach vis-à-vis the sector) and potentially pervasive. In a way, both strands of thinking return to the basics of good governance: professionalism for bank senior and mid-level **12.17**

17 Bank of England, 'Bank of England Statement on Central Bank Digital Currency' (2021) available at https://www.bankofengland.co.uk/news/2021/april/bank-of-england-statement-on-central-bank-digital-currency.

18 S T Omarova, 'The People's Ledger: How to Democratize Money and Finance the Economy' (2021) 74(5) *Vanderbilt Law Review* 1231.

management and effectiveness and accountability for the FCA. As obvious as these prescriptions might be, they are both aspirational targets that the UK financial system has not yet achieved.

12.18 Professionalism is crucial because navigating the challenges that lie ahead will ultimately depend on the honesty, integrity, ethics, expertise and experience of individuals with leading positions within the financial services sector. Both senior and mid-level management are crucial actors that shape and give reality to governance processes and constantly create and re-create the organisational culture of a firm. Professionalism engenders two main qualities that have traditionally distinguished 'professions' from other occupations: possessing a special body of knowledge and skills and acting in the public interest as well as the interest of clients and employers. These two elements are of fundamental importance for bank management. Professionalism would require raising the profile of relevant industry bodies, broad acceptance of a set of qualifications required for each type of position and the enforcement of rigorous codes of ethics within each professional community in the sector. Much of this can be achieved through voluntary action by financial firms, with encouragement and, if necessary, pressure from the regulators (who can leverage their powers under the SMCR) and government. Enhanced professionalism would hopefully deliver a more balanced skillset encompassing people's skills and a genuine commitment to stakeholders and public benefit.

12.19 With respect to the effectiveness and accountability of regulatory bodies, particularly the FCA, there remains considerable scope for improvement. A report published in November 2024 by a group of MPs and peers criticises the FCA for a series of alleged failings and characterises the authority as 'incompetent at best, dishonest at worst'.[19] The report evidences the lack of confidence among firms in the FCA and widespread failings in its regulatory enforcement. This is a significant finding, as for the FCA to have a chance of being effective at changing the problematic culture that prevails in many financial services firms, the FCA itself must have a healthy and sound internal culture.[20] The findings of the parliamentary report add to mounting evidence that this is not the case. For the FCA to improve, it will be necessary to provide it

19 The All-Party Parliamentary Group (APPG) on Investment Fraud and Financial Fairer Services, 'Report on the Call for Evidence about The Financial Conduct Authority' (November 2024), 355 available at https://www.appgifffs.org/wp-content/uploads/2024/11/FINAL-Call-for-Evidence-Report-PUBLIC-1.pdf.

20 A Keller and A Kokkinis, 'The Senior Managers and Certification Regime in Financial Firms: An Organisational Culture Analysis' (2022) 22(1) *Journal of Corporate Law Studies* 299.

with more extensive resources, as one of its greatest limitations is the limited number of staff and the difficulty in attracting staff with relevant qualifications. Accountability must also be enhanced and, to that effect, the role of the UK Parliament and of the relevant committees is crucial. The parliamentary accountability of UK regulatory bodies would be improved if a new statutory body were introduced to scrutinise the reports of independent regulators and collect relevant evidence to support the functioning of the relevant parliamentary committees.[21]

These developments, which we hope to see take place in the next decade, will **12.20** ensure that the rise of culture that we are currently witnessing will ultimately lead to a more effective and socially oriented financial sector. Otherwise, there is a risk that the rise of the culture that we have identified in this book will amount to little more than the rhetorical repositioning of the sector to shield itself from political, market and social pressures and resist any real change.

21 A Kokkinis, 'Response to HL Industry and Regulators Committee Call for Evidence' (2023).

INDEX